If ever there was a marriage centred on socialist conviction and campaigning, it was that of Max and Margaret Morris. Max as President of the National Union of Teachers fought for the right of all children to a full education. Margaret focussed on housing and widening access to universities. She was an early member of CND. Later, they both opposed 'Blair's Wars'. Their stories illuminate nearly 100 years of—yet to be won—class struggle.

This book is in memory of Max Morris and the members of the NUT and SEA with whom he campaigned; and of Jack Jones and other Trade Union and political colleagues who shared the battle against Margaret Thatcher. It is a thank you to Harold Wilson for not sending British soldiers to Vietnam and to Michael Foot for attempting to maintain the role of the State against the rising tide of neoliberalism.

Margaret Morris

Campaigning for Socialism
Memoirs of Max and
Margaret Morris

Austin Macauley Publishers™
LONDON · CAMBRIDGE · NEW YORK · SHARJAH

Copyright © Margaret Morris 2023

The right of Margaret Morris to be identified as author of this work has been asserted by the author in accordance with sections 77 and 78 of the Copyright, Designs and Patents Act 1988.

All rights reserved. No part of this publication may be reproduced, stored in a retrieval system, or transmitted in any form or by any means, electronic, mechanical, photocopying, recording, or otherwise, without the prior permission of the publishers.

Any person who commits any unauthorised act in relation to this publication may be liable to criminal prosecution and civil claims for damages.

All of the events in this memoir are true to the best of the author's memory. The views expressed in this memoir are solely those of the author.

A CIP catalogue record for this title is available from the British Library.

ISBN 9781398420496 (Paperback)
ISBN 9781398420502 (Hardback)
ISBN 9781398421561 (ePub e-book)

www.austinmacauley.com

First Published 2023
Austin Macauley Publishers Ltd®
1 Canada Square
Canary Wharf
London
E14 5AA

I would like to thank Anita Prazimowska and Jan Toporowski for their encouragement over many years and fellow members of the Socialist Education Association over the past 20 years. I could never have finished it but for Don Morrese's patient assistance, whenever I had computer or technical problems nor for the support of my family especially my daughter Georgia and grandson Dharam, and my "Jean of All Trades" helper Rakma.

Table of Contents

About This Book	11
Max: Early Years and Student Politics	16
Max: Beginning As a Teacher	25
Margaret: Early Years	36
Margaret: Hidden History	47
Max: Struggles Around the 1944 Education Act	50
Max: Birth of the Comprehensive School	57
Margaret: Widening Horizons	65
Max: Member of the Communist Party Executive Committee	73
Max: Visits to Socialist Countries	83
Max: Salaries, Equal Pay and the Ban Against Communist Heads	93
Max: Breaking Out of 'Genteel Poverty'	100
Margaret: Ten 'Start-Stop' Years	108
Margaret: The Labour Party Activist	124
Margaret: From First Meeting to Marriage	134
1961: Our First Year Together	144
Max Becomes a Headmaster	157
Women's International Democratic Federation	162
Max: Campaigning for the NUT Executive	174
Max: The Comprehensive School System	183

Max: Setting Up Willesden High School	191
Family Ties	198
Communist Party Activities	204
Margaret: Hornsey Housing Campaign Association	219
Max: Sanctions—The Union's First Steps in Action	235
Max: From Strike Leader to President of the NUT	243
Max: The President and Mrs Thatcher	253
Max: Foreign Trips as NUT President	261
Margaret: Resuming My Career	266
Max: Farewell to the Executive	270
Acquiring a New Family	277
Max: The Mandarins Rampant	284
Margaret Enters Management	300
Max Joins the Labour Party	314
The Blair Years and After	329
In Retrospect	342

About This Book

Although structured as Memoirs, our focus is the history of left-wing endeavour since the end of the First World War when the Labour Party adopted a new Constitution and clarified its Socialist aims. Max, the future teachers' and children's champion, was born 17 years before me, and our Memoirs begin in 1918 with Max aged five putting Labour Party leaflets through letter boxes in Glasgow. Because of the fluke of my longevity, our memoirs cover the whole period since 1918 and end with the fall of Boris Johnson, the war in Ukraine, the publication by the Labour Party of the Forde Report and the outbreak of mass strikes.

The teachers' campaigns were an integral part of Labour's challenge to the dominance of Britain's traditional ruling class. The years have gone by and most of the changes Max or I worked to achieve, although partially successful in the short term, were later abandoned. The situation of children in Britain today is shameful: over a third of them are undernourished and often hungry, the education system remains class divided and many children are alienated or mentally ill by an early age. The professional expertise of teachers is ignored and we have failed to train the skilled workers the country needs and rely on people trained abroad. **It need not have been like this**. The question is why after a more than a hundred years since 1918 is Britain in such a dreadful condition and the Tories in power?

The aim of this book is to enhance understanding of the campaigns of left-wing socialists since the Labour Party became the main challenger to the status quo and the rule of the Establishment. Although struggles over educational developments have taken prime place in our lives, we both became socialists at an early age and involved in general political activities. Max believed all his life, and I still do, that inequality, exploitation, poverty and the dehumanising effects of unbridled capitalism will only be ended when society is reorganised on socialist principles.

After we were married, our personal lives went on happily without much incident other than ones connected to political activity. Our childhoods, especially my experiences as an evacuee and a TB patient, and the 'Hidden History' of my grandmother, may be of interest to social historians and our courtship provides a romantic element, but it is our political activities which dominate these memoirs. Max and I were historians and enjoyed writing about the events we lived through and linking past and present in our analysis of them. This is not a formal academic history but a view of key moments in the past century through a kaleidoscope with two lenses.

The writer and educational journalist, Francis Beckett, described Max as "probably the best known and most influential President that the National Union of Teachers ever had and one of the most influential of the radical educationists of the 1960s and 1970s" (Obituary in *The Guardian* 9.9.2008). He raised searching questions about the purpose of education and became a guiding figure for a whole generation of teachers not just because he won them more money but because he gave them confidence in the social value of their work and a sense of professional pride. He achieved recognition not only within the NUT but throughout the wider world of education and within the Labour Movement. This was despite being a member of the Communist Party and serving on its National Executive Committee during the height of the Cold War.

After he retired, he wrote a number of autobiographical essays. He denied wanting to write a personal autobiography: "my story is only about myself as an actor in the changing fortunes of education and of the teaching profession and about how as a left-wing 'militant' I helped shape them. It is also about the quirks of left-wing politics both in general and as they impinged on education and teachers. I aim to link them all as they were linked in my life where I always saw them together." Especially for those on the left, improved education was seen not just as a means of providing better economic opportunities for working class children within existing capitalist society but with preparing them to exercise power within a socialist state. Max was deeply imbued with that tradition and did not believe that his educational work could be understood without an understanding of his commitment to socialism.

He consulted publishers who thought his essays would be of wider interest if he put some flesh on the bones and turned his narrowly focussed story into more rounded memoirs. This advice went against his nature. Max was a witty and compelling platform speaker and wrote with equal verve, but he had one disadvantage as a memoir writer, he was extremely buttoned up about his emotions and personal life. Indeed, he had an almost fanatical sense of privacy. During the nearly fifty years of our marriage in any discussion about early sexual experiences, if he was asked about his own, he always replied in an embarrassed way, "that's my affair." The potential witness to the sexual mores of Glasgow teenagers in the 1920s was not prepared to speak out! In line with this aspect of his character, his autobiographical essays were thin on human interest. In the earlier part, he refers in passing to "my wife Barbara" and later there was a similar passing reference to 'my wife Margaret', but no account at all of how or when this changing of the guard came about.

So, his manuscript lingered in a drawer for several years. He wanted me to get it out and edit it so that it would be accessible to a younger generation of teachers and help them understand the struggles of the past. I dearly wanted to do as he wished but I could not see a way forward during his lifetime. Eventually after his death I decided to include my own role and do my best to bring them to life.

The first part of this book retains almost unedited the early sections of Max's autobiographical essays describing his upbringing in an intellectual Jewish household in the slums of Glasgow: all chapters headed "Max:" are in his own words.

His father was a keen socialist so it was not surprising that he became a student and later teacher politician, nor that like many of his generation he joined the Communist Party in the mid-1930s. That he stayed in it after the war was less usual.

In contrast, politics were never discussed in my childhood home in a lower middle/upper working-class suburb of Birmingham. My mother loved her garden, poetry and listening to classical music and my father was interested in sport. My happy, uneventful life was abruptly disrupted by the outbreak of the Second World War and on 3 September 1939, I was evacuated and didn't live again with my parents until three years later. My experiences of evacuation and of being separated from my parents made me self-reliant at an early age and aware of class distinctions.

I was a young teenager in 1945 and inspired by visions for the future. We were taught at school how the United Nations was being set up to prevent future wars and the Declaration of Human Rights would bring about the liberation of oppressed people and the recognition of the rights of women. We learnt about the Beveridge Report and how the Welfare State would end poverty, homelessness, ignorance, ill health and unemployment. I was young and optimistic. Now I am very old and reflect about why none of the hopes of 1945 in which I so fervently believed have been fulfilled. Why do the same problems repeat themselves year after year? The Labour Party remains disunited, Old Etonians still dominate the Government and senior Civil Service, inequality is worse than in other developed countries, housing shortages and high rents mean young people can't afford homes, students must pay to study, wars and famine are rife—the list goes on. Now the effect of climate change has become the dominate challenge.

I've not been a good historian because after writing a book on the General Strike of 1926, I became caught up in institutional politics and organisation—a writer of memos instead of books. Although not a public figure like Max, I played my part in the last quarter of the 20th century in the movement to widen access to higher education and to make degree courses more flexible and student centred. Unfortunately, the current commercialisation of Higher Education is eroding much of what was achieved.

Max was a Party loyalist and belonged to the Communist Party from 1935 until 1976 and to the Labour Party from the following year until his death in 2008. I have been very consistent in my belief in socialism and hatred of war but have only sporadically belonged to a political Party. I first joined the Labour Party in 1956 but after several years as an active member and Council candidate I left over Gaitskell's declaration that he'd fight and fight again against nuclear disarmament. I was also alarmed by the watering down of the role of the state in Anthony Crosland's 'The Future of Socialism'.

Later, I joined the Communist Party, six years after the majority of intellectuals had left it. Some may see such a decision as idiosyncratic but it made sense to me at the time. I left it again after it became clear that the Soviet Union, which retained the support of the 'tankies' in the British CP, was not becoming more democratic. I re-joined the Labour Party in the early 1990s but left it over the war in Iraq.

I went back after Brown became Prime Minister but have long believed that Britain won't be able to move forward without changes in our political system including a more democratic voting system than first past the post. I have made an attempt in the final section of this book to analyse why the hopes of 1918 have never been fulfilled.

At NUT Conferences in the 60s and 70s after Max had made one of his more scathing polemical speeches, female delegates would sometimes come up to me and say sympathetically, "how do you cope being married to such a firebrand?" All I could say was that it was actually a lot of fun and certainly never dull. He was a warm, caring and loving husband, if not always the model of patience. Despite coming from different backgrounds and spending our formative years in very different political and social climates, throughout our marriage we were on the same political wavelength. This didn't mean we always saw everything in the same way and our different reactions are explored in the later chapters of these memoirs. We were temperamentally very different; he was a Marxist scholar and theorist while my socialism, although influenced by Marxism and the ideas of Rosa Luxemburg, was a more emotional and pragmatic response to the current state of the world.

The intertwining of our lives over nearly fifty years is at the heart of the second part of these memoirs which I have written in the first person but with many quotations from Max's writings. I can imagine him grumbling and protesting that I have written about things of concern only to us, to which I would have replied that a glimpse into our personal lives might improve understanding of our political activities and help a younger generation, reared on neo-liberal ideology and the demonising of everything and everybody deemed socialist, to appreciate that Communists and Socialists were human beings like everyone else. Since I began work on this book attitudes towards socialism and capitalism have changed. Younger readers may better understand our political campaigning than those who grew up to adulthood in the Thatcher or New Labour years.

Max could quite legitimately complain that my approach gives me a chance to have the last word and comment on events with hindsight but I've tried to restrain myself from imposing my views on his. Because of his aversion to any exposure of his private life—an attitude which members of the generation reared on Facebook and Twitter may find hard to understand—I do not know if he would have been won over by what I have done with his autobiographical essays, but I hope he would have been.

Margaret Morris
25 July 2022

Max: Early Years and Student Politics

Though I was not born in the Gorbals district in Glasgow, my family moved there when I was about a year old and we stayed there until fifteen years later. The Gorbals was notorious for its slums, the worst in Europe my father used to say outside Warsaw. Our own street was not itself a slum but it backed onto one of the nastiest parts of the city into which we youngsters were afraid to venture. There were many Irish in the surrounding streets though they did not impinge on me as Irish, but as Catholics because of the inevitable (as it seemed) St Patrick's Day riots between Catholics and Protestants; those days we kept off the streets to avoid the challenge: "Are you a Billy or a Dan?" to which we quipped to ourselves "or an old tin can?"

I suppose that was my first introduction to politics, though, of course, I did not understand it as such. But politics were regularly talked about in my family, especially by my father who was a Labour voter. The Gorbals was the constituency which the famous Communist John Maclean fought in 1918, though my father would never vote communist and thought Maclean was mad. It was one of the first in the country to go Labour. During the 1918 election, at the age of five, I helped to deliver leaflets for Labour, climbing up the tenements' stairs; it was great fun.

One could not help being political in the Gorbals for though we were comparatively not poor (my father earned a reasonable living as a Hebrew teacher), we were surrounded by much poverty and squalor. I remember how amused I was much later to be told by an eminent academic that the frontages to the tenements in my own street (South Portland Street) were beautiful examples of Georgian architecture, relics of Glasgow's late 18th-century wealth. We lived two stairs up in a 'two room and kitchen', so I never noticed the beauty. What I remember is the poverty, a substantial number of my schoolfellows coming to school barefoot and in ragged jerseys.

When I left my elementary school, I went on a bursary to one of Glasgow's best-known secondary schools, then situated in the heart of the Gorbals, in Crown Street, a 17th-century foundation with a great reputation, Hutcheson's Boys Grammar (known colloquially as 'Hutchy' and its pupils as 'Hutchy Bugs'). Many years later, an article in the *Sunday Times* described it as a school unsurpassed in Britain in academic achievement. I would not know about that, but it was certainly an academic forcing house whose alumni took a substantial share of Higher Education places. It was ruled with a liberal use of the leather strap—and I don't think there was a day when I was not beaten, sometimes getting six of the best on the hand (with wrist covered), for though I was a bright pupil, doing particularly well in the classics, history and English, I was talkative and bubbly, and that merited punishment. I always think that the argument that corporal punishment produces sadists is a bit suspect. In me and many others, it produced what I like to think of as humanitarians.

Hutcheson's was, I suppose, pretty typical of the Scottish academic diet in those days. If you were among the brightest, it was the classics, English and maths that took priority. French was my third language—it was the first only for the lower streams. As for science, that ranked comparatively low—for the duds, as we used to say, especially Chemistry. So, to my intense regret later on, I did practically no work in science.

But they pushed us hard and I was astonished when we moved to London to find myself a year ahead of my age group in Kilburn Grammar School. I matriculated quickly, and was put into the sixth.

As a new boy at 'Hutchy', I had my first real political experience, an example of *chutzpa*h more than devotion to the cause. John Buchan, the distinguished writer, had just been elected as a Tory MP for the Scottish Universities and Rector Scott in morning assembly told us how proud we should be—this was the first Old Boy to be elected to Parliament. Now there was a tradition in the school that Jimmy Maxton, MP, leader of the Clydeside Reds, was also an Old Boy and indeed his name was carved on one of the ancient gnarled desks at which we sat. So that day, after school, I penned an anonymous postcard to the Rector: "You said John Buchan was our first Hutchy MP. What about Jimmy Maxton?" Next morning, I waited in trepidation in Assembly for the response I was sure would come. And indeed, it did. Scott embarked on a tirade against pupils who wrote him anonymous and untruthful letters. The culprit had better beware for he would surely be found out. For a long time after, I was terrified but nothing happened.

During my teens, I was being informally educated in my family and by older friends in both socialism and Zionism and I was also learning to debate. It was all very rudimentary, especially the socialist part, but included Wells' *New Worlds for Old*, and the book whose impression on me was to remain for many years, Shaw's *The Intelligent Woman's Guide to Socialism and Capitalism*. As I recall it, his theme was that socialism meant equality and I was startled by his paradoxes till I was educated out of his ideas by Marxism.

Zionism was taken for granted in my very Jewish family, but its main impact on me was the long hours spent in evenings and weekends studying Hebrew and Jewish history. At one time, my father intended me for the Jewish ministry and wanted me to compete for a place in a religious training school. I was able, happily, to avoid that fate. It soon became clear this was not my vocation and, indeed, it was not long before I declared myself to be an atheist. All in all, mine was a very hard-studying boyhood and my mother used to say that whatever my faults (and they were many) I was a worker—a premature workaholic. But I also had a very active social life with lots of fun in Glasgow's teeming streets full of youngsters precocious in many ways. Among them were some to become very well-known professional folk, including my elder brother, Professor J.N. Morris. Glasgow, I have always thought, was a great city to live in.

Among my earliest memories are observing the turmoil caused by the 1926 General Strike in the city; trams overturned and noisy demonstrations. I was passionately on the side of the miners and I remember my horror at the country being apparently more concerned with the Test Match results that with the starving miners in that long summer when they were beaten into the ground. A picture remains in my mind of a Low (or was it Dyson?) cartoon of a lovely cricket greensward and in the background a starving miner.

My political interests were by no means shared by most of my schoolfellows who mainly came from Tory middle-class, professional families, so I was in this respect very much the odd boy out and considered to be somewhat strange.

This lack of interest in politics among my schoolfellows was confirmed many times by later experiences and helped to create my strong convictions on the uselessness of teaching politics in school. Politics is for adults, not children. Indeed, trying them on children will turn them off not on. It is wasted effort.

I spent much time reading and, by the time I was sixteen, I was well acquainted with Shaw, Wells and Bennett and quite well-versed in Dickens and Galsworthy, both family favourites. The house was full of books. My father took us to the occasional concert to hear the famous Scottish Orchestra, but he failed to turn me into a pianist, though all of us became devoted listeners. I saw my first opera, 'Fidelio', but with the catholicity of youth, was just as keen on pantomime (for which Glasgow was renowned).

By the time we moved to London, I was a convinced socialist and an eager Zionist, as well as quite an accomplished speaker for my age. And I continued my political education, largely by reading, but also by participating while still at school in the chores of the local Labour Party in Willesden, where we lived, though as a schoolboy I could not be a member. I worked hard in the catastrophic 1931 election, an event which deepened my political education and turned me decisively towards the Left.

Like so many young 'intellectuals', I was caught up in the upsurge of the student movement in the thirties. I went to University College, London, in 1931 on one of the few entrance scholarships then available. I took an active part in the radical political activities that were so marked a feature of student life in Oxford, Cambridge and London. Though repeatedly pressed, I did not join the Communist Party because of a dislike, not of student communists, but of the harsh stridency and crude propagandist tone of the Party's publications. My own inclination turned towards the party's rival on the left, the Independent Labour Party, of whose politics and attitudes I had strong and favourable recollections from my Glasgow days. I remember going to a public debate between the Communist leader, Harry Pollitt and the I.L.P. leader, Fenner Brockway, in Farringdon Hall, central London, and being rather disgusted by the intolerant behaviour of Pollitt's supporters. But another reason for my resistance to the Party was that I was a Zionist and could not accept the Party's attitude to that movement.

Nevertheless, I was also very attracted as a history student to Marx's theories on historical development and avidly enjoyed reading such of his historical writings (and those of Engels) as were then available. I also attended meetings and lectures on Marxist theory and philosophy and, like many of my fellow students, saw in the 'world outlook' it advanced something like a clear explanation of a bewildering world situation. It all seemed to me to be an appealing version of socialism, all the more so because of its simplicity and clarity. Moreover, in the attitude of communist students to what was happening around us both at home and abroad, I found an echo in my own feelings and thoughts. So, though I was not a member of the Communist group whose conspiratorial ambience somewhat amused me, they regarded me as friendly and the feeling was, on the whole, mutual. If I can speak of 'conversion' to Marxism it was finally after listening to a lecture by that brilliant working-class intellectual, T.A. Jackson on, of all forbidding topics, 'Dialectical Materialism'!

During 1933, with the Nazi take-over in Germany, student activity intensified, and, as Secretary of the College Jewish Students' Society and a known left-winger, I became the organiser of Britain's first major student anti-Nazi rally, a mass meeting in the University Union (then a temporary building in Malet Street) with such outstanding speakers as J.B.S. Haldane, Lancelot Hogben and the poet and *literateur* Lascelles Abercrombie—all shining stars in the university world and determined anti-Nazis. Our meeting was a huge success, packed to the doors, and helped to rally student opinion in these early days to the fight against fascism.

It was about this time, too, that we set about forming a socialist society in University College on non-party lines, that is, including non-members and supporters of the Labour Party, which in practice meant communists. The problem to be overcome was that the College regulations did not permit political societies, a curious anomaly for an institution founded on radically liberal lines in the early 19th century, when it was known as 'the godless institution in Gower Street'. The moving spirit among us was the future Labour Party Leader, Hugh Gaitskell, then a young economics lecturer and a dedicated socialist. I did not know at the time, but read later in Philip Williams' biography, that Hugh had been prepared to flout College rules openly by meeting illegally within the college boundaries, but was persuaded by his professor to draw back. In the event, we formed the society in his Regent's Park room and then met regularly at the Lord Wellington pub round the corner from Gower Street.

I got to know Gaitskell well because, although I was an Honours History student, I received unusual permission to attend economics lectures after both his Professor and Gaitskell himself had failed to persuade me (rather irregularly, I thought) to transfer to their department. This was entirely because I had won one of the few entrance scholarships to UCL and so was considered to be a potential high flyer. Later, after I graduated, he suggested I research on Chartism (on which he had written a very good little WEA booklet) and gave me an introduction to Harold Laski at the LSE who, in turn, sent me next door to H.L. Beales, who was to supervise my research for some years, a most pleasurable as well as instructive experience. I used to see Gaitskell occasionally years later, after the war, in the Swiss Cottage music shop where he and Dora, his wife, went to buy jazz records. Though he knew that I had gone communist (and he had gone very right-wing) he was the soul of courtesy and we used to chat about my Chartist research.

My involvement in student politics led me to my first experience of international gatherings. On my return from a two months' journey and tour of the Mediterranean, Egypt and Palestine (all done on the £80 University Scholarship in History that I won at the end of my first year) I was a 'delegate' (I cannot remember from whom) to the 'World Youth and Student Congress against War and Fascism' in Paris, towards the end of September 1933. The British delegation contained all the leading communist students and the leaders of the Young Communist League (it was here that I made the acquaintance of John Gollan, later to be leader of the C.P,) but to show how 'broad' they were, I was chosen as the British representative on the Presidium and so had to chair one session of this multi-lingual mass gathering.

Paris was not a very friendly place to anti-fascists at this pre-Popular Front time and, after an excursion somewhere outside the city, our long line of taxis (the taxi drivers' union was 'red') was held up outside the centre of the city by the police for a considerable time, apparently intent on making arrests. None of the British were arrested but, when we returned to England, we were adjured to hide all our documents in our shoes and other secret places for fear of confiscation at the channel port. Nothing happened, either on leaving France or on entering Britain. I suppose we were suffering from a kind of persecution paranoia. At the conference we were merely demonstrating, making speeches— we were hardly organising revolution. But these were tense times and paranoia, in retrospect, seems excusable even if we grossly exaggerated the influence our activities had.

My experience at the Conference did not take me into the Communist Party. What brought me closer was disillusion with Zionism created by the visit I had just made to Palestine, where I spent some six weeks. I had excellent opportunities of seeing everything I wanted to within the Jewish community in the cities and the Kibbutz settlements. I was at the time Vice-President of the University Zionist Federation which gave me very good contacts, and my passage was smoothed by my Palestinian Jewish student friends in London whose families were well-to-do and influential.

Before I set off, I was approached by Ned Warner, the leading communist student in University College (later a distinguished establishment figure) to ask me if I would meet a prominent party member, Hugo Rathbone, active in the anti-imperialist movement, 'The League Against Imperialism', for a discussion about Palestine. I agreed and was given a 'briefing' on Zionism (I was, of course, known as a very left-wing Zionist) and, in particular, on the Palestinian Arabs and their problems. I was then asked if I would take a message to the illegal Palestine Communist Party in Tel Aviv. It showed, I suppose, both my broadmindedness and naiveté that I said I would try to deliver the message but could not guarantee to do so if it meant compromising my Tel Aviv prospective hosts. The message, which I insisted on seeing, was simply one of solidarity and an appeal to keep contact with the British anti-imperialists who were on their side in 'the struggle' against the British Mandate. But making any contact could be hazardous for me as it meant searching out a leader of an illegal organisation, and that could land me and my hosts in trouble.

When in Tel Aviv, I discussed the matter with the leader of the left-wing Socialist Zionists (a Marxist grouping) to whom I had been given an introduction by British friends. Although they were opposed to the communist party (a very tiny, disorganised group) they knew them, and they actually helped to arrange a brief clandestine meeting for me with an Arab who would pass the message on. Though I was suitably exhilarated by the conspiratorial atmosphere of it all and was glad to be of help in circumventing the police, looking back I have often laughed at this brief encounter with international revolutionary politics when I was twenty!

What was far more important to me were my reactions to what I saw. These were inevitably mixed. On the one hand, I was full of admiration at the pioneering successes of the young Jewish community, especially in the Kibbutzim where I stayed. They had done wonders in transforming the barren or swampy countryside and in developing Tel Aviv.

But I became increasingly disturbed by an almost universal underlying attitude of assumed national superiority, an incipient chauvinism towards the Arabs. Palestine at that time (1933) was receiving large numbers of German refugees from Nazism (my ship from Marseilles was full of them) and one would have thought, logically, that this would have led to the opposite kind of feelings. But no—Jewish nationalism was intensified. It brushed off into an anti-Arabism which I could not ideologically stomach, and which upset me very much, though I was not 'pro-Arab' in any way.

I could not yet say that I was turned against Zionism but I was certainly heading that way and, paradoxically so, after a visit to Palestine which normally had the opposite effect on Zionists from abroad. My friends, when I returned home, thought me very perverse and my family was flabbergasted. But I did not go around shouting about 'conversion', I just went on thinking about it all, and soon withdrew from Zionist public activity. The impact of my change of thinking, which was accompanied by a closer identification with the group of communist students in college, was softened by a decision to concentrate for the next few months on my studies as degree-taking time approached.

I had been neglecting my work through a combination of different kinds of college activities, including the student union, the College Magazine (of which I was business manager and sub-editor) and the Debating Society (including the University of London Debating Team), the 'illegal' Socialist Society and the Jewish Students Society which I had founded and led. All these activities, which led my professor to describe me in a reference as "outstanding as a student," were not helping me in my history studies, in which I was really very interested. So, I buckled down to the job and was able to pull off a First.

When I graduated, I had the problem of 'What next?' Professor 'Jimmy' Neale interviewed me at once, as he did my two fellow-students who had got Firsts—it was a vintage year for UCL as we got three of the six History Firsts in the University—and offered me a place researching on some part of his own special field, Elizabethan history, in which he was then Britain's premier specialist. I rather suspected that this would happen and had already decided to ask him if he would help me, rather, do research on a subject I was intensely interested in—Chartism. His reply was: "It's all been done!" The atmosphere, which had been warm, cooled and the interview ended quickly—he would not even give me an introduction to the appropriate Professor at LSE. Later students of working-class history, looking at the lack of research studies and writings on Chartism at that time, will wonder at Neale's remark. He knew nothing whatever about the area and was interested only in developing his Elizabethan research factory for his own greater glory. It is very sad to record this.

So, once again, what to do? My father kindly offered to subsidise me if I wanted to concentrate on research, but I was unwilling to accept this generous offer—I preferred to begin earning my living as soon as possible. So that is how

I fell into teaching. I applied for a place at the Institute of Education though, to take it up, I had to ask for a loan—I think it was £26—from the Middlesex Education Committee to cover my fees. I got both place and loan; the latter I had to promise to pay back as soon as I started work. Remember we were a long way off the system of mandatory awards that prevailed after the war and that has now been destroyed.

So, I started at the Institute, but with the determination to pursue research in my chosen field at the first opportunity. The Institute at that time was regarded as the premier teacher training centre. Its staff basked in the reflected glory of its director, Sir Percy Nunn, whose book—'Education: Data and First Principles' was the bible of aspiring teachers. It was Sir Percy's last year before retirement and we were lucky to hear him talk. He was down to earth, spoke in clear and comprehensible language and seemed to make sense. Academically it was easy to anyone who had been through the tough regime of the UCL History Honours School. And the practical side, which obviously concerned us most, was very well handled. Though I did not hit it off with Mr Jeffries, the History tutor (later Professor at Birmingham), to watch him demonstrate a lesson was a pleasure; he was a born teacher from whom one could really learn.

Pretty soon, I made up my mind to attend the minimum number of lectures I could get away with. I had by then acquired a very attractive girlfriend and we spent a great deal of time together avoiding college lectures, which did no harm to our eventual results.

My interest in politics, however, increased and, towards the end of the course, I joined the Communist Party—on May Day 1935. Though my 'conversion' had originally been to intellectual Marxism as a philosophy, especially of history, I fully appreciated that joining the CP meant more than taking on board a set of ideas. I knew it would mean becoming a political activist in a small organisation. It was a conscious decision not to join the Labour Party, whose record in 1929–31, and in the years that followed, had estranged me and many other students of my generation. What I was not to know was how all-absorbing Communist Party membership would become and the close political and personal friendships it would create—Harold Wilson, years later, pejoratively, if accurately, dubbed it a 'closely-knit group'. My comrades were on the whole of high intellectual calibre, including some of the best students and graduates of my generation.

Max: Beginning As a Teacher

When I finished at the Institute of Education in the summer of 1935, I found myself unemployed. This was not unexpected in spite of my 'First' and good Institute reports. I was simply in the same plight as very many others in a classic situation where there were more teachers coming out of training than jobs in schools—a product of the chronic 'economies' which plagued an education service grossly under-provided with resources and so enduring large classes and overcrowded buildings. I just had to wait and hope for the best. I spent part of my time editing a student journal in the control of the communist student organisation, with the typical title 'Student Front'. It seems that I had already acquired some sort of reputation and I was flattered when G.C.T. Giles, the leading communist teacher, asked me to edit a booklet, 'Schools at the Crossroads', in which I was to write the English chapter entitled, unoriginally, 'The English Schools in Crisis, 1935'. (How many 'crises' have we had since then to the present day!)

I enjoyed doing the research involved and it gave me a taste for handling educational facts and statistics which I have never lost. I wrote and edited under a pseudonym (M Robinson) as was frequently the case in our circles then, so as not to prejudice my job prospects. We did not believe there was equal access to jobs for communists.

So, I had a busy summer. And, at its end, I had a stroke of luck. The English tutor at the Institute, Dr Gurrey, though I had only taken English as a subsidiary subject, recommended me for a temporary part-time vacancy at Harrow County School for boys, a very prestigious Grammar School. I was to take the classes in English and Latin taught by the Head who was off sick for some six weeks. I jumped at the chance and enjoyed very much not being unemployed and earning some money (I was fed up with being paid for when we went out by my girlfriend who had a good science job). Also, it was a 'good school' to have taught in.

When my job ended and no other teaching post was available, I was free to concentrate on the General Election in November 1935, where I worked hard for the left-wing Labour candidate, Morris Orbach, with whom I remained friendly till he died in the late nineteen-seventies. Communists were proscribed at that time by the Labour Party but Morris made no bones about seeking our assistance and I even spoke from his platform. The 1935 Election was a bitter disappointment to us all but I gained a lot of political experience in the campaign.

Before the end of the year, Middlesex County offered me another temporary post, this time in a Junior Mixed and Infant School. With great misgiving I accepted—I was so hard up I could not afford to turn anything down. So, I entered into what was probably the hardest three months' teaching in my life. I had absolutely no training or experience of juniors or infants, yet I was flung into the classrooms and expected to get on with it. The Headmistress, a tough but kindly Welsh woman, guided me when I asked for guidance—which was frequently. Teaching infants nearly killed me. At the end of each week, I returned home and lay down on a sofa, where I stayed utterly dead to the world for several hours. That experience led to my enduring and never-changing admiration for teachers in primary schools, the most hard-done-by of our professional colleagues in pay and conditions. I don't think I could have survived a second term.

That winter, with no prospect it seemed of a permanent post, I played around with a number of possibilities. To my surprise, I had been asked to allow my name to go forward for a Commonwealth Scholarship in History at a mid-western American University. My sponsor was Hale Bellot, Professor of American History at University College, who had been impressed by my 'First' and who was very influential in Anglo-American academic relations. I agreed, and all went smoothly till the Professor, a dyed-in-the-wool Tory, learned of my communist affiliations and I heard no more. Bellot even refused to see me again!

I then had a go at two other possibilities. Professor George Counts, to whom Giles introduced me—a very distinguished academic with left-wing views at Teachers' College, Columbia University asked me to apply for a studentship at Columbia, then probably the most prestigious educational faculty in the world, and I began taking the required tests. At about the same time I was introduced to Kingsley Martin, Editor of *The New Statesman,* through the agency of that wonderful communist agitator, Isobel Brown, who was renowned for her anti-Nazi work, and he asked me to write two articles as a test of my journalistic ability. He received them favourably and I was considering a career in journalism. Then, by a stroke of luck, as it seemed at the time, a permanent job was advertised in my own borough and I put in an application.

It was for General Subjects, which meant English, History, Geography and Maths in the Junior Technical School, a new College in Willesden. I went for interview by a large roomful of the Willesden Education Committee, presided over by the Chairman of the Middlesex Education Committee, John Catlow, a Tory and famous progressive figure in the educational world. I got the job, as a result of which I cut short my Columbia application and thoughts of journalism.

I look back on my work in the school in those pre-war days with almost undiluted pleasure. It was a happy and united staff of a very special kind which only a technical school could put together. It received me very well and I took to its unusual qualities just as well. I was an academic, with a 'working-class' political orientation. Expecting by training to belong to an academic community, I found a mixed academic/industrially experienced staff. For we not only had teachers of high academic calibre, but also 'technical' staff of top quality in engineering. Add to this that we shared a staffroom and some classes with a Secondary School of Building which included highly skilled practitioners in all the building crafts. Many of our teachers in both schools worked part time in the Technical College which housed us and which had staffrooms common to both College and schools and you had an unusually ideal mix, rich in the experience it offered.

I found the work hard—I was learning to teach! But I got plenty of help, especially from my own senior colleague, Walby Knight, who later went into administration and ended up as a brilliant CEO in Harrow. I had disciplinary difficulties to begin with, though not like those of another newly-appointed colleague whom I once found being chased round the room by the children using the desks as stepping stones. Few teachers begin without disciplinary troubles and I always, as a Head, used to describe my own early problems to young colleagues to encourage them to persevere. I know of few jobs, perhaps none, where sheer experience counts for more and where, in course of time, the day dawns that brings with it confidence and success—and happiness in the work.

While at the Willesden J.T.S., I became more deeply involved in trade union work and my political activity became increasingly—though by no means exclusively—orientated that way. I was soon to become Secretary of the 'Teachers' Bureau' of the Communist Party. I was active in both the Middlesex

Secondary Teachers' Association of the NUT (MSTA), considered to be a 'militant' association of Grammar and Technical school teachers in which C.T. Giles (see below) was the moving spirit; and in the Willesden NUT Association, about as un-militant as one could imagine.

These two associations typified the sharp contrasts in professional attitudes which were still embryonic on a national scale but which were increasingly to express themselves as the years rolled on and our activities bore fruit. These attitudes are perhaps best understood by looking back at the earlier development of trade unionism among teachers.

The First World War and its aftermath of social upheaval saw a quite considerable teachers' movement including a very substantial volume of support for affiliation to the Labour Party, and for strike action. This succeeded in winning a system of negotiating machinery, the Burnham Committee, composed of representatives of the main teachers' unions and the LEAs (as the direct employers) under a government-appointed chairman. The resultant Burnham scales established lower salaries for elementary school teachers, the bulk of the profession, who taught working-class children, and higher ones for secondary (mainly grammar) school teachers, who were largely university graduates and whose pupils were mainly middle and lower middle-class children.

There followed a period of relative quiescence in spite of repeated attacks on salaries by reactionary governments. For even the elementary school teachers were appreciably better off than industrial workers, who suffered not only from very low wages but from short time and unemployment: Students might find it hard to get jobs, but once appointed security was virtually assured and their jobs were pensionable. There were relatively few redundancies because entry into the profession was regulated by control of admission to training. So, there was no urgent incentive for teachers' organisations to join in the sharp struggles of the working class which marked the period. As for secondary teachers, though the aristocracy of the profession, their salaries were still too low for them to consider themselves on a par with other professions, such as doctors. The education service was under constant attack from the right and subject to almost unending economy waves, hardly the atmosphere for encouraging professional self-respect.

In these conditions, political 'neutrality' flourished in the teachers' unions and every backward political tendency, including keeping aloof from the Labour movement, or even the parents, gained strength. It was relatively easy to persuade teachers, better off than the industrial workers on one hand and not so well off as the professions on the other, that as an organised body they belonged to neither side in the class struggle.

When a major attack on salaries took place in the economic crisis of the 1930s, the unions, while roused to indignation, fought mainly against discrimination which would have cut their salaries more than others. They did not challenge the government's general economic policy so that, in the main, militancy was limited and not comparable in scope with the mass movements of the workers, from which the organised profession kept away. Nevertheless, there was considerable bitterness and discontent as well as some experience of local militant leadership.

Left-wing teachers emphasised the need for the unions to be active in winning educational advance and to fight for a basic scale for all teachers instead of the separate scales that bred disunity and weakened the general salaries movement. These policies helped to educate teachers in political realities: the demand for educational advance showed up Tory defence of class privilege, while the fight for the basic scale highlighted Tory opposition to improvement in the pay of elementary school teachers whose jobs lay with working-class children. Both policies were clearly linked: economic advance for the teachers depended on educational advance for the workers' children.

I was, as a young teacher, one of Willesden's delegates to the NUT Conference in 1938. I put my name in to speak on an issue of educational expenditure (Government support for Local Authorities, still in one form or another a hardy annual!) and had my first experience of the 'question being put' before I could be called.

At the 1939 Conference, in Llandudno, I got to know the General Secretary, Sir Frederick Mander, who dominated teacher politics in the years before and during the war. He could, without difficulty, keep control of the kind of mass conference that the NUT has, just setting the tone by his keynote address at the beginning and making sure behind the scenes that the Executive he both served and dominated did not spoil the unfolding of the scenario he had planned.

Sir Frederick, a Liberal in politics, passionately hated the Left. I had been put up to second an amendment to a motion which referred to the critical international situation. The introduction of such a topic was anathema to Sir Fred who got more and more agitated, one could see, as the mover of the amendment proceeded with his speech. Just as the President was about to call me, I saw the

General Secretary lean over and whisper in his ear. Lo and behold, the President changed tack and announced the interruption of the debate to hear the fraternal greetings from the Cooperative Union—a speech guaranteed to send the Conference to sleep! I had to do my seconding next day when the momentum of the debate had totally dissipated.

Sir Frederick was widely believed to have handed a list of 'communist' teachers to MI5. There was, of course, no proof of this, and it could have been communist paranoia to believe it. But it was certainly true that, shortly after I took up my post in Willesden in 1936, a member of the Special Branch visited the Principal of the College to warn him about me. The College Secretary was so disgusted (he was a staunch Tory) that he told me. Also, I had a special visit from H.M.I. who came in 'casually' to watch me teach. Later, when I was doing adult education lecturing for the WEA and the University of London Extra-Mural Department, I was also visited and was given advance friendly warning by the Director, the genuinely liberal socialist, Barbara (later Baroness) Wootton, who disliked political snoopers.

Incidentally, after the war, when Mr Chuter Ede was Home Secretary, an unguarded remark of a friend of his on the NUT Executive (Chuter had been a union official for many years and was a regular attender at Conference, even as a Minister) revealed that he (Chuter) had a numbered list of 'communist' teachers for the use of the Special Branch of which he was, as Home Secretary, the boss. This created a furore and the usual crop of official denials.

There was the amusing side to it all as left-wingers tried to guess not only who was on the list but the order of importance from No. 1 down. As Secretary of the Education Advisory Committee of the Communist Party—as I then was—I was assumed to be a contender for the premier position which gave me great joy.

By 1939, I represented the 'Extra Met' (the Committee covering the non-LCC part of Greater London) on the National Young Teacher Committee of the union and got involved in one of the earliest attempts to influence it to take an active interest in the dangerous world situation—of which the Fred Mander incident was an example. To my surprise, my leading opponent was not a reactionary Tory but a fiery Welsh socialist delegate called George Thomas, who made a pacifist speech opposing collective security against the fascist governments. George was soon to make a reputation as a fire-eating Executive member from the Welsh valleys, opposing teachers taking part in school meals supervision and the relevant clauses of the 1944 Act. I met him many times later, of course, and occasionally reminded him of this youthful political 'deviation' After being Secretary of State for Wales, George ended up as Lord Tonypandy and Speaker of the House of Commons.

The mid and late thirties was a period of growing influence for communists, the era of the Spanish War, the moves towards a popular front and the general struggle against fascism and the Nazi war menace. This was the time, too, of Mosley's prominence and I took part in the famous rally against him in the East End—the Battle of Cable Street—when Mosley was stopped in his tracks. I greeted the Hunger Marchers and described in the *New Clarion* (predecessor of *Tribune*) the police attack on the crowds of demonstrators outside Hyde Park when I had the doubtful pleasure of being chased by the Mounties from whom I escaped by climbing up the railings in the Bayswater Road. The article, entitled 'They Left Singing', was intended to capture the spirit of the marchers. It was all very exciting.

More humdrum, when the M.S.T.A. initiated a campaign for educational advance, I was given the job of organising a conference in Friend's House to which we invited the Labour Movement as well as the world of education and industry. This was then a novel approach for an NUT association and turned out to be a huge success. Our speakers, apart from Giles, by then on the NUT Executive, included Professor R.H. Tawney, historian, Christian Socialist and a major influence on the development of education policy within the Labour Party for whom he produced, 'Secondary Education for All' in 1922. Tawney was always effective since, though not an orator, he impressed everyone with his elegance of style, his knowledge of the social objectives education should have and his burning sincerity.

In July 1938, I went with Giles to Paris and had another experience of those world jamborees attracting a very broad clientele but organised behind the scenes by the Communist Party, a World Conference against Fascism and Japanese Aggression in China. The oratory was resounding but seemed interminable and repetitive. Even then I did wonder what practical good it was all doing, but we all believed in the value of propaganda in achieving results. What hope was there otherwise in those dark days? When I heard Nye Bevan in the Conference Hall foyer holding forth eloquently that conferences such as this were a form of 'international masturbation' I was horrified. I was much happier in a great demonstration in the Velodrome d'Hiver, listening to the heroine of the Spanish War, La Passionaria, rouse the vast audience to frenzied enthusiasm for the cause.

Attracted to the Conference were a very varied gathering of intellectuals, artists, trade unionists and politicians. One encounter I found so strange as almost to be bizarre. Crossing one of Paris' lovely bridges with a group that included Cecil Day Lewis, I was astonished to hear him exclaim loudly and passionately how wonderful it all was—he had never been to Paris before! What a restricted life some of our upper-class comrades must have led, I thought, for this was my third or fourth visit on a young teacher's salary! That unselfconscious outburst endeared the future Poet Laureate to us.

In spite of the pressures of political work, I was spending many Saturdays and part of my long teacher's holidays in research on Chartism, under the benign tutelage of H.L. Beales at the L.S.E. where I was registered as a part-time PhD student. At his suggestion, I was working on a biography of Bronterre O'Brien, the great Chartist leader and theoretician, precursor in Britain of Marx in many of his ideas. It was very enjoyable work, mainly in the Newspaper Repository of the British Museum at Colindale, but also in the main library, a place I loved going to. In the course of this study, I became familiar with the then largely unknown chartist press, a truly fantastic phenomenon, and I must have read almost the entire file of the *Northern Star* as well as the various papers edited by Bronterre including the magnificent *'Poor Man's Guardian'*.

I was still considering a possible career as a historian and had gained a reputation in the movement as a Chartist expert. I wrote the centenary article on the 1839 Chartist Convention for the *Daily Herald* and a number of articles in the newly-created *Tribune* for which I also did educational articles (using sometimes the M. Robinson pseudonym). If I may jump ahead, when the war ended and I returned from India, I intended to complete the work and the PhD but discovered to my horror that the Colindale Repository had been bombed, and the Museum authorities told me it would be some seven or eight years before its material could be put in order again. They were wrong, but I was not to know that, and for better or worse I decided to cut my losses, published (in 1948) in a new series a volume of historical documents, *'From Cobbett to the Chartists'*, based on my voluminous notes—and reluctantly left Chartism behind me, apart from the occasional article.

The book turned out to be a success, and, unusual for such a work, had a second, hardback edition—the only one in the series to do so—and a German translation. I thought then, and still think it is a good book and, to my surprise, I heard—in 1983—that some schools were still using it, though it was not produced for that purpose. At the end of 1991, I was astonished to receive a call asking me to lecture to a Scottish seminar based on the book. By then, Chartism had become a growth industry as indeed had working-class history in general, with a vast literature—including work on Bronterre, my Chartist hero. Chatting to G.D.H. Cole shortly before he died, we gossiped nostalgically of the days when only a few of us were working in this field now so well cultivated. He, of course, was the master gardener.

Alongside my Chartist research I was writing a 30,000-word book on the education system for the Left Book Club. Gollancz gave it to Kingsley Martin and R.H. Tawney to read and it passed for publication. As a historical curiosity I recall the agreement we all had not to include discussion of the views of those who thought extending school life meant extending capitalist ideology and should therefore be opposed. This daft sociological approach belonged then to a few sectarian 'Marxists'. Happily, '*The People's Schools*' was well received and nicely reviewed.

But I think the soundest comment came from H.L. Beales who said that it had all the faults of a good first book—it was too jam-full of facts. Anyway, it is now unobtainable as all copies were destroyed in the Second Great Fire of London during the blitz when Simpkins and Marshall's huge books' storage centre was burned down.

'*The People's Schools*' would today, I suppose, be described as a work on the sociology of education. There were very few such books in those days, especially books such as mine which were avowedly political in objective but attempted an accurate, quantitative survey of the educational structure from what I would still call 'a class point of view'. Though I was a Marxist, '*The People's Schools*' was not a Marxist book in any doctrinaire or dogmatic sense. It tried to describe simply and accurately the facts of the educational structure at the time, to bring out its gross inequalities and the consequent deprivation of those who were later to be dubbed the 'underprivileged' or 'disadvantaged'. In those days, we still talked about the workers and the working class.

What did the education system look like in the years immediately before the war? It is summed up by the following table for 1937:

1. Average no. of pupils on registers 5,248,260 in public elementary schools
2. No. of ex-public elementary school pupils 358,863 in grant-aided secondary schools
3. Approximate no. of ex-public elementary 21,000 school pupils in university institutions

The table reveals a blatantly class-structured system which needed a major expansion of resources to rectify. It highlights what Tawney called, ironically, the 'golden sentence' from the notorious May Report on Economies in the Public Services in 1931: "Since the standard of education, elementary and secondary, that is being given to the child of poor parents is already in very many cases superior to that which the middle-class parent is providing for his own child, we feel it is time to pause in this policy of expansion."

Of course, the pre-war structure was not the only expression of class bias. The amenities and resources of the people's schools were hardly the darlings of the Establishment. A ruling class, none of whose scions ever set foot in a public elementary school, was not likely to worry much about the state of its buildings or the way it was equipped unless they were pushed by irresistible, external pressures.

Size of classes was a key criterion of cheap and nasty provision. 'Overlarge' classes in elementary schools before the war were classes with more than fifty children and, in March 1937, there were still 2,646 of them. In spite of this, the Government, in face of falling rolls, demanded smaller staffs not smaller classes. At least 2 million children were still being taught in classes with between forty and fifty children—over two-fifths of the total. Classes in secondary schools (i.e., grammar schools) were considered overlarge, however, if they were over 30 strong, showing the bias against the overwhelmingly working-class 'senior elementary' schools (11–14) where the fifty-figure operated. One sad comment: in 1939, the annual cost of educating a child in a primary school was £17—this was all working-class children were deemed to be worth.

To change all this was the aspiration of the Labour Movement and the teaching profession. Perhaps the greatest contribution to the development of left professional thinking came with the social upheaval arising from the Second World War and the creation of the Council for Educational Advance in which the NUT decided to join with the Trades Union Congress, the Cooperative Union and the Workers' Educational Association to demand a more democratic education system. This led to the great campaign for a new Education Act. As the result of tremendous pressure and sharp argument the Act reached the Statute Book in the Summer of 1944.

Margaret: Early Years

I was born in July 1930, the only child of Reginald Louis Howard and Edith May Howard, familiarly known as Reg and Edie, who lived in a modest, lower middle class/upper working-class suburb of Birmingham. The first nine years of my life were happy and uneventful. I was the apple of both my mother's and father's eye. This might imply that I was spoilt but such a term doesn't seem appropriate to my memories of life as a young child. It was rather that I was cherished, the more so as I was somewhat delicate suffering from eczema, bouts of sickness and indigestion as well as measles (which made me seriously ill) and chicken pox.

My parents were warm and affectionate and, as far as I can recall, were never openly angry or irritable, either with each other or with me. The only quarrel I can remember my parents having was when my father pruned our privet hedge close to the ground and my mother, who was a keen gardener, burst into tears. I can remember this because it was a unique event. Obviously, my parents didn't agree about everything but they sorted things out quietly. So, I was brought up to keep good-tempered at all times and not to respond to provocation.

In addition to loving her garden, my mother loved reading both novels and poetry. I still have a copy of Tennyson given to her on her 20th birthday and her collected works of Longfellow. She also liked listening to classical music on the gramophone and I remember winding this up for her and sharing her pleasure by dancing around the room. Her mother had been an elementary school teacher, starting at the age of 13 as a 'pupil teacher', but my mother had not been allowed to stay on at school beyond the leaving age of 14.

My father was cheerful, fun-loving and quite incapable of being deferential to anyone. He loved sports and would sometimes go to watch Aston Villa or Birmingham City (he supported both with impartiality). He was interested in horse racing, studying form and having a little bet from time to time. His keenest interest was tennis, which he played at a small club near us, often winning the men's singles title in its annual championships. He also adored swimming and one of the happiest times in these years was our annual fortnight's holiday by the sea—I can still see him rushing into the waves and challenging them to break over his chest.

Like most children in the 1930s, I spent my first five years at home where my mother read me all the usual children's stories and taught me to read for myself. This had its downside when I went to school because I found it boring to be taught to read when I already could. My father had played mental arithmetic games with me from an early age, so addition and subtraction were quite literally child's play to me. But my time at home had been isolated and I had missed out on opportunities to play with children my own age, so I was excited to be able to do so at school.

Classes in my elementary school were large but I benefited from what I realise in hindsight were very skilled and committed teachers. Just how good they become clear when I was evacuated and went to a rural school to find that the class of nine-year olds were learning things I had learnt at least three years earlier. Even when moved up straight away into the top class, I was far ahead. It had clearly not been thought necessary to give the children of agricultural workers much schooling.

My mother enjoyed cooking and had no time for people who economised on food in order to spend their money on clothes or furnishings—she referred disparagingly to one of our neighbours as "just kippers and curtains." Our Sunday lunch was a ritual, beginning in summer with the picking of fresh vegetables and soft fruit from her allotment. At Christmas and birthdays, my mother's two bachelor brothers joined us and sometimes mother's married brother and his wife and son came too, but Gordon, my only cousin, being seven years older, had no great desire to play with me. The practice on these occasions was to get out a pack of cards after eating. The favourite game was solo whist, played for pennies or counters. By the age of five, I was demanding to be allowed to play. I became quite skilled and have enjoyed card games all my life.

In this account of my childhood, the word 'politics' has not appeared. I doubt if I had even heard the words 'politics', 'socialism', or 'Labour/Conservative/Liberal Party'. Yet I had picked up certain facts and ideas by endlessly asking questions: Q, why hadn't I got any brothers or sisters? A. Because Mummy and Daddy couldn't afford any more children. Why? A. Because just after you were born, Daddy lost his job.

Why? A. Because there was a world slump and mass unemployment, etc. Another question I asked my father was why he was missing a toe and wore a rubber divider. He relied "but for that neither I nor you would be here." He explained that as a soldier on the front line in the First World War, he was digging trenches when a fellow soldier swung his pickaxe straight through his toe. So, he was sent to hospital while the rest of his group were sent over the top and many of them were killed.

Then to my Uncle Bert—why was he blind in one eye? And to my Uncle Bill, why did he work in a factory not an office? Out of all these questions and answers, I built up some understanding of the social history of our family and the way events in the wider world had impinged upon it. Unlike Max, as a child I was not brought face to face with extreme poverty either in our neighbourhood or at school.

My father was extremely reticent about his early childhood and brushed aside questions. He said he never knew his mother. While writing this book, I commissioned research into his family background and discovered that he was hiding a very sad story. After the war, he was sent to an ex-servicemen's commercial college and trained as a clerk. He obtained a post with Thomas Cook's Travel Agency and made a modest living arranging rich people's holidays. He was not satisfied with this and already had tickets to immigrate to America when he met and fell in love with my mother. So, he got married and stayed at Thomas Cook's.

My mother had worked in offices since she left school and had become a skilled secretary. She had saved her earnings and for those days had a tidy sum put by. As my father was in regular work, they were able to begin their married life by buying a small, modern 'two-up, two-down' end of terrace house, flimsily built but with a bathroom and a garden, fairly typical of the four million new houses built in the inter-war years.

They married in 1929, the year of the Great Crash. The travel industry, geared as it was to the middle and upper classes, was hit by recession. So not long after I was born my father became unemployed. This lasted until he was rescued by passing the examination for a post in a growing public outfit, 'The Unemployment Assistance Board', later renamed 'The National Assistance Board' (today's Social Security). He remained there until his retirement, moving up from clerical assistant to Executive Officer.

I learnt more about my mother's family background. Her grandparents had owned a pub and when they were young her uncles had to get up early to help lay out the drinks for the workers in the factory up the road; the hooter summoning the workers went at 6 a.m. and at 10 to six they all poured into the pub to swallow a glass of hot tea and gin, coffee and rum etc. in lieu of breakfast. Her father owned a saddler's shop and I can remember going there as a toddler and seeing the horses being brought in to have their harnesses fixed. My uncles had helped with the work from an early age and Uncle Bert's blind eye was the result of sticking a needle into it while trying to sew a leather saddle. Both Uncle Bill and Uncle Bert won scholarships to grammar school but were taken out at the age of 13 to help in the workshop, which they did until called up to fight in the First World War, though Uncle Bert with his blind eye was sent to build tanks in the Austin Motor Works instead.

The demand for saddlers' work dwindled with the advent of the motor car but after the War my uncles' leather-working skills were in high demand in the upholstery section at the Austin motor factory Both rose to be foremen and they seemed to me as a child to be among the rich because they were able to buy a car, something neither my father nor our neighbours could afford. So, I asked, was everyone who worked in factories rich? I was obviously thoroughly mixed up! Maybe Max by the age of nine would have said that the rich were the capitalists who lived off the backs of the workers but it was to be some years before I learnt the words 'capitalist' and 'working class', which were never part of my parents' vocabulary.

My calm life came to an end on 3 September 1939, the day war was declared, when I was suddenly whisked away from home, my parents and our cat to live in the countryside. It was a lovely autumnal day and began in an exciting way. My uncles came round in their new 'Austin Seven' and we all climbed in. It was the first time I had ever been in a private motor car. We drove out into the countryside and I remember stopping at a roadside inn where a large crowd had gathered to listen to a loudspeaker broadcasting the announcement by Neville Chamberlain that Britain was now at war with Germany. Every time I hear replays of that speech, I remember when I first heard it and the shocked silence of those listening. 'War'. The very word inspired dread and memories of 1914–18.

My father said, "We have no choice now but to go on to your aunt and uncle's house and leave you there. Birmingham will be a prime target for German bombing and we want you to besafe." I had never previously heard of Uncle Sam and Aunt Lily, not surprisingly as the connection was indirect: my mother's aunt had married the brother of Uncle Sam. They had never had children and in retrospect it was very brave of them to offer to take charge of me. We arrived at Cleobury Mortimer, in Shropshire at the foot of the Clee Hills, and were directed to the gates of a large house in its own grounds. The gates were open so we drove in, though I could see that my parents were a bit intimidated. The middle-aged couple who greeted us couldn't have been nicer, but it was a big shock to me when my parents and uncles drove off and left me alone with them. My only consolation was that there was a cat with kittens and I remember crouching by a log fire cuddling them.

Children of nine are very resilient and, although I missed my parents, I adapted fairly quickly to country life. Never before had I had such space to roam in or the possibility of trees to climb. The garden was a children's paradise with fruit trees of all kinds—apples, pears, damsons and best of all a large mulberry tree which had delicious fruit and was ideal for climbing, Near the bottom gate by which we arrived there was a willow tree with branches sweeping down to the lawn and I appropriated the area inside as my house.

Not long after my arrival, a second evacuee arrived: John, aged 11, the son of my aunt's youngest sister. I had always yearned for a brother, but now I leant of its disadvantages. He wanted his way and I was used to getting mine. Uncle became very skilled in getting us to laugh away our disputes. When the bombing began in the summer of 1940, a Birmingham school teacher was also billeted upon my uncle and aunt; she was not really welcomed by John and me, but we were told firmly that in wartime everyone has to help everyone else. There was plenty of room for us all and my aunt, with the help of fresh produce from uncle's large vegetable garden and greenhouse, provided us with wonderful food despite rationing. I learnt later that during the First World War she had volunteered to work in a large hospital for wounded soldiers and by the age of 20 was its Head Cook and in charge of all its catering.

I had grown up in a socially homogenous suburb but I soon learnt that in the countryside people belonged to different social strata and that this depended on family background ('breeding') more than money alone. My uncle came from 'respectable' farming and land-owning stock; he himself was the district relieving officer (i.e., responsible for the operation of the Poor Law in the area) but also owned a number of houses and cottages. Above him were the county gentry, the 'Sirs' and 'Ladies', who appeared from time to time to open the village fete and who held the top positions in local organisations such as the Hunt or the Women's Institute, of which my aunt was the local chairwoman. At the very top was the Lord Lieutenant of the County, whom I heard talked about but never met, though my uncle did from time to time. Below were agricultural labourers, factory workers (there was a small light engineering factory nearby), shop assistants, domestic servants, etc.

My uncle and aunt were polite to everyone but I was given to understand that I must choose my friends from the right class. Among them were the bank manager's daughter and the daughter of a gentleman farmer (her older brothers went to a public school but she was sent to the local school), both were made welcome by my aunt. She tolerated my friendship with another evacuee from Birmingham whose father was an extremely rich businessman, though he was somewhat uncouth in my aunt's eyes. A problem arose, however, when I became friends with a very nice girl who lived on the Council Estate at the bottom of the village. I invited her to come and play with me in my willow-tree house. We had great fun but afterwards my aunt told me that I must not invite her again because she was not an "appropriate" friend for me. I was bewildered and upset—I felt I couldn't possibly tell my friend she wasn't welcome any more. It is the one bad memory I have from that time. I had come to love my aunt, who had a lovely gentle sense of humour, but I brooded about her snobbery over the children from the Council Estate.

My parents came to visit me whenever they could. My uncles were working night and day at the Austin factory as part of the war effort, so my parents had to come by two buses, with a change at Kidderminster. They could never stay long before having to leave to get the bus back. My mother was slightly intimidated by my aunt but was very happy to go round the gardens with my uncle, who enjoyed being with someone as keen on gardening as himself; all my father wanted was to see me and find out how things were going. In any case, he was never awed by social distinctions: he had the egalitarian view that he was as good as anyone else. Mother used to say the reason he rose no higher in the Civil Service was because he was outspoken and his superiors saw him as 'cheeky'. He said he saw no reason to pretend to like golf or go drinking in the clubhouse. Be that as it may, I later adopted his view as my own. Books about evacuation usually dwell on the hardships of evacuees and those who took them in. Little has been written about the frustrations of the parents left behind. It was hard for mine not to be able to bring up their only daughter—they were happy to see me settled and enjoying life in the country but could not help feeling a little jealous of my aunt and uncle. This was made worse by the latter's offer to adopt me in case my parents were killed in air raids—an offer, however well meant, which upset my parents. They did not want to give me up.

My parents did indeed get bombed and it was only through a piece of extraordinary good luck that they were not killed. They were saved by the existence of a main sewer below the house. No-one knew it was there but when a high explosive bomb landed in the back lawn ten feet from the house, it travelled down to the sewer and exploded into it. The blast travelled along the sewer and caused houses for half a mile to tremble. Our own house was lifted up and dropped back on the same foundations, cracked but still whole. My parents were shaken but unharmed. Only our cat was hurt—a section of his fur was caught in a crack when the house dropped back down leaving him with a bald patch. His fur grew again but for the rest of his live he hissed and arched his back whenever a plane flew overhead.

One aspect of life new to me was going to church every Sunday. If asked my parents would have said they were C of E. but their attendance at church was limited to marriages, christenings and funerals. I liked the services especially the singing, and became quite religious for a while. When three years later I returned to Birmingham, I went regularly to Sunday School and was confirmed. I even became a Sunday School teacher for smaller children. This did not last—when I was sixteen or seventeen, I resigned from the Sunday School and told the Vicar that I did not believe in God anymore. This was mainly because of my growing political awareness that the Church played a political role and had supported Franco. I also objected to singing the hymn *All things Bright and Beautiful; the Rich man in his Castle, the poor man at his gate. He ordered their estate.* What brought the matter to a head was that I had a very literal mind and was nauseated at the idea of drinking Jesus's blood, even symbolically. I have been an atheist ever since.

As I approached secondary school age, there was much discussion about my future education. John was leaving to go to boarding school, a minor public school. My parents were determined that I must go to grammar school. The nearest one from Cleobury Mortimer was in Ludlow, 11–12 miles away by bus over the top of the Clee hills. When younger I felt sick in buses and was sick if not allowed to get off. No-one knew whether I had grown out of this. I loved going around in Uncle Sam's car but that meant sitting in a bucket seat in the open boot.

Was it a risk worth taking? My parents came up with an alternative suggestion. The Birmingham grammar school to which they hoped I would go when the war ended had an arrangement to evacuate children to Burton-on Trent High School and they decided I should take advantage of that.

All this was based on the assumption that I would pass the 11+. My mother turned up at the Birmingham junior school I had been attending before the war and asked if I could take the 11+ as its pupil at the school in Cleobury. She got a frosty reception. "As I'd been attending a village school, I'd be unlikely to pass, certainly not win a scholarship. Could my parents pay the fees if I passed?" *(Free secondary education only began in 1944).* There were no League Tables in 1941 but the school evidently cared about its reputation by only submitting candidates who would be successful. However, mother persisted and I was allowed to do the tests in Cleobury. I did win a scholarship and mother used to laugh about how differently she was treated when she went to get the results—a red carpet welcome!

So, my life went through another upheaval, this time with less happy results. Burton-on-Trent High School was for "young ladies" and the staff assumed that the girls evacuated from Birmingham were anything but. So, they segregated us as much as possible. At morning Assembly, the George Dixon girls stood at the front, not with their classes. If there was any trouble or complaint about the behaviour of girls from the school, it was put down to us. We were a small minority and were put in the lowest streams. Our classmates took their lead from the staff and treated us with condescension. In the year I was there, I did not make a single friend in the school.

The billeting officer responsible for finding the Birmingham evacuees a place to live suffered from similar ideas about our social standing. My first billet was with a family similar to my parents. This would have been fine except that the mother was in the middle of a nervous breakdown and was sent to hospital. It worried me that my arrival might have been her tipping point. I was then moved into a council house with a couple who had several children. It was very jolly there and I enjoyed the happy-go-lucky atmosphere. It was extremely cramped— I shared a bed with another girl—and the food was very stodgy, none of the fresh fruit and vegetables I'd been used to in both Birmingham and Cleobury. All the same I enjoyed being there. I do not remember it being unclean but the sad fact was that after I'd been there a few weeks I developed impetigo. My mother came to see me and was furious—she marched me straight to the billeting officer and demanded that I be moved, then and there. She was usually a mild, rather timid woman but that day she turned into a virago—how dared they put her precious daughter into an impetigo-ridden slum?

Under this onslaught the billeting officer did find a new house for me to stay. It was a small, very clean and tidy house owned by an elderly couple. The husband, although past retirement age, worked in one of the breweries. They were kind to me but had little to talk to me about and I felt very lonely. I began to resent my parents having taken me away from Cleobury to dump me, as I saw it, in Burton-on-Trent. My parents too must have felt that they had made a big mistake: there was less danger of bombing by 1942, so they hurried along the repair of our house and at the end of the summer term took me home.

Before the war, I'd been a cosseted child, sure of where I belonged. For three years, I'd had to live without my parents and had moved up and down the social scale. Although I'd learnt to be self-reliant and socially adaptable, at ease chatting away happily with people of all classes, I'd become rather too self-contained and had lost a sense of emotional security or permanence. I'm not sure I recovered it until I married Max nearly twenty years later.

For the moment, however, I settled back into life with my parents and our cat. I started going to George Dixon Grammar School for Girls as arranged. (The boys' school was next door and there were adjoining playing fields, but we girls were forbidden to go nearer than 10 yards towards the fence!). Term had already begun as I'd been in hospital having my tonsils out and groups of friends had already formed, but I soon became great friends with a girl called Jo Holzinger. I knew about the Nazi persecution of Jews but did not realise for a long time that she was Jewish nor that her parents had put her on one of the children's refuge trains to escape from Germany. I knew she was an orphan and that her adoptive parents were strict Christedelphians, which may be why I didn't realise her background. She did eventually tell me her history but didn't make much of it, maybe because she was very young when she was separated from her parents or found it upsetting to remember it. Her adoptive parents were very strict and insisted she go straight home after school: they didn't allow her to come home with me, nor did they allow her to take me home with her. So, we chattered and played together only during the school day. When she left school at 16, I was not able to keep in touch with her and I've often wondered what became of her.

I found the year in Burton-on-Trent had put me behind and, somewhat to my chagrin I was put into the B stream, where we learnt German not Latin. At least, we were supposed to learn German but at that stage of the war (1942–3) we felt that it would be unpatriotic to do so. We decided that our contribution to the war effort would be making our German teacher's life a misery. If she'd been cannier, she could have told us that we needed to learn German so we could be spies and go behind the enemy lines. I enjoyed school and was shocked when a girl I liked was taken out of school on reaching 15 because her family needed her to earn money. Our teacher told us that she had visited her parents and begged them to let her stay on and take her school certificate but they told her they needed her earnings. I hadn't realised that there could still be poverty now that there was a "Welfare State" nor that some parents didn't value education in the way mine did.

At home, life was dominated by listening to the news on the radio and I sometimes went with my parents to the cinema, which showed the Pathé News. So, although there was not the immediacy which television now gives, we were able to follow events fairly closely. Bit by bit the Allied cause began to prevail— we cheered each victory and mourned each setback. As there were now hardly any unemployed, my father's work was mainly concerned with helping those made homeless by bombing. When the V2 bombs began to fall on London, he was sent there to help, leaving mother and me at home. She had been working in an office since soon after the outbreak of war so I was a 'latch-key' child; when I got home from school, my friends and I had wonderful games of 'ship-wreck'. leaping from chair to chair and climbing the banisters.

Another pleasure after I came back to Birmingham was visiting my aunt and uncle. This meant taking the same two buses my parents had used, with a long walk to reach the bus stops both in Birmingham and Kidderminster.

I was doing this from age 13 onwards and no-one seemed to worry about my safety—which sadly would not be the case today. On one occasion as I was walking home, a man came alongside me and offered to carry my case but when he began to fondle my breasts, I grabbed the case back, swung it against his legs and ran the rest of the way home.

When the war ended and I asked my father how he was going to vote in the General Election, he replied "Labour, of course" but didn't go into why. My mother said she would see which candidate she liked most. I realised if I wanted to understand more about politics and the reasons for wars and poverty and people being divided into different social classes, which by then I did, I should have to look for help elsewhere.

Margaret: Hidden History

My father said he never knew his mother and that from an early age he was brought up by his grandmother. I had always assumed that his mother had died young, although in retrospect that was not what he said. He always quickly brushed aside questions about his childhood, so to avoid upsetting him I learnt not to probe. It was only after I began compiling these memoirs that I thought I should perhaps check out exactly when and why his mother died. A silver teapot presented to her on her wedding had been sitting in our display cabinet since my parents died 50 years ago so I picked it up and by chance looked inside. To my surprise I found a faded newspaper cutting with an article about the wedding of Miss Tamar Howard and Mr Lotzrich at Farnborough on 23 December 1896. This reopened my curiosity so I set out to see if I could discover what had happened.

The facts I unearthed are very sad. His mother did not die young but lived until 1940 when she died of 'apoplexy' in a Poor Law Mental Asylum in Waterford in Ireland to which she had been admitted in 1909 with 'mania' and confined for over 30 years. What I have not been able to find out is how this came about or what happed to her between my father's birth on 5 June 1899 and 10 years later when she was admitted to the Asylum. Nor have I been able to find out whether or when my father knew what had happened to his mother and when he thought she had died. His reluctance to talk about her suggests he knew something unfortunate or shameful had happened to her.

Before her marriage, Tamar Howard had for several years served as a Wesleyan Church Sunday School teacher and was highly regarded judging by the gift of the silver teapot and many other gifts according to the newspaper report of their well-attended wedding. So, what happened? Did she suffer from post-natal depression and become ill immediately after my father was born in June 1899? This might account for my father having no memory of her at all. By the time he was a toddler living with his grandmother, he would surely have had some, even if very limited, memory of her had she been around.

In the early 20th century, and indeed for long afterwards, there was a horror of mental illness: it was seen as a terrible stigma. Poor families sent their mentally ill relatives to Poor Law asylums while the middle and upper classes hid them away. The Howard family in Farnborough were fairly well off so if she had become mentally ill soon after my father was born it seems likely that she was at first privately cared for. His father or his mother's relatives may have thought it best to keep her away from her infant son either to protect him from being upset by her condition or because they wanted to avoid him growing up with the stigma of having a mentally ill mother. The cost of private care may at first have been supplied by the Howard family to protect their reputation as my grandfather was a non-commissioned officer in the Army Catering Corps so not as well off as they were.

Two other facts have come to light. First, the 1911 Census records that my father was then living in Waterford with his father, who was based there, and recorded in the Census as an unmarried man. Secondly, that his father remarried in 1921, as no divorce is recorded, this was bigamy. This may suggest that he thought no-one, including his son, knew that his first wife was still alive.

On reflection, I think at some point in his childhood my father may have been told that his mother was mad or crazy and had been shut away for safety and nobody must find out because it would bring shame on the family. It was one thing, however, to hide away a member of a middle-class family with mental illness but a different matter to put her into a Poor Law Mental Asylum. At that time, a husband had the power to do what he wanted with an ill, or allegedly ill wife. Maybe the marriage had not been happy even before my father was born and my grandfather took advantage of an opportunity to get rid of my grandmother for good. Maybe the cost of private care was a factor. It was not unknown at that period to leave unwanted wives confined in asylums for years, whether it was justified or not. Indeed, right until the Mental Health Act of 1990 many women were confined in Mental Hospitals who were capable of living in the community.

My father was 10 years old when she was admitted, but had probably not yet gone to live with his father. Two years later when he was living with him, his father was posing as an unmarried man. My father must have thought that his mother was already dead. He was old enough to know that Mental Asylums were places of horror and drudgery, whose inmates stayed there until their death. So, if he found out that his father had incarcerated his mother in Waterford Asylum, it would explain his aversion to him. His father was brutal and bullied him but his determination to avoid seeing him after he came out of the army suggests a more profound reason for his feelings.

I don't know for certain if he did find out or when. One thing I feel sure about is that he didn't have any idea that she might still be alive when he married my mother because they would have wanted to go and find her and see how they could help her. Nor do I know whether he changed his name to disassociate himself from the memory of his father or, more simply, because as English patriots he or my mother didn't like having a German name. Maybe it was because of his unhappy childhood that he was such a loving and caring husband and father.

Max: Struggles Around the 1944 Education Act

From the moment I entered educational politics, I became convinced that the ending of the divided post-primary system and the abolition of privilege within it was the crucial step that was necessary to give working-class children their birth right in education. The Government's priority for most of the inter-war years was to cut, or at least keep down, the cost of education. The result was that opportunities for working class children were very little different in 1939 from what they were in 1918, when a forward-looking Education Act was passed but little implemented. The division of the elementary schools into stages after the Hadow Report of 1926 enabled some Local Authorities to develop central or technical schools (such as the one in Willesden where I taught) and provide more specialist teaching in 'senior' elementary schools, but most children were still leaving at 14 and receiving very inadequate provision from 11–14, many in all-through, overcrowded and dilapidated schools.

The Education Act of 1935 had provided for raising the leaving age to 15 but this had not been carried out when the War started. There had been little increase in the number of free places in the rate-supported 'secondary' schools, which modelled themselves on the endowed grammar schools and had a normal leaving age of 16. The Spens Report of 1938 had as its theoretical foundation the division of youngsters into types requiring different kinds of education. In short, the situation was exactly as I portrayed it in *The People's Schools*.

During the war, the Norwood Committee (1942) went even further in recommending the rigid stratification of the future secondary structure according to 'types', reflecting supposed abilities and aptitudes, each requiring a separate education, with the basic premise that the majority were of a type not really capable of a full secondary education.

This Report was the basis of the tripartite recommendations in the 1944 Act for schools to be created to provide for the "Age, Abilities and Aptitudes" of all children. No fees were to be paid in maintained secondary schools, which the Act said should be "sufficient in number, character and equipment to afford for all pupils opportunities for education offering such variety of instruction and training as may be desirable in view of their different ages, abilities and aptitudes, and of the different periods for which they may be expected to remain at school, including practical instruction and training appropriate to their respective needs."

The Act provided for the raising of the school leaving age to 15 from 1 April 1945, which was not to be postponed for more than two years, and the Minister was to bring before Parliament an Order in Council raising the age to 16 as soon 'as he is satisfied that it has become practicable'.

On nursery education, the Act merely said LEAs had "to have regard to the need" for provision for the under-fives in nursery schools or nursery classes. No duty was imposed. However, there was a wider conception than before of the welfare of the child.

As part of a comprehensive health service LEAs were obliged to provide free treatment, milk and meals (not specified as free) and boots and clothing and transport (where necessary). LEAs also had powers to prohibit or restrict the employment of school children out of school hours.

LEAs were permitted to provide maintenance allowances for the over 16s and compulsory attendance for one day a week at County Colleges for school leavers up to the age of 18 was to commence on a date to be appointed. There was to be an approved list of private schools 'recognised as efficient'. The dual system of church and state schools remained but under very favourable financial arrangements for the former.

Fees for higher education were not abolished but a duty was imposed on the LEAs to provide grants for all able to obtain places. Such grants were not mandatory for 'further education' as technical education came to be called.

Despite some improvements as a result of the Act, it failed to end discrimination against working-class children. Of course, the efficacy of the Act in this regard could only be assessed some years later in the light of what had taken place. Clearly there could be no change of any significance without the injection into the system of very substantial resources, not only to make good the damage and destruction of the war years but to provide for the expansion of educational opportunity and a leap forward to greater educational equality.

One development showed imagination. This was the Emergency Training Scheme (ETS) intended to crash-train in 13-month courses 30,000 teachers to make good the gaps caused by the war and to provide for raising the leaving age (R.O.S.L.A.) in 1947. I took part in the scheme as a Senior Lecturer in the largest of the colleges and was in it from its beginning to its end; some four years later. I can say that, for myself, any doubts I had because entrants did not have to possess the normal formal qualifications were soon dispelled because of the quality of the recruits and the eagerness and rapidity with which they set about acquiring the educational attainment essential for any teacher. Very many, if not all of them, had there been no war, would have gone through the educational sausage machine; it was just opportunity that had been taken from them. Others brought to the profession what so many think desirable—non-academic experience and maturity, much of it gained in the crucible of war.

Of course, there were some misfits and these existed too among the staff, often hastily recruited and pedagogically inadequate for the task. But if my own experience is anything to go on the training was down to earth, caring and genuinely educative. We were not prepared to foist on to hapless children teachers who could not teach, though some slipped through the net. Only a small number of staff (often from the old training colleges) were addicted to educational fantasising; by far the majority knew what schools were like, what they were about and the kind of practical expertise teachers needed, and this they tried to provide while, at the same time, partially filling the gaps created by lost educational opportunity.

Crucial to the new education dispensation was raising the leaving age to 15 (R.O.S.L.A.), which in the Act was to come into effect not later than two years after April 1945. Shockingly, for a Labour Government, sharp controversy developed over this because of the resources necessary. Many accounts have been given of the divided views within the Cabinet.

Ellen Wilkinson stood her ground in face of Cripps and Morrison and also of a press campaign initiated by *The Sunday Times* which produced some incredible arguments. Nastiest of all, however, was the 'progressive' Liberal *News Chronicle* which insisted that industry needed the 'nimble fingers' of our fourteen-year-olds if Britain was to compete in the brave new post-war world. What hypocrisy, to call in the very arguments used by the 19th century factory masters and repeat their self-same words! In those days, Lord Macaulay, with contempt, asked in Parliament if the country's greatness depended on the exploitation of little children. I wrote to the 'liberal' editor saying I would never buy his paper again—it had up till then been my 'daily'—and indeed I never did.

Happily, the Cabinet decided against postponement, but the essential further advance to 16 was indefinitely shelved. At my first post-war NUT Conference in 1947 in Scarborough, I moved a resolution demanding the implementation of R.O.S.L.A. to 16. It was carried with full support of the Executive and was about as ineffective as any of the demands for educational advance in the years that immediately followed.

The implementation of the Act required new schools as well as new teachers in order that all children could attend a secondary school. Although there was a formula that could be interpreted as meaning that the same conditions should pertain to all schools, its actual words allowed a different interpretation. I described them at the time as "a Pandora's box which was to reveal not hidden treasures but the most controversial collection of bones of contention ever to be provided by parliamentary drafters." Education according to 'Age, Abilities and Aptitudes', such innocent and common sense-sounding words, became the foundation of a tripartite secondary system every bit as divided and class-biased as in the bad old pre-war days. And it was put over by the con trick of renaming the senior schools 'Modern Schools'. Whoever thought up that title deserves the accolade due to genius for it was a brilliant cover-up for second-class schooling for the masses in a tiered system. Modern? It was modern apparently to leave school earlier than the old grammar schools considered normal. It was modern to have large classes, to lack specialist teachers of maths and science or modern languages. It was modern to spend less per head on those who needed education most.

True, because of the basic statutory need to provide 'roofs over heads', some of the new Modern buildings—and they grew in number—were fine and well-equipped. And many of their teachers daily falsified in practice the nasty typology of the ever-so-respectable Reports as well as the mass of 'evidence' produced by the fake and fraudulent educational psychologist Cyril Burt and his academic acolytes 'confirming' working-class mediocrity.

One event made an enormous impact. With incredible stupidity, the new Ministry under Ellen Wilkinson took over from the Tories the notorious Pamphlet No. 1, *The Nation's Schools*, produced by the civil servants, which embodied all the worst features of 'typology' in yet another golden sentence. It declared that the education of the overwhelming majority of children was to be determined by the fact that "their future employment will not demand any measure of technical skill or knowledge." They were to be the hewers of wood and the drawers of water in our capitalist society! No formulation could have been more deliberately calculated by the civil service mandarins, public school alumni almost to a man, to raise every hackle in the Labour Movement.

There were stormy scenes at the first Labour Party Conference after Labour took office in which, to everyone's astonishment, Red Ellen, in tears, defended the abominable monster produced by her Tory predecessors.

The fact is that she was muddled on what constituted progressive educational policy. She was one of a long line of Ministers of Education who were easily manipulated by Public School officials.

Some of the offending passages in this classic statement of class-ridden education were to be 'revised' after the Conference defeated both platform and Minister. I doubt whether that revision ever took place. Enquiries at the DES have failed to produce any version except the original, so once again the mandarins prevailed and a Labour Conference was deceived. It was to become all too plain that the ghost of *The Nation's Schools* still walked; it was the spectre which haunted the development of post-1944 Act secondary education. But though the mandarins had won, this had the salutary effect of wonderfully concentrating the minds of the Left in the profession on the need for radically restructuring the system.

As I wrote at the time, free secondary education and ROSLA were the peak of implementation of the 1944 Act and of Labour's devotion to its pre-war promises for education. They also seemed to register the end of the period of post-war advance. That was the way it looked to those of us on the left who, while not expecting miracles, were appalled by Cripps' cuts in 1948. Hugh Gaitskell, Cripps' successor as Chancellor, whom I'd known so well when a student, astounded us by actually proposing for Cabinet discussion cuts even more serious than Cripps's: raising the starting age and lowering the leaving age back again. Happily, these were not implemented.

When the Government was defeated in 1951, the Tories needed only to continue what Labour had begun in cuts. At the Easter 1952 NUT Conference, I gained some notoriety by calling the Minister, Florence Horsburgh, Madame Gradgrind. It was not really an accurate parallel, but it caught on. It should really have been Madame Guillotine. for she set to with her axe with such gusto and what seemed almost like sadistic pleasure, beginning with her notorious 5% cut 'request' to LEAs for 1952–3, which was supposed not to harm 'the essential fabric' (was this the first time this weasel phrase was used?) of the system—a claim which Sir William Alexander, the leader of the Local Authorities, tore to shreds in *Education*.

A curious feature of this attack on the schools was, of course, that Churchill's Chancellor was none other than Rab Butler. Did he weep tears over his first-born now being sacrificed on the altar of economy when only a few years earlier it had seemed such a lusty child? Cabinet Papers for 1953 show that he produced a list of savings from the education budget that included charging fees in state schools, raising the starting age to six and lowering the leaving age back to 14. (Was this perhaps the origin of 'Butskellism'?) This was too much even for Madame Gradgrind and Butler did not press his case to the end. The reasons were not educational but that the proposals, e.g., the leaving age of 14, would create 'serious political opposition' and could only remove enough teachers to make the savings worthwhile at the cost of keeping classes 'excessive' lower down—a politically dangerous course.

It is time the full facts of this episode in Butler's career were more widely known. He is not such a hero after all. He went on, of course, guffing about the glories of the secondary modern schools, "the most interesting and distinguished feature of the 1944 provisions…giving our democracy a fuller meaning and new vigour." Indeed!

I wrote at the time, quoting J L Hammond, "The poor never lost a right without being congratulated by the rich on gaining something better." Why, I asked, did they not send their own children to these schools if they were so wonderful?

Disillusionment set in as the facts took their toll. In 1953, nine years after the Act, I felt obliged to give a very negative assessment of the effect of the Act in my book *Your Children's Future:* "Nursery schools, the leaving age of 16, County Colleges, genuine secondary education for all—the major part of the proposed reforms have remained dead words while even of the advances made some have been whittled down and others seriously threatened." One weakness was the lack of provision of technical education: within the tripartite system few technical schools existed and there was no financial support for students at Further Education colleges, unlike for university students who received mandatory grants.

In 1953, there were still nearly 600 schools on the Blacklist of unfit schools, many of which were described in 1924 as "incapable of improvement" and these were the tips of an iceberg of continuing old and very unsatisfactory premises. Even worse, classes could not be reduced in size. Though the definition of 'overlarge' had been amended to 'over 40' there were still, in 1952, 1240 classes with over 50 children and 47% of the children were in classes of over 40 in primary and over 30 in secondary schools. Butler, who had eloquently proclaimed that until classes were reduced in size the teacher was "more a circus master than a prophet" was actually the circus master as things were turning out, helping to whip the system whose reform he had fathered.

One could go on giving indices of the low level of educational provision in the early fifties which overshadowed the earlier advances, the negative side of things that seemed so overwhelming, the collapse of so many visionary hopes. Interestingly enough and typical of the ambience, my sharply critical book was given a very favourable feature article review in the establishment *Times Educational Supplement* by Jennie Lee.

Was the education structure more deeply rooted than one had imagined, more resistant to change? Or was it just a question of lack of clear thinking about class and education and the political will to face the problems and try to solve them? We on the Left took the latter view and, at the time, we blamed Labour for betraying the promise of the post-war years. There was no-one in the Attlee Cabinet to fight for the people's schools as Bevan fought for the people's health. True, Ellen Wilkinson had shown some spirit in raising the leaving age, but she did not understand what made the system tick. Her successor, George Tomlinson, has a quite undeserved reputation for being a progressive Minister—his was a typical case of being enveloped by the Whitehall mandarins in their aristocratic embrace while they undermined Labour's progressive aspirations.

Max: Birth of the Comprehensive School

Within the NUT before the war, though much strengthened after it, there had grown up a keen group of left-wingers who were concerned not only with general socialism but with socialist educational reform. Some were members of the National Association of Labour Teachers (the precursor of today's Socialist Educational Association), others were in the Communist Party and there were Labour M.P.s such as W.G. Cove and Leah Manning.

Among the issues we discussed was what sort of schools would be needed if the long-standing aim within the Labour movement of "Secondary Education for All" was to be fulfilled. From our left group discussions emerged the idea of what we called the multilateral school, either a single institution with modern, technical and grammar streams across whose boundaries transfer would be easy and within which there would be parity of conditions; or the three different streams in separate buildings on a single campus site. Some of us wanted to go beyond this to 'L'Ecole Unique', the single or Common School, a title which we borrowed from our French left-wing colleagues and which more clearly expressed what we wanted to achieve. But so strong was our feeling for the art of the possible and our conviction that the Labour Movement which, with the teachers, was to be the engine of progress that we united with our Labour colleagues on a policy of the highest common factor of agreement we could achieve. That explains why, in *The People's Schools (1939)*, in the programme of reform at the end, I did not go farther than demanding experiments in multilateral schools. I'm afraid I was a premature politician in thus subordinating the views of my closest colleagues and myself to the need for building a wider movement that could advance towards our goals.

(Footnote Max's group seemed to be unaware that after the publication of the Hadow Report an NUT pamphlet advocated a single 'multibias' school and the term 'a Common School' was used in discussion at that time but sputtered

out in the 1930s faced with the struggles against economy cuts and the ideological pressures from the Conservative Party and the Board of Education against any fundamental change in the education of the majority of children. See Brian Simon, The Politics of Educational Reform (1974) chapters 3 and 4.)

By the time the war ended, the previous ideological confusion on the Left was largely dispelled and there was among left-wing teachers, if not among Labour Councils, a pretty general consensus that went beyond multilateralism and adopted the restructuring solution implicit in the Comprehensive School. 'Comprehensive' as a descriptive term that became generally accepted dates from Circular 144 of 1947 in which the Ministry defined the different possible types of secondary school. It is a clumsy and dull word which we accepted to avoid confusion in preference to either Single or Common.

Reasons for the consensus around the Comprehensive Idea are not difficult to find. There had been a growing realisation that the pre-war Hadow reform which had been heralded by many as the way forward (was not Tawney a member of the famous Committee?), in practice imposed on secondary education iron chains by separating different types of secondary school. And the Spens Report of 1938, though implementation of its secondary proposals would have created better opportunities for working-class children than Hadow, had as its theoretical foundation the obnoxious division of youngsters into types requiring different kinds of education.

The Norwood Committee (1942) went even further than Spens in rigidly stratifying the secondary structure according to 'types', reflecting supposed abilities and aptitudes, each requiring a separate form of education, with the basic premise that the majority were of a type not really capable of a full secondary education. This stupid formula was the spirit which informed the Ministry's interpretations of 'abilities and aptitudes' in the 1944 Act, with predictable results in rigid tripartism.

In his book in 1954, Petch, perhaps Britain's greatest post-war expert on examinations, revealed how Norwood 'rigged' his committee to ensure its final recommendations. He describes the circumstances in which the Norwood Report was published as a "perfect example of that departmental procedure which, to the uninitiated, seems like official chicanery." The department was, of course, the Board of Education. Thus, the Report was published without reference to the Secondary School's Examination Council which might well have refused to accept its recommendations. The Board wanted the unadulterated Report as 'the tablets of law'.

Another Committee, the Fleming, set up to examine the relationship of the public schools to the maintained system reported for creating closer association by having the public schools take in up to 50% of their pupils from the maintained sector. The Fleming 'democratic' solution was a mirage that was to appear time and again throughout the post-war years, whenever the public schools found themselves under pressure—political, social or financial. It was, of course, never on, for the simple reason that you could not by tinkering make a root and branch class institution democratic. As I have always argued you cannot mend the public schools; you have to end them.

Taken together, Norwood, Fleming and then the row over *The Nation's Schools* served to harden progressive opinion for hard solutions. In the event, those, who like myself, were advocating fundamental change received what mattered more than anything else—the imprimatur of hard facts, the fiat of the realities of the post-1944 system as it was, not as it had been imagined by rosy-eyed progressives. In the brave new world under a Labour Government with a pretty nifty record of social reform (Health Service, Social Security à la Beveridge, housing programmes, etc.), the education structure remained as class-stratified as ever.

Despite the strength of the case, it took twenty years of campaigning to achieve a consensus that the Comprehensive School was the route to educational progress. Ideas were canvassed, arguments developed and fed into the small but active and influential National Association of Labour Teachers and from it into the Labour Party; into Communist Party educational pamphleteering and campaigning; and into union educational discussions.

A policy of more grammar schools continued to attract support for a long time after the war and Labour-controlled LEAs had to be persuaded that this was not the way forward. As late as 1955, Gaitskell could still say he "saw no need to be 'violently dogmatic' about the Comprehensive School." And it was no off the cuff phrase of Harold Wilson when (in answer to a question of mine at a public meeting as late as 1963) he said the grammar schools would be abolished over his dead body. Many working-class children had found their opportunities via grammar schools, even though they formed a minority of their pupils. This explains why it took such a long time not only to win the NUT for the Comprehensive School but for the Labour Party to become firmly committed.

The Labour Party was not fully committed till 1958 and the NUT not fully so till 1966.

We were not helped by some of the 'progressive' educationists. They were wrong even if for progressive motives. Typical of the 'progressive' literature of the time was the 1949 book by Roger Armfelt, 'Education—New Hopes, Old Habits' (1949) which stated: "Education will be harmed if it places an exaggerated emphasis on knowledge, on memory, on analysis, on researching and on the expression of thought in written words." It was such theories that I was to rail against throughout my life. In the late forties and early fifties, a number of us on the left conducted a sustained polemic against those who lauded the 'freedom' of the Secondary Moderns from Grammar School 'restraints' such as examinations—they failed to understand the inferior social role in adult life for which this 'freedom' was a fig leaf.

Alas many of our colleagues on the left followed this false trail and were completely sold on 'progressive' methods which denied the need for systematic learning. An example was the concentration on 'project methods', not as an aid to study in particular cases, but as a total substitution for a systematic curriculum. Another was the growth of 'Look and Say' methods of teaching reading. In a notable contribution to this important debate John Daniels (one of our group) and Hunter Diack of Nottingham University produced a set of readers, *The Royal Road Readers*, based on phonic methods. (It is interesting to see this debate resuscitated in recent times).

At the time, I summed up the new 'theory' of the modern school in the words: "It doesn't matter what you teach them, it's how you teach it. Content doesn't matter as long as you keep the children happy. High attainment, sound knowledge, the avenue to the seats of power, are not for the masses. Keep them happy with 'practical' work—you don't need brains for working a lathe or the tools of the 'modern' equivalents of the hewers of wood and drawers of water." The sad fact was that the 'progressive' movement, even if unintentionally, played ideologically into the hands of the right who did not believe that the workers' children either needed or were capable of a fully comprehensive education.

Intelligence Testing was the intellectual fig-leaf used to cover up the nakedness of the class-biased educational structure, especially the secondary modern school. From early in the 20th century, the study of eugenics and psychology was based upon the concept that intelligence was innate, fixed and could be measured. Professor Spearman argued that each person's inherited mind power could no more be changed than his height.

And in 1909, Cyril Burt's comparative study of test results from children in private preparatory schools and those from public elementary schools was used as proof that working class children were less intelligent than those from the middle and upper classes. Later the alleged intellectual inferiority of the masses was used as the theoretical justification for Churchill's 'Labour is unfit to govern' slander.

Looking back on those days, one can feel pride to have belonged to a group of left-wingers who took on in theoretical combat the pillars of the educational establishment: that dared to examine critically the mighty Professors, Spearman, Burt and Vernon. I remember how small I was intended to feel when, bold enough to utter a few words of doubt on Spearman's views on intelligence at a conference at the London Institute, the Director, G B Jeffery, lambasted me from the platform for daring to question the master. Spearman was not a crook like Burt, but he was wrong, terribly wrong in his theories that placed the working-class in permanent intellectual servitude.

No-one has yet told the full story of our campaign, for such it was, against Intelligence testing, and it is time the omission began to be repaired. In the course of our discussions on educational policy in the Education Advisory Committee of the CP, we had begun to feel the need to develop our understanding of the intelligence theories then prevalent. Paradoxically, it may be thought, intelligence tests were advocated in the inter-war period as a way of proving that many working-class children were being wrongly deprived of secondary education and, therefore, there should be increased working-class entry to Grammar Schools. When, however, after the War, we became wedded to the Comprehensive as the way forward, testing was correctly seen as an obstacle to the new system we wanted—one totally unselective. Testing served the purposes of those who denied the possibility of such a system being viable. So, we were drawn to challenging what we saw as the theoretical foundations of selection.

We were aware of the resolution of the Soviet Communist Party of 1936, attacking 'pedology', i.e., testing, and we began looking at the Soviet material, psychological writings, etc. But we developed our own critique and had the advantage of having in our midst highly intelligent and psychologically sophisticated comrades such as John Daniels, then a teacher in Nottingham and later to become Deputy Director of the Institute of Education at Nottingham

University. John had worked in Personnel Selection during the war and had rumbled testing for what it was worth, and he tutored me, a psychological ignoramus, on its essential phoniness. Others, such as Joan and Brian Simon, played an important part in our discussions. But perhaps most important of all, we developed close links with the Communist Party Psychologists Group which included some who were later to become Britain's leading academics in the field, particularly those centred in the Maudsley Hospital.

I organised joint discussions between the teachers and psychologists and we clarified our thinking on the essence of intelligence theories and the work of the leading intelligence testers. Our aim was to dethrone I.Q. as an instrument used in group testing for educational selection: we could not reach total agreement on the possible clinical use of I.Q. for individual diagnosis but this did not seem so important to us. What was agreed on most of all was what I expressed in the sentence: "The job of education is to change children, not to classify them."

Highlight of our campaign was a public conference organised by the Party's Cultural Committee, led by Sam Aaronovitch, at the Beaver Hall in the City of London in 1950 at which I delivered a theoretical/practical/political statement of some length (later published), followed by a discussion from the very large audience drawn from academics, teachers and the Labour Movement. The conference was widely reported in the relevant press and made a substantial impact. We carried on the campaign in articles, letters to the press, union discussions, meetings, etc. and can truthfully say we shook the Testing Establishment and, perhaps more importantly, began to convince Labour Local Authorities and teachers at large of both the falsity and wickedness of testing as an instrument of selection. We decided to prepare a substantial theoretical work, which Brian Simon wrote and which was discussed at every stage by our committee. *Intelligence Testing and the Comprehensive School (1953)* proved to be an excellent work of major importance and is still, deservedly, widely read.

I have always regarded our campaign on intelligence testing as the most successful waged by Communist teachers and psychologists. We changed the face of educational psychology—no-one today can advocate testing for educational selection in the manner that we had to endure in the forties and fifties. Without our campaign the movement for Comprehensive Schools would have been considerably weakened and I look back with pride on my own inexpert role.

We fought the good fight for high standards, for raising the educational level and demanded first that all artificial barriers be removed from secondary modern children staying on and entering for the examinations hitherto exclusively oriented towards the grammar school minority; and secondly, by intensive propaganda for the Comprehensive school. We had many allies in the profession and among educational administrators—among the latter J.J Dempster in Southampton, Alec Clegg in the West Riding and Sir William Houghton in London stand out as showing what children could accomplish with the theoretical shackles removed.

In the mid-fifties, while the main educational effort among left-wing teachers was directed towards turning the clock of educational advance forward again—buildings, size of classes, teacher supply and such like issues—the group of Labour and Communist teachers continued to meet informally, including a larger gathering at the NUT Conference. But it lost much of its steam after 1956, not only because of the Soviet Twentieth Congress revelations and the Soviet occupation of Budapest (which weakened the Communist element considerably) but because our Labour colleagues were confident of winning their battle for the Comprehensive in a future Labour Government.

What helped us most was the mounting evidence of what a blunt instrument for selection the 11+ was. Teachers, both in the Grammar and the Modern Schools were able to show from their daily experience that selection at ten plus for a transfer the following year could be a hit and miss affair. Many children were being denied success in the grammar school because they were kept out, just as many were not succeeding because they were selected in to a narrow form of education unsuited to their talents.

Selection also took place in some areas for admission to technical schools at 13-plus, again using blunt instruments for making the choice.

On one occasion in my own school, we were asked to take an extra form by the Middlesex LEA because, through a clerical error, twenty-five extra children were notified that they had won a place. I got a lot of fun quipping about 'Selection by Clerical Error'. It highlighted the absurdity of the whole process.

A growing movement towards a broad consensus against selection so early in the child's life was pushed forward by the undermining of confidence in intelligence testing, not just its procedures but its whole theoretical foundation in the false concept of immutable innate intelligence. Intelligence Tests, we said, tried to pour the holy water of 'science' on the essentially reactionary political and social process of selection.

All the evidence seemed to be pointing in the same direction—that the eleven-plus should be abolished. And, with this, almost inevitably, support for restructuring the system on Comprehensive lines grew. Slowly, the number of Comprehensives increased up and down the country. The example of London, Middlesex, Anglesey, Coventry and the West Riding was followed elsewhere. But legislation was delayed until 1965, by which time the case against the 11+ appeared irrefutable.

Margaret: Widening Horizons

When Max returned to teaching after the war and immediately resumed trade union activity, I was still at George Dixon Grammar School for Girls. I really had very limited contact with the world outside home and school. My parents were not very much interested in either British politics or world events, so what I learnt at school was the dominant influence on the development of my ideas and the widening of my cultural horizons. Looking back, I have gratitude to my teachers in the George Dixon Grammar School for Girls, and above all to Miss Player, the senior history teacher. This does not make me support the return of selective Grammar Schools—I just want all schools to be good within a Comprehensive system catering for the learning needs of all pupils. I doubt if the supporters of keeping our remaining grammar schools have in mind what was one of the most permanent contributions of George Dixon Grammar School to my future life—my conversion to socialism.

Even now, when asked how I became a socialist despite coming from a totally non-political family, I find it hard to explain. I doubt whether any of the teachers at my girls' grammar school were in the NUT or even the women's grammar school teacher's union, and only one of them had the reputation of being a socialist. This was Miss Player. She was very shy and reserved and would have been horror struck at the idea of indoctrinating her pupils. But just by teaching history in a very matter of fact way, and recommending books to read, she opened my eyes to socialist ideas—not Marxism apart from Engel's 'Condition of the Working Class in 1844' and later 'The Communist Manifesto', but Bernard Shaw. Like Max, I read 'The Intelligent Woman's Guide to Socialism and Capitalism' and Robert Tressell's, 'The Ragged Trousered Philanthropist'.

Reading about trade unions led to my first militant action: at the age of about 16, I led a walk-out from school dinners, when for the second day running, we were served mince followed by semolina—two plates of slop! So, we all walked out. Oh, how I got told off!—this was the era of rationing and I was told it was criminal to waste food at such a time. I noticed, however, that we were never again offered mince followed by semolina, so it seemed militancy was effective!

The history syllabus at that time ended with the First World War and had significant gaps: it was both English and West European centric—never a word about Scotland, Ireland, the East of Europe or most of Asia, Latin America or even America after its independence in 1773. A large section of the syllabus for both the School Certificate and Higher School Certificate dealt with the British Industrial Revolution and I was inspired by the development of the trade unions and their struggles to win better conditions and a living wage. In the Sixth form we also specialised in the Tudors and Stuarts, and were required to read R.H. Tawney's 'Religion and the Rise of Capitalism'—which I found hard going but food for thought.

The founding of the British Empire—four fifths of the world was pink on the map—was extolled in our text books but we learnt from Miss Player that this was at the cost of the exploitation and oppression of local people, to the extent of the virtual wiping out of the Australian aboriginals and Maoris, and large-scale massacres during the suppression of the 1857 Indian Mutiny and during the Zulu war in 1879. She told us briefly also about the slave trade to America. So, I came to deplore jingoism and was shocked at the story of how Lloyd George, an opponent of the Boer War, came to Birmingham and had to be smuggled into the Town Hall to protect him from being set upon. In European history, we studied France from Louis XIV to the French Revolution and its call for 'Liberty, Equality, Fraternity', the Revolutions of 1848, Germany under Bismarck and the abolition of feudalism in Tsarist Russia, but stopped short of the Russian Revolution.

Coverage of what had been taking place more recently was limited to one period a week of 'Current Events' provided for all Upper Fifth and Sixth From classes as a group.

The teaching was not searching or critical in any way but we learnt about the setting up of the United Nations and the Declaration of Human Rights and were introduced to the Beveridge Report and its aim to fight 'the five giants of squalor, ignorance, want, idleness and disease', which was why the Welfare State was being created. Some doubts have been expressed in recent times about whether the mood of national solidarity and sense of community at the end of the war was really as strong and universal as portrayed in writings about that time. I can only say that it was axiomatic in my school that a better life should and could be created for the benefit of the whole population now that the war was won. Everyone had sacrificed and everyone should benefit. That was what we were brought up to believe.

The radio and visits to the cinema, which always showed the latest newsreels, filled in some gaps. I remember my horror at the pictures of starving children during the Indian famine in 1943/4, and later the appalling pictures of the entry into the Belson Concentration Camp. A freed inmate from the prison camp returned to live with his parents in the road next to ours. He was all skin and bones and wandered around talking to himself. I wanted to be nice to him but did not know how to approach him,—in truth I felt embarrassed and out of my depth, so tried to avoid him.

Long before the end of the sixth form, I had decided that I was a socialist. Emotional sympathy with the "have-nots" of the world played a major part in this decision but that could have been subsumed into support for generally agreed policies for improving conditions for everyone in Britain within a Welfare State. But from the books I had read and from my own small encounters with class divisions and prejudice, I had come to the conclusion that the core problems of the world—poverty, exploitation, inequality and lack of freedom—were the result of the class divisions of the capitalist system and that control of the economy must be taken out of the hands of capitalist corporations and run under democratic control for the benefit of the whole community.

As I saw it, the war had been won using a planned economy and that should not be abandoned nor economic decision-making revert to the search for profit by those who owned capital. Instead, the needs of those who created goods and services by their work should determine the direction of economic policy, together with the needs of the young, the old and others who were unable to work. In short, I believed that for the world to be made a better place it was essential to establish socialist ownership and control of economic life. I am a natural organiser by nature (i.e., somewhat bossy—my Head Mistress told my parents that I was destined to end up as a Headmistress), but I have never been able to see things in a mess without wanting to sort them out. My ideas were vague and lacked a systematic theoretical base—indeed I was still almost totally ignorant of the writings of Marx or his followers. Nor was I much influenced by the Soviet Union—Communist Russia under 'Uncle Joe' had been our ally in winning the war against Hitler but, unlike for Max's generation, it was not my main focus.

Had I known that Marx said that interpreting the world was not enough, the task was to change it, I would have agreed. I wanted to be part of that and have in a modest pragmatic way, and despite many set-backs, gone on wanting to do so ever since. The main drawback to my naive idealism was that I had absolutely no idea about how to put it into practice. I knew no-one politically active, no-one who belonged to a political party or organisation. Maybe Miss Player did, but there was no way I could ask her. None of my friends at school had become as interested as I was in politics. I went two or three times to all-Birmingham Sixth form debates but, like most of the girls there, did not have the confidence to participate. I began to have quite strong opinions on current events, but no-one to share them with.

One discussion I do remember with my parents took place just before I left school over the Yangtze incident when a British warship was attacked by Communist forces during the Chinese civil war:

I expressed the view that the ship oughtn't to have been there and Britain should not be getting involved but my father thought this was a pro-Communist anti-British view and that anyone having it should go back to China. I just went quiet—no point in quarrelling with my father who, although he continued to vote Labour, had become more and more right-wing after the end of the war, perhaps because his only political reading was the *Daily Express* and *News of the World.*

My interest in politics did not stop me having many other interests and benefitting from all that the school did to widen its pupils' horizons. Organised trips to the Town Hall to hear the City of Birmingham Symphony Orchestra and school trips to the Birmingham Repertory Theatre, then in its heyday with Paul Schofield playing the key roles, encouraged me and my friends to go to concerts and the Rep in our own time, and also to the Shakespeare theatre at Stratford on Avon, where we picnicked by the river before going into matinee performances. I loved reading and read widely, not just our set books. A film club at school supplemented my occasional outings to the cinema—I must have seen all of Charlie Chaplin's films many times and particularly liked 'The Great Dictator' and 'Modern Times'; I remember, too, 'Metropolis' on the dehumanising effect of industrialisation and 'Dr. Caligari's Cabinet' about psychological illness, which gave me nightmares. Special favourites were the French films from the 1930s such as 'Quai des Brumes'.

An exchange visit to Paris in 1947 certainly extended my horizons and in ways not foreseen by my teachers. When I arrived at the Gare du Nord, I looked in vain for the schoolgirl who was supposed to meet me. Eventually the platform cleared and left a tall, elegant young lady wearing very smart clothes and platform heels—this was my exchange. We were both just under 17 but the difference in our life styles was even greater than in our appearance. She took me home and dressed me in some of her clothes and took me dancing at the 'Moulin Rouge', the famous Montmartre night club. I had never before been to a dance hall, let alone a night-club, but once I got the hang of it, I happily jived the night through. Her parents seemed to think this quite normal and were kind and welcoming; among other things they introduced me to wine. They also took me to the cinema to see 'Les Enfants du Paradis' which I found very moving even though I didn't understand it properly until I saw it again some years later. The problem was the return visit. How could I possibly entertain this sophisticated French girl in the manner to which she was accustomed? Quite simply, I couldn't, and she was clearly bored to death when she came to Birmingham a few weeks later. This was not one of those exchanges which led to a life-long friendship.

On the down side at George Dixon, and probably typical of Girls' Grammar Schools at that time, science was not well taught and I never really understood what it was all about. I made it difficult for myself by always asking "why," but no-one helped me grasp the basic principles of scientific knowledge. I was really floundering but passed with credit in the School Certificate exams—which just shows how a facility for rote learning can mislead examiners!

This was very much the era of "The Two Cultures" (i.e., the Sciences and the Humanities) and at the end of the fifth form everyone staying on had to choose. My problem was that my two favourite subjects were history and maths. I suggested that I should do these two subjects in the 6th form with the aim possibly of studying economics and economic history at university. "But," said my teachers, "you can't do that. Economics is not for girls. If you are going to be a teacher, you need to choose between the humanities and the sciences." Maths was bracketed with science, so as I had no confidence about grasping what science was about and no wish to go on with it, I chose History, English and French.

I was sad to give up maths—I was no mathematical genius but I'd obtained distinctions in both maths and advanced maths in the School Certificate exams and I wanted to go on with it.

The maths' teacher was very annoyed—I suppose not many girls wanted to do maths and she'd looked forward to having me in her small 6th-form group. For the rest of my time at school she cut me dead, which saddened me because I felt it had not been my fault. I'd truly wanted to do maths. Although it meant I never formally studied economics, I've always taken a serious interest in economics and read widely in that field later in life.

Just as my parents had assumed I would go to grammar school, they assumed I would go to university. I also wanted to go, especially if I could leave home and see a bit more of the world. The school mainly sent its pupils to Birmingham University but about ten years earlier, a girl had got into Oxford so it was suggested to my parents that I stay on an extra year as Head Girl and take the Oxford entrance exams—which I did, but without success, I also applied to King's College, London, which wrote back asking for a photograph, and then a week later rejected me. This caused me some anguish—was I that unattractive? Only later did I realise that if you apply to a Church of England college, it is not helpful to describe your religion as "atheist." Fortunately, Birmingham University offered me a place as a history scholar and I started there in October 1949.

Outside school, a great treat was the annual visit of the Carl Rosa Opera Company to Birmingham. At some time in the past, my mother had made friends with one of the singers in the chorus of the company and from when I was about 13, she arranged for me to go back stage and even on stage when they needed a crowd of children. This didn't involve singing, which was just as well as I've never mastered the art of making my vocal cords produce the sounds I can hear in my head—I've always loved listening to music, especially opera, and can easily spot a wrong note, I just can't sing very well. Mother's friend said that everyone who is not tone deaf can learn to sing if properly taught, but I'd been inhibited by an incident at primary school—I still remember the look of embarrassment on the class teacher's face when a visiting inspector picked me to demonstrate singing scales. I've always regretted that I let this early discouragement prevent me ever trying to learn to sing.

I was also active in the Girl Guides, which I enjoyed for its opportunities to go camping. I learnt to put up tents and cook over camp fires. At 16, we transferred to the Sea Rangers. It may seem strange that there was a company of Sea Rangers in Birmingham, about the most landlocked city in Britain, but some rich philanthropist with a large estate including quite a sizeable lake allowed us to go rowing there. I had always enjoyed swimming (I don't remember learning to swim, I just toddled in after my father on our pre-war seaside holidays), so now I qualified as a life-saver and was able the next summer to have a free holiday in the Isle of Wight as the life-saver to a Girl Guide camp. The sea was very shallow and I didn't need to rescue anyone, but I taught quite a few girls to swim.

It will seem strange to present-day teenagers that I have not mentioned going out with boys, but the fact is that until I went to University I just didn't come across any. None of my friends had brothers the right age nor did any live in our road. One school friend had an elder brother who was at Oxford with Kenneth Tynan (later a famous theatre critic), and I remember meeting them at her house, but to describe their behaviour to us as patronising would be an understatement. I was far from unique among the girls in our sixth form in this isolation from the other sex.

My first romantic experience came during the summer before going to university when I visited France again. This was arranged through my school: a family near Orange in Provence had a 17-year-old son who had failed his 'Bac' in English and they wanted someone who would coach him over the summer. What I didn't know until I arrived was that he had two older brothers so that I would spend the summer dancing on the terrace every night with Yves, the eldest son,—always under the watchful eye of his mother. It was really an idyllic time. Every morning I would spend two hours coaching my pupil. Then the four of us would go off to the River Rhone and swim before returning for lunch on the terrace. I was enchanted by the blue sky, the colours of Provence and the warm climate—as well as by Yves. His father was a lawyer and drove me round to see all the Roman remains—Orange itself, Arles, Aix and the Pont du Gard. My French certainly improved, though I made an embarrassing gaffe at dinner one evening when pressed to have more, I replied, "merci, je suis plein." There was a moment's silence and all eyes swivelled to Yves. Then conversation resumed. Later Madame took me aside and explained that in slang 'plein' meant pregnant.

She knew I wasn't (she'd been too careful a chaperone, never going to bed until I had turned in). Despite—or maybe because—of our enforced sexual restraint, it was a lovely romantic summer with stolen kisses. I kept in touch with the family for some years—Vincent, my pupil, passed his Bac, and Yves won admission to the Ecole Normal d 'Administration (the elite H.E. institution for future politicians, diplomats and top civil servants). He visited me once in Birmingham but then I became ill and we drifted apart.

Max: Member of the Communist Party Executive Committee

Though my work and interest was increasingly concentrated on education and teacher politics, I was also deeply involved in the general political activity of the Communist Party. At the Easter 1952 Congress of the Party, I was elected to the Executive Committee under the system of democratic centralism. At first, I found the EC interesting and often stimulating. Its method of operation over a bi-monthly weekend was roughly as follows: on the Friday night there were various committees on different areas of work and policy. I sat on two, the Social Services, of which I was later to become Chairman, and the Cultural Committee. Both were widely representative of their field, the former included experts in education, medicine, building and architecture, social insurance, housing and local government. The documents we produced were factual, well-informed and I still consider sensible as practical socialist policy for the Labour Movement. Some of our members were, or became, leading public figures in their areas of work, e.g., medicine, architecture and education—the general public later would hardly believe that some of these distinguished figures were once Communists!

Work in the Social Services Committee was taken very seriously indeed as, even though we had no parliamentary and small local government direct input, we could hope to help shape Labour Party thinking through our numerous political and trade union contacts. Thus, there was a minimum of hot air and 'ideological' expression on the committee and a maximum of hard factual analysis as well as an effort to be realistic about policy and proposals. We were the first political grouping on the Left, for example, way back in the late forties, to examine carefully and advocate a form of local income tax to replace rates and this is still regarded by many hard-headed reformers as the right policy. Our education policies (most of which I wrote or drafted) were far from being propaganda exercises and put forward eminently practicable proposals acceptable to the Labour Movement, e.g., in building-up support for the idea of Comprehensive Education. And we were foremost in our detailed critique of the private sector and of the shortcomings of Government policies on resources for educational development.

Much of our time was devoted to housing problems and policies where we had the advantage of considerable expertise among our members and their groups in the building industry, especially architecture, as well as of the hard work of our small 'cadre' of local councillors in working-class areas. Our output on housing was voluminous though some of it on hindsight was not as well-founded as was thought at the time. Thus, faced with the severe shortage of homes, we were among the earliest advocates of styles of building that were later to be critically questioned—massive blocks of flats that could be put up speedily and cheaply. In the forties and fifties, these seemed a progressive way of using limited resources and the courses of action we were proposing had wide expert backing.

We were particularly fortunate in the experience we could command on health problems, especially from a group of devoted doctors and nurses working in the Socialist Medical Association in which there was no ban on Communists.

Persistent advocates of Health Centres, a hoped-for feature of the National Health Service which unfortunately was cut short, we were possibly the first to win support for the idea of group practices which became a growth point in progressive medical treatment and a practical 'second best' to Health Centres. And among our members at that time was the pioneer of the 'smoking damages health' research, Dr. Richard Doll, who was to become the leading authority in the field.

These were some of the areas of work in which we became immersed; others included social insurance, rents, town and regional planning—all subjects on which we could call for and received the assistance of knowledgeable and experienced people. It was far removed from the empty sloganizing and theorising of which the Party's general political propaganda was so often accused. When I produced a 'Report' for a Party Congress in the sixties which tackled the whole issue of the social services and the welfare state from both a theoretical and practical standpoint, it was, I still think, a very workmanlike statement of socialist policy, free of jargon, and credible.

On the Cultural Committee sat a varied collection of intellectuals who reached out to comrades or sympathisers among writers, musicians, historians, scientists, and leading figures in the drama and film worlds, indeed to almost every area that could be described as cultural. I suppose the most distinguished writer in the Party in those days was Doris Lessing; the best-known historians were Christopher Hill and Rodney Hilton; the outstanding scientists J.B.S. Haldane—and one would include J.D. Bernal who never held a 'card' but was considered a Communist; George Thomson and Benjamin Farrington were renowned classical academics; Alan Bush our best-known composer, along with a fair number of other very well-known musicians including Benjamin Frankel and James Gibbs; there were many good artists and, in the world of theatre, Mark Dignam and Beatrix Lehman, along with a fair number of fellow-travellers, were most active. With such 'contacts', the Cultural Committee felt itself to be in close touch with its world.

But, unlike the Social Services Committee whose discussions were fairly humdrum and down-to-earth, it was often the scene of sharp controversy. Intellectuals did not easily submit to discipline nor accept, in their daily work, ideological bonds. And it often seemed that the committee was presuming too much on the acceptance of what became known in the movement as 'Zhdanovism' after the Soviet cultural boss who had tried to dictate to his Soviet comrades what they should be writing or painting, with what many of us believed to be pretty awful results on the quality of their work. I remember the look of horror on Doris Lessing's face at a meeting when the Committee Secretary seemed to be trying to dictate what the writers should be writing about and relished her attempt to tell him that creative writers did not operate to order—Doris was then at the height of her deserved reputation as a novelist.

Nor were the scientists happy with the attempt, for example, to impose the genetic theories of Lysenko as correct. I always wondered why it was necessary for us to take a line on such matters, which I found it difficult anyway to understand at all. Let the Russians have their arguments, I said, but don't let's divide ourselves on issues of genetics which only one or two of us could follow. Haldane, to his credit, refused to conform and later left the Party. Trying to follow the Zhdanov line did us untold harm and it was some time before the lessons were learned.

Let me say that I never liked Soviet painting and became bored with most Soviet novels and films of that period, and always said so. My own tastes were different and no Party line would or could change them. I could not criticise Dr. Zhivago to order!

But the Cultural Committee was the organising force behind a successful campaign on American Comics which resulted in legislation banning these obnoxious and obscene attempts to brainwash children into accepting violence and war as acceptable ways of life. I am proud of the part I played in organising this campaign behind the scenes—one which attracted wide public support. As an educationist I was particularly pleased with our efforts to undermine intelligence testing and its theoretical base.

On Saturday morning, the full EC met and international Communist practice demanded that the first and main item on the agenda for discussion was the Political Report, either a general analysis across the board or one directed with particular emphasis on an outstanding issue. But whatever the title, this statement, usually delivered by a member of the Political Committee, presented the line of the PC which was rarely if ever altered in substance and always 'took account of' the comments of the EC members who spoke, or rejected criticisms unless they were pretty powerfully backed. Not that any of this made much difference in practice. Political statements were the lifeblood of the Party, the vital force of our existence. It was the statement that mattered, the adoption of a 'correct' position. The word was the centre of our existence.

I recall how, on the fortieth anniversary of the Party's birth in 1920, we were presented with a voluminous document on the course of political events since our formation and our place in them. I commented that the paper was full of jargon, polysyllabic formulations, and would be barely comprehensible or even readable to a 'worker'. Back came Harry Pollitt's reply from the Chair that this did not matter, the document was there for the record—that was what mattered. And we never heard of it again. Nothing was really expected to happen as the result of the 'lessons' of the forty years in preparing which endless hours of time must have been spent. Even if we could not act correctly, we were at least right thinking. We were the victims, as I used often to say later, of our own propaganda which confused the word with the deed. Revolutionary words were a substitute for revolutionary action. Of such an attitude is eternal optimism born.

While we realised the limitations of the power we had over current events and developments, the discussions nevertheless were invariably conducted on the assumption that what we said mattered and that the words would result in deeds. The Party would 'swing into action', would 'mobilise' the workers or tenants or whoever, and our resolutions would change things. Without this conviction, of course, there would have been eternal and endemic frustration not only among the EC but in the membership at large. And it is true, and was the object of envy among many local Labour Party comrades, that for some years after the war, small as it was, the Party could command the devotion of a fair number of activists who were prepared to canvass, demonstrate, attend their union branches and vigorously pursue the Party line there.

I had been on the Executive Committee for four years when the traumatic events of 1956 took place in the Socialist world. I did not attend the 1956 Congress of the Party since, as usual, I was at the NUT Conference. But, on returning to London, I learned what many others already knew, that for the leader of the Party, Harry Pollitt, it was a harrowing experience, causing what some described as a breakdown.

The reasons, of course, were the rumours that had been appearing in the press of a secret session of the Soviet Party Congress (which he had attended as our representative) addressed by Khrushchev, in which he had denounced Stalin. Foreign delegates did not attend the secret session Harry and other Communist leaders throughout the world asserted, nor had they been given any text of the speech, if it really happened; and though many doubted this story I found it absolutely credible knowing something of the high-handed way the Russians operated.

But, alas, I was wrong. Very much later (after I had left the party) it was revealed that the speech had actually been sent to the party leadership by a British comrade resident in Moscow. So, the professions of total ignorance were false and a deliberate deception of the Executive Committee by its leaders who repeatedly lied to us. If the lies had been exposed, then it would have destroyed the party.

When the E.C. met, Harry's resignation as General Secretary was confirmed. He was translated to the Chairmanship and John Gollan, the Party's 'favourite son', always the putative successor, took over. There was a great deal of to-ing and fro-ing about the Khrushchev speech of which truncated versions had been appearing in the world's press, but the line from the top was still to cast doubt on the more lurid accounts or even the very existence of the speech and to try to allay the unease which was spreading throughout the Party. This was very unsatisfactory and many of us were very annoyed when we were told that the Russians would not confirm or deny anything. It seemed we could all stew in the juice they were creating. The truth was that we all feared the consequences if the stories proved even partly true.

When the speech was published in *The Observer* in full and was obviously authentic, all hell broke loose in the Party. Already in view of the circumstantial evidence of authenticity, members had been rumbling with revolt and reacting to the growing turmoil. The Executive had published some equivocal statements hoping to allay discontent. But we were tied down by our leaders' continual insistence on their ignorance of the speech.

I recall how, on the day of the publication of the speech in *The Observer*, I was fulfilling a Party engagement in Oxford and called in for tea afterwards at Christopher Hill's—then a don at Balliol, but not yet Master. He reflected very accurately the internal turmoil among the many intellectuals still in the Party and I tried to convince him—and myself—that the Party leadership would, in the light of the revelations, 'reform'. I failed to convince Christopher, but we parted very amicably and at least a bit mutually comforted. It was clear we were in for a tough time ahead.

My own reactions were coloured by opinions expressed indicating that the traditional solidarity of the leadership was not as firm as usual. Thus, there were strong criticisms being expressed of the Party's leading theoretician, the famous (or notorious) R. (Raji) Palme Dutt, renowned even more than Harry Pollitt for his unshakeable adherence to the Soviet line on everything. Raji did not command the same affection as Harry, an almost legendary working-class leader, whom we all loved.

I was dared to challenge him on the Executive by others, much senior to me, who would have been more influential but who hadn't the stomach to do it themselves. And I did, over a notorious leading article he wrote in *Labour Monthly* in which he compared Stalin's crimes to "spots on the sun."

Would his colleagues be as impervious as Dutt to the horrific facts that were now regularly appearing in the press as myth after myth about the USSR was exploded, and which could no longer be dismissed with the customary 'anti-Soviet lies'? Dutt did more damage to the credibility of the Communist Party and to its internal cohesion by that article than anyone apart from Stalin himself. He responded to my challenge with icy cynicism and typically Talmudic prevarication.

When I suggested his removal from the 'Polit bureau', to my disgust I got no support. Dutt was described to me by a Party leader who had known him much longer than I as the Party's 'evil genius'. His influence from now on steadily declined; he no longer commanded the intellectual respect he had previously enjoyed. My own personal and political relations with him steadily deteriorated.

A bad situation, with members leaving in droves, worsened with the impact of incontrovertible evidence of Soviet antisemitism, hitherto described by the Party as 'impossible'. We had a fair number of Jewish comrades, including a business men's group who supplied a lot of money, which was shattered if not destroyed by this evidence.

But not even this had the destructive effect that followed the Hungarian events of October and November. Mounting discontent forced the summoning of a special 'extended Executive' on the eve, as it turned out, of the Soviet occupation of Budapest, with leading comrades attending from all over the country. The atmosphere was electric: the criticism and condemnation (including my own) were widespread and Harry Pollitt, as chairman, to our disgust, closed the meeting, leaving conclusions to be decided by the Executive itself next morning, in the hope that the situation would be contained through that much smaller body. That Sunday Soviet tanks entered Budapest.

I remember arriving and finding that, instead of beginning the meeting, the majority of the Executive had to wait while upstairs the Political Committee tried to hammer out an agreed line to put to the Executive. I was one of a group who sent upstairs a strong protest at this procedure. It was our responsibility, I said, to discuss matters collectively and not wait to receive a line from on high before we could form conclusions. But most of my colleagues were prepared to accept this 'democratically centralist' way of making decisions. The truth was that they were stunned by the Hungarian events on top of everything else, punch drunk and utterly bewildered and would welcome a 'lead' from our heavyweights. My rebelliousness was disapproved of by most of my colleagues—the Party's leaders!

When the meeting finally began with the most perfunctory of apologies from an obviously nerve-racked Pollitt, it took an extraordinary form. For the discussion of the Political Committee's line was repeatedly interrupted as we stopped to listen to radio accounts of the events in Budapest. These unfolded the well-known brutal intervention by armed force in the affairs of a 'fraternal' Communist country in order to impose domination by the USSR, and in my own brief but emotional contribution I was unequivocal in my condemnation, and demanded that we reject the line proposed which was equally unequivocal—support for the Soviet Communist Party.

While many doubts were expressed—the previous day's discussion could hardly have been forgotten—even the dissidents among us were not prepared at this critical moment in world history to reject support for the 'Fatherland of Socialism' which Gollan, Pollitt, Dutt and others insisted must be given.

We broke for lunch, and I took Arnold Kettle back home with me instead of having a bite in the neighbourhood as we would normally have done. He had taken the same line as I had and, gloomy and miserable, we wanted to talk matters over. Arnold was one of the Party's outstanding intellectuals, a university don with a national reputation as a brilliant literary critic. (He was later to become Professor at the OU and one of its pro-Vice Chancellors). Over lunch we agreed that the majority line would be overwhelmingly carried and would lose the Party massive support, certainly in the circles in which we mixed and probably also among the working-class members who still formed the Party's solid foundation. But we would stick to our guns.

When we resumed after lunch and the vote was taken, we found ourselves in a minority of two. Our point of view was routed; the Party would fight to the end to maintain its pro-Soviet line, 'right or wrong'. All signs of dissidence from the doubters seemed to have dissipated under the strains of the crisis and they had rallied to support the Political Committee of elder statesmen, the Party's full-time officials. Even such temperamental dissidents as Brian Behan (Brendan's brother), a vigorous and talented young building workers' leader, caved in. For me, the conclusion of the meeting presented the ultimate irony. For we were urged to join the massive demonstration then taking place in Trafalgar Square, a couple of minutes' walk from our King Street headquarters, protesting against Eden's Suez adventure! (During the meeting I had questioned what credibility we could have if we opposed Suez while supporting the invasion and occupation of Hungary). I joined the huge crowd being addressed by the right-winger Hugh Gaitskell, sad and dispirited by what my Party comrades had just decided.

About a quarter of the membership left the Party, a massive blow to an organisation whose numbers had been steadily declining since the war. But it was not only quantity that was affected but quality. In the nine months after the 20th Congress revelations, we lost substantial numbers both of our professional and industrial workers. It is a myth that it was only the weak-kneed, yellow-bellied 'freedom fighters' of the Party's middle classes, e.g., academics, teachers and such like, that resigned. We lost many horny-handed sons of toil and 1956 marked a serious decline in our trade union influence.

I have been asked many times why, in view of my attitude on the Hungarian events, I did not resign, especially as I was in such a minority on the Executive. Stripped down to its baldest nakedness I suppose the answer is that, being a political animal, I did not like the alternatives. I revolted against the crude Trotskyism that some of my ex-colleagues embraced: that cure was worse than the disease, indeed it would have made the disease fatal. And, having a long time before made my decision not to join the Labour Party, on grounds of socialist theory and practice, I could not, in honesty as I examined my own ideas, bring myself to do so now when the Party was, under Gaitskell, taking an increasingly right-wing stand, even allowing for Suez. Moreover, a fair number of Labour folk, including Bevanite MPs, though neither Bevan nor Foot, were, in private taking a similar line to the CP!

Twelve years later I found a similar pro-Russian line among such Labour comrades in the Czech situation, even though then the CP opposed the Russian occupation). These comrades were obsessed (this is the only word I can use) with anti-Gaitskellism which, for them, was the main enemy to be fought, and seemed to be spending most of their energies attacking the Labour leadership. There was always another alternative, which many embraced, to leave active politics altogether. But that was not in my nature.

I argued it all out with myself and with friends and the conclusion I came to was to stay in and fight for change from the strong position I occupied, personally, in the Party. But there were two other factors which were to condition this conclusion. One was that I would have to be accepted as a critic within the Party leadership (I was not muting my critique) and the other was my increasing absorption in my political work in education where the general political controversies seemed to be only marginal.

When the Executive met again almost immediately after that traumatic Sunday in early November, my criticisms, indeed sharp attacks on what we had decided and on what I considered to be obnoxious features of Party organisation now were taken as inevitable. Nobody seemed to expect me to toe the line and conform— so long as I accepted the Party norm of no public attacks, which I did. Indeed, if I did not, then there was no point in staying in and trying to change things.

The debates were often fierce, there was still considerable dissidence on what was happening in Hungary, including strong criticisms from J.R. Campell of the Old Guard, and in interpreting what had happened and was still far from being changed in the Soviet Union. I was sometimes one of a group, sometimes alone, in expressing my views. But gone were the bad old sectarian days when such expressions of dissident views automatically meant expulsion or resignation. It was recognised that divergence of views had to be accommodated—the monolithic approach had, regretfully to the Dutts and their ilk, gone. Gollan, for all his coldness of manner, fully appreciated this and his main concern was to hold the Party together not invite further defections. But this more liberal policy operated only within limits and some very talented and valuable comrades, e.g., Edward Thompson, were expelled for 'going too far' in public opposition.

I decided to soldier on, trying to keep my own conscience clear, and a very uncomfortable bedfellow for many, saying what I thought very sharply. Paradoxically, though I was a rebel, or maybe because I was, sometime in the late fifties as the result of a conversation with Pollitt (of whom I was very fond personally) he asked me if I would like to work full time for the Party. Changes were pending at King Street and he would like me to consider the proposition. I did consider the matter seriously—I was then teaching in Willesden, had been at the same school for some years, was happy there, but somewhat restless for more reasons than one. So, I went to see Gollan. But even by the time of our talk I was veering away from the prospect. What was on offer was taking over the Party's propaganda department, a very important, indeed key one for the Party's public image.

When I pointed out my own 'dissident' record this was brushed aside with the emphatic point that I would be a member of the HQ team which worked together. It was an indirect way of telling me something—I felt that Gollan would not be unhappy if I refused!

He added that I would not automatically be a member of the inner Party leadership, the Political Committee—at least not yet. Clearly, I would have to work my passage and show my amenability in teamwork. Fair enough, I thought, but not for me in the mood I was in. So, I refused. In any case, by this time I was deeply involved in education politics, which seemed a far more constructive and worthwhile use of my time.

Max: Visits to Socialist Countries

In the post-war years, when I was Secretary of the Communist Party's Education Advisory Committee, I got to know the leaders of the various teachers' unions in Eastern Europe, 'behind the iron curtain'. It was a time when (contrary to media propaganda) these countries were eager to show off their 'socialist achievements' and hence for visitors to come and see them. Private visits were discouraged; what they wanted were representative delegations, especially from trade unions and cultural bodies. But individual visits from political or otherwise prominent personalities were also encouraged and facilitated, and with the contacts of the various missions in London largely confined to left-wing circles, I suppose I ranked as one of these.

I was nevertheless surprised to receive an approach in the early summer of 1948 from the Bulgarians to make a combined holiday and work tour of their country. I would have to pay my own fare, of course, but would be offered hospitality when I got there. So, with my wife, Barbara I set off in August for the fascinating journey on the Orient Express, in the rail carriage from Paris to Sofia, though third-class, not in the luxury conditions of Agatha Christie's travellers—nor with the same doubtful kind of company!

In Sofia, we were treated as VIPs—something I got used to in all my subsequent visits to the socialist countries—and were lodged in what was then the only good hotel in the city and shown around by a personal interpreter. It was a difficult time for the Bulgarians, just after the war and three years of bad harvests. There was not a lot to eat (apart from in the Sofia hotel largely reserved for foreigners) nor much to drink and life seemed to be pretty tough all round. This was especially so for my teacher colleagues, as we learned when spending a week in their holiday centre by the Black Sea in Varna; it was a red-letter day when meat was available and we lived largely on lime tea, occasional eggs, vegetables, bread and some very rough goat cheese.

But the people I met were enthusiastic about the changes taking place and looking forward to a richer future. I was very impressed with what they were trying to do in education. Though Bulgaria was a backward country economically, there was a strong educational tradition because of the part Bulgarian culture played in maintaining the national identity in the long period the people endured under the 'Turkish yoke' until the late 19th century. So schooling was more advanced than one would expect in a Balkan rural economy just beginning to be industrialised. I wrote two articles on Bulgarian education when I returned for the *Times Educational Supplement* probably the first they had ever received and published on such an esoteric subject.

One incident impressed itself on my mind and helped to shape my attitudes in those days to some of the severities of the regime both there and elsewhere in the East. On a visit to the famous Rila Monastery, I met the Minister of Justice and listened fascinated to the conversation (interpreted) at the dinner table (the monks did themselves and their visitors quite well!). "Can you imagine my feelings," he was saying, "when as Minister I had to deal with the case of the very man who had tortured me in prison?" Indeed.

Poland was to be my next visit, the following summer, as the result of relations established with Paul Delanoue, the future General Secretary of what was to become that year the Fédération Internationale des Syndicats de l'Engseignment (FISE). My friendship with Paul lasted till his death in 1983 and became very close and personal. He was quite the most outstanding teachers' leader I ever met, a man of enormous talent and energy who dominated his part of international teacher politics for a generation. He had been a leading resistance fighter during the war, became a teachers' union official and then moved over to run the Teachers' International created as the result of the split in the World Federation of Trade Unions in 1948, itself a major consequence of the cold war.

I went as an unofficial visitor to the FISE foundation meeting, the first of a series that was to last till the late sixties when I voluntarily ceased to attend, though by then I was not as persona grata, particularly with my Russian colleagues, as I had been earlier. I found Poland even more fascinating than Bulgaria, and was well-looked after by the Polish teachers' leader, Eustachy Kuroczko, who told me he had been released from gaol as a political prisoner under the pre-war fascist Colonel Beck regime by the protest of the NUT. He was an enormous, fat man who used to pat his tummy and say in German to me:

"I have the whole proletariat here!" with a laugh that roared like a peal of thunder.

Warsaw was a sad sight. In 1949 it was still largely rubble though rebuilding was progressing fast. There were no suitable hotels and we were lodged in the Parliament House. But we met in a magnificent Teachers' Union building, far grander than Hamilton House, an indication, of course, of state support. It was early days of such meetings for me and I was very interested in what went on, not yet too blasé to appreciate the clichés and the unreality of much, even most of the politics of international teachers' relations. But even then, it seemed a bit remote from the day-to-day problems a union like the NUT was handling and I wondered how one could relate these top-level discussions to what I was actually involved in at home as a teacher.

I saw a fair bit of Poland and was so well-briefed on the Polish school system that I was able on return to repeat my Bulgarian effort for the *T.E.S* and publish two articles. But what a lot they had to do to rebuild their destroyed country! And, I must add, to re-educate their teaching corps. For it became clear to me in direct conversations—many teachers we met could converse in English or I could understand them with my imperfect French and German—that there was far from universal support for the regime in the profession, especially among the old grammar school types.

One thing stood out in the education policy as described to us. This was the very deliberate effort to change the 'class composition' of higher education to increase sharply, and rapidly, the proportion of working-class and peasant entrants to the institutions. This, of course, struck a chord of strong sympathy with western left-wing visitors. I wondered, nevertheless, how it would pan out as it would take time to alter the school base sufficiently to make the change permanent. Just insisting on 'class' credentials for entry, irrespective of the country's needs would hardly be enough and this, I believe, is the way it largely turned out. We were assured that there would be no political discrimination in dealing with HE staff. I was sceptical, and justly so as later events were to prove.

As we left the country, we became involved in an incident which was to have interesting repercussions. We got onto the plane and it was empty, apart from one other traveller. This was not so surprising in those Cold War days for a flight to London. When I looked round a few minutes later, however, our fellow-passenger had disappeared. That was that. I had not noticed anything in particular about him and forgot all about him.

It will be recalled that we were at the beginning of that dreadful period in Communist history marked by the series of East European trials, Kostov, Slansky, Rajk, etc., caught up in which were two American brothers, the Fields, who seemed to be *personae gratae* with the various Communist governments, travelling freely on various missions with government approval. Then they disappeared. One of them, Noel, was to languish in a Hungarian jail till 1956 on trumped-up charges as it turned out, and the other, Hermann, just disappeared! One morning, many months after my Polish visit, I opened the Sunday left-wing newspaper, *Reynolds News*, to read on the front page that the wife of the disappeared Hermann had, by dint of patient and obviously very difficult investigation, traced her husband's last known moves to Warsaw Airport and the plane on which we had travelled. We were named in the story and she was trying to trace us. Later that morning she telephoned me, obviously in great distress, and all I could tell her was what I have written above. I could not even be sure, because the incident had made no impression on me, after the lapse of time, that there was another passenger—it could have been an airline official—and I was quite unable to describe the possible passenger, if there was one. She understood this, and was very disappointed. I would have been ready to help, though I was a little alarmed at being even so indirectly involved in what was already (and was to become even more) a rather nasty-sounding cause célèbre: the fate of the Field brothers was the subject of continual comment in the international press till the late fifties. The East Europeans involved (Polish, Czech and Hungarian) denied all knowledge of the missing brothers while making more than hints about 'imperialist agents' and espionage. But lingering doubts in my mind nagged me for a long time. Had I really been a witness to Hermann Field being spirited away?

In the summer of 1951, I attended the FISE Conference in Erfurt, East Germany, the Thuringian city made famous by Martin Luther's defiance there of the Pope. It had not been easy to get into East Germany from the West. A group of us had to hang around the Soviet Embassy in Paris for days, waiting for visas (there was no East German mission yet) and then we had to travel to Frankfurt and change for the 'iron curtain' under the suspicious eyes of the anti-communist officials. I cannot say I ever took to East Germany, though my colleagues there were at great pains to impress on me how the old Nazi Adam was being eradicated by education. And, indeed, the educational effort was formidable—as was the task to be achieved in 1951, so soon after the war. My later visits were to leave me with very strong appreciation of work in the schools of the German Democratic Republic, as the country was later called. I once spent several days in Berlin just checking their English textbooks to remove mistakes and solecisms, such was German thoroughness. I was particularly *persona grata* as being both an experienced teacher and politically sound! I wrote from time to time in their teachers' or pedagogical journals on British education.

London had not only a Polish Cultural Institute with a busy programme but also a Hungarian one, a bit off the beaten track in Notting Hill, which I used to visit from time to time. I became friendly with its director, George Buday, an old-style Hungarian intellectual, who was to stray from the fold, like so many others after the 1956 Soviet tank takeover of Budapest. Interestingly enough, the Director of the Polish outfit was also an old-style intellectual and a major poet, Anton Slonimski, with whom I was also very friendly. He too, in the fifties, became an influential dissident. People like Buday and Slonimski were examples of how the new regimes had to rely for their public face in the West on the pre-Marxist generation of intelligentsia. They were, because of their reputations, excellent propagandists for the 'liberalism' the regimes still attempted to profess in cultural affairs. Actually, it was all very deceptive; those of us who knew Slonimski and Buday well and liked them, easily saw through the facade of sympathy with Marxism they appeared to show.

At the Institute, I met two young Hungarian student historians, one of whom, Eva Harazsti was, 30 years later, to become the third wife of A.J.P. Taylor. They were both delightful girls and very capable historians, with the same interest as I had in Chartism, and along with Buday they suggested I visit Hungary to lecture on Chartism under the auspices of the Hungarian Historical Institute; the lecture would fit into the programme of continuing celebrations of the centenary of 1848, a notable revolutionary date in Hungarian history and with strong British links through the Hungarian national hero, Kossuth, who had been fêted by London East End workers. I soon received an official invitation from the Hungarian Association for Cultural Relations and my wife and I went off to spend the Easter vacation in Budapest. I developed a liking for the country which I have never lost, made many friends and became acquainted with the strange, lilting Hungarian tongue and the marvellous Hungarian wine and delicious food. But, in 1950, I had no illusions about the severity of the regime, then dominated by Rakosi, and the cultural drive towards Marxist conformity. Here again, as in Poland, it became clear that there was a long way to go before the teaching profession, especially in the secondary schools and higher education, was 'converted'.

But the educational effort was formidable and was of high quality professionally. So impressed was I that, when I returned, I not only produced two articles for the *T.E.S.* but also one for the equally respectable *Year Book of Education*, as well as writing a little booklet for the Institute which was very well-received in educational circles. My lecture to the historians was chaired by the leading Hungarian historian, Erzbet Andich, wife of Hungary's 'Chancellor of the Exchequer' and a pillar of the regime who was to suffer a sad fate in 1956.

By now, I was a pretty well-known 'expert' on East European education but I had not yet penetrated the holy of holies, the Soviet Union. The opportunity came in the summer of 1952 when the Society for Cultural Relations with the U.S.S.R. (the S.C.R.) decided it was time to organise the first post-war delegation of educationists. Chris Freeman, the Secretary, consulted with me closely on how to get as representative and 'broad' a delegation as possible but also one with some political stiffening in view of the sensitivity of the Russians during this very freezing period of the cold war. It was agreed that G.C.T. Giles and I should go (with our wives), as well as the expert on Soviet education, Deanna Levin, and we got the adherence of the Secretary of the National Association of Labour Teachers, Peter Ibbotson and, as leader, Professor Lewis of Nottingham University with his novelist wife who was also keenly interested in special schools.

Others, too, leavened our Communist lump and it seemed a good crowd to have assembled. But, even under S.C.R. auspices, and with myself, a CP Executive and Giles, a former Executive member, we had trouble with visas. Right up to the last moment before departure, when we had given up hope of the delegation ever taking off if there were no visas.

At that moment, I insisted on a personal intervention with the Ambassador, the formidable Andrei Gromyko (future Foreign Minister and President), to whom I painted a horrific picture of the terrible publicity they would get if the delegation was cancelled, as it must be—our colleagues would wait no longer in suspense and would go to the press. The visas were immediately available, but I could never understand the stupid brinkmanship of the Soviet bureaucracy in these Stalinist days. Even then, at the 59th minute of the eleventh hour, a visa was refused to one of our leading Communist colleagues, Eric Godfrey. I could only conjecture it was because he had worked for some years in the U.S.S.R. as an engineer and was a victim of the ridiculous suspicion of foreigners working in their country that prevailed under Stalin. Eric was a devoted Communist and became shortly after a distinguished President of the Technical Teachers Union (the A.T.T.I.).

Received with the lavish hospitality customary under the Stalinist regime, the delegation travelled quite widely and got a pretty thorough appreciation of Soviet education, though presented with a good deal of unnecessary propaganda. We were all hard-bitten professionals, whatever our political views, which varied widely, and asked searching questions, refusing to be fobbed off. I remember Giles, a devoted adherent of everything Soviet, but a teacher to his fingertips, roaring with sceptical laughter when they told us there were no juvenile delinquents in the country—all youngsters were 'educated' out of crime! What we found amusing was one expression of what was later to be dubbed 'the cult of the personality'. Shown round Moscow on a sight-seeing trip, the guide would say: 'Look at that building. It used to be here. Stalin moved it back there!' Stalin was responsible for personally shaping the contours of the streets, it seemed.

But we learned a lot. In spite of all the silliness, the visit was more than worthwhile and no-one could see Soviet education, whatever its weaknesses, without leaving full of admiration for advances being made after years of such a devastating war. There was no need for the Russians to try to gild the lily. The whole world was, in time, to pay tribute to their educational progress. One thing the visit convinced me of was the viability of a common curriculum, a genuine core, something we had not yet achieved in advanced Britain. Never having been a 'child centred' fan, I found quite agreeable the ordered discipline and the strongly 'teacher centred' educational approach.

As the visit progressed, unfortunately agreement of everyone on everything we saw regressed. We could not disentangle education from politics. The sense of propaganda was too powerful for some of our colleagues to stomach—even theatre visits, the merits of a Bolshoi production (pretty marvellous) or the 'realist' style of a Turgenev play (terrific, again, thought I) would arouse controversy and sometimes even tempers. So, towards the end, we could not agree to a 'communiqué', except in the blandest of terms, which the Russians did not like at all, nor did some of us. I suppose we had all underestimated the pitfalls of such a delegation in the lowest trough of the cold war with the U.S.S.R. in the last months of Stalin.

One incident on this delegation visit caused me great concern. During our periods in Moscow, we were given great attention by a senior official of the International Department of the Trade Union Centre who used to join us at meals in the hotel and take part in our chat—his English was very good indeed. What seemed to interest him was that, although we were composed of various political tendencies, no-one seemed to be a supporter of the then Tory Government and when we discussed British politics, on which he asked, naturally we thought, many questions, he was fascinated by our (politically) derogatory remarks about the Prime Minister and his policies. (The Tories had begun imposing severe education economies.) One of our number was particularly abusive. Towards the end of the visit when, I think, he had had more than a few drinks, he called me aside and, to my astonishment, told me that he had been approached by the international trade union functionary and asked if he would work for Soviet Intelligence. I found this unbelievable. For though I was hardly a political innocent and was as aware as any layman of the existence of intelligence networks, the crudity of the approach was incredible—it even included, according to our colleague, instructions on a clandestine meeting in London if he pursued the offer. I strongly urged him to forget the whole thing and not be a fool and there we left it, though I took good care to have the minimum of conversation with the Russian concerned for the rest of the visit.

I was sceptical of our colleague's story. I knew he was not very discreet and I had no high opinion of his political sophistication and found it difficult to believe that the Russians could put their trust in an individual who, after a few drinks, could not hold his tongue: such behaviour did not lead one to have a high opinion of Soviet Intelligence (with or without the capital 'I'). Did the mere expression of anti-Tory or anti-Churchillian sentiments indicate a willingness to spy? And what use could this fellow be to them anyway? I used to joke later, when there were all the revelations of the 'Cambridge Circle', that I had very close relations with a number of Russian diplomats and had revealed to them all the secrets of the operation of the wicked eleven plus!

But gnawing doubts remained. Such behaviour towards an important official delegation, as the Russians evidently considered us to be, could undermine, if revealed, the credibility of all the political efforts to lessen the tensions of the cold war which we all thought so menacing. Delegations being used for intelligence recruiting! So, when we returned, I decided to see Harry Pollitt and tell him about it. When, at the beginning of our conversation, I indicated to him what it was about he immediately walked with me over to the big window in his room—away, he said, from any possible bugging devices (C.P. Headquarters, we all suspected, was riddled with bugs). I told him the story which he received quite impassively, but with agreement about the dangerous adventurism of the Russian concerned, if the story were true. I, of course, added my own estimation of the credibility of the colleague concerned. Harry asked me to leave the matter with him, giving me an assurance that he would, in his own way 'take the matter up' and would make as strongly as he knew how the necessary representations politically in the right quarters. I trusted his political judgement, as he more than anyone would appreciate the politically disastrous consequences for the Communist Party—always eagerly pursuing the extension of the 'delegation movement' as an important part of its international work.

    I often thought about it, especially in later years when the various Cambridge stories began to proliferate. As a student and after, though I was not an Oxbridge character, I knew quite a few of the former members of the Cambridge University Socialist Society (the famous C.U.S.S.). They mostly seemed to me, as the years went by, to be anxious to forget their left-wing student past. In fact, the one I knew best who was later to be exposed, John Cairncross, I met only socially and he did not seem to me to be at all a political animal. Conversation was almost exclusively about literature even though he was working in the Treasury. But I remember being very surprised to hear that he had resigned his job and was going to live abroad and devote himself to French translation, of Racine, I think. He was a brilliant linguist. When the exposure came, much later, after the Blunt sensation, I must admit, rather naively perhaps, my utter astonishment. He had never in my presence expressed any left-wing sentiments: on the contrary, if anything he had seemed to me to have opposite views, and never referred to any involvement with C.U.S.S., though in the company we met in it would have been natural to do so.

In the years that followed, I was to make many more visits to the East and could not but conclude that, in spite of differences of form, the pattern was pretty much the same, even in education. Differences of form were, of course, historical in origin with the Czech stage of development, for example, being way ahead of the Rumanian, and bearing more similarities to what I was accustomed to at home. But what all had in common was a massive input of resources for educational development and a fervent (and quite un-Marxist) belief in the perfectibility of man through education. Alas, it was a flawed argument, if only through the conformism the system produced.

Max: Salaries, Equal Pay and the Ban Against Communist Heads

In describing my entry into the teaching profession, I gave an account of its divisions between elementary and secondary teachers, the economic background which led to its quiescence in Government policy and the dominance of the right wing on the NUT Executive. The creation in 1942 of the Council for Educational Advance which brought together the NUT with the Trades Union Congress, the Cooperative Union and the Workers' Educational Association posed every educational question politically, and though the union played on the whole a restraining role, it was a big advance on its previous 'neutral' attitude. One result was the official McNair Report, which declared that teachers were 'seriously underpaid' and recommended considerably higher salaries.

Following the 1944 Education Act, a basic scale of salaries was created in 1945, though on top was built a structure of differentials mainly intended to appease the higher-paid grammar school teachers. Nevertheless, the ordinary class teacher received a lift up, and from these changes grew an entirely new atmosphere in the profession, especially among those working in the old elementary (now called primary) or secondary modern schools.

Four major factors played a part in the post-war years in developing teachers' militancy. First was the improved position of industrial relative to white collar workers as the result of war-time and post-war full employment and trade union organisation. This acted as a spur to teachers seriously to reconsider their policies and methods. Secondly, some professional groups, particularly the doctors, were adopting aggressive attitudes on remuneration and demanding upgrading of pay at least sufficient to maintain pre-war relativities. To teachers this was a salutary lesson, for if the doctors, an overwhelmingly middle-class group, could adopt such postures and with success, why should not they? Thirdly, inflation, especially after 1949, brought home to teachers the fact that pay recommendations made during the war had not been implemented and that they were in general worse off than before, not only relatively but even absolutely. Fourthly, the deeper public interest in education helped to increase the profession's self-confidence: one did not apologise so often for being a teacher, it was even something to be proud of. The 1948 salary agreement gave English and Welsh teachers an increase varying from £15 to £30 a year; an indication of change was the demand in the following year by the Scottish teachers (first in the field) for an increase of £150.

Continuous ferment among teachers and within the NUT marked the years after 1948, and discontent was increased by salary agreements which emphasised the differentials at the expense of the basic scale. But it was a complex situation involving seemingly contradictory pressures. With their new-found confidence, teachers openly compared their work and pay with those of doctors and other highly-paid (by comparison) professional groups. The word 'profession' appeared increasingly in teachers' vocabulary, and salary aims were summarised as 'a professional scale'. Professionalism, however, was often translated as meaning 'peaceful and constitutional' methods of negotiation. Professions did not strike.

In that case how was the professional scale to be achieved, since employers showed no signs of granting it during the normal routine of Burnham negotiations? It was obvious that industrial workers were managing to keep their end up, because they either held in reserve the power of withholding labour or actually used it. Put simply, industrial employers were afraid of industrial workers. But teachers held no terrors for their employers. At one and the same time, teachers wanted to be a 'profession', but very many of them wanted to behave like a 'union'. This seeming contradiction had to be resolved. Subtly, slowly, but surely attitudes of mind and habits of thought began to change, destroying old social prejudices and preconceptions.

The pace was quickened, even forced, by the activities of 'militants'— Labour, Communist, progressives of all colours and creeds. This group consisted of a number of elements. There were leading members of the National Association of Labour Teachers, mainly Londoners. Then there were the communists who, in the early post-war years, were at their peak of membership. They were quite well organised in local groups throughout the country under the leadership of the Party's Education Advisory Committee, of which I was the Secretary and G.C.T. Giles was Chairman. In addition, were union activists, a varied collection including militant Catholics, educational progressives of all kinds, some 'liberals', some whom I used to describe as 'Adullamite's', teachers discontented with the state of the profession and with our conformist public leaders.

Our very loosely organised group always worked pretty harmoniously together and the political disputes that rent the world of socialist politics were usually kept outside our relationships. We stuck to our common aim of changing the 'non-political' 'neutrality' stance of the union as the main voice of the profession in very practical ways, including changing the composition of the Executive, which during the most virulent period of the cold war moved sharply to the right. We were a very undogmatic crowd, pragmatic rather than ideological, evolving policies on the firm basis of the hard facts about teachers as we intimately knew them. Our aim was the achievement of a salaries policy that would unite as many teachers as possible.

G.C.T. Giles was the chief victim of a cold war barrage. Former Head Boy of Eton and a Scholar of Kings College, Cambridge, he had been converted to socialism during the First World War and to communism in the mid-twenties. As Headmaster of a Grammar School in a union composed almost entirely of elementary (later primary and secondary modern) school teachers, he stood out professionally. His communist beliefs made him the target of considerable abuse, but his positive qualities marked him out as a leader whom the union establishment could not ignore and indeed feared. His manner in debate was quiet, thoughtful and reasoned, free of rhetorical flourishes and fireworks, the very opposite of the stereotype of a revolutionary agitator. He became President of the NUT in the crucial (for education) year 1944–5 and played an important role in the negotiations on the 1944 Act. He was a man of considerable personal charm, down to earth in speech and manner, free of can't and humbug, qualities which earned him a wide circle of friends and disciples, of whom I was to become the closest of all. I sat at his feet and learned what teacher politics was all about as well as a great deal about schools and education. Trying to follow his example was an education in itself.

Giles' and my base was the Middlesex Secondary Teachers' Association. A solid core of active members had enough in common to maintain the Association's reputation for progressive policies within the union, especially on economic issues.

Unity was further encouraged by opposition to the Middlesex Education Committee which had fallen into the hands of a group of virulent Tory politicians who had broken with the old progressive traditions of the Authority. The Association soon became the main focus for the organisation of activist policies within the union and the main platform of the pressure for change both professionally and educationally.

It was not a good time for the Left within the union and the profession and especially in Middlesex, where the Tories launched an attack on left-wing teachers unprecedented then and since in British educational history. It began with the refusal of the County Council in 1950 to confirm the selection of Reg Neal, a Communist, to a primary school headship after his due appointment by the Education Committee. This was followed up by the introduction of regulations banning Communists from promotion to Headships and Deputy Headships or appointments to teachers' training colleges. (To create 'impartiality' fascists were also included in the ban but as none were known to exist this was taken as a purely cosmetic gesture). The operation became known as the 'Middlesex Ban'.

The Middlesex Ban became a running sore which bedevilled relations between the Union and the County Council till it was removed when Labour defeated the Tories at the County Council elections in 1958 and faithfully redeemed its promise to repeal the obnoxious regulation. I say 'the Union' because the issue became national. Not only Middlesex teachers but the national conference opposed the ban and the Executive was instructed to take all measures necessary to remove the ban which was seen as an attack on the freedom of teachers as citizens to hold views and carry out political activities within the law. Needless to say, all union pronouncements emphasised objection to political activities within the classroom and throughout the entire period of the ban (and indeed before and after) no Middlesex teacher was ever accused of misusing his professional position for political ends, though every effort was made by our enemies, including in Parliament, to find evidence of such impropriety.

Union pressure failed to move the Tories and a ballot of Middlesex teachers for industrial action failed to win the necessary very large majority required by the rules for such action; though I always thought it was remarkable how many were prepared to put their principles to such a severe test. Remember that the NUT had not engaged in industrial action since the early twenties for teachers' own living conditions! It is extraordinary how the first ballot in the NUT, post-war, on industrial action, was held not on pay but on an issue of fundamental principle of civil liberties. This must be the only such example in trade union history. It was too much to expect teachers to strike on such an issue and in the prevailing cold war atmosphere.

For me, personally the choice was clear. If I wanted promotion, I would have to leave the county. My answer was equally clear. I preferred to stay on and fight rather than enjoy the sweets of promotion which not only I but many of my colleagues felt I well deserved. I felt morally superior to the Middlesex Tories and showed my lack of deference and indeed contempt for them at every opportunity. They did not love me but could not sack me without causing a furore. My aggressiveness towards them gave me excellent training in how to handle obnoxious bosses and helped to win for me a reputation for forthright, principled and tough attitudes, a reputation which was to stand me in good stead throughout my professional life.

The Ban was at last lifted in 1958. For me, it meant the opportunity for promotion which I received towards the end of 1959 when appointed as a Deputy Head in Tottenham. The fight against the Ban, in particular winning such massive union and political backing (among both Labour and Tories) was, looking back, a key factor in winning the battle against political discrimination in education. No future local authority or government could or did reimpose such a ban.

The left in the union carried on with its activity in defence of its own pay and conditions and of the education service. We saw these two as going hand in hand and I was later to adapt a notorious phrase from American politics when I said what was good for teachers was good for schools and vice versa. Size of classes was the most obvious case in point. It was not always easy to see the best way forward and we made mistakes especially when we plugged issues for doctrinaire reasons instead of tuning in to what really concerned our colleagues.

A good example of this was when year after year at Conference we made an issue of the union's international relations, which was really part of our anti-American orientation, feelings certainly not shared by most of our colleagues. We were trying to expose the cold war attitudes of the World Confederation of Organisations of the Teaching Profession, of which Ronnie Gould was President and which was Yankee dominated, and at the same time build a bridge between W.C.O.T.P. and FISE, the International of teachers' unions in the Communist countries—plus some sympathetic fellow travelling unions outside.

Our tactic, for which I was the spokesman, was to expose the almost total lack of information given to the union by our leaders on the union's international activities, which we hinted broadly were politically inspired by our American colleagues. My annual speech on the issue received exceedingly loud applause but, alas, hardly any votes. The issues seemed remote, even stratospheric, to the classroom teacher who was prepared to trust the Executive on these esoteric matters.

The truth, too, was that the leaderships of both internationals were to blame for the failure to build bridges between east and west. It was revealed later on that W.C.O.T.P. had been taking subsidies from the C.I.A.—who hardly gave away money for nothing. But at the same time the other teachers' International was the instrument of Soviet policy as I knew from personal experience as I attended its gatherings unofficially for many years. It was to take a major change in the international atmosphere in the post Stalin and Churchill periods for any progress to be made in international teachers' relationships.

But for us in the fifties it was a good and progressive fight, part of the 'fight for peace'. The teachers were however content to leave these issues in the hands of the trusted Ronnie Gould, who seemed to keep even his colleagues in ignorance of what was going on. This ignorance was typified by a union President, Granville Prior (a close friend of Hugh Gaitskell) who led a union delegation to the USSR. On his return, I asked him what had impressed him most. "Oh, Max!" he cried out ecstatically: "The smoked salmon!" For this kind of approach Sir Ronald must take his full share of responsibility—no-one else on the Executive had the slightest clue about the issues involved in international teacher cooperation. I did not know whether to cry or laugh when, in a social function at the Polish embassy, the Chairman of the Union's International Relations Committee told the Polish Ambassador how much she was looking forward to seeing Dubrovnik during her forthcoming Polish visit.

But if opposing the cold war produced nothing very tangible, fighting the bread-and-butter issues were showing some results. One very important development deserves special mention. This was the success that crowned the union's efforts to win equal pay, the same salaries for the same jobs for both men and women teachers. The profession had a majority of women but, until 1956, they were paid on an inferior salary scale. In 1956, after many years of agitation, an agreement was finally concluded between the public service unions (civil servants, local government, teachers, etc.) and the Government for a phased introduction of equal pay to be completed in 1961. Until the war, it was normal for local authorities not to employ married women teachers and to dismiss women on marriage, and only after the war was the change formally effected. I remember the annoyance of the 'management' at the University of London Institute of Education before the war when, as editor of the college magazine, I had published a provocative article from one of our women activists under the title 'Shall I lose my job, my swain, or my virtue?' The pre-war employment discrimination certainly did not encourage marriage and conventional morality among those responsible for the education of the young, as the article pointed out. The NUT played a big part in achieving what, in spite of the phasing, was a signal landmark on the road to the end of sex discrimination in employment. Achieving a good salary for all teachers took longer.

Max: Breaking Out of 'Genteel Poverty'

In order to secure a proper level of remuneration for all teachers, the most important single function of the union, we on the left believed it was necessary to break with the traditional methods of conducting salary negotiations. Under the practice, long current, the negotiations were shrouded in secrecy from the moment they began till the deal was presented for ratification. Our members did not know what was being demanded and the public was sublimely unaware that the teachers were asking for anything at all. Figures may have been discussed at conference, but the Executive had always succeeded in preventing themselves being bound by any target figure for which to negotiate. In practice, this meant that they set targets—which were too low and ended up with poor settlements.

So, the 'fight for figures' became a major issue in the union—not just for the actual target figure, important as this was, but for the figures to be publicly known and campaigned for as the objective of the negotiations, one against which success could be measured. In choosing it, we did our own careful research, usually making comparisons with the pre-war scales. The demand for figures gained increasing support and, at the Margate Conference in 1954, the battle was won with the adoption of a resolution from the floor, demanding that the Executive press for a basic scale of not less than £500 to £900, which it had resisted.

But, of course, it was not as easy as some had supposed. Time and again, the union leadership was to attempt to slip out of any firm commitment and Burnham awards usually fell short of what we felt could have been achieved by more active policies. In September 1958, in spite of the fact that two years earlier teachers had received the largest increase for many years, I wrote that: "Teachers are worse off at the minimum, the maximum and in the value of the increment than in 1938. Teachers have not shared in the sizeable productivity achieved since 1938." In truth, teachers could be described, so long after the end of the war, as living in a condition of 'genteel poverty'—a phrase I used which caught on and became widely quoted.

In the cold war atmosphere that pervaded British politics and trade unionism at that time, it was very difficult not only for communists but also for any left-winger to win office. But our advocacy won increasing support locally and on the floor of the Conference. An NUT Conference is a very tolerant body if it is listening to what it considers to be a good case well put, and, without undue modesty, I can say that I soon became a conference favourite which the press, always out for copy, soon took notice of and gave our policies good publicity. And so, the battle for a detailed salary policy openly discussed and voted upon was won, even though the details did not necessarily satisfy us.

I have concentrated on the broad outline of the issues debated rather than the details because of the importance of the principals involved. Once there was open debate and democratic decisions (and that means acceptance of majority verdicts—winning some and losing some) on the major issue of pay, it was like a release of new energy into the deliberations of the union.

It was not too far ahead to victory on public campaigning, which was met with equally dogged and ultimately unsuccessful resistance. It is not too much to say that the atmosphere throughout the union was transformed.

Throughout the fifties, signs of change, as in the fight for figures and publicity, multiplied and, indeed, on one occasion in 1959, an award was actually rejected. It was also in 1959 that I had my first major public encounter with the redoubtable Sir William Alexander, the LEA leader. You could always rely on him to say something provocative enough to enrage the teachers. His strongest suit was contempt as when, as an NUT Conference, he compared the parallel progress of the number of teachers and the growth of juvenile delinquency in a throwaway 'funny' remark—which he had obviously carefully prepared. But in 1959 he got more than he bargained for when, just before Easter, in a speech opposing increased pay, he spoke dismissively of teachers as part-time workers: how 'nine to four' at school allowed many of them to do odd jobs, including serving as barmen in the evenings. At our Conference which followed soon after I took the mickey out of him by referring to his well-known love of propping up bars—he should be pleased that teachers were so hard-up that they were able to service him in the evenings as well as working for him during the day. The press took up my riposte in a big way and Sir William did not like it at all, but the incident was helpful to the union.

Most of our energy in demanding higher salaries was concentrated on winning increases on the Basic Scale, a higher minimum, maximum and a shorter progression between the two. This meant opposition to money in salary awards being spent on the very complex system of 'above scale payments', which had been introduced into the salary structure at the instance of Sir William Alexander. These at relatively small cost bought off, in our view, influential sections of the profession who benefited from these allowances. A big minority within the union had opposed these innovations, foreseeing that they would serve to depress the Basic Scale which was common to the whole profession. Our argument was that increases on the Basic helped everyone and so was the most unifying demand. The counter-argument, which repeatedly won the day, was that these allowances formed a promotion structure which was a necessary part of especially secondary school work and was a small price to pay for the support of the grammar school teachers for our demands on the Basic. Tactically, this carried weight because, it was argued, the union never needed to force through policies by using its majority vote on the Burnham Committee, irrespective of the wishes of colleagues, which would have been bad public relations.

Both this argument and our own had one considerable weakness—they ignored the very real disadvantage suffered in the allowances structure by teachers in primary schools, who were the majority in both the union and the profession. This disadvantage was encapsulated in the phrase 'the primary/secondary differential' and in ignoring its importance, both practically and psychologically, advocates of 'the basic and nothing but the basic' (the policy that all moneys won should go to the Basic Scale) were making a big mistake and weakening the thrust for higher salaries. It took some time for this to sink in among the Left, many of whom thought that any move to improve the allowance system to give primary school teachers (and especially Head Teachers) better treatment was contaminating the pure milk of egalitarian theory.

I fought hard among my colleagues to change this attitude and eventually succeeded. When it came to planning our tactics for the 1961 claim, I won my colleagues for a change in our salary strategy; and henceforth it was to include not one demand but two.

We would go for the necessary big Basic Scale but also for righting what so many primary school teachers regarded as a fundamental injustice. The purists and dogmatists were unhappy, but we had adopted a strategy as well as a policy that was to prove a winner, and in the not-too-distant future. For we had united in a single force the main elements of the profession that were justly discontented and they amounted to a majority of the teachers—an enormous potential for change the most 'durable and powerful alliance hitherto in the annals of the union', I called it.

Symptomatic of the situation at this time was the casting of big minority votes against salary agreements, demands for 'interim awards' between dated agreements, insistence on public campaigning for specific demands, the holding of strike ballots (not for specific strikes, but on the 'principle', a typically abstract way of doing things) among the grammar school men teachers in England and Wales and the Scottish teachers—probably the most 'professional' in outlook of the unions. Another example was the resistance to the government's proposal to increase teachers' superannuation contributions by one per cent; on this occasion (1956) an NUT conference passed a resolution instructing the Executive "to use the full resources of the union" to oppose the proposal. As it turned out this 'full resources' was whittled down by the right-wing leadership to the withdrawal of teachers from the school savings movement. But feeble as this sanction was, it made a big impression because it was an action and not just a verbal protest. The one per cent issue, seemingly small, became the focus for more fundamental discontents. It had an extraordinary effect in enraging otherwise passive and conformist teachers whatever their political views. Fuel was added to the rising flames when the Minister, the bland, suave and urbane Sir David Eccles, accused the teachers of making a 'song and dance' about a trifle. This injudicious remark created an explosive reaction which 'Song and Dance' Eccles was never allowed to forget. At the same time, demands multiplied for direct action to end the irritation of dinner duties. And shortly after, in a remarkable decision, a Special Salaries Conference in 1958 rejected the Executive's provisional acceptance of a 5% offer. This had never happened before but its impact was weakened when, in January 1959, the offer was accepted subject to the promise of further negotiations.

Discontent smouldered in staff rooms and local associations following the 1959 agreement. Not only the minority who had been ready to strike but many others felt that an opportunity had been lost in conditions of a severe shortage of teachers and coincident with a major public clamour on Britain's backwardness in science and technology. No wonder an explosion occurred when, with unexampled cynicism, the government decided to increase policemen's pay substantially above the level rejected for teachers. Although the current agreement was due to last till April 1962, a new claim was put in January 1961. Almost simultaneously the Scottish teachers found themselves in conflict with the government and a strike was planned (and later took place) by the Glasgow branch of the Educational Institute of Scotland (the equivalent of the NUT) with the support of the national body.

Events moved rapidly. At Easter, the NUT Conference in a carefully planned move, against the advice of its top leaders, insisted on expressing their solidarity with the Scots in the clearest possible way, fully appreciating the moral position thus created by supporting someone else's strike.

Negotiations were, therefore, conducted in the Burnham Committee by teachers' representatives' conscious of a growing militant force behind them determined 'to fight this time'.

So that, when the outcome was the customary unsatisfactory provisional agreement, for the first time in professional history a majority of the NUT Executive rejected the recommendation of their own representatives, and decided to propose to a Special Conference the reopening of their negotiations backed up by the threat of a one-day national strike without pay, and a series of area strikes in the autumn with strike pay of 95% of salary. Strike pay was to be provided half from the relatively small union 'sustentation' fund and half from a national levy of 5% of gross salary from all members of the union in the country, a very big commitment for an indefinite period. At the Conference on 17 June, however, while the rejection of the pay offer was carried, the proposals for strike action were merely left to the Executive to pursue.

Then in late July came the 1961 Selwyn Lloyd (Chancellor of the Exchequer) pay pause and cuts and the extraordinary response in an outcrop of teachers' unofficial strikes on the one hand, and the acceptance by the union leaders on the other of an offer which the Special Conference had already refused. To their consternation Sir David Eccles immediately rejected this agreement, standing firm on the pay pause and an even lower figure, but also proposing to destroy the established negotiating machinery and replace it by a government-controlled body. Clearly the immediate need was to defeat the government's policy as a prelude to going on to fight for the full professional demand. This should have involved a major battle with all the weapons previously proposed by the Executive, and even more. Instead, the 'non-political' leaders of the teachers emphasised 'political' persuasion and dropped all mention of strikes.

But when Eccles still would not budge the NUT Executive, under pressure in which we played a large part, decided to call another special conference, proposing for the second time the sanctions already outlined at the previous one, but also a ban on school meals supervision and a programme of political action by 'constitutional' methods. The school meals ban amounted to a campaign of civil disobedience, since the duties to be banned were statutory obligations. Referenda among members on these proposals and various weaker alternatives suggested by the officers were organised in late September and the Conference took place on 7 October. It carried most of the Executive's proposals and added the important recommendation to union members to join opposition political parties or, failing that, to join the Conservative Party to oppose government policy. This was indeed a revolution in professional thinking, a very far cry from the days of 'political neutrality'. The Conference, however, decided to drop the proposal for area strikes following on the announcement that the ballot figures in the selected areas did not reach the required 75% majority of the total membership.

Actually, the high, if not high enough, figures both for strike action in the areas and for the levy confirmed emphatically the tremendous change that had taken place in the outlook of the profession. It was the success of the ballots not their supposed failure, as they falsely claimed, which alarmed the right wing, and the press fully appreciated the significance both of the ballots and of the conference by its subsequent concentrated attack on the profession for failing in its traditional 'sense of responsibility'. Praise was lavished on the grammar school unions whose refusal to follow the line of the NUT reflected the fact that the Government's salary cuts deliberately left untouched increases in differential payments of which they were the chief beneficiaries. This disunity seriously weakened the struggle in progress.

All this had a profound effect on the public, and especially on the Tory Party, which met in conference a week later. This saw the unprecedented defeat of government education policy presented by Eccles: the delegates, traditionally loyal to Ministers under fire from outside, made it clear that they were acting under the strongest pressure from teachers in the localities, masses of whom, till then active Tory workers, had declared they were finished with the Conservative Party. Add to this the LEAs' statement that the school meals ban would result in closing many schools (something not originally anticipated) and it seemed that the teachers were set for success and Eccles for defeat.

At precisely this moment, following on a new meeting with him, the teachers' leaders by a majority vote completely capitulated without gaining a single concession of the slightest value, accepting everything they had publicly denounced. Truly they had 'snatched defeat from the jaws of victory'. Eccles was saved (and in Parliament a few days later showed his contempt for his saviours by repudiating even the worthless concessions claimed). The teachers, cried the Press, were sound after all.

But were they? Only the wrath of the members which they were terrified of facing, and which the extraordinary unofficial strikes and unprecedented mass demonstrations (including an 'occupation' of union HQ) in the following days confirmed as the prevailing feeling, prompted the brazen decision of the Executive to ride the storm by refusing to call a conference to ratify their actions. There were very profound reasons which prompted such an open and risky betrayal. High stakes were being played for. It has been shown that if the programme of action had been operated its success was very likely. A new factor would have entered the political situation, one highly dangerous for the Establishment—the factor of a highly organised and influential opinion-forming body of professional people committed to industrial action. The possibilities of consequent links with the Trade Union movement not only for the teachers but for other white-collar bodies were incalculable.

It is plain that the entire thought and behaviour pattern of most of the teachers' leaders would cause them to shrink from the prospect before them: it was a case of 'after this the deluge'. One must, however, admit that though the secret ballot figures were, in the circumstances, remarkable (and should have evoked pride), they did not universally appear to be so to a profession lacking in experience of action. So, there was a large body of confused and dispirited members in addition to the substantial numbers who would never support any action. The remarkable fact was the steadfastness of the overwhelming majority of local union leaders throughout the country.

1961 was the turning point in professional post-war history. Though the union leaders had ridden the storm, things were never the same again. New powerful forces had been unleashed at the grassroots—to use today's jargon. It was not just the credibility of the leadership that had been decisively undermined, but a whole ideology and approach to union activity. At the annual conference that followed in 1962 and for which the unprecedented (before and since) number of 800 resolutions were received, the Executive, already partially changed by elections which reflected the new situation, was on the defensive throughout and important decisions were taken to prevent a recurrence of the 1961 betrayal.

(I shall always remember the apology of one mildly-left member of the Executive, the gentle Emrys Powell from Wales, when I accused the Executive of treachery—"No, not treachery, Max, betrayal.") New rules were passed stating clearly the supremacy of conference in policy-making and the requirement to have all Burnham agreements ratified by a conference. It seemed that democracy had triumphed, if somewhat belatedly.

But there were wounds that could not be healed. Thus, though every effort was made to conceal the truth from the membership, the fact was that the union lost some 10,000 members to the NAS in an emotional reaction to the betrayal. This was a windfall on which the NAS built up its subsequent substantial increase in membership for it included many good militants who refused to be reconciled with their old organisation and who were able to attract young men teachers in the staff rooms. It also helped to build the myth that the NAS was 'militant' while the NUT was always in the end quietist because of the domination within its ranks of women. Founded on this myth, which until then had little actual practical effect, the NAS was to become a force in teacher politics that could no longer be ignored. Their biggest victory was to be given membership of the Burnham Committee by Eccles. Cynically, because of a deal just as disreputable as the NUT leaders' betrayal, they agreed to call off any plans for action in 1961 as the price of their reward.

We had suffered an ignominious defeat at the hands of an 'own goal' leadership, pusillanimous, gutless and unctuous. It was a pity that it was the membership who would suffer its effects. The whole operation was an object lesson on how not to run a union.

Margaret: Ten 'Start-Stop' Years

While Max was becoming a force in both Communist and teacher politics, I was entering with zest into the spirit of student life at Birmingham University. I went to the required history lectures, but mainly passed my time in the Edmund Street Common Room, the bar or the Student Union at Edgbaston. I successfully ran for the Undergraduate Council and was elected assistant editor of the student newsletter. I joined the 'Socialist Society', which was non-party political and brought together Communist and Labour Party supporters and other less committed socialists. There my somewhat naïve ideas came up against much more informed views.

Most of the male students were ex-servicemen and among them were a number of committed Marxists with a clear 'world view'. Politics they insisted was about the working-class achieving power and mocked my 'petit bourgeois' idealism. They said those who were benefiting from capitalism would do everything possible to maintain that system, and that governments in Parliamentary democracies when it came to fundamental economic choices would always support the interests of the rich. Every trick of propaganda would be used to play upon ordinary people's caution about change and persuade them that socialism was a threat to their way of life. Surely, they said, I realised how the press always portrayed Communists as people to be feared?

So, I started reading the Marxist classics or, to be honest, shortened versions of the main texts—I have never been a Marxist scholar like Max. I also read Lenin's 'Imperialism the last stage of Capitalism' and made an effort to understand more thoroughly what was going on in the world.

Life wasn't all politics. We were required to take a sport so I chose fencing and learnt to hold a foil and 'stand to'—great fun. I also joined the Scouts and Guides Association, and spent a lot of time just meeting people and chatting. I went to Saturday night hops—I was somewhat uncertain about how to behave with the other sex, and very cautious (in those pre-pill days the fear of pregnancy was a real deterrent). I noticed that there were class distinctions even in the common room, with a group of ex public school students from rich families who obviously considered themselves superior to the rest of us.

There was also another distinctive group, the older ex-servicemen, who played a lot of cards. One day three of them shouted out that they were looking for a fourth to play solo whist, so I offered my services. They may have thought I would be an easy victim and suggested stakes much higher than I expected. I'd been playing solo whist since I was five years old, so I agreed and ended up with a nice little addition to my grant. They didn't invite me again and, my family had taught me never to gamble more than I could afford to lose, a precept I didn't want to break again. In addition, I began to play bridge, which I found more challenging than solo-whist.

All in all, I was thoroughly enjoying myself when after seven weeks it all suddenly came to an end. New students were required to attend the mass X-ray department to make sure they hadn't got TB, then very common. I was called back and told that I must go into hospital. By a coincidence the other new history scholar, Malcolm Yapp (later Professor Yapp of SOAS and a world expert on Kurdish history), was in the same predicament. So, there we were in the Queen Elizabeth Hospital—Malcolm in the men's TB ward and me in the women's. He managed to persuade the nurses that in the evening they should push both our beds into the 'day room' so we could talk. We exchanged whatever books our visitors brought and discussed them together.

A little sexual frisson crept into the room but our situation was hardly propitious and I wasn't really Malcolm's type. After about a month, the doctors decided to insert something like ping pong balls into our chest cavities to try to collapse our lungs so they could heal. In Malcolm's case, this was successful, though it was two years before he could return to university.

In my case, they found it impossible to open up my chest cavity and so decided that the best approach would be a period of bed rest and a high calorie diet (lots of butter and cream). If I had come from a crowded home, I would have been sent to a sanatorium but because I had a bedroom to myself, I was sent home for my unfortunate parents to look after.

It's never been in my nature to feel sorry for myself, but back in my bedroom at home I felt caged and also perplexed—had I really got TB? And if I had, how did I get it? I had no cough and found it difficult in hospital to produce sputum samples. Nor did I have night sweats, the other usual symptom. As far as I knew,

I had had no contact with anyone suffering from TB. It was true that I had been having period of extreme tiredness. I had never had a great deal of stamina but this feeling of weakness was far more extreme. I realised it had started after I'd had a bout of pneumonia about three years earlier and so I assumed that the holes in my left lung shown in the X-rays must have started then. But was it really necessary for me to lie in bed all day long?

My bed at home was comfortable but the room was a bit Spartan with a linoleum floor covering, just a one-bar electric radiator and a small rug by the bed. The only warm room in the house was the living room with a coal fire. It also had a radio (a large cumbersome contraption). My mother had had an operation for breast cancer followed by radiotherapy two years earlier, and though she was clear, the last thing I wanted was her running up and down stairs with meals for me. She was a believer in doing exactly what the doctors said, but I negotiated with her that I could get up mid-morning and sit quietly downstairs until after lunch and then go back to bed, then get up at tea-time and stay until after supper. This gave me a chance to listen to the radio.

The highlights of this period were visits from some of my new University friends, especially Gill Walmsley and Harry Houghton. Gill and I had met in the Freshers' queue to register for the Socialist Society and immediately took to each other. She was a born rebel, despite coming from a military family and going to Cheltenham College for Young Ladies. Her elder sister was in the Communist Party and her younger sister was married to Sam Aaronovitch, then a full time Communist Party official. Harry, on the other hand, came from a working-class family and had a strong 'Brummie' accent. He had won a scholarship to grammar school but had felt an odd man out. His friends were leading lights among the trade unionists from the Austin Motor Works in Northfield, where he lived. He had spent his National Service period as part of the occupation forces in Germany and was critical of their involvement in black market activities and connivance at ex-Nazis taking on administrative roles.

All my visitors brought me newspapers and magazines. Gill brought me *The New Statesman* and *Tribune;* Harry brought copies of the *Daily Worker* and articles from *Labour Monthly.* The General Election of February 1950 was a topic of conversation but only Harry had a vote as Gill and I were not yet 21. Harry saw it as his mission to improve my understanding of politics and would lecture me on Marxist theory, the evils of imperialism and why America and Britain were to blame for the Cold War. I had plenty of time to ponder over what he said but felt

I needed to know more before fully accepting his point of view. But his visits stopped me feeling that lying in bed was intellectually a total waste of time.

After several months of this regime, I was taken back to hospital for more X-rays, which showed some improvement. The doctors said I no longer needed to lie in bed all the time but must live very quietly. I should never run or take exercise, and should walk as little as possible. I should not stand if I could sit, and I should not sit if I could lie down. I did my best to do as I was told, and was happy when the weather allowed me to sit in the garden or walk slowly up the road to watch my father play tennis. I was told I could go back to university in the autumn if I continued to improve.

So, in October 1950 I started my course again, but I was a subdued student compared with a year earlier. I re-registered with the Socialist Society and attended its meetings but gave up staying on afterwards. I noticed we seemed to have more funds than most societies and was told this was because a year earlier the treasurer had staked all our funds on 'Russian Hero', who had won the Grand National at 66-1. This was a new insight into practical Marxism! I could not help being amused also at one of our leading lights, Trevor Taylor, later Secretary of the Anglo/Russian Friendship Association, who displayed his solidarity with the working class by wearing a cloth cap—made by his West End tailor. I liked the fact that the Society was non-sectarian and debates could be open-ended, although Communist Party members were the dominant group and did their best to persuade others to accept their views. As, like them, I opposed the Korean War, high defence spending and, rearmament, they targeted me as a potential member, but I resolutely refused to join, both then and during the rest of my time at university.

I told them that it might be a weakness on my part, but I was still finding my way and too independent-minded (individualistic in their terms) to be able to toe a Party line or accept the discipline demanded from Party members. Nor could I go along with their veneration for the Soviet Union because I could not dismiss as mere capitalist propaganda stories about the existence of gulags and the persecution of political dissenters. I worried too about Stalin's denunciation of Tito, whom I saw as a wartime hero and the founder of a socialist Yugoslavia. My belief that capitalism must be replaced by societies based on socialist principles was in no way dented, but I was not convinced that the Soviet Union had the right template. I do not wish to claim prescience about the deformations of socialism outlined in Khrushchev's 1956 speech, but I was deeply uneasy.

Despite the publication of 'The British Road to Socialism' in 1950, which sought to stress respect for British democratic traditions, I saw the British Communist Party as still a rigid adherent of the Moscow line. This stood in the way of my committing myself to membership. So, I was spared the anguish and sense of betrayal which afflicted so many members in 1956.

As I was forbidden to do most other things, I dutifully attended lectures and seminars. Our tutorial groups were never more than four—usually only two or three—which meant we really got to know the lecturers and received a lot of individual guidance. At the end of the year my results were very good—much better probably than they would have been if I'd been able to participate fully in student life. I did ease up in the summer term as I felt stronger. I began travelling over to the Student Union to play bridge, and I went to a few Saturday night hops, though I limited my dancing. The most adventurous thing I did was to go sailing with the Scouts and Guides Association which had hired a large sloop to sail across the Channel. Our Captain was an ex-naval officer, who knew exactly what he was doing, and it was understood that I would not do anything at all strenuous like hauling in sails. I was allowed to hold the rudder sometimes and I remember my excitement when a large liner loomed up out of the mist and I had to take evasive action.

Once more, however, things were about to come to a full stop. Was it my fault? Had I really done too much? So much bed-rest had enfeebled me and I'd not had the muscular strength to do very much until the summer term, but should I have done even less? Would it have made a difference? Anyway, my September check-up showed that my lungs had deteriorated, so instead of going back to University I must go back into the Queen Elizabeth hospital. Before going, I went to see Professor Cronne, Head of the History Department, to ask him whether there was any way I could continue studying while in hospital as I couldn't face interrupting my course a second time. He knew me well as I had been in his tutorial group and was very sympathetic. He said he would see what could be done. I also went to see Rodney Hilton, the Communist Medieval historian to ask him if he could help me get a place in the International Union of Students sanatorium in Czechoslovakia. He too promised to do what he could.

Back in hospital I was immediately put on a regime of complete rest plus fresh air. This meant being in bed on a balcony outside the ward. I was not allowed to get up even to go to the toilet. Birmingham is not a warm place so I and a fellow patient on the balcony had to wear a scarf and gloves to survive.

From my bed, I could see across to the University buildings and couldn't help feeling wistful, especially on Saturday nights. Fortunately, when autumn turned into real winter, I was taken back inside. Both Professor Cronne and Rodney Hilton did what they had promised. Professor Cronne arranged for the Statutes of the University to be supplemented by a clause incorporating the Queen Elizabeth Hospital "as part of the Department of History for the purposes of study of Miss Margaret Howard," and I began to be sent books and essay topics for the main second-year courses. About once a fortnight a member of staff came to tutor me; very often this was Dr. Geoffrey Templeman, who I saw as very right-wing but the soul of kindness.

It took some time for Rodney Hilton to organise the offer of a place in the IUS Sanatorium but early in December it arrived. I was delighted. I immediately told my doctors that I should like to be transferred but they were strongly opposed. They said I was not fit to travel and needed an operation to collapse half of my left lung by removing some of my ribs, which they were planning to do shortly. I think they felt a certain professional pique that I had thought I would be as well off elsewhere. There was no way I could oppose them, especially as it would have worried my parents' stiff. So, I had to thank Rodney but decline the offer.

Queen Elizabeth Hospital had a team of doctors specialising in the treatment of tuberculosis, headed by a tall, imposing-looking surgeon, who used to sweep through the wards surrounded by a large retinue of other doctors and nurses. I was led to believe that if my lung was not collapsed, the TB would spread, especially as it had apparently started to affect my right lung. I still had no cough but was shown my X-rays (not that I could really understand them). So, a two stage 'thoracoplasty' was performed just before and just after Christmas 1951 to remove my left ribs. This was major surgery: the operation not only leaves a large scar on the back, it also leaves a big hollow between the neck and shoulder blade, one shoulder higher than the other, the head slanting to one side and, in women, a sinking in of the breast. To counter these effects, patients on emerging from the anaesthetic find a mirror at the foot of their bed and are told to try and keep their neck straight. I'm afraid my first reaction was to burst into tears and say, "no man will ever look at me now" (I was only 21 and had already been ill for two years).

Time was to prove this fear unwarranted, but the physical after effects have stayed with me all my life—shortness of breath, the development of curvature of the spine, back and neck ache in middle age and limited strength (not to mention the more frivolous need always to wear high necked dresses and padded bras and swimming costumes. For most of my life I did my best to ignore these problems and never classed myself as 'disabled'. It has only been as middle age passed into old age that I've become resentful of my back aches and lack of strength due to this surgery. My experiences were used by Linda Grant in her novel, *Dark Circle*, about life in a TB Sanatorium in 1950-1. Alongside the surgery, for the next three months I was given daily streptomycin injections along with large quantities of enormous, hard to chew tablets known as PAS. I now believe it was the streptomycin more than the operation that cured me, but at the time I accepted that the doctors were saving my life. I thought it was doubtful whether I would reach my 30th birthday even with the surgery. People were still dying of TB—George Orwell had been the best-known victim a year earlier.

In retrospect, I was very unlucky to have been diagnosed with TB at that point in time. Streptomycin, which was to become an effective remedy, was still in an experimental stage when I was first diagnosed in 1949, and was only used as a last resort because of serious side effects, including deafness.

However, these problems had been overcome by the time I returned to hospital in autumn 1951 and patients were being cured by 'strep' in combination with the tablets known as PAS. Neither I nor my parents was aware of this but the doctors in the Queen Elizabeth must have known.

In hindsight, it was clearly wrong of the surgeons to operate: I was not dangerously ill, so why did they not pause and reflect upon the physical harm being inflicted on a young woman by what might well be unnecessary surgery? Were these very eminent doctors just trapped in rigid thinking or were they subconsciously trying to postpone the reality that their high status within the medical profession was about to be lost as their skill became redundant? I had been brought up to believe that doctors know best and it was many years later before I faced the reality that they had betrayed my trust and had not acted in my best interests. At the time, I thought I ought to be grateful still to be alive and that the setting up of the National Health service had enabled me to have a standard of treatment that my parents would never have been able to afford for me. I was only 21 and my social background had not prepared me for questioning authority. If I or my parents had been more worldly wise, we might have known that patients had the right to reject surgery in light of the known existence of effective drugs.

Three months after my operations, I was allowed to get up. Needless to say, I could hardly stand so atrophied were my leg muscles. It was arranged that I would go to a sanatorium in Midhurst, Sussex, to convalesce. Only patients thought likely to 'fit in' were selected to go as NHS patients to what had previously been a very upmarket private sanatorium set in beautiful grounds with every facility. In practice, this meant only middle-class patients. Because I was a university student I must have been thought to qualify despite my modest social background. The NHS was set up to provide access to medical care for everyone, but a process of social selection was being applied over access to this high-quality provision. There were no blue-collar workers among the patients when I was there.

Many of my fellow patients had been there before the NHS and came from upper middle class or aristocratic backgrounds and so I got to know a mixture of people I would never have come across in normal life. I felt particular sympathy with the regular army officers, whose careers had been brought to an abrupt end by developing TB. One of them, an extremely handsome 30-year-old Colonel, took a fancy to me and made it his mission to teach me to play snooker. Another fellow patient had been in the Irish National Bridge Team and gave classes to those of us interested. I also became friendly with a young Irish aristocrat, a 'Lady', who invariably had done the Times crossword by mid-morning, and who wore a quite fabulous dressing gown. One day, the Director came round and seeing that my name was 'Howard' asked me if I was related to the Duke of Norfolk—so I replied deadpan, "no, a different branch of the Howard family."

The grounds were very beautiful and as I and my fellow patients gathered strength we were allowed to go walks. The male and female patients were supposed to go out of separate gates and stay apart—a rule often broken. Nor were we supposed to drink alcohol, but most lockers contained a bottle of dry sherry, a drink I learnt to appreciate. The only sad aspect of this time was that there were still patients hanging on to life by a quarter of a lung, some of whom didn't make it. However, most of us believed we would get better and be able to resume normal life, so the atmosphere was generally optimistic and very different from that in most accounts of life in tuberculosis sanatoriums.

After my transfer to Midhurst, I continued to receive books and essay topics from the University and in June I sat some of the second-year exams in the Sanatorium. I did well enough for the History Department to decide that I was qualified to enter the third year. So, in October, I went back to Birmingham and resumed my studies.

Again, I re-joined the Socialist Society but generally took things quietly. My only new activity was to make use of my bridge lessons at Midhurst to qualify for the University bridge team—only the second team but I enjoyed playing competitive bridge and the coaching we received. The students with whom I had started, including Gill and Harry, had already graduated: Gill had gone off to London to train as a teacher and Harry had become a trainee manager in the food department of a large store. Later in life he became a VAT Tax Inspector, which suited his ideological convictions about the importance of taxation to fund public enterprise and the Welfare State—no attempt at evasion got by him!

I was welcomed back by my new fellow students. It was the height of the Cold War and a difficult period for impartial study at the borderline of history and current events, my main interest. The Professor in Modern History was an expert in American History and took a very pro-American stance. Fortunately, I was not in his tutorial group but in that of a young lecturer in French History, Douglas Johnson, a friend of Rodney Hilton and a socialist, though not a Communist. He supervised my dissertation which I chose to do on the history of Trade Unionism in Birmingham, 1900–1906. For variety and as a form of escapism from cold war pressures, I chose as my special subject a paper on Anglo-Saxon archaeology, which was being taught by a visiting lecturer from the British Museum.

All I wanted at this stage in life was to graduate and get out into the world. In March, Professor Cronne asked me to see him. He proposed that I should take an extra year in order to obtain a First (something much rarer and more prestigious in those days than today). He pointed out that although I had been deemed qualified to continue into the third year, I had not done all the course and this might disadvantage me in the final examinations (in the days before credit accumulation, degree classifications were entirely decided by 3rd-year exams). I thanked him but said I would rather do the best I could and graduate so that I could move on. My decision was influenced by a lack of confidence that I knew enough to get a First.

This conversation prompted me to consider how I would earn my living after graduation. It had always been assumed by both me and my parents that I would become a school teacher, but no-one with a history of TB could be admitted to a post-graduate teaching course or employed as a teacher. I saw an advert in *The*

New Statesman for a graduate trainee in a publishing firm in London, applied, was interviewed and offered the job. So, all I needed was to finish my degree. The Coronation of Queen Elizabeth took place in the middle of the final exams, which I found a great help as it saved me having to do exams while suffering period cramps. After the exams were marked, everyone had a viva, but I was relaxed—just glad it would soon be over.

When the results were posted, I was listed as having a First, only the 4th one in 25 years in the History Department. I could not believe it and for the next 24 hours suffered deep anxiety about how embarrassing it would be when the mistake was discovered and the list was changed. The next day my name was still there and I also received a letter offering me a post-graduate scholarship. I felt confused and strongly doubted that I deserved such a high mark—I felt troubled at the thought that I must have been given a sympathy upgrade. In the current credit accumulation system, I would certainly not have obtained a First, but in the 1950s awards were much more subjective and what was looked for was 'first class quality' in some answers in a majority of papers. I went to see Douglas Johnson who said my dissertation and special paper fully met this criterion and, as for the general papers, "never has so little knowledge gone such a long way." That made me feel better—a bit less of a fraud. So, I relaxed and even did a little basking in the glory—my parents were extremely happy. This was not the case with one male student with whom I had occasionally gone out, who came up to me and solemnly said that he would no longer be able to take me out now I had a First, as he had only got an Upper Second.

This was a reflection of the extraordinary importance given to degree classification as well as the male chauvinist attitudes prevalent at that time.

I was in a dilemma about what to do over the scholarship. Should I stick to my plan to go into publishing, or take advantage of the opportunity to do post-graduate work with the possibility of an academic career? If I took it up and wanted to do research in modern history, I would have to work under the tutelage of the Professor whom I saw as 'a Cold War Warrior'. How could I cope with that situation? It just didn't seem to me a viable option and I hadn't the courage or self-confidence to try to take it on. Britain was not America where McCarthyism reigned. Here established Communist historians like Rodney Hilton were in a safe position, but the reality of the Cold War years was against new young Marxist or left-wing research students gaining an academic post. I was drawn to trade union history but there wasn't a specialist in Labour history in the Department and, fond as I was of Professor Cronne, I did not want to pursue his type of medieval history. I had enjoyed Anglo-Saxon Archaeology as something finite and happily non-political, but it wasn't really my main interest and there was no-one in Birmingham who could supervise research in that field. It was then suggested to me by the visiting lecturer in the subject, Rupert Bruce-Mitford, Keeper of Anglo-Saxon archaeology at the British Museum, that Birmingham University would probably allow me to hold the scholarship at Oxford University where I could be suitably supervised and where my First would gain me admission to one of the women's colleges. I succumbed to this idea—maybe it was escapism but it had other attractions. It allowed me to leave Birmingham and stretch my wings, and, having been rejected by Oxford earlier, it assuaged my ego to be offered a post-graduate place at any college I chose. So that autumn I enrolled at Queen Anne's College on a B.Litt. degree in Anglo-Saxon Archaeology (a 2-year research degree unique to Oxford) with Professor Christopher Hawkes as my supervisor.

It has to be admitted that I took life very easily at Oxford. At my first meeting with Professor Hawkes it was agreed that I would make a study of the incidence of Anglo-Saxon saucer brooches, as had been suggested by Bruce-Mitford, and that I should go to see him once a term. At these meetings he would walk round and round me until I felt quite giddy, telling me the results he thought I would obtain. He showed his goodwill by providing tea and biscuits or a glass of sherry before saying he must rush off. Such 'research supervision' was not uncommon and reflected a belief at the time that postgraduate students ought to be left 'to sink or swim' as a test of their worthiness. Fortunately, the then Director of the Ashmolean Museum, Dr Donald Harden, was more helpful. He said my first task must be to familiarise myself with Anglo-Saxon collections and suggested I make a catalogue of those in the Ashmolean. This provided him with free assistance and gave me an opportunity to meet other post-graduate researchers or undergraduates interested in archaeology. So, my days were spent drifting along to the Museum for a mixture of cataloguing and socialising.

St Anne's College organised social events for its postgraduate students and the History Tutor, Dr. Marjorie Reeves, later Principal of the college, took me under her wing. She was sceptical about my field of research and urged me to go back to being a historian. Later I regretted that I hadn't taken her advice; maybe I would have listened more carefully if she had been a modern historian but she was a medieval specialist. I thought also that my scholarship was tied to studying

Anglo-Saxon archaeology, and, anyway, at the time I was content with what I was doing. I had a small but comfortable attic room in post-graduate lodgings in Merton Street and enjoyed wandering round the colleges and Christchurch meadows. I began to spend quite a lot of my leisure time in Magdalan College with a tall, red-headed undergraduate called Andrew Saunders, who was a leading light of the Undergraduate Archaeological Society.

He had been passionately interested in archaeology since the age of nine when he had taken part in excavations near his home in Cornwall.

At the end of the summer term, we were both accepted for the whole summer as expenses-paid assistants at a Viking Boat excavation near Oslo, where our relationship developed further. Despite my continuing fear of becoming pregnant, my hormones could be denied no longer—with his curly golden red hair, blue eyes and wide grin Andrew was too sexually attractive for me to resist. But the risk worried me, so I felt more secure when we became engaged a few months later. We married two years later when we both had obtained jobs in London.

Looking back, I see my two years in Oxford as a hiatus in life, a pleasant, self-indulgent one participating in the life of Oxford's 'Gilded Youth'. I remember especially May Day 1954: Andrew was able to take me with him to the top of Magdalan College Tower to hear the Choir sing in the dawn before we went punting with a glass of champagne on the river below. He had a friend with a car which he used to pack with students sitting on one another's laps and drive out to one of the inns in the surrounding villages for dinner. As Andrew's fiancée I was often invited along. I learnt to watch cricket and relax for hours. I had no money worries, no fees to pay and my postgraduate scholarship adequately covered my modest needs when not being invited out. I met people from all sorts of backgrounds, some of whom had a self-confidence in the right to be eccentric which was a complete contrast to the timidity and conformism of most of those with whom I had grown up. I was amused at the deference a particular professor showed towards titled students. Like my father, I had no time for deference but at that stage in life had not been able to shake off a tendency to be diffident, a frequent trait of female students even at Oxford. Diffidence I realised was not a problem for any of the male ex-public-school students, most of whom radiated self-assurance and a conviction that they were bound to get to the top.

Although I did not lose my interest in politics, and continued to read *Tribune,* the *New Statesman* and sometimes *The Daily Worker*, I decided to let politics lie dormant for a while: I felt inhibited from active involvement by the tension between my wish to support policies more wholeheartedly socialist than those of the Labour Party and my worries about Stalinism. I would have liked to link up with the group of post-graduates around G.D.H. Coles, the leading socialist and trade union historian, whose writings I admired, so I dropped in two or three times on lectures by him but was too diffident to introduce myself.

What I did not anticipate, and what my family had been too inexperienced in worldly matters to raise with me, was that research in Anglo-Saxon archaeology might be a dead-end. The academic world was still small in the mid-1950s and there was little expansion until well into the sixties, but most people who got Firsts and went on to do research found a niche (though, as explained above, it was more difficult for known left-wingers, a fact which had influenced my decision to escape to the long-ago past). Bruce-Mitford had told me that there would be an Assistant Keeper's post in the British Museum for which I could apply towards the end of my time at Oxford, but he did not warn me that this would be the only post on offer in Anglo-Saxon archaeology for several years. Nor did he warn me of the male-chauvinist attitudes I might encounter were I to apply for the BM job, which I did, but the post went to a postgraduate from Cambridge, David Wilson, already a friend of mine, who later went on to become Keeper of the Museum. David was probably a better candidate and I wouldn't have resented it at all but for the way I was interviewed by the Chair of the Panel, Sir Mortimer Wheeler, who insisted that the key requirement for the post was a knowledge of Greek (which I obviously didn't have) and who generally made me feel patronised and not taken seriously. This wasn't just sour grapes on my part, I felt discriminated against, but I would have shrugged my shoulders if there had been other jobs to apply for, but there weren't. So how was I to earn my living?

I was rescued by an advertisement for an Assistant Editor of the Wiltshire Victoria County History, a position located within London University's Institute of Historical Research and involving more research and writing than editing. The series had reached the point where someone was wanted to compile a gazetteer of Anglo-Saxon remains in Wiltshire. As most students were more worldly wise in choosing their fields of study than I had been, there wasn't much competition. I could not have been more fortunate than in having as my immediate boss an extremely gentle and understanding historian called Elizabeth Crittall. The overall Editor was Ralph Pugh, a man so meticulous that he filed his laundry bills for five years. He taught all his staff the necessity to be absolutely accurate in every detail. After I had finished the Gazetteer, I was asked if I would like to stay on to work on the economic volume which would be covering the history of Wiltshire's industries. I really enjoyed this except for the day when the manager of the Harris Bacon Factory thought that before examining their archives, I might like to see how pigs were slaughtered. I refused as tactfully as I could. I used to go home loaded with sausages and pork pies. After bacon, came dairy products, tanning and gloves. I very much enjoyed this period of my work with the VCH and was sorry when the economic volume was ready to go to press.

For the next volume, I did some work on nonconformity in parts of Wiltshire but after that the main area to be covered was parish histories. My first one, Fugglestone St Peter, taught me the technique, but I quailed at the thought of spending my future researching manorial rolls. It was time for me to move on— yet where to? Back to archaeology in the hope some posts would eventually open up, or could I build upon my work on the history of industries and switch to economic history, even though I had no research degree in that field? The aspect of archaeology I most liked was taking part in excavations, which I had continued to do in holidays on digs that Andrew was directing. I was doubtful about whether I could make a career in this field but thought I'd have one last attempt. So, I applied for and was awarded a Senior Scholarship at Westfield College in London in order to do research on the continental background of the Anglo-Saxons. I left the VCH in the summer of 1959 and was able to get work directing a small dig of my own on the Ryknield Roman Road near Buxton before taking up the scholarship in the autumn.

Andrew and I had married in March 1956 and in the early autumn moved into an extremely nice flat, comprising the top floor of a large house near Hampstead village, which we rented unfurnished from Professor Phelps Brown, a well-known economist. Andrew had achieved his ambition of a post in the Department of Ancient Monuments and was totally enthused by his work. His dedication to a career in archaeology, which had impressed me at Oxford, seemed less appealing when I was living with it. Not that I was uninterested in the things he wanted to do: I had enjoyed our wet and muddy honeymoon exploring Celtic crosses in Ireland, and was happy to spend holidays excavating or looking at old fortresses. We both had a love of opera. Andrew had been a boy chorister at Magdalan College School and enjoyed hearing good singing, so we found the money for upper circle seats at Covent Garden; the most memorable of the productions we saw was Joan Sutherland in the original production of Lucia di Lammermoor. But there were other things I wanted to do and to talk about—especially politics. Anyone who has lived with a partner totally absorbed in his or her own field will understand the problem.

After the 1956 Suez debacle, we agreed that we would both join the Hampstead Labour Party. The whole international communist movement including the British Communist Party was in complete turmoil at this time over Khrushchev's revelations about Stalinism and the Soviet invasion of Hungary, so it seemed that the only viable choice for political involvement was the Labour Party, which had actively opposed the attack on Suez.

Andrew had never been drawn towards communism but had a family background of non-active support of Labour (his father was Town Clerk of St Austell which precluded him from party politics). The effect of our starting to attend meetings was to bring to the surface a difference of view between us.

Andrew was only marginally interested in politics and tended to support the established leadership. My views, on the other hand, were very much on the left and, as explained below, I quickly became deeply involved in Labour Party activities.

Our differences of view might not in themselves have mattered but during the next three years our interests increasingly diverged. We got on well enough but saw less and less of each other. I was not unhappy when with Andrew but I was beginning to be bored in his company. By early 1959, I began to worry that I had rushed into marriage in the same way as I had rushed into Anglo-Saxon research—over anxious to get on with life. In retrospect, this 'live for the day' approach reflected suppressed uncertainly about my health Although I had been told my TB was cured, it took me some time to trust that it wouldn't come back again. By 1959, I had recovered my confidence and began to think ahead. Andrew and I had had a great time together as students, and it had seemed only sensible to get married in case I became pregnant—no one trusted birth control methods before the pill came into use. On the eve of our wedding, I had suddenly had doubts about whether I really wanted to marry Andrew. Indeed, I was not sure whether I wanted to get married at all. All the arrangements were already in place; in deference to his family, we were being married in church and they had come up to Birmingham for the occasion. I felt it was too late to draw back and dismissed my doubts. Three years later they were returning. Andrew wanted children and I thought that it would be irresponsible to start a family if there was any danger of our marriage not lasting. I began to wonder whether now that our sexual ardour was cooling, Andrew really wanted to be with me. My reputation as a left-winger worried him in relation to his role as a Civil Servant, but I did not want to draw back from political activity. At a different level, I noticed that at the parties we went to or gave, he seemed to enjoy flirting with other women as, indeed, I did with other men. I thought that giving up the VCH and going off on a research trip would clarify matters in relation to my personal life as well as my future career.

Margaret: The Labour Party Activist

I had done nothing at all to put my socialist convictions into effect since leaving Birmingham University, but was galvanised into action by the Suez crisis. I attended the 'Law not War' rally against the British bombing and invasion of Egypt and heard both Gaitskell and Bevan speak. I went with my old University friend Gill and after the speeches we started to go down Whitehall towards Downing Street but were held back by police on horses. The pressure of those arriving from behind meant everyone was being squashed and I was finding it difficult to breathe until I managed to climb on a small wall and cling on to some railings. Eventually the crowd thinned and I got away and went home. I had done all I could that day. Because of the after effects of my TB surgery, I was always short of breath and I had been frightened at one point but I was determined not to be daunted: I would take part in many other demonstrations in the future but would take care not to be crushed again.

The following week, I applied to join the Labour Party and along with Andrew became a member of the Central Ward of the Hampstead Labour Party. I experienced a surge of adrenalin on doing this. My Communist friend Harry had always said that not being involved was endorsing the existing capitalist system, so now I would no longer be guilty of that. Not that I had any illusions about the Party I was joining, despite its stand against the Suez invasion. As Foreign Secretary, Ernest Bevin had committed Britain to the Cold War and support of America, which led to Britain supplying troops for the Korean War. And despite granting independence to India, the Labour Government had continued to keep forces abroad to maintain the commercial interests of the British Empire. Thus, the Malaysian 'insurgency' beginning in 1948 was brutally suppressed without protest from the Labour Shadow Cabinet. The consequence of these foreign policies was rearmament and high defence spending to the detriment of spending on the National Health Service and fully carrying out Beveridge's proposals for social security. The setting up of the Welfare State had improved the lives of the great majority of British citizens, but needed extending and better facilities, which would only be possible given additional resources.

The choice between defence spending and spending on the NHS and welfare had come to a head in 1951 when Hugh Gaitskell as Chancellor of the Exchequer introduced 50% charges for false teeth and spectacles, took £100m out of the Insurance Fund and restricted increases to some old age pensions. Aneurin Bevan, John Freeman and Harold Wilson resigned in protest. As one of the first beneficiaries of the NHS, I applauded their resignations. If as defenders of the cuts argued, there was "too much" demand for glasses and false teeth, it was because of the extent of the need. My hospital experiences were showing me how many things still needed to be improved not cut. One minor example: I nearly caused one Sister to have a nervous breakdown by persuading a junior nurse to change the covers on all the five pillows which I needed to use, not at all realising that only one pillowslip a week per patient was the allowance, however grubby the others!

There was constant inner-party strife between the leadership and the Bevanites for the following four and a half years. I read Tribune and on all major issues agreed with its views. While a student at Birmingham, I had read 'In place of Fear', Bevan's account of his background, and shared his conviction that a better life for the working class could only be achieved through socialism and the use of the fruits of industry for the benefit of all. I thought Bevan was correct to argue for the nationalised industries to be run on democratic lines. When the Coal mines were nationalised, the Miners spend a day marching to celebrate but the next day the same managers were in place. On foreign policy, the Bevanites led the opposition to German rearmament and argued for negotiation for a peaceful détente in place of Cold War antagonism, a demand given added urgency by the development of the hydrogen bomb.

In this period, whenever I had considered joining the Labour Party, I had been shocked at the virulence of the opponents of Bevan and the various attempts to silence him and other Bevanites by accusations of breaking Labour Party rules. The majority of constituency parties voted in support of the Bevanites at Labour Party Conferences but the block vote of the unions led by Arthur Deakin and other right-wing union leaders outweighed them. Matters came to a head not long before the 1955 Election with an attempt to expel Bevan. In the end this was side-lined, but in the face of such disunity it was not surprising that the Conservatives won the election. This was the first election in which I had a chance to vote but I saw little point in doing so as it would have meant travelling to my home town of Birmingham to vote in a constituency which was solidly Conservative whatever I did. In any case, why should I vote for a party that stifled free speech and differences of view?

Some months before the Suez crisis, the balance between right-and left-wing views began to alter. After the retirement of Attlee in December 1955, Hugh Gaitskell was elected Leader of the Party with a solid right-wing vote, but nine months later there was a complete reversal and Bevan won the election as Treasurer by a substantial majority. Equally important, there had been a change in the leadership of the Transport and General Workers Union with Frank Cousins, a keen advocate of socialism, replacing Arthur Deakin. The automatic support of right-wing policies by all the key union leaders had come to an end. In his acceptance speech, Bevan said he would continue to urge reform of the Party's structure, a leftward movement in policy and for greater emphasis on public ownership. My awareness of these changes made joining the Labour Party easier, but I doubt I would have done so without the Party's stand against the Suez invasion.

In the weeks after I joined, political debate both locally and in Parliament was dominated by the aftermath of the Suez invasion. The speeches of Gaitskell and Bevan taken together were described by Michael Foot as "the most brilliant display of opposition in recent parliamentary history." Both also condemned the Soviet invasion of Hungary, though their analysis of its deeper causes differed. Bevan urged that the priority was to negotiate with the Soviet Union, in the interests of peace in both Europe and the Middle East.

Christmas was not far away and it was made clear to me that the first duty of a new Labour Party member was to turn away from discussion of high politics and help out at the Christmas Bazaar. So, I dutifully pushed leaflets through doors and turned up to help man the stalls.

I used the occasion to buy a selection of Labour Party pamphlets: "Homes for the Future," "Personal Freedom" and "Towards Equality." These statements of policy had been drawn up while the Gaitskellites were the dominant force, so I was encouraged, and somewhat surprised, by their forthright content. Over half of all houses were privately rented at the time and 'Homes for the Future' begins by stating "private landlordism has failed to provide the majority of our people with the houses of the standard they deserve" and advocates its replacement by public ownership along with making it possible for those who wish to buy to be able to afford to do so. I very much agreed with all its proposals. Slum clearance and house improvement, the provision of council housing and controversies over rents would feature as major issues for the rest of the 1950s, especially in Hampstead whose MP, Sir Henry Brooke, became Minister of Housing and Local Government early in 1957.

The Christmas Bazaar, various social events, ward meetings and turning up to help at the Party Headquarters in Broughton Gardens enabled me to get to know many of the Hampstead Labour Party's leading members. They were to my 26-year-old eyes, a high-powered, middle-aged, middle-class group, deeply versed in the details of Labour Party Policy. As well as various MPs and their wives (Tony Greenwood, Sydney Silverman, Stephen Swindler, John Beard), there was a sizeable cluster of London County Councillors and the formidable Hampstead Alderman, Flo Cayford, the sole 100% working class member I got to know, although we also had a leading trade unionist, Geoffrey Drain, who later became General Secretary of NALGO. In this company, I did not think it appropriate to throw my weight around in discussion, but I listened and occasionally commented. The most important item on the agenda for the constituency party was choosing a Parliamentary candidate but I was too recent a member to be qualified to participate in the hustings. I was delighted, however, at the result—Dr David Pitt, originally from Grenada and a practising doctor in London. He was a warm hearted and extremely eloquent socialist, who in his acceptance speech spoke out in support of everything I believed in, including that social services should be run "on the principle of each according to his ability to each according to his need," that the forthcoming H-bomb tests should be cancelled and that Britain should not develop its own H-bomb. He said he was against "the crazy state of foreign affairs with the world divided into two camps, each relying on weapons so destructive that their mere testing could bring an end to mankind." (*Hampstead and Highgate Express,* May 1957).

Looking back, I recall how very real at that time was our fear of nuclear weapons—I used to look out of our sitting room window with its view of a vast swathe of West London and imagine the horror of everything being destroyed by an H-bomb, which would cause even more annihilation than the A-bomb used at Hiroshima. A Hampstead Committee for Nuclear Disarmament was set up and organised a meeting, 'No place to Hide', at the Friends Meeting House. The initiative came from Quaker peace activists not the Labour Party but I went along. As I remember it, there was no formal membership and I had no contact with the Committee as such, but a small group of local supporters used to meet in a café near to where we lived and I occasionally popped in for a chat and to fold leaflets or stuff envelopes.

This was the period when I was working on the history of the Bacon Industry in Wiltshire and was going there for days at a time to look at factory records, but whenever I could I attended Labour Party meetings or just went along to the Committee rooms where the Agent, Andrew Campbell, always had something which needed doing. As well as canvassing against the forthcoming H-bomb tests on Christmas Island, there was a major campaign against the Rent Bill going through Parliament which would decontrol rents of houses above a certain gross value. Landlords were giving tenants notice to quit but delaying offering them new leases, thereby causing many long-standing tenants great anxiety over whether they would be able to afford to stay in their homes. Blocks of flats just round the corner from me were affected and there was talk of a march of protest to Henry Brooke's house in Redington Road, but I must have been away if this happened. We argued that housing should be regarded as a social service and landlords should not be set free to profiteer from the shortage of homes, many of which were dilapidated and lacked basic amenities.

One other meeting I remember was addressed by Sydney Silverman, whose private members Bill for the abolition of capital punishment had been passed in the Commons but rejected by the Lords (he finally achieved abolition in 1965). Something I found missing was any discussion of trade union actions: when I suggested we should give support to a bus strike in May that year, I was firmly told that strikes were not Labour Party business. I did not feel well enough briefed to argue the point but I felt that the Labour Party policy document 'Towards Equality', which was limited to state actions only, although excellent in itself, should not have missed out the key role of Trade Unions in levelling up workers' incomes with those of other classes.

The major economic debate within the Labour Party that year and in the following years centred around a policy document entitled 'Industry and Society', published in July 1957. It was based on the ideas put forward the previous year by Antony Crosland in 'The Future of Socialism', which became the bible of right wing 'revisionists' for the next 50 years (almost to the present). I read this book from cover to cover—all 500+ pages of it. *(for a quick summary the Wikipedia entry can be recommended)*. I warmed to the argument that the aim should be the reduction of inequality and the balancing of Britain's class stratified society. Yes! But I was not convinced that Crosland's argument that nationalisation and state control of the 'heights of the economy', Labour's policy until then, were no longer necessary or that capitalism had been tamed by state regulation and its inadequacies corrected by the welfare state. Scepticism overcame me when I read the following much quoted sentence:

"The most characteristic features of capitalism have disappeared—the absolute rule of private property, the subjection of all life to market influences, the domination of the profit motive, the neutrality of Government, typical laissez-fair division of income, and the ideology of individual rights."

Crosland argued that these changes were irreversible, which made me think of Mill's statement "The price of liberty is eternal vigilance." Of course, I was not able to anticipate Thatcherism, the victory of neoliberal ideology and globalisation, but my instinct that this analysis was altogether too complacent was correct.

I had accepted that Britain had become a Mixed Economy but thought that without further socialist consolidation even the advances already won could be undone. "Industry and Society" proposed buying shares in capitalist enterprises instead of nationalising them—I voted and spoke against this in local meetings. Opinion was divided but the nature of our Hampstead membership led to a somewhat laid-back, intellectual style of discussion. However, the Bevanites in Parliament reacted bitterly and *Tribune* called it a betrayal of socialism.

Despite these reservations, I was sure I had been right to join the Labour Party and believed it was mainly moving in the right direction. Aneurin Bevan, the advocate of negotiations and disengagement from the Cold War had become spokesman for foreign affairs. Our local candidate was a passionate nuclear disarmer and 'Industry and Society' had not yet been passed by Conference. I was becoming well integrated into the local Party and was starting to receive encouragement—especially from the leading women members—to think of taking on some public role and of becoming a candidate for the Council at the next round of elections in 1959.

I became a Governor of an LCC Secondary School near Kings Cross, Sir Philip Magnus School. I remember my reactions to my first school visit: the Head took us into a classroom and I began moving around the desks showing an interest in the children's work when the class teacher said at the top of his voice, "I wouldn't bother doing that, this is the E stream so you can't expect much of them." I was outraged and blew my top off at the Head when we were back in his room. Fairly soon after that I was on the panel to appoint a new Head and did my best to help choose a Head who would not condone such disparagement of slower learners.

My honeymoon with the Labour Party came to an abrupt and unexpected end in October, although I continued to devote all my spare time to party activities. There was a motion before the 1957 Conference seeking to commit the Party to unilateral renunciation of the H bomb, but it was lost because Bevan spoke against it. When I heard extracts on BBC radio that evening, I could not believe it—I and thousands of others including many of his closest allies. He said he did not want to go "naked into the Conference Chamber." But logically this meant that he was prepared to threaten nuclear annihilation for hundreds and thousands of people, even if we were attacked with conventional weapons. To do so would amount to a crime against humanity. And if this was to be just a bluff, would it carry any force? Some said it might provoke a first strike from Communist Russia and that they would rather be "red than dead." Others, including myself, did not believe that the Soviet Union, which had plenty of problems within its own sphere of influence, posed any real threat to countries outside the Soviet bloc. On the contrary, it had every reason to want to negotiate a nuclear free zone in Europe, as Khrushchev was offering. Bevan's statement would make negotiations more difficult—surely the constructive way forward would be to take a moral stance against the development and stockpiling of such weapons?[1]

In response to this volte face a mass campaign arose, the Campaign for Nuclear Disarmament. This swallowed up the Hampstead Group and became a national and then an international movement. A Central Hall meeting was held and a lobby of Parliament but the main focus for several years became mass marches at Easter to or from the Atomic Weapons Research Establishment at Aldermaston.

This took four days, camping out on route. Political commitment was to be allied with an outdoor adventure, a physical challenge and the companionship of shared experience. By March 1958, there was a mood of excitement and enthusiasm about the first march which was to go from London to Aldermaston. I badly wanted to go but knew there was no way I could cope: I was leading a normal life and my fear of TB returning had abated, but I became breathless

---

[1] That the Cold War was based on a non-existent Soviet threat is now largely accepted by academic historians: see Andrew Alexander 'America and the Imperialism of Ignorance: US Foreign Policy since 1945'.

going up even gentle hills and could not walk and talk at the same time—let alone sing songs or shout slogans. Where I to attempt to go, I would soon fail to keep up and would become a drag on others. I never explained this to anyone: it may have been over sensitive of me to be embarrassed, but I didn't want to be seen as making feeble excuses, so I stopped going to supporters' gatherings. I felt much more upset and left out, less reconciled to being unable to participate, than I had felt 7 years earlier when listening from my hospital bed to Saturday evening dance music from the Students Union. The following year, when the March ended in London, I could at least show my support by being there to cheer its arrival.

For CND's objectives to be achieved, the Labour Party would have to reverse its position and then win the next general election, so I had no hesitation about continuing being active within it, even though my confidence had been shaken. One solace was that the majority of those active in the constituency party shared my views on the bomb and one of the MPs living locally, Tony Greenwood, was a leading member of CND. Our candidate, David Pitt, was also firmly committed. The position was less clear-cut on the other major issue of principle, public ownership, so arguments over "Industry and Society" continued. However, there was unity on the need to win elections. Immediately after the Suez debacle, Labour had a clear lead in opinion polls, so the question was whether it could be maintained and not weakened by the split in the Party over unilateral disarmament and/or by confusion over the economic policies advocated in 'Industry and Society'.

There were three elections in the next 18 months: the 1958 LCC election, the 1959 Council elections and the 1959 General Election. I canvassed vigorously for all three. I was chosen as one of the candidates for the Council elections in the West End Ward, which it was hoped could be taken off the Conservatives as a by-election in an adjoining ward had recently been won. I found that housing and rent rises were the dominant issues on the doorstep. To my disappointment, although the Conservative lead was reduced, I was narrowly defeated. I still remember one incident which rather nonplussed me: one day a woman opened the door and after listening to my spiel said, "It depends on what my husband decides." I explained to her about how the suffragettes had tied themselves to railings so she could have a vote and she ought to be independent and make up her own mind. Looking rather furtively over her shoulder she replied, "I am independent—he tells me what to do and I vote for the other one."

All efforts were then concentrated on the General Election to be held early in October. I had been elected as Social Secretary for the Constituency and in that capacity organised a dance at the Town Hall with Humphrey Lyttelton's Band, which performed on a cost only basis as a contribution to the Election Fund but, sad to admit, my organisation was amateurish, and although enjoyable and not a disaster, the dance was not a great money-raising success. I did better at organising that year's Christmas Bazaar which raised over £300—a good result in those days.

I found canvassing for the Parliamentary election somewhat frustrating. I was pleased that I never encountered any racist views about our choosing a black candidate, but the issue of unilateral disarmament kept being raised both by those who supported it and were still upset by Bevan's "Naked into the Conference Table" speech, and by those who didn't and were reluctant to vote for David Pitt because he was a well-known unilateral disarmer. The 1959 Manifesto tried to paper over the cracks and gave far more attention to domestic and economic policy than to foreign affairs. It promised to renationalise steel and road transport and to retain the right to take failing industries into public ownership, while at the same time adopting the 'Industry and Society' policy of buying shares in private companies. It promised a massive Council House building programme and to abolish the 1957 Rent Act. There were many other positive and detailed proposals for ending the gap between the 'Haves and Have-nots', and for improving life for the population as a whole. It promised to abolish the 11+ and develop a comprehensive system of secondary education. The Manifesto ended with a statement about Labour's commitment to taking part in negotiations to bring about international nuclear disarmament.

It was all to no avail. The Conservative Party under Macmillan with his slogan "you've never had it so good, don't let Labour ruin it" won both in Hampstead and nationally. I felt this was a setback for world peace as well as for hopes of a better life for the majority of the British people. Could it have been avoided? David Pitt attributed his defeat to the Labour Party "overplaying material issues and failing to concentrate on the more important moral issues…socialism must be raised to a higher plane; it must be the conscience of the people."

Later, looking back as a historian, I realised how much the election of Harold MacMillan as leader of the Conservatives had helped that Party slough off memories of its indifference to unemployment and poverty in the interwar years, something which had not been possible while Churchill and Eton were still in power. Macmillan was a longstanding 'One Nation' Conservative who had published 'The Middle Way' in 1938, and had Keynes's economic views. His 1959 Manifesto was a very detailed 'One Nation' programme, including proposals for tackling local unemployment and ambitious housing plans. His record as Housing Minister gave credibility to these proposals. Although a supporter of retaining British nuclear bombs, he advocated negotiation to ban them and achieve peace. What he said was true—most working-class people were better off than they'd ever been: wages had been keeping ahead of inflation and he pointed out that conscription was ending. All in all, it was not surprising that the Conservatives won the election. They had a clear majority of the popular vote on a turnout of 78.7%

I felt very disheartened: I had thrown all my energies into Labour Party activity in the hope that I could make some small contribution to keeping it on a socialist course. It was a relief that just after the election was over, I was due to set off on my research project on the continental roots of the Anglo-Saxons. I only returned in time to organise the Christmas Bazaar.

Margaret: From First Meeting to Marriage

I first met Max in early November 1956 just after the climax of the British invasion of Egypt over Nasser's nationalisation of the Suez Canal and the simultaneous Soviet invasion of Hungary. The occasion of our meeting was a social organised at his and his wife Barbara's flat for the Bulgarian Dance Group of which Barbara and Gill, my closest friend from university, were both members. Barbara and Max lived round the corner from us, so Gill took Andrew and me along.

I had been a participant the previous week at the mass protest in Trafalgar Square and Downing Street over the British action in Suez and because my main focus was on Suez, I had not followed events in Budapest with much attention and felt confused about whether counter revolutionary elements were indeed taking over the reform movement—hanging communists from lampposts as claimed in the *Daily Worker*. I was bursting to ask Max, the well-known Communist and teachers' leader, for his views but assumed that he would be extremely unhappy over the use of Soviet tanks whatever the alleged justification, and not at all anxious to discuss the situation at a social gathering with someone he had never met before. So, to avoid being intrusive or making misinformed comments, I moved away from him after the initial introductions. I found out later that my instincts had been sound. As he explains above, he was strongly opposed to the Soviet action and at the CP Executive meeting he and Arnold Kettle voted against endorsing the invasion.

I don't remember meeting Max again for probably a year or so but during 1958 Andrew and I began to bump into him at Jack Straw's Castle, a pub on the edge of Hampstead Heath which was the Sunday mid-day drinking venue of some of my Labour Party friends and other left-wingers. Max was very friendly with two Labour MPs living near him, John Baird and Stephen Swingler, and I remember meeting him at a social at John's house. If I were writing a romantic novel, I would be able to invent details of such encounters, but all I remember is having lively political discussions at which he was occasionally present. Sometime in early 1959 I became aware that he was seeking me out at these gatherings, so I was not surprised when he offered to canvas when I was a Council candidate at the beginning of May. My fellow candidate was a relative of his, Myron Morris, who when Max appeared at the Committee Room greeted him by saying "How very kind of you to come and support my campaign." Max and I had a laugh over that as we both knew he was there to support me, not Myron. During the Whitsun break Max invited me to have lunch with him near my VCH office. From then on, we did all we could to meet and spend time together, often walking on Hampstead Heath together after he left school. A month later we became lovers.

We moved in fairly Bohemian circles and neither of us felt fulfilled in our marriages, but nor had either of us been seeking a new serious relationship. So, we were just not prepared for the intensity of our desire to be together. I've often pondered over why Max, who had numerous female followers and had disappointed at least one by refusing to leave Barbara for her, was so captivated by me. Much later in life he told me jokingly that it was because I was kind, intelligent and had bright eyes—and that he'd always had a soft spot for blonds!

I know I was just bowled over—totally enthralled—but I couldn't have explained why. At that time, Max was 45, seventeen years older than me, but there was no hint of middle-age in either his appearance or behaviour. He was short and slim with a mass of dark, wavy hair, and he moved and spoke very quickly. Some psychologists claim women look for a husband who reminds them of their father, but I'd never been attracted to older men and the only things Max had in common with my father were a mischievous sense of humour and a lack of deference. Maybe those two attributes were important. Max and I had many interests in common—politics, history, theatre, reading and opera going. I found his company intellectually stimulating and lots of fun. However, before we had time to take breath, the summer holiday period was upon us and we felt we had no choice but to go off as prearranged: Max went to an International Communist teachers' conference in Hungary and I went with Andrew to visit Bulgaria where Gill had taken up a position as a teacher in the English School in Sophia.

September came and back in London I became busy canvassing for David Pitt but arranged to meet up with Max. We found our feelings had not changed. After the General Election, I was scheduled to go off on an archaeological tour of the Anglo-Saxon homelands, so we agreed that I would be in Amsterdam at Max's half term, and he would join me there.

In Amsterdam that October any film director wishing to create a typical image of young love might have taken a long-distance shot of us walking hand in hand up and down the canals and their bridges. Every so often we stopped, turned towards each other and smiled. If the camera had zoomed in for a close-up, it would have shown that these were not youngsters at all but a man of 46 and a woman of 29—but, yes, in love. We did not talk very much, not a word about politics, but that weekend, without any discussion of should we, shouldn't we, or any formal proposal from Max, we decided that we were going to find a way to live together. At that period, if we were to be socially accepted and continue to be politically active, convention required us to get married.

The problem, of course, was that we were both already married and would need to get divorced. Max said he thought Barbara would accept their splitting up without problems as their marriage had been one of convenience for some time. He was more worried about what Harry Pollitt, the previous General Secretary of the Communist Party, would say as divorce was looked down on in the Communist Party and he thought everyone would be very critical of his leaving a good Communist wife, respected by everyone, for "a young flibbertigibbet blond" in the Labour Party. He was right about Barbara, who was cooperative and stayed friendly with Max, but needlessly anxious about his Communist friends, all of whom quickly accepted me once we were married. My worries were about Andrew—I felt guilty because although we were drifting apart, and I suspected he was having sexual adventures, we had had good times in the past, and still rubbed along without open discord. I thought his pride would be hurt and he might resist ending our marriage. I was not worried about my friends, although I assumed that any idea of my becoming a Labour Parliamentary candidate, an idea which had been suggested to me, would be scotched if I married a well-known Communist. I was somewhat worried about how my conventional parents would react to my getting divorced, but it turned out they were rather pleased as they had never been fully at ease with public-school educated Andrew (although with great self-control, they had never let on about that to me).

Max did not give much thought to his parents' reactions but in the event his father strongly opposed his marrying me and for nearly two years refused to meet me. His sole reason was that I was not Jewish—he said that he had put up with

Max marrying one Gentile but it was insufferable of him to marry a second one. His mother, however, visited us as soon as we were married and couldn't have been more understanding.

Before Max left Amsterdam, we agreed that we would bring our marriages to an end during the Christmas holidays. This would give time for Barbara to find a flat of her own. During the intervening weeks we would have to continue living as before. When I returned to London, I would be busy organising the Labour Party Christmas Bazaar. Max would be busy as usual with school and meetings. The only problem was that when chatting at some social event in the summer, we had arranged for the four of us (Max and Barbara, Andrew and me) to go to hear Boris Christoff sing Boris Godunov at Covent Garden. I felt awkward about going as a foursome but as the tickets had been bought before Amsterdam, we went as planned. It was a glorious performance, so I forgot my scruples and we all enjoyed it immensely. I arranged to visit my parents at Christmas and intended to find a bedsit in January. I persuaded Andrew that he should visit his parents without me at Christmas (his mother disliked me so he was not surprised I suggested visiting my parents instead of his). He was very preoccupied with his work, and out of cowardice, I delayed telling him that my proposal to spend Christmas apart was because I wanted to leave him. I finally told him this just before we went off to visit our separate parents. He was angry and threatened to beat up Max. I don't think he would ever have done that but I was very nervous about his making a public scene or refusing to divorce me. I felt I had been the one who had originally been keenest for us to get married and his agitation made me feel guilty but not enough to deter me or change my mind.

Max and I spent a few days together over the New Year in Brighton but I was not very good company as I was still feeling guilty and nervous. We decided I should avoid Hampstead for a while to allow Andrew time to come to terms with the situation, so I went to stay with Barry Rose, a VCH colleague, and his wife, Madeline, in Arnos Grove in North London, while I looked for a bedsit. My friends were wonderfully hospitable and understanding to us both but had limited space, so I found a bedsit with acquaintances of Max in Parliament Hill, on the other side of Hampstead Heath in North St Pancras. Max, who was just starting his new job as a Deputy Headmaster in the London Borough of Haringey, returned to his own flat once term began as Barbara had cooperated and moved out. I needed to continue travelling under the terms of my scholarship, but before I left, I went back to see Andrew. This was a turning point because, although still angry, he admitted that while I was away in the autumn, he had begun an affair with our student lodger, Hilary, and although not originally intending it to be serious, he was now committed to her. Never has a wife been so happy to hear of her husband's infidelities! My feelings of guilt about leaving him were lifted and the path to an arranged divorce opened up.

Getting divorced is a miserable business even today and in 1960 the only way to get divorced in under 5 years was on grounds of proven adultery or cruelty. As a result, there was quite a thriving business of hired "co-respondents" willing to spend a night or pretending to spend a night in a hotel room with those wanting to get divorced without attracting unwanted publicity.

With the help of a lawyer friend, we used this procedure to make sure that neither Max, as a well-known public figure, nor Andrew as an up-and-coming Civil Servant, had their reputation endangered by a prurient press. Discretion during this period meant that Max and I could not openly live together, so I continued to live in bedsits, moving in the late autumn from Parliament Hill to one in nearby Highgate Village. The highlight of 1960 was our summer holiday in Greece an unofficial pre-honeymoon during which we combined sightseeing and relaxing on beaches. We discovered we had another passion in common— we both loved swimming in the sea.

Once I left Hampstead, I could no longer be active in the Hampstead Labour Party and after explaining to my friends there that I was leaving Andrew and moving away, I just quietly dropped out of sight. Disappointed though I was with the rightward trend in the Labour Party, I did not decide to leave it at that point, but there seemed no point in joining a branch in St Pancras when my stay there was likely to be short; in any case my scholarship meant I was travelling a lot. My bedsit hosts, Joyce and John Keyes, were keen members of their local Communist Party branch, which met in their house, so they invited me to sit in on two or three meetings as a visitor, which I found interesting with a high level of informed debate. I was not considering joining but was sparked into sharing their activities by the St Pancras Rent strike.

The origin of the disputes over the level of Council House rents in this period was the ending of the post-war arrangement for Councils to borrow money cheaply from the Public Works Loan Board in order to build the new housing desperately needed after the war. The shortage of homes was a national problem which the private sector could not solve alone, but the Conservative Governments of the mid to late 1950s wanted to reduce the costs to the Exchequer of subsidising the Council building programme. However, forcing Councils to borrow on the open market at a time of rising interest rates soon led to a vast increase in the amount of debt Councils owed. The Government had a simple solution for these rising debts—make existing Council tenants find the money by putting up rents.

Faced with rent rises, many very substantial, Council tenants naturally felt a need to defend their standard of living, but their resistance was above all based on a sense of unfairness. Why should Council tenants rather than taxpayers as a whole pay the costs of solving the national post-war shortage of homes? Council tenants were mainly working class and living on limited incomes. Long-standing tenants argued that their rents had long ago covered the cost of the accommodation they occupied but they continued paying rent, unlike owner-occupiers who after clearing their mortgages had no more to pay. More recent tenants rejected the argument that they were a highly subsidised group, because it wasn't the building costs of their own homes which was eating up the money, but servicing the cost of new building. Why should money be so dear and financiers be allowed to make huge profits from lending money at high rates to Councils? Why should landowners be allowed to charge sky-high prices for land for building? The Government's policy on housing was seen as tailored to the interests of the owners of capital. Such was the strength of feeling that many tenants and residents' associations sprang into being to oppose the rises.

Many Labour Councillors sympathised with these arguments but faced surcharges by the District Auditor if they did not comply with instructions to balance their Housing Accounts.

In St Pancras, a Labour Council had tried various manoeuvres to limit rent increases with the result that the Councillors were surcharged in March 1959. (Footnote; See Peggy Duff, *"Left, Left, Left"*) When the Council was won by the Conservatives that May, rents were raised again and a differential rent scheme was introduced in January 1960. Many tenants faced a doubling or more of their rents, which in many cases became higher than private rents, even though the 1957 Rent Act had opened the door to increased rents in the private sector. Large-scale marches and repeated mass lobbying of Council meetings failed to achieve meaningful negotiations. The campaign against the increases went on for over a year and was at its height when I was living with Joyce and John.

After the Council refused to negotiate, the St Pancras United Tenants Movement organised rent strikes with many tenants either stopping paying rent altogether or reducing their payment by the increased amount. Eviction notices were issued by the Council. The United Tenants Movement decided to fight two cases and Don Cook, their leader, and a cheerful character called Arthur Rowe barricaded themselves into their flats on the day they were due to be evicted and called for fellow tenants and sympathisers to man barricades to guard the approaches to their blocks. I totally sympathised with them—this was a class struggle. So, I joined the rota to man the barricades where Arthur Rowe lived. There were plenty of volunteers and a shift system was set up. This continued for almost three weeks but when I turned up for duty early in the morning on Friday, 22 September, I found the area swarming with police and heard that the bailiffs had broken in during the night and enforced the eviction. We surged forward to try and re-enter the block but were roughly manhandled out of the area by the police. That was the end of my first small attempt to support direct action.

Meanwhile, the end of our divorce proceedings began to be in sight and Max and I were able to make plans to get married early after the New Year. I did not want to live in the flat Max had shared with Barbara and, in any case, only 18 years were left on the lease, so it made economic sense to sell his flat and find a new one. But this was a very difficult time for house hunting in London. Max was extremely busy with his job, the NUT and the Communist Party, so it fell to me to deal with all the practical issues. This was not a problem as my scholarship had finished and I was at a loose end. I'd completed the agreed programme, but there was still no prospect of a post in Anglo-Saxon archaeology becoming available.

Not only was I unemployed, I was worried about the direction I should take for the future. It was clear I needed to draw a line under the Anglo-Saxons, and probably would have been wise to have done so a year earlier instead of giving it one last chance. Academic posts in all fields were scarce and despite my First without a research degree in modern history I felt I stood no chance of appointment despite quite extensive research on the economic history of Wiltshire for the VCH. It would have been better to have spent the previous year starting a PHD in Economic History but I could not have afforded to do that. But what was I to do? School-teaching was still ruled out because of my history of TB. I didn't want, and was not qualified, to work in a library, local archives or a small museum. I thought I was too old to become a trainee publisher as I'd originally planned and

I was too inculcated with academic snobbery to consider a career in business where at that time the role of women was limited to being short-hand typists.

Although I was brought up at a time when it was assumed that getting married and motherhood was the natural future for girls, I had been financially independent for several years and did not want to ask Max for money. After my scholarship ended, I drew out the superannuation contributions I had accumulated at the VCH (short-sighted but necessary at the time to pay my rent and cover other expenses). Several years earlier I had been influenced by the writings of Simone de Beauvoir and become a feminist. I had hesitated about getting married to Andrew because of my desire to be independent and it was important for me that during that marriage I had been an equal breadwinner. As Max was older and already established, I knew that would not be immediately possible but as a matter of principle, I did not want to be totally financially dependent on him. I told him he was getting a bad bargain with me, but he laughed it off and told me to give it time. He said that we would be able to manage on his salary since he was about to become a Deputy Head. We would be far from rich but his mortgage was nearly paid off and the sale of his Hampstead flat should enable us to buy a permanent home without a mortgage in a cheaper area.

Despite his reassurances, I wanted to find work. While at the VCH and during my senior scholarship year, I had done a small amount of WEA lecturing and had run short courses for the Tutorial section of the London University Extra-Mural department. I made approaches there and was able to get two courses a week. This was far from what I wanted and precarious (although it never happened to me, courses closed if the numbers fell off). The Extra-Mural Dept offered a 4-year part-time Diploma in Sociology, which was very popular with unqualified social workers, charity workers, even some policemen and many married housewives who regretted they had never gone to University. I was accepted as a regular lecturer on the first-year social and economic history component. As this involved marking essays and exams, it was better paid and more secure than WEA or Tutorial work. This meant I would have an income of my own but it was still far from a full-time salary. I felt frustrated and disappointed to be in such a position and today feel strong empathy with the growing number of part-time or unemployed graduates and post-graduates.

I was more successful on sorting out somewhere to live than job seeking. I sold Max's Hampstead flat to the novelist David Storey, who was even more monosyllabic than the characters in his novel, "The Sporting Life": he left after viewing the flat without any indication that he liked it, let alone intended to buy it. But buy it he did and at our asking price. Finding a home was more difficult but was eventually achieved. After weeks of traipsing around, I looked at a converted maisonette in Crouch End, Hornsey. The first time I called the smell of dogs and damp was so off-putting that I didn't even go inside the door, but Max suggested we go back and look at it together. This time we went inside and immediately saw its advantages.

Although derelict, it was a lovely flat, half of a converted late Victorian house. It had a large sitting room with high ceilings and decorative cornices which we could use for holding meetings as well as parties, and a bedroom with a view over East London as far as Epping Forest. Among other original features was a beautiful willow-pattern toilet bowl but it was cracked and gave off an abominable stench—rather typical of the flat as a whole. The renovation needed was enormous but Max's ex-colleagues in the building department at the Technical College happily organised it for us.

We took possession in January 1961 and for several months lived in one room, sleeping on a mattress in what became the study, while the place was torn apart around us. Dealing with all that took a great deal of my time and energy, leaving me no time to brood about my lack of full-time work.

There was another reason why I decided to be satisfied for the time being with my part-time position: Max and I both wanted to have children and at that time wives had the major responsibility of child care except in families who could afford to employ a nanny. The idea of paternal leave was almost unheard of and despite my feminist views about the right of women to be equal partners in marriage, I realised that marrying Max meant that it would be my task to care for our children should we have any. Although I had resumed normal life after my recovery from TB, I was far from robust and although I wanted to bear Max a child, I was frightened about the physical strain of childbirth. This did not deter me from wanting to conceive, but I recognised that I would find it difficult to combine starting a new job and a family at the same time. Also, I held the then conventional view that it was best for children while infants to receive individual attention at home rather than be sent to full-time nurseries; I would want to do whatever was best for our children should they arrive. I thought it interesting that in some socialist countries at that time mothers received an allowance for staying at home to care for their children, which was thought to be better for the children as well as saving the state the cost of nurseries. While supporting the right of mothers to go out to work full or part-time if they want and think they can cope, I thought then, and still think today, that time spent nurturing children in their early years should be a priority and that for the future, shared parental care and opportunities to work part-time must be developed. But in 1961 that was not on the agenda.

We finally were able to get married on 18 February 1961 during Max's half term. It amused us to do so at the St Pancras Town Hall, where the red flag had recently been flown. An added bonus was that the Registrar was a Communist member who plied us with sherry even before beginning the official ceremony. We had two witnesses each—a doctor friend of Max, a pioneer in setting up health centres, called Hugh Faulkner and his wife Maggie, and my friend David Wilson, later the Director of the British Museum, and his wife Eva. Hugh drove us across the West End for lunch at the restaurant near Oxford Circus where Max had taken me on our very first date together, 21 months earlier. Then, somewhat inebriated, Max and I left to go to Torquay. The weather was fine, the daffodils were out and we spent our days just as we had in Amsterdam, strolling along hand-in-hand, turning from time to time to smile at each other. So began our life as a married couple.

1961: Our First Year Together

At the time of our marriage, I had never heard Max speak at a public meeting and was looking forward to hearing him in action at the first opportunity. I knew he was renowned as a compelling speaker: retired teachers still reminisce about how you could hear a pin drop when he was making a speech. Clive Griggs, co-editor with Max of 'Education: the Wasted years 1973–1986', has described first hearing Max at a packed NUT meeting at Friends House in 1960:

"Conversation died down as a small dapper man walked to the end of the stage. I was not sure what to expect for this was a formidable audience to face. He began to speak and from the first few words he had gained the full attention of the audience. He produced a few statistics, spelt out the substance of the matter and then had everyone in the palm of his hand as his witty remarks brought laughter from the teachers attending because it was clear he was a teachers' teacher. He really knew their situation from his own classroom experience. It was a master class in public speaking."

So, full of anticipation, I went along with him to the 1961 Easter NUT Conference in Brighton. This took place at the height of the salaries campaign described above in 'Breaking out of Genteel Poverty'. The atmosphere in the Brighton Pavilion was heightened and there was a buzz of excitement in the hall at the formal opening session, which I was able to attend as an observer. To my disappointment, all discussions of the key issues on which Max was planning to speak were held in private sessions which I was not eligible to attend. I knew exactly what he was planning to say because from the beginning of our marriage I became an audience for the rehearsal of his speeches. Although he gave the impression of speaking spontaneously, he meticulously prepared his speeches, including the timing, so they would end on a strong note before the red light came on. But I would have to wait for a while to see the performance.

Max spent every minute not in the Conference Hall busy lobbying delegates as we walked up and down the front. Everyone we met wanted to hear his views and I was amazed how many people he knew by name and association. I was not surprised that he achieved his main objective of obtaining the suspension of standing orders so a motion could be carried supporting a strike by the Scottish teachers' unions. This was a clear signal to the NUT leaders on the Burnham Committee that if they failed to stand firm in the negotiations then taking place there would be support for militant action.

Conference over, we returned to our flat with its gaping holes in the walls and out-of-suitcase living. It might be thought that we could have found a home requiring less renovation but that is to underestimate the acute shortage of housing both to rent and buy. My support of the St Pancras Rent Strikes a year earlier had made me aware of the underlying reasons: the dilapidation of Britain's 19th-century housing stock, the weakening of rent control and Councils being forced to pay market interest rates on borrowing for building new houses. This had led both to rising rents and to a reduction of new Council building. Private building wasn't sufficient to make good the shortfall so the shortage was exacerbated, leading to rising rents and house prices, and to the exploitation of that by landlords, later dubbed 'Rachmanism'. The effect this had on us was that it had taken us weeks of searching to find anywhere at all either to rent or buy. So, we were grateful for what we had found.

We were grateful too that the buying price and costs of renovation were within our means as the escalation of house prices was still at an early stage. Hornsey at that time was known as "the poor man's Hampstead." Housing was still seen in terms of providing homes, not as a financial asset. Over 50 years later I still live in the same flat and the younger generation, now completely priced out of buying such a home in London, cannot believe that a teacher and part-time lecturer could have bought it, such has been the inadequacy of the housing policies of nearly all Governments from the 1918 "Homes Fit for Heroes" promises to the present day.

So, we thought ourselves lucky and made fun of camping out—until the day when an electrician put a nail in a water pipe and a hot water fountain shot up in the hall and the joke wore thin as we tried in vain to stem the flow. As my only commitments were two half days of lecturing, it fell to me to take charge—not that I minded as I enjoyed planning how the flat was going to be and finding ways to let in more light in some of the rather dark and gloomy rooms. I also had to do the cooking as I discovered that making tea or coffee was the limit of Max's culinary skills. Jewish mothers tend to pamper their sons but I was surprised that his first wife, Barbara, a successful professional woman, had not taken steps to remedy his ignorance in her own interest. He was always eager to help and over the years learnt to make good straightforward meals but for the time being I was head cook and chief bottle washer. As Max was juggling with his new job as a Deputy Head, the NUT Salaries Campaign and Communist Party responsibilities, this didn't worry me: pragmatic common sense overcame such feminist principles as I had about how domestic duties should be shared. Anyway, I was far too happy that we were now able to live together to niggle about anything, but I did take one stand: to my astonishment, on our first night in our new home, he discarded the clothes he had been wearing and left them on the floor. What on earth, I thought, had his mother and Barbara been thinking of to let him get away with behaving like some upper-class milord with servants to pick them up? So, I kicked them into a ball and said, "let's have a game of football with these and see who can score a goal by getting them to the dirty clothes basket first." He got the message.

While sorting out the flat and unpacking our possessions, I had discovered Max's library and every day I found books I wanted to read. There was a whole shelf of Left Book Club editions, and many books not only on history and education, but also on economics, not just Marxist theories, but Keynes and his precursors and classical economic writers. I had been thwarted when I was sixteen and told economics was no subject for girls, so now I had the chance to catch up. Usually when Max came home after whatever meeting he'd been speaking at, he found me curled up with a book. As I tend to become oblivious of time when reading, this meant he sometimes had to wait for supper but he found that a small price to pay for not having to feel under any pressure to cut meetings short because I was time-watching at home.

The salary campaign within the NUT had reached a new stage because the awaited negotiations had resulted in such a paltry offer from the Government that even the right wing on the NUT Executive were affronted and recognised that the forthcoming Special Conference would not accept it, so they voted to reject the offer and consider what actions the NUT could take to put pressure on the Government.

The Conference took place on 17th June. Max returned home late and far from satisfied. True the conference had endorsed the Executive recommendation to reject the pay offer but no formal vote had been taken on proposals for strike action.

NUT Associations had been holding meetings all over the country urging that this was the only way to budge the Government. In Middlesex, 1200 teachers had attended a meeting two days earlier at which Max had been the principal speaker. Even the Executive, usually under Sir Ronald Gould's thumb, had by one vote put forward proposals for a one-day National Strike followed by local strikes. This would surely have been carried, which Sir Ronald wanted to avoid, so by his wily manipulation of the agenda the issue was left in the air—not defeated but not formally endorsed, just left to future meetings of the Executive to pursue. This left Max and other militant delegates frustrated: at informal discussions after the Conference, they agreed to stress that strike action was still on the agenda but had little confidence that the Executive would put it into effect.

After Max had unloaded on me his disappointment about the outcome of the Conference, I somewhat naively made matters worse by asking why the NUT leadership was so timid about striking whereas a small rival union, the NAS, had called a number of local strikes the previous month—why couldn't the two unions work together? Through gritted teeth, Max replied that they had opposing objectives: the NUT wanted a salary settlement which would benefit all teachers by raising the basic scale and distributing differential payments fairly across primary as well as secondary schools, whereas the NAS wanted as much as possible of the available money to be concentrated on maintaining the differential scales of 'Schoolmasters', i.e. male secondary school teachers, who felt that the recent introduction of equal pay for women teachers would drag down the general level of pay. The main aim of the NAS was to pressurise the Government into awarding it representation on the Burnham Committee, even though this would enable the government and Local Authority Leaders to play the teaching unions off against one another, so weakening the negotiating position of teachers as a profession. (The future was to prove this only too correct!)

Having vented his frustrations and made sure I understood the reasons for his antagonism to the NAS, Max switched off. I was always amazed at his ability to do this: if upset about anything, I tend to go on turning it over and over but Max could let it lie and move on to another of his many different interests. As it was a Saturday evening, he wanted to relax and so we probably went up to Highgate to visit Connie and 'Siggy' Seifert, who kept open house and offered hospitality to an enormous range of people—Communists and other left-wingers, trade unionists, Jewish friends from all walks of life and writers, artists and film makers, including American escapees from McCarthy's blacklists. I loved going there because of the warmth of the welcome and never knowing whom we would meet. I enjoyed also the company of their four children and their friends and the natural way in which they as teenagers took part in conversations. I was grateful for the way the whole family welcomed me from the first day Max took me to meet them after we were married. Although neither religious nor Zionist, the Seiferts identified themselves as part of the Jewish community, but I was never made to feel an outsider there, which I appreciated because Max's father was still refusing to meet me.

Max had known Connie since their schooldays because her brother, Ezra Shine, became his close friend soon after the Morris family moved to London. Connie later became a teacher. Like Max, she joined the Communist Party in 1935, along with her future husband, Sigmond, always called Siggy by his friends.

He was a solicitor and specialised in helping tenants cheated under the Rent Acts and along with his partner, Richard Sedley, became financially successful as a result, despite resisting bribes from landlords to represent them instead of their tenants. (See Noreen Branson, *Britain in the 1930s.*)

During the McCarthy period in America, he began to represent those blacklisted who came to England and needed help with the British immigration authorities. He worked in collaboration with an American lawyer, Richard Treuhaft, who defended the Hollywood Ten and other targets of McCarthy and who was married to the English writer, Decca Mitford, the left-wing member of the famous—or some would say infamous—Mitford sisterhood. Richard and Decca, together with Lester Cole, the screen writer who was one of the original Ten, were among the many distinguished guests we met at the Seifert home. As both Max and I were avid cinema goers, we were fascinated to meet also Carl Foreman, who wrote the script for *High Noon* and co-wrote *The Bridge on the River Kwai,* two films which we had seen more than once.

Another new aspect of social life for me was going with Max to receptions at the Russian and East European Embassies. He saw these as opportunities to have discussions with other British trade unionists and left-wing MPs, alongside having a swig or two of whisky and nibbling at the usually lavish refreshments provided. I found it encouraging how many of his target group were keen to hear his views in general and not just on education. Listening to some of the Labour MPs made me a little nostalgic for my Hampstead past as part of the inner party debate—I was mulling over whether or not to renew my Labour Party membership once properly settled into our new home. As it is not in my nature to stand meekly by listening quietly and I didn't want to butt into Max's conversations at this point, I wandered off to find new people to talk to and usually ended up having conversations with some of the Embassy wives. Many of them had held senior positions in teaching or public service and were frustrated at being stuck in London with only a supportive role, so they were pleased to find someone they could confide in. This way I learnt a lot about quite different aspects of life inside their countries from that printed in the English press. One aspect of Embassy parties I found amusing was the tactic for indicating to the guests that they'd drunk and eaten and talked enough so it was time to go home: first the lights would briefly dim, a few minutes later, they would dim for a little longer, then after another ten minutes they would dim for even longer—by which time they hoped everyone had got the message.

At receptions, our diplomatic hosts were too busy to have long conversations, but over the next few years several ambassadors or cultural secretaries made this good by inviting us to dinner parties. Either they wanted to understand British politics in general or the English educational system if they had children and wanted advice about sending them to English schools—the Hungarian Ambassador sent his daughter on Max's advice to Haverstock Comprehensive School, where later the Miliband brothers would go. I once nearly caused an incident at a dinner Party at the Hungarian Embassy when at the end of the meal it was indicated that it was time for the women present to withdraw. I just sat still. This was a Socialist Embassy not a British aristocrat's party! Judith, the Ambassador's wife eventually came, whispered to me and begged me to go with her. I did but felt I had made my point. Max said we'd never be invited again but he was wrong and the next time the women present were not asked to withdraw. I hoped the Embassy had revised their practices and it was not just because I was there.

After the first Party, we went to I said to Max that our hosts seemed to have an inflated idea of what an important person he must be as a member of the Executive Committee of the Communist Party. The British Security forces must have shared this view as was demonstrated by a curious incident at our home. One morning the bell rang and two men in suits said they had come to repair our telephone and offered to show me their credentials. I said it's working alright, what needs doing? They said that the wires leading into the house were mixed up and they wanted access to sort them out between where they entered the house and the telephone. So, I showed them into the yet-to-be-renovated front room. The wires ran under the floor; half the floor boards were up so I pointed out they would need to climb down into the cavity below, which needless to say was full of dust and dirt—altogether filthy. My two well-dressed visitors looked taken aback and said they would need to come back in suitable working clothes. The next day they turned up in brand new boiler suits. Nothing could have better demonstrated that they were not real telephone operatives at all, which I had suspected the previous day. So, I waited until one of them was down below in the cavity and asked him whether he thought tapping law-abiding citizens' phones was an honourable way to earn a living. He didn't deny that this was what he was doing but said I must have a guilty conscience. Not at all, I replied. The exchanges continued until they both beetled out of the house as quickly as possible. When Max came home, he was not at all surprised and said he'd expected it would happen but not so blatantly.

Max had been an honorary member of the Communist International Federation of Teachers (FISE) from its inauguration onwards and one of its leading figures with whom he became friendly, Fan Min, the Vice-President of the Chinese Teachers, invited him along with me to visit China for three weeks during our first summer together. We saw this as a fascinating opportunity and regarded it as a belated honeymoon. This was the period of "The Great Leap Forward" in China and of the growing ideological breach between Mao and Khrushchev and competition over the leadership of world Communism. At this point, relations had been temporarily smoothed over but leaders of the teaching unions on both sides considered it their duty to brief us with their viewpoint. As Max wrote later:

"We were met en route in Moscow by the entire Soviet teachers' leadership for the few hours' stop-over in the airport and, because of the Soviet-Chinese dispute, the tensions tingled. It was a most uncomfortable experience and I was not surprised when the Russians asked us if we would stop over for a few days on our return, some three weeks later, for a 'discussion'."

From the moment we stepped out of the plane into the opaque heat of Peking airport (as it was called at that time), we had the most fascinating travel and political experience of our lives. We travelled to Shanghai, Nanking and Hangchow, received if anything too much care—they would not let us (both good swimmers) use a swimming pool in case we drowned! We talked politics and education from morning till night with the aid of a brilliant young Australian-

Chinese female interpreter, and filled books with notes of impressions, conversations and events. Max gave a lecture on British education to an assembly of 'cadres' in Peking which evoked well-informed and highly intelligent questions.

But—there was always a "but." Ours was typified in a conversation Max often quoted humorously. "But," he said to Fan Min, while boating on a very beautiful lake full of lotus flowers in Hangchow, "But you've still not given me, nor has anyone, the answer to my question as to what time you begin the school day." A very boring, mundane question. (I should say we were in China during the school holidays when no schools were in session.) "Ah," he replied, "the world is divided into three camps, the socialist, the imperialist and the underdeveloped (sic)" and, Max's highly intelligent friend proceeded to give us the stereotyped 'script' as the interminable preliminary to any answer—the real question never seeming to be reached.

This stereotyping created a uniformity of response from nearly everyone and there was as well a hierarchical order of reply according to the seniority of those present, which we found irritating. A junior official would never speak without the permission of a senior, if present. Even our delightful interpreter whom Max teased unmercifully—being an Australian she was accustomed to Western ways and did not object—could rarely unbend and be natural in our company. When we returned after a few days away from Peking and he asked her jokingly next morning how her newly-wed husband had received her, she replied deadpan, "He asked me if I had been criticised!" How could such talented and intelligent people be in such a groove, we wondered.

Yet we were astounded at the material progress even then when China had just gone through a very bad economic patch and was still feeling the effects of famine and food rationing. Not long after our visit the country embarked on the 'Cultural Revolution' and Max confessed later to not being surprised at its atrocities. The cult of Mao was just as overwhelming as the cult of Stalin. During that harsh period his friend, Fan Min, disappeared and we lost contact with him. We were delighted to see his name mentioned again years later when a group of British educational correspondents visited China. He had been cast out and was now apparently rehabilitated.

Our hosts knew we were going to stop over in Moscow on our way back and they were none too happy, but discreet. They showed their feelings more when, while in Peking, we received an invitation to shorten our visit in order to visit

Ulan Bator in the Mongolian People's Republic, a Soviet satellite, on our return journey. We decided to refuse the invitation, much to our Chinese hosts' approval.

My memories include some pure "tourist" days—visiting the Emperor's palace in Peking and the Great Wall of China—and a number of social encounters. In Shanghai, we were touched to see children clustered round lampposts eagerly taking advantage of their light to read. Their homes had neither electricity nor running water, but clean water was available from standpipes in each street; we were told that installing these standpipes and covering over sewage drains had reduced the death rate to a fifth of what it was before the Revolution twelve years earlier. It was very hot everywhere but we saw few flies and were told that as a public health drive, children were encouraged to trap flies and paid a small reward. One interesting encounter we had was with an expropriated factory owner, who said he was happy to have been brought back as manager of his old factory. He told us that his salary was four times that of the ordinary workmen and that this was the maximum permitted differential since the Revolution. *(Not the case in China today!)*

We had two memorable meals. First, a simple meal at the home of Fan Min—this was a signal honour and something very unusual for official visitors. So, we met his wife and children. On our return, we named our new kitten after his daughter, Sho Wei (Little Sunbeam in Chinese). The other meal was given officially by the teachers' union to celebrate Max's birthday and featured a 'longevity cake'—years later as Max reached 90, we would joke that there must have been magic ingredients in that cake.

Then back to London and for Max, school and the NUT. For myself, I felt the time had come to become politically active again in my own right. As our home was more or less sorted out, I wanted to get back into the fray. I had not formally left the Labour Party so I had to decide whether to become active in the local Hornsey Constituency or not. I mulled it over for a while. After losing the 1959 General Election, the Labour Party had been rent by divisions. Proposals to abolish 'Clause Four', the symbol of the Party's commitment to public ownership, had eventually come to nothing, but were an indication of right-wing thinking. There were also suggestions about breaking the link with the trade unions, whose block vote at Conference was no longer guaranteed for right-wing motions. The October 1960 Conference had voted to support Unilateral Nuclear Disarmament but only by a small majority and Hugh Gaitskell had pledged "to fight and fight again" until it was reversed. Gaitskell's domination of the Party seemed set to continue. In later years, I reflected that if I had been able to foresee that he would die under three years later and that Harold Wilson would become Leader my decision would probably have been different, but no-one can foresee the future.

At the time, I doubted if anyone would take much notice of my views if I joined the Hornsey Labour Party. I was clear about where I stood but I knew nobody in the local Party and thought that my past service as a Council Candidate and Hampstead Constituency Officer would not be enough to counteract distrust of me as the wife of a leading Communist. In 1961, Cold War antagonisms were far from over. The alternative would be to join the Communist Party, something I had refused to do in the Stalinist era. That was over but would joining now after so many members had left, serve any useful purpose? The Communist Party had initially been reluctant to support CND but was by then fully backing it—if it had not been, I should not have considered joining it.

Max was reluctant to put any pressure on me so I had to insist that he explain why he had not left the CP after Hungary and why he still thought it worthwhile to give up his time to serve on its Executive. So, he explained his attitude exactly as he does in the extracts from his memoirs above. In addition, he talked about the opportunity it gave him to work with other trade unionists. As he wrote later:

"For we did have influence, sometimes substantial, on the trade union movement and on particular unions. There we could claim we were a force. The Industrial Department, under various proletarian leaders like Peter Kerrigan and J.R. Campbell, was the real power in the Party. It organised willing volunteers in the various unions in separate committees, aiming to win positions of influence on policy-making. All conferences and elections in unions where we had members were planned for and progress recorded.

"Influence in the unions had a further objective: namely to influence through them Labour Party policies from whose affiliation we were excluded. The CP leadership had a timetable for when resolutions had to be submitted to national TU conferences. A particular motion or motions were always considered as suitable or not for them to put into the TUC and, most importantly, to Labour Party annual conference. So that, on occasions, the Industrial Department could boast to the EC that it knew what motions either had a fair, or good chance or were certain to appear on the Labour Party Conference Agenda. Apart from the passing of particular resolutions on home or foreign policy, the composition of the Labour Party National Executive could be influenced through the elections to the trade union and women's sections. It was, therefore, of crucial importance at one time or another to be able to influence how the miners' or the engineers' or any other union vote would be cast in these elections.

"In trying to affect these outcomes we were at one with a number of Left Labour MPs and other Left elements in the Labour Party. We had close personal and political relations with a goodly number of these, particularly a group of the Bevanite MPs (though not with Bevan himself, who was very anti-communist, nor even with Michael Foot who was not). There was no need to arrange clandestine meetings. Numerous parties thrown by the Embassies of the socialist countries provided opportunities for the mixing of Communist and Left-wing Labour politicians (and others too) to talk and discuss informally and convivially. The Labour MPs were in my experience very careful not to involve themselves organisationally in any way—they were not in any sense crypto-communists. What we all had in common was a desire to turn the Labour Party in a leftward direction and an understanding of the importance of winning big unions for this objective through their elected leaderships."

Max himself acknowledged that the way the CP worked was not ideal: he said "I sometimes reflected that, for a Party whose ideology preached mass action as the engine of change, we were too concerned with manoeuvres, manipulations and even machinations over individual positions, on this or that office through whom in practice the changes could be pushed, even if the movement down below was not all that 'pushful'. It did not accord at all with orthodox Marxism on the limited role of the individual in history."

Despite Max's reservations I thought the importance given by the Communist Party to the work of the trade unions was a possible reason for joining it. The trade unions had created the Labour Party to act as their political arm, yet ever since the first Labour Government under Ramsay MacDonald, the political leaders of the Party had sought to distance themselves from trade union struggles. This had disappointed me at Labour Party meetings in Hampstead. Not that I thought the Labour Party ought to get involved at a detailed level in every dispute, but it ought to take a generally more supportive stance. The Communist Party had become a pressure group rather than a political party seeking to win power directly, but its focus was changing the Labour Party in a direction I supported. So, I decided that on balance my best choice was to join it, a decision certainly influenced by our visit to China and my visit two years earlier to

Bulgaria, where my friend Gill was still teaching. Although I had never thought that the USSR provided a model for other countries to follow, it was encouraging that changes were taking place under Khrushchev.

Max meanwhile was fully engaged in renewed struggles over the Government's refusal to grant the teachers a satisfactory pay offer. The situation had deteriorated during the summer because after Selwyn Lloyd introduced his pay pause in late July, the NUT leaders became anxious to settle and not to pursue preparations for strike action. This was opposed by meetings, a ballot for strike action, and a Special Conference, but to Max's disgust, it all came to nothing because the NUT Executive agreed to capitulate, call off all action and accept a reduced offer. So, there were more protests and meetings. I drove Max down on 23 October to a major demonstration at Hamilton House when the Executive was meeting—this is often referred to as a "sit-in" or 'occupation' but in fact only a small group including Max marched in and demanded to be heard, while about 1000 members waited outside. Eventually Max and the others came out and had to report a lack of progress. It was a defeat that had long term effects. As far as Max personally was concerned it led to a number of militants including him deciding to stand for the Executive in order to reverse its right-wing majority with its subservience to Sir Ronald and his fellow officials. Max stood at the first opportunity and, although not immediately successful, set off on his route to becoming President of the Union.

Life calmed down in November and December but one major development for Max was that he was appointed to a Headship of a Secondary Modern School in Willesden, to begin in January. Meanwhile our social life expanded as we could now invite friends to visit us—in the 1960s most entertaining was done at home not in restaurants. It was the era of dinner parties and as I liked cooking, we bought a large round table and set out to take our turn in playing host. We both enjoyed the cut and thrust of political discussions, and our social circle expanded. We also now had a spare bedroom and could put up friends, including Harry my ex-Birmingham University friend or, on CP Executive weekends, one of the provincial members, sometimes Dave Bowman, a future President of the National Union of Railwaymen who, by coincidence, a few years later teamed up with Max's first wife, Barbara. Whenever we could we went to the theatre or opera, or more occasionally a concert. Sunday mornings we relaxed and sometimes as a joke followed the example of the notorious Horatio Bottomley with a breakfast of kippers and champagne. So, the pattern of our married life for the next few years was set.

Max Becomes a Headmaster

Having been held back from promotion for years by the 'Communist Ban', Max was keen to have the chance to run a school and put to the test his ideas about how schools should be run. Chamberlayne Wood was a small secondary modern school in Kilburn, then part of the Borough of Willesden. He later described the challenges he faced and how he dealt with them.

"Having spent two years as a Deputy in Tottenham, at Down Lane Central School, in January 1962 I began my first Headship—at Chamberlayne Wood Secondary Modern School. We were situated in Kensal Rise, a mixed area—a minute or two away on one side was the HQ of the Willesden Conservative Party; nearby were some of the lushest houses in North West London and, in the other direction, there was a solid working-class district and adjacent to it a relatively slum area with a very tough reputation. Much of the last two areas was becoming multi-occupied, mainly due to a rapidly growing immigrant population, largely West Indian, especially from Jamaica.

"I came into the school with a reputation as a well-known 'red' and as the most prominent spokesman of the militants in the union and indeed the profession after the traumatic events of 1961—and with my hat thrown into the ring as an Executive candidate in the Easter elections to follow. But I would be unable to be any kind of figure, let alone an active controversial one in the Willesden NUT Association because Willesden had the most reactionary leadership in the whole NUT (only then beginning to be successfully challenged). It had actually changed its rules to prevent me becoming a member; it did so constitutionally by refusing to accept as 'local' members those who belonged to other Associations, which applied to me because I was a member of the famous Middlesex Secondary and Technical Teachers' Association. No other Association in the country had such a rule.

"As far as I was concerned, my union activity would lie elsewhere though, of course, as a Head, I was bound to play a part, and it proved to be an increasingly large one, in the borough. My intention was to make a success of the job, build a second reputation as a Head running a difficult working-class school, and that I set out to do. I knew there would be difficulties with possibly biased staff but I also knew that the Willesden Authority responsible for running the school under the Tory Middlesex County Council was a staunch Labour bastion and would support me in doing all I could for the deprived children of the area. In this I was proved right—I got the fullest backing from both the political and administrative leaders of the borough. Leader of the Council was Reg Freeson, a brilliant and courageous young politician soon to become an MP, with whom I had established a friendship some years earlier, and I had other friends on the Council, including its future Chairman of Education, Gordon Richards, who had been an active member of the MSTA. I soon saw that my main job was to unite the staff on our educational objectives. The school was in a poor state of morale, partly due to some unfortunate publicity only very recently and the absence of a Head for a whole term, but it had had a good reputation in the past which I was determined to restore. There were disciplinary problems especially among the potential school-leavers and the staff were looking to the Head to exercise firm control.

"We were also at the beginning of the great wave of 'immigrant' entry to which teachers were, as yet, unused—some 28% of the children were black and most of them had not passed through the Willesden primary schools and so had to be acclimatised to our ways of working, a task which we had all to learn together to accomplish.

'It took some time, but I can claim that, by the time we had ended the school year in July, things had settled down. Major indiscipline had been overcome after an outbreak of hooliganism at the end of my first term when the leavers, stupidly organised in a special 'leavers' group (which I would see never happened again), had broken many of the school windows as a parting gift. I was determined that future leavers would have a different attitude and would feel more grateful. I refused to dismiss the 'Kensal Rise mob' as intractable. I had already handled some of the toughest individuals simply by being tougher than they, or their families, in my own way. I kept one young hoodlum waiting outside my door for three days till he had cooled off before I agreed to honour him with a conversation—he had been able, up till then, to intimidate staff. He did not like this at all and his parents came up, called me a 'jumped up Glasgow keelie', to which I took no exception, showered me with other intended insults and went away empty-handed. Some years later, meeting the culprit outside the school, I shook him by the hand, enquired after his career and asked him to come in and see me. He was polite, respectful and pleasant—no trouble. It was his family, not the school, that had made him so 'tough'.

"I found problems of discipline fascinating. Early on, I had encountered my first fire-raiser, a tiny lad who, a case conference concluded, just liked lighting matches, though they did not know what they could do about it. That conference confirmed my scepticism about the part psychologists, psychiatrists and social workers could play in constructively solving the problems of difficult children. They could always find reasons for something happening but rarely, if ever, tell you how you could stop it happening in future. It was the teachers who were in the front line and had to cope as best they could. I used to enjoy talking to difficult children and they seemed to enjoy being taken notice of in this way, but whether I did them any good I could never be certain.

"One attitude of mine the staff certainly appreciated—and future staffs too.

"On principle, I always backed up the teacher publicly in facing the pupil. If I thought the teacher wrong, I dealt with that privately because nothing is more destructive of staff morale than the Head who, for whatever reason (egalitarian, democratic, 'justice', etc.), undermines his staff's authority. Of course, this means that mistakes are made, but these can be mitigated in various ways and the alternative attitude is worse. Let it be known that the Head will back a pupil for whatever reason against a teacher and you can say 'goodbye' to an ordered regime (I don't mean a harsh, 'authoritarian' one). It's the Head's job to deal with staff who behave badly to children, not the child's job, nor, may I say, the parents. The teacher is not perfect and can do wrong but, overwhelmingly, teachers do their best and the balance sheet is in their favour. I am all for sacking other incompetent workers—and bosses. Teachers are more vulnerable than most other workers, which is why their unions make it so difficult to remove them. I've torn a strip off many colleagues privately for weakening the collective reputation of the school by being wrong. That is the way to improve their performance—not 'democratically' weakening their authority as the 'trendies' (who don't have to face the music) would like us to do on phoney egalitarian principles.

"School children and teachers all benefit more in the end from my kind of approach—of that I have never had any doubt.

"By the time I finished my five-year stint at Chamberlayne to go to fresh pastures at the new Comprehensive a mile away, the school had a first-class reputation in the borough—or, I flatter myself, I would never have got the Headship of what was expected to be the borough's largest school. Chamberlayne had 380 pupils, a large fifth form of stayers-on, considering the size and character of the intake, and even a very small sixth (which I had no intention of continuing—in the selective set-up these pupils would be better off transferring to Grammar Schools). Ethnic minority children now numbered 55% and, in 1966, we would not have been surprised to find that we were the only secondary school in the country with a black majority. We ran a full curriculum to GCE 'O' Level and CSE standard (with the exception of metalwork) for the early 1960s were fully unstreamed (an enormous benefit to the discipline of the school and the general relaxed atmosphere) with options operating **metalwork** after that for examination reasons.

"I had already begun my personal campaign to put remedial *(the term used at that time for dealing with children with special needs of all kinds)* work on the curricular map: we had a first-year special remedial class, plus a separate group receiving practically full-time remedial attention, as well as a remedial maths group, while withdrawal groups operated throughout the school, including the fifth form, for remedial attention. In fact, some of our children would have been better off in Special Schools, so blatant were the problems with which we tried to cope. I wonder how many secondary moderns in the country were doing any remedial work at all at that time.

"Of course, the school had a wide range of extra-mural activities, including community service, a school magazine, foreign school journeys, and our star turn was an annual fifth form formal Christmas Dance—which was prepared for by lunchtime dancing lessons. It had become famous in the borough and local VIPs eagerly sought invitations. We had a fine sports record, in spite of having no playing fields of our own and having to share a playground with the infant school which was the joint user of our 1904 building.

"We took careers guidance very seriously and had little to learn from an HMI who came to see us in one of those formal visits which I found irritating because of his well-intended waffle. We were doing so much without benefit of a trained careers' teacher, but HMI was not very interested in the provision of this necessary 'resource'. He waffled on about how we ought to do it, regardless! Talk about making bricks without straw! We were expert at improvising what we believed to be educationally necessary and did not require advice without extra resources from HMI/DES.

"In my final Speech Day in November 1966, I reported on how visitors who came to see us because of our very large proportion of ethnic minority children, had commented on the 'normalcy' of the atmosphere. I don't know what they expected! In those days, before the multi-cultural lobby had begun to form, our main concern was to integrate many children who had only recently arrived in Britain into our school community, as I put it 'breaking children into our habits, our methods of work, our routine, while trying to improve the educational standards of the children…nothing very special, just getting on with our job of running a decent school'.

"Today, there are those who would criticise these objectives, about which I am quite unrepentant. Needless to say, the black parents were enthusiastic in the school's support, and when the local MP, Laurie Pavitt, PPS to Michael Stewart, speaking to our parents joked about our numbers and suggested that I had opened a recruiting bureau in Kingston to increase my salary, they roared with laughter.

"One interesting aside: my Speech Day in 1965 was on November 15th, a notorious day in our history, the day when Ian Smith declared UDI in Rhodesia, and Reg Freeson, the other local MP, came from the Commons to tell a tense, largely black audience of the Government's determination to oppose Smith. Reg, of course, was utterly sincere. Few then would have forecast Wilson's prevaricating pusillanimity. It was all very exciting—a fascinating experience for a school function, all the more because our Guest of Honour that evening was none other than the cricketer Leary Constantine, perhaps the most popular and distinguished West Indian in Britain. Was I a pioneer in this, too? All in all, it was a memorable night."

Women's International Democratic Federation

Max's appointment as a Head meant that I had become a 'Headmaster's Wife', traditionally expected to attend various functions such as Concerts and Speech Days and act 'graciously'. I was happy to go along but not so keen on the gracious act; rather, I saw it as a chance to chat informally with teachers or pupils and listen to their comments. I found it interesting to meet those whose exploits or problems Max had told me about.

A month or so after Max became a Headmaster, I myself acquired a new role as an advocate of girls' and women's rights on behalf of the Women's International Democratic Federation (WIDF). The WIDF had been set up following an international Congress of Women held in Paris in November 1945 attended by delegates from 41 countries, many of whom had been involved in pre-war anti-fascist and popular front women's organisations. Women had borne much of the brunt of the war and the delegates were united in their hopes for peace and a better life for women in the future. The WIDF had as its aims "to fight for peace and to prevent wars; for women's political, social and economic rights; and for conditions for the happy development of all children and future generations."

Britain was represented at this Congress by women who had been working in the International Women's Day Committee set up during the war. This was widely supported by an amazingly broad list of women holding public positions in social and political organisations: trade unions, peace movements and women's rights organisations. Among them was Elizabeth Acland Allen, Vice-President of the Women's Liberal Federation and General-Secretary (1942–1960) of the National Council for Civil Liberties, who became head of the British delegation to the WIDF founding Congress and Beatrice Webb. The event was given added lustre with telegrams of support from Mrs Churchill, Eleanor

Roosevelt, the wife of the U.S. President, and Mrs Smuts, the wife of the president of South-Africa.(38).

Later allegations that the WIDF was set up as a Soviet front organisation in no way fit the facts: it was a world-wide organisation of women wanting to consolidate peaceful relations between countries and improve the life of women and children in every way now that the war had ended. This was recognised by the United Nations which gave it Consultative Status with the UN Economic and Social Council and its Commissions, including the Commission on the Status of Women. However, campaigning for peace and to avoid future wars, the initial priority of the WIDF, meant establishing friendly contact with women in Communist Countries who had the same concerns, and this led to it being proscribed as a Communist front during the McCarthy period in America. One result of this was that the WIDF was deprived of its UN Consultative status between 1954 and 1967, when it was restored.

After the founding of the WIDF, women's organisations were set up in many countries to support its aims. In Britain, the National Assembly of Women (NAW) was set up at a Meeting in St Pancras Town Hall on International Women's Day, 8 March 1952.

Women came from all over England, Wales and Scotland: the Chair, Monica Felton, a leading figure in the Labour Party, announced that 1398 delegates were present. They represented, trade unions, political organisations, women's guilds, peace organisations, street groups, women's rights organisations etc. Among them was Connie Seifert who became a member of the new organisation's committee. Like the WIDF, the NAW included Communists among its members, and the British Communist Party was affiliated to it.

Soon after marrying Max, I had been to a NAW party to celebrate International Women's Day held at the Seifert home and was told all about the organisation. I certainly supported all its aims and would have been happy to join it as an individual on the spot if I'd been asked. I did not think any more about it that year. Then in February 1962 I got a phone call from Connie saying would I go to see her, she had urgent need of my help. She said that the NAW had a problem: they had been asked by the WIDF to find someone with a background in education to join a delegation to Ceylon (now Sri Lanka) to support the development of women's education there. Would I be able to go as I was not working full time and would be able to take time off?

I felt obliged to point out that I was a very junior member of academia and up to that date had not been involved in NAW meetings although I could have done so as a member of the Communist Party even though not an individual member. But she said time was too short to find someone else because the mission was leaving in three weeks' time. I felt embarrassed because I had done nothing to deserve such an opportunity—it was purely by chance that I knew Connie, but I agreed to go. On reflexion later I realised that Connie's difficulty in finding someone more experienced, better qualified or more involved in the NAW was a symptom of how the Cold War was beginning to impinge on support for both the NAW and WIDF. Anyway, I packed my case and went off.

Ceylon had achieved its independence in 1948 as a British Dominion; it became a Republic within the Commonwealth in 1972 and changed its name to Sri Lanka. A Parliamentary system had been established during the Colonial period and in 1962 the radical socialist Sri Lankan Freedom Party (SLFP) headed the Government and the Prime Minister was Mrs Bandaranaike, the world's second woman Prime Minister. The Ceylon Woman's organisation affiliated to the WIDF had close links with the SLFP and our visit had been agreed with Mrs Bandaranaike and near the end of our visit we had a meeting with her to discuss our findings.

As I had anticipated, the two other members of the WIDF team were senior figures and experienced members of international missions. Our leader was Anna Gyanchand, a high-level educational administrator, who lived in Delhi, and was supported by Doctor Olga, nicknamed 'Mother Moscow' both because of her large matronly appearance and because she was in charge of all maternity and child care services in Moscow. Despite my youth and lack of equivalent status, they welcomed me warmly as a member of the team. We met up in Delhi early in March. While waiting for Olga to arrive, I was invited to stay with the Gyanchands. From that moment till I left for home nearly three weeks later, life was a non-stop round of visits, meeting people, talking and discussing, often till midnight. I was surprised how many Indian and Ceylonese women were well informed and interested in British politics.

Although our formal mission was to investigate and encourage women's education in Ceylon, Anna took advantage of our presence to arrange for us to visit a large secondary school for girls in Delhi and I found myself speaking to an open-air gathering of 1500 girls about the history of women's struggles in Britain to get secondary and higher education and the obstacles they had to overcome to become doctors. It seemed to go down well and there were lively questions. I had time as well in Delhi to explore the town and was full of admiration for the Red Fort and the Great Mosque but I was troubled by the poverty and obvious malnourishment of many of the people. I still can visualise seeing four labourers struggling to lift a plank which I could have lifted myself with the aid of another woman.

When we arrived in Colombo, the capital of Ceylon, we were met by an official reception with garlands of flowers, and taken to the Mount Livinia Hotel, just along the coast, where it had been arranged we would stay. The hotel had not changed since colonial times and was cluttered with elaborate furniture and attendants in ceremonial dress. It was right by the beach and we were able to swim there in beautiful warm water. This idyll did not last, however, because Anna discovered that the daily charge for staying there was far above the allowance given us by the WIDF for our costs (although officially organised, our visit was not being paid for by the Ceylon Government). So, Anna discussed the problem with the Ceylon Women's Federation who promptly arranged for us to be given hospitality in the house of one of their members. So, on Day 3 we paid our bill and decamped. By then, I had discovered another far from idyllic aspect of the Mount Livinia Hotel: after swimming from the beach, I asked why a line of young boys with poles were swimming a little further out and was told it was to protect hotel guests from being bitten by sharks—the boys would be attacked first giving time for the guests to get out of the water!

On our first morning, we met an official from the Dept. of Education who helped us plan our schedule of visits and gave us a brief introduction to the history of education in Ceylon. Early in the period of British Colonialism a programme to establish new schools was set in motion, and this was very greatly extended in the period of power sharing with an elected Parliament in the years just before Independence. In 1942, schools run by the state were made free and the aim of providing a school for all children was agreed. Most of the early non-fee-paying schools were elementary schools, with teaching in Sinhala or Tamil but new single sex secondary schools, called Central Schools, were established alongside the existing secondary schools from the Colonial period, which had provided an English education for the sons and some of the daughters of the elite members of society who held positions within the Colonial regime. The Central Schools were modelled on the original Royal College in Colombo, but taught in Sinhala or Tamil, along with a strong emphasis on learning English. The

University of Ceylon was also established in 1942, although Colleges for studying Medicine, Law and Agriculture had been set up much earlier, and the Royal College of Colombo had been converted into a University College attached to London University in 1921.

A problem had arisen in 1956 when the Government, then led by Solomon Bandaranaike, made Sinhala the only official language for education and commerce.

This had led to riots by the Tamil minority and Solomon Bandaranaike's assassination. This law still existed at the time of our visit but we were told it was being soft-pedalled.

It was agreed that we should visit three girls' secondary schools in Colombo, the University, a teacher training College and an orphanage. Then we would be taken through the rural highlands to Kandy, visiting on the way a rural secondary school, a self-help community centre, a Buddhist charity organisation, a tea factory and a children's hospital.

In addition to this official schedule, the Ceylon Women's Federation organised various meetings with groups of their active members, our participation in an International Women's Day Celebration, a meeting with women members of the Tea and Rubber Trade Union, a visit to see elephants dancing in Kandy and to a Ceylonese Ballet there, a welcome dinner in a typical restaurant in Colombo and a farewell dinner on an island in the middle of a moonlit lake. Everywhere we were made welcome and everyone we met wanted to discuss their views and hear ours. We were certainly kept busy!

I agreed with Anna and Olga that I would take notes at the more formal meetings to help us with our final Report but unfortunately, I don't have copies, nor of our final Report to the WIDF, which seems to have been lost along with a lot of other WIDF archives. I would have had only my memories to rely on had I not recently discovered in a closed cupboard behind Max's desk 4 long letters and 12 postcards which I had sent to him describing what we were doing, which he must have kept for their sentimental value (we had only been married for a year and they were not all about my travels). In one of the letters, I said that the Government were not exaggerating about the importance being given to education. The population was growing fast and everywhere we went we saw new schools and thousands of children, the girls in white dresses 'looking very fresh and dainty'. Whether as many girls as boys went on to the Central or other secondary schools we could not tell, probably not, but we saw a considerable number of girls' secondary schools. At secondary level, all schools seemed to be single sex.

Olga was impressed with the level of community services and the health of the children we saw. She had been part of a WHO mission previously to a poor area of India and commented on the contrast. The areas we saw in Ceylon, especially the central rural highlands, were both beautiful and fertile, with fruit and coconut trees everywhere. Some of the coconut trees seemed to be wild and anyone could pick up the fallen fruit—we were told this was one of the reasons we did not see hungry children. We were aware, however, of the enormous gap in living standards and opportunities between the mass of the population and the British-speaking elite, including the members of the Women's Federation and most other people we met, who occupied positions in Government service or political organisations.

The core of this problem was explained to us when we visited the self-help Community Centre near Kandy: put simply, it was lack of employment opportunities. The Ceylon economy was based on exporting tea, rubber, coconuts, cinnamon and fruit. There were a small number of processing and oil companies but nearly all manufactured goods had to be imported.

Although literate and numerate, many young people, even those who had attended secondary schools, had nowhere to work except in agriculture, domestic service or on tea or rubber plantations, most of which were foreign (mainly British) owned.

The Community Centre was trying to help young women by teaching them skills in weaving, mat and trinket making, so they could make a living by selling their artefacts to the growing tourist market, but this was very small scale, not a national solution. The organisers of the Community Centre complained that the curriculum in the schools, both at primary and secondary level, was too academic and failed to equip young people for useful work apart from teaching, but the essential need was a more balanced economy. The ruling Sri Lanka Freedom Party had begun to nationalise foreign owned assets, including the oil companies, but their socialist aims were handicapped by lack of investment capital.

For me, the visit was a fascinating and stimulating experience and opened my eyes to aspects of colonialism not taught in British Universities at that time. I was less sure that our advice, such as it was, had much impact on the future of educational development in Ceylon, but hoped that our visit provided encouragement and solidarity to the women we met. Although most of them belonged to a privileged elite and often came from families in which fathers, sons or husbands held positions in Parliament or other Government positions (Mrs Bandaranaike was the widow of the previous Prime Minister, Solomon Bandaranaike), the members of the Women's Federation selflessly devoted their time to doing what they believed would best help the well-being of children in all strata of society and raise the status of women. They were Singhalese nationalists who had supported the struggle to gain independence from British rule and nearly all of them were socialists or communists. My only reservation was that our programme had not allowed time to visit the Tamil areas and our hosts obviously didn't want us to discuss the problem of recent conflicts between the Singhalese Government and the Tamil minority. I felt uneasy about not probing into these issues but felt constricted by our position.

We returned together to Delhi and wrote our Report. Olga was homesick and wanted to get home quickly. So did I, but I was invited to go to Agra to see the Taj Mahal and thought Max would not want me to miss such an opportunity. So, I spent a day admiring one of the Seven Wonders of the World before catching the plane back to London, Max and our cat.

In between my visit to Ceylon and a second last minute trip on behalf of the NAW, the Cuban missile crisis took place and for ten days many Londoners lived in fear of nuclear annihilation. The danger was averted but increased awareness of what a terrible disaster a nuclear war would be for the population of all countries involved was leading to support for policies aimed at restoring peaceful relations between East and West. It was in this context that the Soviet Union hosted the World Women's Congress of the WIDF in Moscow in late June 1963, which was attended by over 1,500 women from 113 countries, including Great Britain, whose delegation included a number of leading figures from the Quakers, CND and other peace and women's rights groups. The NAW was to be represented by Molly Pritt, one of the Vice-Presidents of the WIDF and the wife of D.N. Pritt, the left-wing defence barrister and an ex-Labour, later Independent, M.P. Three days before the Congress was due to begin, Connie phoned me to say that Molly Pritt was ill, so would I go in order that the NAW could be represented?

My own health was under question at that time because I was about to go into hospital to have a suspicious lump in my breast removed, but I felt well and had the time before my hospital appointment, so I jumped at the suggestion.

My trip to Ceylon had whetted my appetite for international contacts, so it would be interesting and I thought—mistakenly—that I wouldn't need to do anything but listen and meet women from other countries—perhaps Olga would be there.

So, I arrived in Moscow two days later and was officially greeted with flowers and introduced to a lady who I was told would be my personal interpreter. I was surprised and puzzled at such attention. It then transpired that because I was replacing Molly Pritt, who was a WIDF Vice-President and thus automatically seen by the organisers as the senior British Delegate, they saw me as taking her place as Head of the British contingent. This was not something I had anticipated and I immediately suggested that the British Delegation should meet and choose who should be seen as their leader. Most of those attending were senior and more experienced than I was and it would be embarrassing to be thrust into a false position. But the organisers wouldn't listen—I was replacing Molly Pritt, ergo I was 'Head of the British Delegation' and would follow the programme arranged for heads of delegations. That was that. So, I had to accept the situation. I hardly saw the rest of the British delegates, who were puzzled about who I was, but I explained to them the position—most were amused but one or two were annoyed at having been passed over for someone as junior as I was, but neither they nor I could do anything about it.

Being head of a delegation meant that I attended a reception to meet Khrushchev who shook us all by the hand and welcomed us. I felt I was in the presence of one of the makers of history, the Soviet Leader who had denounced Stalin's crimes, opening the way for change, and who had backed down over the Cuban missile crisis to prevent war; he had very sharp intelligent eyes and seemed to me to exude an aura of power. At the reception, I had meetings with the Heads of some of the other delegations including the Chinese and the Russian delegations. As Max had discovered when we visited China, there was growing tension between the Russians and the Chinese over ideological differences and the leadership of World Communism. My awareness of these problems helped me manage to say the right things to both of them without actually committing myself on the issues in dispute between them, so both saw me as friendly to their countries—womanly hugs from both.

One chance encounter came about in the hairdressers: I found myself sitting next to Valentina Tereshkova, the first woman in space, whose return to earth had been timed to coincide with the World Congress. She still had helmet marks on her face and was having her hair done ready for her appearance at the Congress. We were both under driers so I cannot say I spoke to her but I smiled and she smiled back. Once the Congress began, I realised that I was present at a most extraordinary, indeed amazing, gathering of women. Opening the Congress, Eugenie Cotton, President of the WIDF, said "the role of the WIDF since its foundation is assembling women of the whole world without distinction as to race, countries, social distinctions, opinions or religion, to work together for the realisation of their common ambitions: the happiness of their children, the improvement of the status of women in all spheres and peace. These ambitions answer a great need for justice and humanity."

The Moscow Congress was the largest and most representative yet achieved. Over 1,500 women were present including delegates from 113 countries of which 27 were in Europe, 34 in Africa, 23 in Asia, 25 in Latin America, 2 in North America, Australia and New Zealand.

There was a great range in their backgrounds: there were leading figures from many countries, including 53 Members of National Parliaments, professional women from education, law, medicine, journalism, science and the Arts, women working in peace and religious organisations, trade union representatives, but also ordinary workers, peasants and housewives—plus of course, one astronaut. UNESCO sent an observer and it was clear that the WIDF would soon regain recognition for its work as an advocate for all aspects of women's place in the world.

The meetings of the Congress were held in the modern Palace of Congresses within the Kremlin. They were centred around 4 themes, each with a keynote speaker drawing upon both recent works done by the WIDF and its local affiliates and an assessment of the work still to be done, followed by other speakers on the problems in their own country. The first theme was the 'Struggle for Women's Rights in Society and the Family', introduced by Ana Matera from Italy. Fuki Kushida from Japan then covered the 'Struggle of Women for Peace, Disarmament and Friendship between Peoples'. She was followed by Aoua Keita, Deputy in the National Assembly of newly independent Mali on the 'Struggle of Women for National Independence'. Finally, Vilma Espin de Castro from Cuba introduced the topic of 'The Health, Schooling and Education of Children and Youth'.

All the keynote speakers provided a comprehensive account of the state of progress on their topic and the remaining challenges in different areas of the world according to their stage of development. Fifty years earlier, almost all women worldwide had subordinated to men in all aspects of their lives so there was much to celebrate. The United Nations Declaration of Human Rights had included the right of women to full political and social equality but not all nations had formally adopted this right and, even in countries in which it had been incorporated within the law, its implementation was hindered by social conditions and traditional attitudes. Changes in the position of women had often come about as a result of struggles in which men and women had jointly participated: the fastest recent progress had been in the newly independent countries of Asia and Africa and some of the worst problems were in the remaining colonies—South Africa in particular was suffering from the oppression and mistreatment of women both in their working conditions and as a result of the enforcement of apartheid; and the lives of women and children in Vietnam were being blighted by continued imperialist occupation. There were many countries, also, where women were still used as domestic or agricultural drudges, totally at the mercy of the whims of their husband or master.

Listening to these presentations and the speeches that followed set my mind ticking over furiously. Thinking of Britain, it was true that women had had the right to vote for 35 years but still held only a tiny minority of senior positions in Government, the Law, the press, business, universities etc. I reflected, too, on how the Soviet Union had improved opportunities for women in many ways, including sending Valentina into space, but still had only one-woman member on its 32 strong Politburo—a situation that was not about to change.

I was particularly interested in Aoua Keita's presentation of how political independence in the newly independent countries was being undermined by neo-colonialism and the domination of their economies by Western capitalists, making the elimination of poverty and exploitation a continuing problem despite political independence. Speculators, she said, would rather throw away food than feed it to hungry people in order to keep up the price and protect their profits.

It was hard not to be moved by Fuki Kushida's account of the continuing health problems of the survivors of the bombs dropped on Hiroshima and Nakasi and her call for peace and disarmament not just nuclear disarmament but general disarmament so that the resources released could be used for economic and social development and the elimination of poverty and hunger. There were other moving speeches: a delegate from Iraq described the imprisonment of women for organising in support of women's rights and how the Government forced children to watch their mothers being tortured in order to deter them from 'subversive' ideas. Delegates from Third World countries spoke about their fight against various forms of oppression—early marriage and arranged marriages, genital mutilation, lack of freedom to move outside the house, obstacles to education, lack of voting rights, exploitation, low wages and long hours. Then there was Dolores Ibarrui, 'La Passionata', the Spanish Civil War heroine, who spoke about the continued plight of women living under Franco's Fascist Regime. She has been described as one of the greatest orators of the 20th century and listening to her at the Congress I understood why—it was not just what she said, it was her capacity to convey emotion and commitment so that the whole audience stayed hushed as she finished before breaking into applause.

Halfway through the Congress, I learnt that as Head of a Delegation I was not there just to listen it would be my responsibility to help draft one of the summarising statements for approval at the final session. I was allocated to the one on the Health, Schooling and Education of Children and Youth and was teamed up with Marie-Claude Vaillant Couturier, the leader of the French delegation, and Alba who was deputising on the drafting group for Vilma Espin de Castro, the official Head of the Cuban delegation, who had given the keynote speech on this theme. We had lots of paperwork to help us along and Alba was continually rushing off to consult Vilma on nuances of policy leaving Marie-Claude and me to sort out exact wordings. I found both of them a pleasure to work with: Marie-Claude and I developed a camaraderie, exchanging ideas in a mixture of French and English (we each spoke in our own language but understood enough of each other's to work that way). We had to stay up two nights running far into the night to get it finished. Marie-Claude was very French in always looking well dressed; during one late night session she suddenly realised a button on her blouse was hanging loose and was delighted that I had a sewing kit in my room and could repair it for her. I noticed that she had concentration camp identification tattoos on her wrist but only found out her full story later. This was perhaps as well as I might have been awed and less relaxed working with her if I had known she was a heroine of the French Resistance movement and later, after surviving the Concentration camps, a witness at the Nuremberg trials, and a member of the French National Assembly, including being elected Vice President of the Assembly. Alba later became Cuban Ambassador to Britain and I got to know her well. She used to send me invitations to receptions along with "Mr Margaret Morris" which amused me because Max, although sound in theory on women's equality, was rather conventional and uncomfortable with such a title.

After attending an international Conference before the war, Max expressed scepticism about whether it had been served a worthwhile purpose. I did not feel that way about the WIDF Congress in Moscow. I was sure the delegates' expressions of solidarity with each other's struggles had given comfort, encouragement, and a renewed sense of direction and purpose to many of the delegates attending. I felt privileged to have been there. I was also very tired indeed and when I went into hospital two days after my return, I hardly needed an anaesthetic to put me to sleep before my operation. Fortunately, my lump was a benign cyst, so I was soon home with Max and our cat, who had produced two kittens while I was away. I found out that this had sent Max into a panic because she had previously produced four, so he thought the other two must be stuck and summoned the vet, who had just laughed at him. Normal life was resuming, but my understanding of the challenges facing women throughout the world had been fundamentally enlarged.

Max: Campaigning for the NUT Executive

While I was away in India and Ceylon, Max was fighting his first election for the NUT Executive as a candidate for the Extra-Metropolitan District (Greater London and its fringes apart from the LCC area). After the debacle of calling off the Salaries campaign in October 1961, the leaders of his own Association, 'The Extra Met'. had urged him to run because his record at Annual Conference would in their view outweigh his Communist Party membership and he would have the support of the officers of other local associations throughout the area, who were the people that mattered when it came to organising elections. They proved right and in spite of heavyweight opposition and political organisation against him, to the delight of all on the Left, Max polled extremely well for a first-time contender. As he said, "I've polled well enough to make victory next time virtually certain. The Union Establishment is shaken: they had thought that the Communist Bogey would dismiss the left-wing 'menace'."

Two years later, in 1964, all the evidence pointed not only to a victory but to a substantial one: a letter supporting Max had gone out to every school signed by the leading local association officers in the District, apart from the old guard. It was, therefore, a considerable shock when the result showed Max some 60 votes short of victory. When he came home and told me this result, I'm afraid I just burst into tears of disappointment—so instead of me consoling him, he had to console me! But that was not the end of it as Max wrote in his draft memoirs:

"What followed was of decisive significance in the union's electoral practices. My friends, astonished at a result that contradicted all their information, decided to pursue an enquiry into the way votes were handled at H.Q. The matter was pressed by a prominent Labour teacher, Ron Wallace, the secretary of the Ealing Association.

What happened in those days was that the voting papers (individually signed and either individually posted or sent in in batches by schools or even whole areas) were received by the doorman from the postman or other deliverer, collected in batches by an official, taken upstairs and placed in a box ready to be counted by volunteer scrutineers—local teachers. Before, however, being presented to the scrutineers, the votes were guillotined by officials to remove the signed slip each had at the bottom, to avoid identification which would destroy the secrecy of the ballot. (Officials, it was taken for granted, would maintain secrecy!) What we discovered was that, at no stage in the process from receipt of votes at the door to the presentation to the scrutineers, was there any check whatsoever on how many votes were received either by the doorman or in transition to unlocked boxes upstairs or as presented to the scrutineers, a quite extraordinary position.

Of course, no-one could, or did, suggest that anything wrong had occurred in the election just concluded, but the total lack of security, the absence of rudimentary checks and the consequent possibility of mishap shook members of the union far and wide as the information we had gathered percolated through.

It took some years before the sensible step was taken to place the election in the hands of the Electoral Reform Society, but although only relatively minor changes were immediately operated, we all assumed that henceforth everyone involved would do their utmost to ensure the absolute probity as well as the secrecy of the election and that the previous free and easy approach would end.

I could not help being reminded of what had happened some years before. I used to stand for annual election to one of the union's national committees and, though the poll was small and I was pretty sure of the necessary support, I was never elected. One year I announced that, as a candidate, I wanted to be present at the count which was done in the office. It proved to be unnecessary because I was told I was elected.

One of the reasons I was gaining personal support was that, though teachers liked and wanted my militancy, they were also pleased that shortly after the lifting of the official Middlesex Ban on Communist promotions I had acquired an aura of respectability by becoming a Deputy Head in Tottenham and two years later Head of a secondary modern school in Willesden.

Being a Headteacher, I always held, helped me in the union. I had never taken the sectarian view that some left-wingers held even then and that was later to become fashionable among the Trotskyists, that Heads were the agents of the employers and had interests diametrically opposed to those of assistant teachers. Overwhelmingly teachers took the view that they were a part of a profession responsible for educating children in schools; that there were varying degrees of responsibility within schools and that the ultimate responsibility in the school, whatever the process of consultation might be, lay with the Head.

My support gathered strength, however, mainly because of the growing popularity of the salaries policies and strategies with which my name was associated. I was actively involved in 1963 in the union's dispute with Sir Edward Boyle as Minister under Quintin Hogg. Boyle has, deservedly, an educational reputation almost unique among Tories as a progressive in education on the strength of his tolerant attitude to Comprehensives. What is often forgotten is that this reputation was earned largely when he was out of office and, indeed, politics. He fell foul of the teachers very seriously in 1963, when in office and power, because of a short-sighted and mean interference in Burnham, when he refused to approve the provisional agreement reached. He was prepared to agree the global sum which he described as 'generous' but insisted on amendments to the distribution, the most obnoxious of which was reducing the starting salary for the lower paid.

Of course, this was unacceptable to the union, as indeed were the other changes to be made at the expense of the young teachers and the low paid. So, the union embarked on a public propaganda campaign culminating at Conference a few weeks later at Margate. It aimed at influencing Parliament and included a mass lobby on 20th March of over 6,000 members travelling from all over the country. Three by-elections were pending and the case was put there—an unusual form of political action at that time. We had the support of the LEAs and the other teachers' unions, except for the Heads. But it all was of no avail: Boyle announced his own scales on the day of the lobby!

It was then that I christened the Ministerial team the twin-headed 'Hogg-Boyle', a soubriquet which caught on and which I believe Sir Edward did not appreciate.

The campaign did not, however, involve action and revealed the weakness of such efforts which had no real bite. It certainly did not worry Boyle who carried on regardless, as he made clear at the Association of Education Committees' Conference that summer. As always, taking the mickey out of the Great and the Good, I wrote to the AEC journal, Education (19.7.63):

"Sir—It has puzzled me how a man of the Minister's undoubted intellectual distinction could persist in talking about the 'partnership' that exists in the educational service, while at the same time arbitrarily and dictatorially destroying the machinery of collective bargaining for teachers' salaries. Now, in a striking passage in his address to the AEC, he at last gives a clue to his mysterious processes of reasoning. He reveals his admiration for George Orwell and his acquaintance with 'Newspeak' "which the rulers of Oceana were able to exploit for their own tyrannous purposes." 'Newspeak' is, I believe, less politely known as doubletalk.

While 'de mortuis' is a maxim with something to be said for it, Boyle, like Butler, does not wholly deserve the retrospective adulation he has received. Remember that we were here dealing with the Minister's right to impose salary scales over the head of a statutory negotiating body.

At the beginning of 1965, the new Labour Government foolishly took over almost in its entirety, the Bill for altering the structure of teachers' salaries negotiations which Hogg-Boyle had wanted to pass. My Middlesex colleagues took the lead in drawing attention to what we considered were the evils of the Remuneration of Teachers Bill, now sponsored by the new Ministers, Michael Stewart and Reg Prentice. These were primarily that the Government (the D.E.S.) proposed to become part of the Management Panel of the Burnham Committee with enough votes to dominate its decisions, so making any really independent bargaining by the LEAs, the teachers' employers, impossible; and the introduction of an arbitration procedure in the event of breakdown of negotiations which enabled either side to demand unilaterally and secure arbitration—in effect a system of compulsory arbitration. At that time although there was some confusion among the membership on arbitration as such, opinion was strongly against compulsion and the Executive had reluctantly been pressed successfully to declare against it as well as making noises against the dangers of Government integration into the salary negotiating system.

We militants were appalled that a Labour Government newly elected after thirteen years of Toryism should uncritically accept a draft Bill prepared by the Tories whose salary policies so many Labour MPs had so bitterly opposed. We were even more outraged that the Executive opposition to the Bill was feeble, leaving the pressure to be exerted largely by London and Middlesex teachers who lobbied Parliament and conducted public propaganda on what should have been a national effort. Indeed, Michael Stewart gave us short shrift, telling us that he had been given to understand that NUT Headquarters was in favour of the Bill which was, of course, contrary to Executive policy. On subsequent occasions when I met Stewart, he was very bitter about the union's public opposition to the Bill, though I was never able to get him to give chapter and verse for his damaging allegation and he is silent on it in his autobiography.

But our opposition had one useful result in securing the only material amendment to the Bill (which became an Act in 1965) which made it the responsibility of the independent Chairman of Burnham to decide whether the 'breakdown' was such as to warrant the demand of either side for arbitration.

To this day I firmly believe that private assurances had been given by an official to Stewart (who was an NUT member) to push on regardless of the public position of the union. I was told by an Executive member that Stewart had intimated this to his local MP but, when the matter was raised on the NUT Executive, the establishment flannelled their way out of the 'difficulty' and nothing was done about it. Compulsory arbitration legally enacted must have been seen as the best way of circumventing demands for militant action when salary negotiations produced a blatantly unsatisfactory offer from the Management. We on the Left argued that there was now no incentive for the Management to continue negotiating since, under the Act, they could rely on an arbitration tribunal which would have, so we thought, a built-in tendency to support government policy reflected in the Management's offer through the deciding vote of the government-appointed chairman of the tribunal. This, in the event, proved to be a simplistic and even erroneous view. For, on the one hand, there were arbitrations that were favourable to the teachers and, on the other hand, industrial action was, in fact, taken notwithstanding the existence of the Act.

The point we neglected to take full account of was that arbitration, like every other political act in industrial relations, was subject to the prevailing political and economic circumstances. Thus later, in 1981, the union, after a long period of fruitless opposition to the compulsory arbitration clauses of the Act, objected strongly when, because the circumstances were likely to favour the teachers, the government amended the Act to make arbitration possible only when both sides demanded it—the original teachers' case! And the teachers opposed this change because they wanted to be able unilaterally to secure arbitration. It all went to prove a point I was continually to make: that it is wrong to elevate tactical issues into 'principles'. The job of a union is to negotiate the best it can for its members (in the immortal words of Jack Dash:to separate the boss from his cash) not to take a barren stand on 'immutable principles' which may do its members no good in particular circumstances and may do positive harm. Arbitration was just a case in point.

Success on our salaries policy in the 1965 Conference made my friends confident that the Executive seat was a certainty in the following 1966 biennial elections, especially since I was actively engaged publicly in discussion on two other issues which attracted very much professional and educational attention at the time. One was the public discussion around the establishment of the Certificate of Secondary Education as a new examination which would allow a useful school-leaving qualification to be won by pupils for whom the GCE 'O' Level was unsuitable.

I became the spokesman of the secondary teachers in Middlesex and led the negotiations with the Middlesex Education Committee officials to create the new C.S.E. Examination Board in the County.

Hard bargaining and a refusal to be deferential (two qualities which pleased my colleagues who liked to see 'the bosses' beaten down into agreement) eventually paid off and we secured what a DES official told me some years later was regarded by the Department, with reluctant admiration at the achievement, as the best teacher-controlled constitution among all the Boards.

The other issue was of national significance. Towards the end of his second period as Minister (1959–62) Sir ('song and dance') David Eccles floated suggestions for the appointment to schools of 'auxiliaries', 'teachers' aides' in the classroom, with a few weeks' training. I was far from being the only one who smelt a rat in this philanthropic proposal which was disingenuously presented as one to help teachers with their more menial tasks, such as 'nose wiping'. This was one of the happy phrases for which Sir David had a gift—his ideas of education seemed to be similar to Churchill's 'spanking baby's bottoms'. When questioned at a Tory teachers' conference to explain exactly what the helpers would do, he had replied: "I have no idea. It is ridiculous to ask the Ministry to lay down a schedule of restrictive practices. I am not a trained teacher. I have no idea of what is professional and what is sub-professional." Indeed!

But, as the discussion proceeded, it became clear to very many of us that what was in the wind was a proposal to dilute the profession with 'auxiliaries' who could take over teaching duties in a situation of severe national shortage of teachers. The danger was especially menacing for primary schools which would have a supply of cheap baby-minders 'helping' with reading, for example, a highly-skilled task, or taking over the class when teachers were absent. We were dealing with the thin end of a very dangerous wedge.

When the Executive seemed to be temporising over the issue and prevaricatory statements appeared in the union journal, a number of us became alarmed that the pass might be sold in discussions with the Ministry and LEAs. I ventilated our views in a series of letters to the union journal which aroused considerable national interest in the profession. The alarm spread and the upshot was a clear statement from the union opposing the proposals and making clear the distinction between 'ancillaries' (that is, recognised helpers for specific non-teaching tasks, e.g., welfare, meals, laboratory and workshop assistance) of which we wanted many more, and 'auxiliaries' in the classroom to help with unspecified teaching duties. The proposals were killed, we thought permanently.

Imagine our astonishment when Anthony Crosland resuscitated the Eccles scheme in 1965, making no bones about the relationship of the proposals to the severe teacher shortage but still prevaricating about the auxiliaries' teaching duties. We were horrified at this second example of a Labour Government taking over proposals launched earlier by the Tories. Crosland was easy meat for the mandarins on what to him must have been the rather boring mysteries of teaching. Here was a cheap way of meeting the teacher shortage which he presented with an astonishing lack of subtlety for such an intelligent man.

Once again, I engaged in extensive correspondence in all three major educational journals. The difference was that this time it was quite impossible for the union publicly to prevaricate on the issue as in 1962. When Crosland came to the 1965 NUT Conference, he tried hard to win the union.

But, in spite of vociferous backing from sundry Professors of Education utterly remote from classroom practice on which they were always ready to pontificate, and a far too tolerant attitude from union high-ups, he lost the argument because he could not come clean about the real objectives of the exercise. He did not, however, give up easily.

When the 1966 Conference came round Crosland was still trying. But, taking no chances, a resolution making it clear that the union would have nothing whatever to do with auxiliaries had been put on the agenda by my Association and won high priority for debate. This I moved shortly before the Minister was due to speak and, as expected, it was carried with no difficulty, setting the seal on the union's attitude. As there could be no auxiliaries in the classroom without teacher agreement, the issue was now closed. We had done an important job for both the profession and education. One can only imagine the use that would have been made of auxiliaries, trained for five weeks, in the years of very severe teacher shortage that followed."

In the light of this account of all the issues on which Max took a public stand on behalf of teachers' interests both at Conference and in correspondence in the educational journals, it is not surprising that in the 1966 Elections he not only won a seat on the National Executive but did so on first preference votes alone. That his election caused consternation to the General Secretary was made very clear when Max and I bumped into Sir Ronald and his wife while walking on the front at Eastbourne before the 1966 Conference: Lady Gould vitriolically greeted Max as 'a menace', to the obvious embarrassment of her husband who was more discreet.

To both the left and right in the Union, Max's election was clearly seen as a landmark—a portent of the future. As Max joked, "for some of the old guard it was not only the end of an era, but the beginning of Domesday." Later he commented: "I never ceased to be astonished at this almost apocalyptic view of what was an almost inevitable consequence of the changes that had been taking place in the profession and the union."

As an 'Executive wife' I was pleased that I was at last allowed to attend Conference and watch Max in action. Indeed, it was made clear to me by the then President's wife that it was my duty to do so and she gave me sisterly advice on how to dress and comport myself. I listened politely but had no intention whatsoever of wearing a hat or gloves, which I considered totally inappropriate at a Conference, nor did I want to go to 'ladies' tea-parties instead of listening to Conference. The overwhelming majority of the NUT Executive at that time were men, despite the majority of teachers being women, but I saw no reason to pander to what I saw as male chauvinist social behaviour, even if endorsed by their wives.

From then onwards I did attend virtually every Conference for many years but that was because I found the debates worth listening to. On principle, I never wore a hat, even when Max was President and I sat next to him on the platform. On the other hand, I enjoyed dressing up for another aspect of the role of 'Executive wife'. It was customary in the 1960s and 1970s for almost every local NUT association to have an Annual Dinner to which their local Executive member and his wife were always invited, along with the local Director of Education, Councillors and/or local MPs. These were very formal affairs—black tie and long dresses, a parade of notables when everyone else was seated, waiters lifting metallic covers from plates in symmetry and after dinner speeches. But no-one took all this pomp seriously—it was just a joke.

Max was usually the principal speaker and was good at blending serious issues with witty remarks, and, alas! some standard jokes which I soon knew off by heart. Very often I was seated next to the Director of Education or local MP and was able to have serious discussions about the educational policies and problems of the locality (I was ever a blue stocking!). The menu at these functions was usually roast chicken and apple pie—I used to tease Max about the enormous sacrifice I was making for him eating the same meal on Saturday evenings, week after week, year after year. Of course, I was exaggerating and in truth I found these local events and getting to know his key supporters and their wives or husbands very enjoyable. Although Max was not overtly electioneering for President of the Union, attending these social events helped him to gather support for that in the future.

Max: The Comprehensive School System

Tony Crosland's Circular 10/65 is rightly regarded as the nodal point in the story of Comprehensive education but it was not an outright win for the Comprehensive principle. The Circular 'requested' Local Education Authorities to prepare plans for reorganising their schools within a comprehensive system but it was not made compulsory. The practical politics was that the Government's majority was so meagre that it could not count on legislation being successful. Comprehensive reorganisation would be controversial with even some Labour members opposing—and there was always the hurdle of the Lords. Secondly, not all teachers were convinced of the virtues of root and branch reform, and legislation could have been counter-productive because implementation could have been hindered on the ground by the powerful weapon of resentment.

It was not until 1966 that an NUT Conference unequivocally adopted Comprehensive reorganisation and that decision was helped by the Government's decision to persuade rather than order. The truth is that the argument for the Comprehensive had not yet been won in the country. The *TES* typified much of the confusion when, in an editorial as late as the summer of 1967, it could still argue that "selection is as inevitable as sunrise."

As Max described above, it had been shown without doubt that selection at 11 was based upon the false premise of fixed ability and that the 11+ test was both biased in favour of middle-class children and totally unreliable in choosing between them. Children failed who were fully capable of a grammar school programme while others passed who later struggled. The proportion of places varied from place to place but on average four children out of five were stigmatised as failures and often discouraged from further educational effort. Families were disrupted and divided when one child passed and another failed. In general, confidence in selection by the 11+ test had been destroyed and the psychological damage it did to the children deemed failures was recognised.

Within the Labour Movement, there was hatred of the eleven-plus which was seen correctly as a mechanism to 'select' the working class (and many of the middle class!) out of a full secondary education—the corollary of selecting so few in. And yet there remained an attachment to the concept that grammar schools were needed to provide a ladder for social mobility.[2] This led to some of those in the Labour Party who wanted all children to have an equal chance of a good education to support comprehensive schools as 'grammar schools for all', while others argued that comprehensive schools should have a 'grammar stream' even though this implied selection at the point of entry.

Yet none of the advocates of comprehensive education from RH Tawney's 'Secondary Education for All' in 1922 onwards had thought it meant all children should follow a narrowly academic grammar school curriculum. In some of the senior elementary schools before the war, and more widely in Secondary Modern Schools after it, teachers had developed new types of innovative technical and practical courses alongside traditional academic ones.

A major advance taking place at the time of the 1965 Circular was the development of the Certificate of Secondary Education (CSE) under the auspices of local Boards composed of elected teachers and Local Authority representatives, CSE's were available in both academic and vocational subjects, and incorporated course work assessment, in addition to examinations. They enabled recognition of a wider range of studies than the University-controlled 'O' and 'A' General Certificate of Education.

Another development in the same period was the setting up of the Schools Council in 1964 by the Secretary of State for Education. It took over responsibility for curriculum and examinations previously undertaken by the Secondary Schools Examination Council and the Curriculum Study Group. Initially the Government, then under Sir David Eccles, wanted to set up a new unit composed of civil servants and HMIs with the object of 'helping' teachers in curricular matters. "No-one in the Ministry," he said, "has the slightest intention of forcing anything down the throats of teachers or authorities." But the proposal alarmed Sir William Alexander—after all the schools belonged to the LEAs, not the Ministry. The teachers' organisations were also sceptical and feared politicians trying to dictate what should be taught in schools.

---

[2] Modern research by Professor Selina Todd shows this was very limited in relation to working class children.

So, reluctantly, the mandarins began official negotiations with their 'partners', to explore the possibility of creating a Curriculum and Examinations body in which the Ministry could participate, but not dominate. Sir William, however, made it clear that if the Group continued, it would have to be under the control of any new body set up, not remain under the control of the Minister. So, Edward Boyle, by then the Minister, had to agree to the setting up of an independent and representative Working Party, which led to the formation of the Schools Council and the demise of the Ministry Group. A wide range of educational bodies, including teachers' organisations, were represented on the Council. It was a non-directive body intended to provide leadership in curriculum, examination and assessment development. Its work was undertaken by committees and working parties responsible for different programmes. It commissioned much research into these areas and published a large quantity of reports.

Early after it was set up, however, our union representatives had foolishly agreed to a project for monitoring the results of the new CSE examinations by a battery of aptitude tests—intelligence tests under another name. Many of us saw the danger in linking the exam's credibility with such tests and began a campaign to oppose the whole project, which was highly embarrassing to the Executive but even more embarrassing to the Council staff, who feared a loss of credibility at such an early stage in its life. Max took the lead in this campaign, backed by the Middlesex County Teachers' Association (MCTA) renowned for the powerful punch it packed in the union. So, Derek Morrell, the first Joint Secretary tried to nobble him and invited Max to meet him privately to talk things over.

When he came home afterwards, Max was bubbling with amusement. The meeting had lasted several hours and beer and sandwiches had been provided. Present alongside Derek Morrell were the chief HMI involved in the Council, R H Morris, and Professor Philip Taylor, the Director of Research, a charming but, Max thought, not too convinced supporter of the tests. Stan Jacques, Secretary of the MCTA had gone along with Max and together they explained their pedagogical, psychometric and political reasons for opposing the programme. Neither side was prepared to concede but Max felt confident that their intervention had been effective.

He was proved right: though the issue lingered on until the final reports were published, these were shelved and deposited in limbo. The new CSE would not be lumbered with pseudo-scientific tests.

In Max's 1953 book *Your Children's Future,* he defined the Comprehensive School as having three characteristics: an unselective entry, a full course of studies and the whole secondary age range. That meant comprehensiveness in intake, curriculum and age group 2 to 18. It meant a total break with the concept that there were different types of children who should follow different curricula. Max and his fellow campaigners wanted all children to have the chance to experience a full range of studies, both technical and academic. But some teachers stayed wedded to the idea that academic subjects were of superior worth to practical or technical ones.

The most important points made by the NUT on the draft of Circular 10/65 were to urge additional building and staffing resources and that consultation by LEAs with teachers should precede any decision on choice of type of Comprehensive. Objection was taken to the Circular referring to the Grammar schools as the type of school with exemplary teaching (Max called this "a typical DES solecism!"). On examinations, the NUT wanted to ensure that no school would exclusively take either GCE or CSE as some LEAs wanted. Judgement was reserved on 6th Form Colleges.

Although disappointed with the absence of compulsion, Max and like-minded colleagues were concerned to make a speedy start on what they saw as a revolutionary change. As he wrote later:

"Educational opinion was divided between those like myself and my left-wing colleagues who wanted to push ahead with existing buildings and those whom I described as willing to wait until the Greek Kalends when, hey presto! we would have the resources for purpose-built schools for all. This to me, looking back at the stop-go history of school building, was a pipe dream. If we accepted voluntarism, then we could go ahead, use and adapt existing buildings as LEAs saw fit, and build a new whenever and wherever we could. Insistence on legislation would strengthen the demand, especially from LEAs and opponents in the profession, to wait till everything was ready.

It is a cliché of British educational history that to wait till everything is ready means to wait forever! We were convinced that once the Comprehensives started in a big way, as they would with Government backing, then the pressure for the best possible conditions would help us achieve necessary improvement. Here was a clear case of the best being the enemy of the good."

Use of existing buildings made neighbourhood schools more likely. But it opened the way to different varieties of age range. One could no longer insist on all Comprehensives being 2 to 18; only go on demanding building programmes that would accelerate their coming into existence. So, Max's definition of the essentials of a comprehensive system was whittled down to two—comprehensive entry and a comprehensive curriculum. Practical politics prevented insistence on the third one. But the fact had to be faced that this permitted both concealed and open selection higher up the age ladder than eleven. So, while you had an unselective entry at eleven, some schools for example stopped at 15 or 16, while others went on till 18 and you could, in practice, have a two-tier, class-biased system through parental decisions, especially as the school leaving age was 15 and not due to be raised to 16 till 1968.

Max had no patience at the time or later with two theoretical approaches by sociologists to the issue of the meaning and purpose of comprehensive reorganisation. First was the idea that a comprehensive school must have a 'balanced intake' so all schools would be equal; but for any Local Authority to introduce 'banding' and bussing children around undermined the advantages of neighbourhood schools and was contrary to the principle of abolishing testing. As Max explained: "You had to face the fact that some neighbourhoods were 'more equal' than others and you could have quite distinct working and middle-class schools. This never worried me as my colleagues soon appreciated when I became Head of a Comprehensive which quickly lost all its middle-class children. After all, the Comprehensive was there to raise standards in all schools so why jib at a school where nearly all the intake would have been in secondary modern, second-tier schooling under the old system? Which is not to deny that a balanced intake had educational and professional advantages not least of which was that it made working life easier for teachers. But schools were made for children, not for the teachers, Max used to argue somewhat primly, and some thought strangely for a union leader. He was simply not prepared to make 'balanced intake' a fundamental issue of principle as some keen Comprehensive advocates were doing."

Max was amused and sometimes irritated when educational historians later attributed the major responsibility for Comprehensive reform first and foremost to sociologists. Academics had helped the movement with the publication of evidence, but this only confirmed the first-hand critique of the eleven-plus and the persistence of middle-class take-up of secondary and higher education places which teachers knew because they lived with them daily. He was likewise amused, irritated and scathing about those who advocated comprehensive schooling as a way to change society. As he wrote:

"This was the social engineering objective beloved of the sociologists. The Comprehensive was to create social equality, no more no less. You brought children from different social classes together in one school and, hey presto! you had the classless society. I always remember one of my sceptical Welsh colleagues conceding that, if the Comprehensive meant the classless school, he was all for it. What could be greater bliss, he laughed, than a school without classes!

Schools are neither catalysts of revolution nor dictators of conformity; mechanical agents of the status quo nor major progenitors of social transformation. Neither too much nor too little should be expected of them. They are neither the hope of humanity for a new world nor the ball and chain of the prevailing social system. They are neither the blinding light on the road to Damascus nor the keepers of the dungeon of the old order. This is a basic truth. The process of change initiated by education is inevitably slow. Fundamental social change must come from deeper social forces, not from super-structural elements. The super-structure can and does indeed influence the base but it cannot of itself change it. In fact, Lib-Lab social engineers, unconsciously perhaps, find in claims for education an alibi for not supporting the real forces that can change society. It is all so nice, easy and comfortable to imagine revolution through education. But it is armchair politics, parlour socialism."

When it came to the operation of the reform by Crosland and his officials, it became a case of the blind leading the blind. Max thought Crosland was the wrong man for the job and regretted that he had replaced Michael Stewart whom he had listened to making a brilliant case in Parliament against 'separatism' in secondary education.

As Max wrote:

"Crosland simply did not understand schools and he was easy meat for both the mandarins and the sociologists he listened to, who understood as little as he did about the working of schools. Indeed, what could be more deadly than the combination of a posse of old school tie mandarins and the gallimaufry of academic sociologists administering and advising on a revolutionary change in one of the most conservative elements of the state structure? Neither had any experience of working in the schools they were supposed to be transforming and despised the humble teachers (the lowest rung in the academic ladder) who were looked upon as the P.B.I., the Poor Bloody Infantry, of the educational world."

The consequence was a lamentable failure to prepare in a practical way for the introduction of such a major change. Neither the resources needed nor the training of teachers in mixed ability teaching were given serious attention. Crosland did not even listen to his own Labour teachers who included people very sophisticated in school matters as well as deeply experienced through their union activities in the machinations of the civil service education bureaucracy who had been instrumental in killing off promising Comprehensive developments after the war.

Max argued that if the entire age group were to be given a full secondary education, then surely steps should have been taken at once to control teacher education to ensure the balance of training was right not only as between primary and secondary but as between science, maths, the humanities, technical studies, and so on? On the contrary, laissez-faire reigned supreme with occasional nudges and zigzags about one shortage or another and occasional committees which told the schools what they already knew—that there was a grave shortage of teachers, especially in maths. Yet how could schools offer a comprehensive curriculum for the age groups concerned without priority being given to making good the curricular gaps of the secondary modern schools, gaps which were fully documented? And how also could you do it without an enormous increase in remedial and special needs teaching—a field of pedagogy which hardly existed in teacher training?

The colleges were enormously expanded to include larger departments of educational theory and new departments of educational sociology which spent the students' time theorising about the changes in progress. Young men and women were recruited as academics, often with minimal teaching experience and sometimes with none, to pontificate to future teachers about the social significance of the educational system, when what future teachers needed was training in how to teach slow learners science and maths as well as how to read and write. When these grave faults were revealed, as they were time and time again, little or nothing was done to change things. Educational research continued for a long time to engage itself in such matters as the efficacy of mental testing instead of concentrating on what the schools needed—finding out how children learned and how best to teach them. The ideologists produced the theories, the schools were left with the problems. And the greatest of these was how to advance the attainment of masses of children who had previously been regarded as not worth the effort.

A major trend among Colleges of Education was to regard as inferior anything to do with practical teaching. The job of the colleges, many argued, was to educate, not to train.

Max was one of the few voices raised against this trend and he was frustrated that many members of the NUT Executive welcomed the change because they thought that it would help to raise teachers' status. Max was not suggesting that the DES or the Labour Party should have issued curriculum directives but that a body should have been established, properly constituted and representative, to think out the issues, make proposals and test out whether they were effective, or not.

Max said that it was astonishing in the circumstances that so many comprehensives turned out so well. He attributed this to the freedom given to the teachers entrusted with creating the new schools. They just got on with the job without benefit of high-level pedagogical advice, just relying on their own experience. When Max was appointed as Head at Willesden High School no-one tried to advise him, let alone tell him what sort of curriculum the new-style secondary school should have. He was given an office and a time limit of two terms and told to get on with planning a new, unselective school. Which is what he did. As he said, "Quite frankly, there was no-one in administration locally who was either able to or would have presumed to interfere in what I was doing. I was glad to be left alone and to be judged by the outcome."

Max: Setting Up Willesden High School

Could anyone have started a new job under less auspicious and more daunting circumstances? I was appointed towards the end of September 1966, to the Headship of Willesden High School, one of the new large Comprehensives due to open in September 1967. I had my appointment confirmed some days later by the Brent Education Committee, which had replaced the Willesden and Wembley Councils and the Middlesex County Council in 1965. Then all hell broke loose. A group of Tory Councillors, led by a young man, now long forgotten, Richard Haselhurst, announced that they would seek to have my appointment overturned at the full Council meeting and began campaigning to that end.

Their argument was quite simple—I was a Communist and therefore quite unfitted to be in charge of a school. Ironically it was the Middlesex Tories, who had instituted a ban on the promotion of Communists in the fifties, who had, under the same Chairman, appointed me in 1962 to my first Headship at Chamberlayne Wood, a short distance away from the new Comprehensive, but a few of the Brent Tories now wanted to reinstitute the old Middlesex Ban and who better to start with than me, a member of the Executive Committees of both the NUT and the Communist Party? However. the Brent Tories were far from united in opposition to me and even those opposing my appointment were muddled, in that they expressed flattering opinions of my educational capabilities and, poor politicians that they were, failed to appreciate that the atmosphere had changed since the early days of the Cold War.

So, I suddenly found myself the centre of public attention. There was not a national newspaper, daily or Sunday, that did not feature the move of Mr Haselhurst and his colleagues, usually on the front page and for several days. It became a cause célèbre, the subject of leading articles in both the national and educational press and of comment on the media. There was a harsh and discordant note in the Evening News. 'Balanced' articles or leaders appeared in the Daily Telegraph, Daily Mail and the Sun. Only the Evening News behaved disgracefully. Children in my school were 'interviewed' through the playground railings, random 'parents' (one a lad of seventeen) were intercepted in the street outside the school and were, of course, opposed to my appointment. No parents of my current school nor the new one were approached, or, if they were, their views were not printed.

Sir Ronald Gould suggested an Executive statement which duly appeared and was forthright and effective. The local press, for whom the issue was a natural 'sensation' behaved with commendable restraint in their comment after a discussion the Editor had with me in which he showed his understanding of the harmful effects on a new school that could accrue from irresponsible reporting.

When the matter was raised on the floor of the House of Commons in an unfriendly way by one of Brent's Tory MPs, the chief Tory education spokesman, Sir Edward Boyle, was clearly unhappy about the Tory councillors' move.[3]

But the key factor in the whole sordid business was obviously the attitude of the Brent Labour majority group. They not only refused to budge but the Chairman of the Education Committee, Councillor Gordon Richards, expressed himself in as vitriolic a manner as he was capable of, and that was something! Force was lent to their powerful reaction by the fact that they were far from being a left-wing group. They argued not only the political issue but also my own educational standing and their experience of me as a Head for five years in Willesden of what was commonly regarded as a highly successful school. There had been, of course, no question of my misuse of my position for political purposes. I had been leading the Communist Party's educational work for many years (though I had by then given this up) and had always insisted that teachers must show total professional integrity and an exclusively professional relationship with both parent and child. Politics was a matter for the teacher in his private activity as a citizen. Later, one of my main objections to the Trotskyist crowd in the union was their deliberate blurring of these lines of demarcation on which the public reputation of the profession depends.

The upshot was a heated debate in the Council meeting in which Richards called those challenging my appointment and demanding my dismissal "a squalid and contemptible bunch of political muckrakers." The Tory motion was thrown out and the battle was over.

But scars remained. It was hardly the atmosphere in which to begin organising a very large new school on what was going for a long time to be

---

[3] He later accepted an invitation to give away the prizes at the school's Speech Day.

controversial comprehensive principles. Neither parents nor staff found the situation a pleasant one, and I fully sympathised with them. This kind of political confrontation was both irrelevant to and dangerous for the Comprehensive issue. I had made this clear to John Gollan, the General Secretary of the Communist Party, who had asked me whether the fact that I had requested no help from that quarter during the fracas meant that I did not want any. I said that was precisely the case.

For some people, an unfortunate side issue of the whole business was that, at the same time, an attempt had been made by some on the Left to pillory professionally former MP, Peter Griffiths, a rather nasty type who had defeated Gordon Walker in Smethwick in 1964, after conducting a racist campaign, but lost his seat in 1966 and was seeking a post as a lecturer in a polytechnic. At the time, I insisted that Griffiths' obnoxious views need have no relevance to his professional right to teach which had to be judged on his professional work and on that alone. Some of my 'left' colleagues were muddled about it all as some still are in their attitude to the right to employment of those they dub 'racists', often a term of abuse rather than one of precise definition.

As for the job itself, for me, up till now, it had all been theory; now it was to be practice. Instead of political campaigning for the Comprehensive, I had the job or organising one and the responsibility for running it.

An attempted witch-hunt against my appointment was not the only difficulty I had to overcome. On the first day of term, the NUT began its first militant action—not a strike, but a boycott of dinner duties. As teachers were obliged by law under the 1944 Education Act to supervise school meals, such action involved civil disobedience and so was against the law. Nevertheless, on the new school's first day of operation I opened the school in the morning as its Head and then, as an NUT Executive member, led many of the staff out of school at dinner time.

It was the responsibility of the Local Authority to keep the school meals system going, and although Brent was generally supportive of its teachers, I had been instructed not to leave the premises (as the NUT had advised its members to do); and on the first day of the action, the Chairman of the Education Committee waited in his car outside the school to see whether I would leave the premises or not. I did leave and went off to meet the NUT local Secretary, Derek Tutchell and others. Wisely, the Chairman did nothing about this 'disobedience'—I thought the Director of Education had probably advised him to pipe down and not exacerbate the situation.

I never received another 'instruction' till the day I retired. Of course, if I had anticipated a breakdown of the service in the school due to the union's action, I would have closed the premises after due warning to parents in advance. But this was an NUT action only and there were at that time a substantial number of colleagues in other unions who continued to work normally.

There were serious problems to solve arising from the nature of the entry and the curricular base from which I had to begin. Thus, in the Brent scheme, the Authority had regrettably—from expediency not principle—decided to pay for children who opted out of the system into grammar, denominational, direct grant or independent schools elsewhere. So, a fair number of academically able children were lost to the school. Although my catchment area, as I used to say, stretched from Rolls Royce land to 'slumdom', it was clear we would not have a totally unselective entry; on the contrary, we would become an almost exclusively working-class and increasingly black neighbourhood school. I was not alarmed, as some were, about this. If the job of the Comprehensive was, as I firmly believed, to raise the educational standards of the majority, how better to begin than with a school population previously denied full educational opportunity?

Secondly, we were to be a ten-form entry school, occupying two sites twelve hundred yards apart, amalgamating secondary modern, grammar and technical schools. My instructions from the Committee were to carry out its pledge to continue existing courses for all children in the school at the time of the merger. So, while we could organise a comprehensive curriculum for the new entry, for some considerable time we would be running this side by side with grammar, technical and modern courses for the majority of the children.

Problems enough, one could say. But I was determined; while carrying out the Committee's pledge. not only to create something new for the Comprehensive entry but also to weld the different elements of the existing schools together in every way possible, especially in curriculum.

I was going to maintain the grammar-technical children's standards and offer them new opportunities while, I hoped, substantially improving the education available to the secondary modern school pupils.

I began a long process of consultation. I interviewed every member of staff both to learn what I could about them and to explain what we would be trying to do. I attended school assemblies and social functions, met the PTA of the Tech—no PTA existed in the grammar school and the one in the modern school was defunct. I had frequent and useful meetings with the Chairman and Vice-Chairman of the Education Committee and the Chief Education Officer, all of whom gave every possible help.

May I digress at this point? I have written here in the first person and this must seem rather strange these days when the approach to school organisation and when, in particular, the Head's role is often rather different. The fact is that, having been appointed, I was simply told to get on with the job in the time given to me. No-one suggested that I should prepare plans for the approval, far less the decision of a Governing Body, or in consultation with any organisation of parents. Brent still at that time operated a system of joint Governing Bodies for groups of secondary schools but my experience up till then had been that such Governing Bodies played very little part in the life and work of schools. I was expected to be able to plan all aspects of the school's work and any consultations with staff and parents were entirely up to me. The Authority had appointed me because they thought I could do the job and I was expected to get on with it and produce a viable school organisation by the following September.

Such a modus operandi would be impossible today under the 1980, 1986, and 1988 Acts elevating the role of parents and governors. Thus, I was left to produce my own scheme of appointments and allowances; to interview and make recommendations for all of them that could be filled internally. Other appointments would be made in the normal way by advertisement and the Committee's routine procedures. I recall having difficulty with only a couple of the numerous recommendations I made which, for some reason or other, the Chairman did not approve. A fair number of the grammar school staff left but that was due to unwillingness to work in a Comprehensive or to better promotion prospects elsewhere.

I had no hesitations about staff deployment. We were one school and would be one staff. Thus, my timetabling instructions to Heads of Department (to whom I gave a great deal of autonomy) were to use all their staff throughout the school, especially for the new entry, consistent with the maintenance of existing courses. I also wanted Heads of Departments to teach, if possible, in both lower and upper forms. There was no reason why modern school staff should not take grammar-tech classes where able, and it would be good for the others to get used to teaching the slower learners. The children had to get the best we had to offer.

Though organisation occupied much attention, its only point was to serve the curriculum. Curriculum is all in a school—so much else flows from the right decisions here. The new entry would have a genuinely comprehensive education with everything that anyone could reasonably include in a 'common core'—science, technical and practical studies, art, music, French, as well as the staple subjects. We in fact gave them the national curriculum, as did most schools in the country, without the Baker Act ballyhoo and without externally prescribed syllabuses.

This we wanted to continue for the first three years. We were also planning a course system in the fourths and fifths which would allow the continuation of a broad education consistent with examination demands.

For nearly all the children coming in this was a substantial extension of opportunity over what would have occurred under the old system and, for many in both the grammar and modern schools, we were able to offer new, e.g., technical, facilities. The new entry would also have mixed ability teaching though provision was made for setting French and Maths if the Departments wanted. We could not go beyond this at that stage because of the Committee's pledge.

Having studied the records of the children in the modern school and, later, seeing the composition of the new entry, I made what I believe was the most crucial decision of all, to deploy a substantial part of our staffing allocation in creating what was to become through growth the largest remedial department in the country (later renamed, after the fashion, special education). We estimated a need for seven remedial classes, two (after a term's experience three) in the first year, two in the second, one in the third (soon two) and two in the fourth, plus specialist groups for reading and English as a second language (ESL). The work was to be done in small classes mainly under a single teacher and, in addition, we would withdraw children from ordinary classes for extra reading and maths. Without these arrangements subject teachers, untrained for and unused to coping with what would have been massive and extraordinarily difficult teaching problems, would have sunk into despair and become resentful under the burden. Of course, I was criticised by the dogmatists for "hiving children off" but I was more concerned with helping children to cope through more individual attention than with dogma.

Other problems seemed insignificant beside the immensity of this one. I outlawed corporal punishment, though not everyone agreed. We began building what was to become a highly successful pastoral system based on forms. A PTA was organised. I visited all the feeder primary schools to meet the children coming in and their staffs and Heads. We held meetings for the new parents. We opened in September 1967, with what I hoped and expected to be a smoothly running organisation.

Six months after our opening we held our first Speech Day, christening our brand-new Assembly Hall, with Christopher Hill, the Master of Balliol, an old friend and keen Comprehensive advocate, as my guest who entertained us with superb wit and unconventional wisdom. As I listened to his warm words for what he had seen, I felt relaxed for the first time in fifteen months. Thanks to the magnificent response of my colleagues to the difficult problems they had faced we seemed set fair for the future.

Five years later, when the first entry had completed the statutory secondary school course, I listened to another Speech Day guest, Vic Feather, General Secretary of the TUC, kiss the blarney stone ("the best Comprehensive school I have seen yet") after I had made my fifth annual report.

That had shown conclusively (we had researched thoroughly) that in exam results all those who would have been selected for grammar school education under the old system had done about as well as they would have done under that system, while the rest, the great majority, had done substantially better. Whether a school is a success or not depends on many factors. But, I reflected, we had beaten the Cassandras on the one factual criterion they had forecast we could not fulfil. In that particular aspect of educational attainment, we had beyond any shadow of doubt proved that, while we were advancing the education of the slower, those ahead in the race did not suffer.

Family Ties

I had expected my conventional parents to be shocked at my getting divorced, but they quickly came to like Max when we visited them in Birmingham—perhaps because he could make them laugh but mainly because their darling daughter was obviously happy. My mother, although only in her early sixties, was getting frail and my father was crippled with arthritis, so I took over the main family event of the year—Christmas lunch. For several years not only my parents but also my two bachelor uncles, Bill and Bert, came to stay with us in London over the holiday. Christmas celebrations were not part of Max's upbringing, but he entered into the spirit of it with enthusiasm, getting up at 7 am to put the turkey in the oven and going to the local pub with my father and uncles for a half of beer (my father's one drink of the year) while I got on with the cooking. Max did the washing up in the first year but then, cannily, went out and bought one of the earliest 'washing-up machines'; it was primitive compared with today's dish-washers but no-one else we knew had one.

My father had always loved the sea so in 1965 after he retired, he carried out his life-long ambition and moved to Devon, buying a bungalow in the village of Marldon, just inland from Torquay and Paignton. Marldon has a beautiful situation on the edge of the moors but it is very hilly. My parents' bungalow was not far in distance from the shops and the bus stop but they were up a steep hill. After a couple of years, my father's arthritis made going there a painful process and from the beginning put paid to his idea of taking a bus down to the sea for a swim.

Then my mother developed an illness related to Parkinson's disease which left her unable to make effective use of her muscles—she could move about and use her hands for household tasks, but if she fell over, she was often stranded on the floor. Neither my father nor I were strong enough to lift her but we helped her manoeuvre on to cushions and raise herself on to a chair. She kept remarkably cheerful and did not lose her sense of humour: I remember her joking one day as I struggled to help her, "the old grey mare's not what she used to be."

I went as often as I could to visit them but in those pre-motorway days, it took five hours to drive from London to Marldon, and the same back again. Even though I was still only lecturing part-time, it was not always easy for me to get away and Max could only come with me at half terms and other holidays. We went together when we could as we both liked that part of Devon and had spent our brief honeymoon there. We were able to take advantage of the beach to swim or walk, and my parents enjoyed going for trips with us in the car along the coast.

My parents were resilient and anxious to stay independent. They employed a cleaner and someone to help in the garden and, once a week, a Home Help came to assist my mother take a bath. But she gradually got worse and the situation was not viable without someone on hand to help in the evenings and at night. The next-door neighbours, who were nurses, were very kind and would pop in to help if my father phoned them to say he was in difficulties, but there was a limit to how often it was fair to disturb them. It was a difficult situation for my parents and for me as their only child. All in all, their decision to uproot themselves from Birmingham could serve as a classic warning to people retiring to be very cautious before setting out to live a new life elsewhere.

I could not help thinking that it would have been easier if my parents had stayed in Birmingham, two hours away by train and where they had friends, instead of moving to remote Marldon, where they knew no-one.

As they could not face the idea of being separated, I began to investigate the possibility of finding a nursing home willing to take them both. I found visiting nursing homes very depressing but eventually found one in Paignton where they could have two adjoining rooms; even though they were rather small there was a wide door they could keep open so my father could go and be with my mother whenever he wanted. Neither my parents nor Max and I had available capital, so it was necessary to transfer their bungalow to us so we could take out a mortgage to cover the costs. The Home was clean and the staff were friendly and kind, and my parents seemed reasonably happy once they were installed, though they missed their Marldon home with its wonderful views. They were not enthusiastic about the food but didn't really complain, although one day my father, bent over and leaning on his stick, confided "the problem here is that everybody else is old."

They had been in the Nursing Home nearly a year when in June 1970, my mother had a heart attack. I was able to rush down and be with her and my father as she died. After the funeral, my father moved back into his bungalow. He was very sad and lonely but assured us that he could look after himself, and would have the TV for company. I went down a couple of times and then brought him back to London for Christmas. Unfortunately, while staying with us he had a stroke and had to be admitted to our local hospital. He didn't really recover and remained very confused he often thought I was my mother. However, he insisted on going back to Marldon in the spring, but almost at once he had a second, fatal stroke. His death made me think of the old, anonymous poem: "He, for a little while, tried to live without her, liked it not, and died."

Although preoccupied with the problems of my own ailing parents, I gradually became drawn into the life of the Morris family. Max's mother, who had been visiting us despite his father's disapproval of our marriage, fell ill and went into hospital. Max loved his mother ('Ma') and asked me to go with him to visit her. His father was at the bedside, so that was when I first met him. Ma was happy that we politely greeted each other and the ice was broken. Unfortunately, she was seriously ill and died in hospital, leaving Max's father ('Da') grief-stricken and living alone in their flat in Pinner. After the formal period of mourning was over, I suggested to Max that we should visit him. This we did and I soon realised why he and his father didn't get on very well—they were so alike, full of strong opinions and convinced that they were right. They both had socialist views but Da would launch into a tirade about how Max could have been a Labour Party Minister, if only he hadn't been so foolish as to join the Communist Party. It was rather late in the day, I thought, for paternal guidance as Max had just turned 50, so I decided my role when we visited was to side-track the discussion by talking about music, which was Da's great love.

I had already met Max's brother Jerry, a pioneering Professor of Social Medicine, his wife Galia, and their two teenage children, David and Julie. Galia and I quickly developed a rapport and joked about being married to a pair of workaholics.

I liked the children but Galia was worried that 15-year-old Julie was too advanced for her age in relation to boys; she suggested I might be able to talk to her. I declined this request but actually began to spend a little time with Julie because she was fond of her grandfather and asked me if I could drive her after school to visit him. When I began doing this, I found visits with Julie much easier than visits with Max. Fortunately, Jerry got on with his father better than Max and was able to convert a flat at the top of his house in Hampstead for him instead of his living alone in Pinner.

The brothers got on quite well and respected each other but were not really on the same wave-length. They shared a commitment to socialism but whereas Max remained a trade union militant and anti-establishment rebel all his life, Jerry had become part of the Labour Party Establishment, one of 'the Great and the Good' who served on Enquiries and Royal Commissions (he was later a member of the Black Committee on Health and Inequality whose Report Margaret Thatcher refused to publish). They both lived well into their 90s and never met without disagreeing about something.

I had already got to know another Morris, Myron, when we were fellow Labour Party Council Candidates for the same ward in 1959. Myron wasn't actually a Morris: he was Galia's half-brother and had been adopted by Jerry at the end of the war to enable him to come to Britain. His story was very sad, similar to that of the boy in the film 'Au Revoir Les Infants'. Galia had Russian Jewish parents and lived in Paris but they divorced. Galia and her mother escaped the threat of Nazi occupation by fleeing from France to England in the late 1930s, where she met and married Jerry. Her father remarried a French Jewess, so when the Germans invaded, he, his wife and their son Myron escaped south to near Grasse in Vichy controlled France. In 1943, the Germans occupied the remainder of France and began rounding up Jews and deporting them to concentration camps. The day they came to the village where Myron lived with his parents he was out in the hills playing with friends. The local Catholic priest went to find him and said he must hide and not go back home as the Germans had taken his parents and were looking for him. He never saw his parents again.

He was hidden by the priests for a while and then was moved to share a hiding place with Resistance fighters until the end of the war 18 months later. As a 14-year-old orphan, he was transferred to a displaced persons camp until Jerry and Galia traced him and arranged to adopt him. He arrived knowing no English, but he was a talented linguist, bi-lingual since childhood in Russian and French, and fluent in German, so he soon became English-speaking and adapted to life in England. When after university, he did his period of National Service he was sent for training as a spy on account of his languages, but did not wish to become one, and chose instead to work promoting East-West trade. In the years since we had been fellow candidates, he had acquired a Danish wife and two children and was working with Maurice Orback, a Labour MP. Myron was devoted to his sister and, being a good handyman, made up for Jerry's deficiencies when odd jobs needed doing. Soon after we bought our flat in Menton, Myron and his wife visited us and decided to follow our example and also buy a flat there. We became close friends and for nearly thirty years Myron provided the same service for me as for Galia in relation to Max's DIY limitations. (Not that Max was quite as bad as Jerry who I once found sitting in the dark because he didn't know how to mend a fuse!)

Myron was a great 'bon viveur' and an excellent chef plus a marvellous story and joke teller, both at the dinner table and when Max and I met him on the beach for our daily swim.

Sad as I had been at losing my parents, it enabled me to take a full-time lecturing post. I had decided by 1968 that I should make an effort to develop a proper career before I was too old and had sought the advice of my old tutor from Birmingham, Professor Douglas Johnson. He helped me obtain a commission to write a Historical Association Pamphlet on the General Strike of 1926, which I finished and submitted in late 1970. Although it was not come out until 1973, its acceptance helped me obtain a temporary lectureship in British Social and Economic History at Queen Mary College in the University of London for the academic year 1971–72.

I thoroughly enjoyed my year at Queen Mary. The Head of Department, Professor Robert Leslie, believed that his lecturers were professionals and needed no advice about what and how to teach provided they turned up on time, so he used to stand and watch as both students and staff filed into 9 a.m. lectures. He liked to boast of his open-mindedness in having staff from all political tendencies, and paired me with John Ramsey, a historian of the Conservative Party, to run a Masters course together. We both enjoyed the experience. As a member of staff, I was invited to join the seminars at the Institute of Historical Research run by A.J.P. Taylor, which brought me into contact with other modern historians and their work.

I found some of the QMC students less interested in their studies than the older, Extra-Mural students I was used to teaching. Perhaps they were only there because their families or teachers had pushed them to go to university. Others, however, were delightful: some came from rural parts of England and from families in which no-one had ever gone to University before. I remember one 3rd-year student from Cornwall coming to see me in great distress after the final results were out. He was a good student and had been expected to get a 2.1 (at that time only a minority of students were awarded 1st or 2.1 classifications), but he got a 2.2. "How can I ever go home and face my parents?" he asked me. I told him to go home and tell his parents in a proud voice that he had won the award of a Second-Class Honours Degree of the University of London and the offer of a place to do a post-graduate teachers' certificate. My advice worked—his family celebrated with him and he later became a very successful Head of History in secondary schools.

One of the courses I was required to teach was an introductory course in American Economic History for Professor Maurice Peston's Economics course. This was a challenge because British history degrees at that time were Eurocentric and I knew absolutely nothing about American economic development and very little about general American history. So, I had to buckle down and do some serious studying—enough anyway to keep ahead of the students. I don't know if they enjoyed the course but I felt I had filled in a gap in my own education.

Another thing I learnt at Queen Mary College was to drink vintage wine. All members of staff were eligible to join the wine tasting Club so I signed up. There were extensive cellars and the Club had accumulated over the years a remarkable collection of wines. Every month the Committee decided which wine was ready for drinking and each member was entitled to buy two bottles at original cost price (i.e., next to nothing). I still remember my first allocation—2 bottles of premier cru 1964 Puligny Montrachet. Max and I found them a revelation!

The only problem about my year at Queen Mary was that the lecturer on maternity leave I was replacing was due to return. But the experience would help me obtain a permanent post in the future, and I was able in the meantime to go on attending the AJP Taylor seminars. I would have liked to stay on at QMC but it was convenient that I would be free the next year because Max was by then President-elect of the NUT for the year April 1973–74. NUT Presidents were expected to be accompanied everywhere by their 'consorts' and I was happy to give up a year to support him in his triumph. I would be able to resume my own career in September 1974.

Communist Party Activities

In late autumn 1961, I put into practice my decision to join the Communist Party. As I was not able to contribute to the trade union aspect of the Party's work, I joined the local Stroud Green branch. The Hornsey Communist Party had a long history of activity and had worked closely with the local Labour Party during the war. Initially the two parties agreed to support George "Jonah" Jones, a Communist, as a joint candidate for the 1945 General Election but Labour headquarters insisted that a there should be an official Labour candidate. The CP had failed to anticipate the Labour victory and thought that the wartime coalition would continue, so it fielded few candidates but agreed Jones should stand because of his local support. At the election, he obtained 21% of the votes and the Labour candidate 25%.

When I joined the Hornsey Communist Party was still active with a full-time organiser (Wolf Wayne) and rented premises. Although formal links with the local Labour Party no longer existed, there were ongoing personal friendships and contacts through CND, the NUT and the Campaign for State Education. Max was usually too busy to attend ward meetings so I went along by myself to test things out. Discussion was very erudite with quotations from Marxist and Leninist writings; when I ventured a purely empirical observation, I was advised by one of the male members that I needed to take seven years studying Marxist doctrine so I could back up my points properly. I just ignored this male chauvinist/pedantic putdown and continued to attend meetings and get to know the other members. The Hornsey Party took a stand on local issues and the year after I joined it issued a very well-argued memorandum to Hornsey Council proposing the compulsory purchase of a large site in Highgate for Council Housing. I was encouraged by this as I was already acutely aware of London's acute housing problems.

I was also encouraged that the ward members were as anxious as I was to get rid of British nuclear weapons. After Kennedy's failed Bay of Pigs invasion of

Cuba in 1961, concern had mounted over the danger of the Cold War leading to nuclear war and when the Cuban missile crisis began in October 1962 concern turned to outright panic: Britain would be annihilated in a nuclear war and some Londoners fled to the countryside. Max and I circulated CP leaflets calling for negotiation in the interests of World peace and waited fearfully as Soviet ships with nuclear warheads started across the Atlantic. We did our best to have confidence that Khrushchev and Kennedy would be able to negotiate a compromise. This was achieved with Khrushchev agreeing to dismantle offensive weapons in Cuba and return them to the Soviet Union in exchange for an American declaration not to invade Cuba again. After this crisis, the Moscow-Washington hotline was set up and a period of détente followed gradually leading to the Strategic Arms Limitation Talks in 1970. Both CND and the British Communist Party continued to call for Britain to dismantle its nuclear arms but the sense of urgency lessoned. The cost of Trident continued to be a substantial drain on the British economy.

In 1963, Max was asked to run as a candidate: in the 1964 Parliamentary Election. During the United Front period before the war and from 1941 until the 1947/8 the Communist Party had sought to gain affiliation or an electoral pact with the Labour Party but, as in Hornsey, these overtures were rejected.

Despite this, in the early years of the Attlee Government the CP supported everything the Government did in the interests of raising British production, including discouraging strikes and failing to oppose wage cuts. However, its hope of being formally recognised by the Labour Party waned with the advent of the Cold War and by 1950 the CP had come to see the Labour Party as an instrument of American Imperialism. Its policy document, 'The British Road to Socialism' maintained that Britain could achieve Socialism through democratic means but the Communist Party would need to put forward its own policies and candidates at Elections along with building up support in factories and other workplaces. In the 1950 General Election, it stood 100 candidates. The result was disastrous: in Hornsey G.J. Jones's vote fell from 21% in 1945 to only 1.9% and all but three CP candidates lost their deposits.

After that expensive debacle, the policy was slimmed down to fighting elections in a small selection of constituencies only. This was still the case in 1964 and Hornsey was one of those selected to run a candidate. Max was very busy with NUT campaigning, running Chamberlayne Wood School and attending Communist NEC and Social Services Committees, but felt that it was his duty to do as requested.

We were busy in door to door canvassing when in January 1963 Hugh Gaitskell unexpectedly died and Harold Wilson became Leader of the Labour Party. This caused me to pause and briefly feel a little wistful. Wilson had always been on the left and in 1951 had resigned from Attlee's Cabinet along with Aneurin Bevan in protest over the imposition of NHS charges and pension reductions to pay for the costs of the Korean War. Would it have been better if I had stayed in the Labour Party? Canvassing in 1959 had been exciting because we had thought Labour could win. It failed to do so but maybe Harold Wilson could now recapture Labour for left wing policies and end the long years of Conservative Government?

Despite these thoughts, my reasons for losing confidence in the Labour Party as a route to socialist progress remained. I described earlier how I had been unconvinced by Anthony Crosland's arguments in *The Future of Socialism* that capitalism had been tamed and I had opposed 'Industry and Society'. in 1957. During the 'Butskellism' period the policies that the left-wing members of Attlee's Government stood for in 1951 had been whittled away with continued heavy spending on defence and armaments drastically reducing the funding available for the Welfare State. National Insurance benefits had been meant to provide a floor under which no-one could fall into poverty and means testing and the other humiliations of the Poor Law were to end. However, by 1964 N.I. benefits including pensions had been so reduced that half of those receiving them needed to apply for supplementary benefits from the National Assistance Board. Old Age Pensioners who were too proud to do so were living in poverty. My father had worked for the National Assistance Board since it was set up but said he would be glad to retire soon because relationships with clients had changed. During the war he had been in London helping to supply assistance to the victims of bombing, who were glad of help, but many applicants for supplementary benefits in 1964 resented having to apply. My father sympathised with their frustrations and applied the rules as generously as he could, but sometimes came home upset at clients shouting at him.

I thought that until Britain abandoned its expenditure on supporting America's role in the Cold War, its financial situation would remain in crisis to the detriment of working-class standards of living and adequately funded public services.

Although in the Election Max received a negligible 1258 votes, we thought it had been worthwhile putting up a candidate to publicise the realities of Britain's situation after 13 years of Conservative governments, insufficiently challenged by a right-wing Labour Party.

Before the General Election in October, there were April elections for the newly created Haringey Council and Greater London Council, which would take over from the existing Councils in April 1965. Residents in Hornsey, Wood Green and Tottenham would be voting for 60 Councillors from 20 wards. It was agreed between the Communist Parties of the three boroughs that we would put up one candidate in each ward and I became the candidate for Crouch End. At the election none of the CP candidates got more than 250 votes (my own vote was 190). Haringey Council was won by the Labour Party which took 40 of the seats.

As part of the election campaign our ward had organised a meeting in Rokesley Infants School on 20 February 1964 on Hornsey's housing problems and distributed invitations to attend throughout Stroud Green and parts of Crouch End. We used the Heading "Who Owns Hornsey?" and invited anyone with housing problems such as high rents and house prices, falling in Leaseholds, overcrowding or landlords failing to do repairs to come along. A panel of experts would be available to answer questions. I was the main speaker and the Chair was Ethel Ramsey, our Candidate for the new Greater London Council.

Just before the meeting I circulated a second "Who Owns Hornsey?" leaflet directed specifically at tenants of the London, City and Westcliffe Property Company which owned houses in the roads off Crouch Hall Road and most of the houses in the roads running from Tottenham Lane or Weston Park up towards Ridge Road including the large Rokesley Vale Estate. It said, "Tenants of the company might be interested to know what the 1957 Rent Act has done for the Company:

In 1957, it paid out in dividends—£15,525. In 1962—£100,615.

In addition, it has been making free gifts to the shareholders of extra shares: In 1959-2 new shares were given away for each one held.

In 1960—1/10 of a share was…

In Jan. 62—1/3 of a share was given away for each one held In Dec. 62—1/2.

As a result, the man who owned £100 worth of shares in 1960 owned £660 worth at the end of 1962.

WHAT DID THE SHAREHOLDER DO TO GET THIS EXTRA INCOME and CAPITAL?
NOTHING AT ALL!
WHAT DID THE TENANTS DO TO MAKE IT ALL POSSIBLE?
THEY PAID AND PAID AND PAID!"

When the meeting in Rokesley School took place instead of the usual 10 to 12 at our meetings over 50 worried people turned up bursting with complaints and pleas for help. In face of so much distress, neither Ethel nor I thought it appropriate to use time electioneering. We answered their questions and then proposed that a local campaign led by victims of the housing crisis should be set up. Such a campaign needed to be long term and separated from party politics. Many of the people there agreed. I offered to make the practical arrangements and publicise the date. Less than a month later the inaugural meeting of the "Hornsey Housing Campaign Association" took place. It would become a very active body for most of the remaining 1960s. I acted as its Advisor and 'case worker' dealing with tenants seeking advice. Other CP members supported it in various ways but it was an independent organisation and I kept my role in the Association separate from my Communist Party activities. The story of the Hornsey Housing Campaign Association is told below.

Returning to Communist Party activities both Max and I were pleased Harold Wilson beat the Conservatives but, as we had anticipated, Britain's financial problems soon began to make difficulties for the new Government. Its education policies aroused the opposition of teachers: in particular by taking over unaltered from the previous Government a Bill altering the structure of negotiations over teachers' remuneration. Alarm was raised also over a proposal for using untrained 'auxiliaries' in the classroom. Max was in the forefront of mobilising the NUT's opposition speaking at meetings and writing in the press. By the winter of 1965, he was at the height of his campaign to become a member of the NUT Executive, and was elected early in 1966. He took his seat at the NUT Conference in early April.

Meanwhile Harold Wilson was deliberating about calling a second General Election, which was eventually held on 31 March. Max would gladly have supported someone else as the Communist candidate for Hornsey but as time was too short, he entered with gusto into campaigning, focusing particularly on education. I teased him, "You've already been elected to the NUT, this is a different election," but it made sense because of the large number of teachers living in Hornsey.

The results at the Count were unexpected but an example of the British voting system. Max obtained 1184 votes and the Labour Candidate 20501, so together they had 21.685 votes (45.28%) which was 615 votes more than the winning candidate, the Conservative Hugh Rossi. The Liberal candidate's votes had reduced Rossi's vote but if the Communist Party instead of standing their own candidate had recommended voting for the Labour candidate, Stephen Yeo, a young historian with very similar interests to my own, he might have been Hornsey's first Labour MP. This is conjectural but it caused an awkwardness in our relations with some of the local Labour Party members with whom until then we had had very good relations. Stephen Yeo, disappeared from Hornsey and electoral politics; he had a successful academic career culminating with being elected as Principal of Ruskin College in Oxford from 1989 to 1997. Fortunately, Harold Wilson won by a substantial majority and good relations were soon restored with local Labour Party members.

After Easter Max's CP meetings regularly clashed with NUT meetings, so his attendance at the CP Executive became intermittent and he gave up both the Social Services Committee and being Secretary of the Teachers Advisory Group.

However, he remained on the Executive and continued being concerned about Communist Party developments both in Britain and in the International Teachers organisation, FISE (see 'Visits to Socialist Countries'). Every summer I went with him to its annual Conferences in Russia, Hungary, Czechoslovakia, or Romania and became friends with the Teachers leaders there, some of whom stayed with us when they were invited to NUT Conferences. We were encouraged by developments during the Prague Spring under Dubcek, whom the Czech teachers enthusiastically supported, not least because of a democratic change enabling them to elect their own leaders, whereas in the other Communist countries the teachers leaders were imposed on them from above.

While Max began to focus increasingly on the NUT, I began to give more time to Communist Party and related activities. Noreen Branson, Editor of Labour Research was a member of the Highgate ward of the Hornsey Communist Party and we had become friends working together for the Hornsey Housing Campaign Association. She invited me to join the Editorial Board of Labour Research and help cover housing issues. I was also made a member of the CP Social Services Committee—not to replace Max but because of my growing expertise on housing problems. Then in 1967 I was selected as the Hornsey candidate for the 1970 Parliamentary Election and began publishing its policies in the Hornsey Journal and writing occasionally for the Morning Star. So, I became very busy and happy with the things I was doing. This was not to last.

Max and I were on holiday in Yugoslavia when the Russian and Warsaw Pact armies marched into Prague on 21 August 1968 and arrested Dubcek. We were sitting on a beach and suddenly everyone around us began talking excitedly. We couldn't understand what was going on as no-one spoke English. There were lots of Italians and though neither of us knew more than a few words of Italian, we eventually managed to piece together what had happened. We were both devastated—shocked and disappointed. Our hopes that Dubcek's 'Socialism with a Human Face' would be the beginning of a move towards democracy within the Communist world were shattered. We were on the way home and agreed that if the British CP supported this as they had the Soviet invasion of Hungary in 1956, we would both resign. However, when the Executive met, they passed a critical resolution about the invasion, so we continued our roles within the Party. When Max became President Elect of the NUT in 1971, he resigned from the CP Executive but stayed a member of the Party.

I continued my election campaign but realised that the overthrow of Dubcek would let loose a revival of anti-Communism. "Freedom for the Czechs" and other pro Dubcek slogans were daubed on the façade of the Town Hall and Central Library. Prayers for Czechoslovakia were held in churches. I was relieved when the Hornsey Journal published a letter from me headed "MRS MORRIS CONDEMNS RUSSIAN INVASION." I wrote that the occupation was "a violation of Czech independence and sovereignty and of Communist principles and that there must be "restoration to the Czech Government of full control over their own country, which clearly involves the complete withdrawal of all uninvited troops. As a Communist, I have confidence in the Action Programme of the Czech Communist Party and its proposals for the democratic renewal of Czech Society."

The British Party's own procedures were tainted by Stalinism and after attending its Annual Conference, I was critical of how policy was decided in advance and handed down to the Conference for endorsement. Elections involved voting for a pre-approved list.

So, at a London District Conference, I seconded a motion from a North Finchley delegate seeking to bring inner party democracy closer to that of the rest of the Labour movement. She said there should be more discussion at branches before Congress so that they could put ideas forward for open discussion and initiate policy. I added that instead of "blunt, generally stultifying political resolutions" the District Committee should provide a self-critical analysis for open discussion. Despite the Standing Orders Committee advising against accepting the motion, it was passed—other members must have had enough of being bored to death! Max wasn't there but when I told him he laughed. He was surprised but pleased it was allowed to be put.

My statement of confidence in the Czech Communist Party was totally sincere but Khrushchev's de-Stalinisation programme had been halted by his removal from power in 1964 and the hardliners had returned to power, so I doubted whether the Soviet Government now under Brezhnev was going to allow the Czechs to follow an independent, democratic path. I feared too that although the CP executive statement was firm and clear there would be attempts by some Party members to tone it down. To our disappointment long-time friends of ours, the author Jimmy Aldridge and his wife Deana, broke off relations with us a little later because of our criticism of the Soviet invasion.

Meanwhile preparing for the election went ahead. Looking back, I realise how helpful it was to have a local paper, the Hornsey Journal, which gave full coverage of local political events and treated the political parties equally. The Leader of the Hornsey Conservatives, Douglas Smith, enjoyed controversy and he and I had frequent ding-dongs in the Journal over Council policy especially after the Tories won Haringey Council in the spring of 1968. I also frequently was able to get articles or letters in the Morning Star.

My first article as a candidate was about homes. I said that problems had become suddenly very much worse in the ten years since the Tory 1957 Rent Act was passed. The latest estimate of the number of sub-standard houses in use meant that about a quarter of all families in modern, wealthy, industrialised Britain are deprived of their most fundamental need—a proper home. All women need a home fit to raise children; this was true in faraway Vietnam where war meant that their homes were being blown to bits; and in the Middle East where Arab women were living in refugee camps and Israeli women could never be secure in their homes until Israel was accepted by the Arab Countries, which can only be achieved if Israel withdraws from the areas it has won by force and treats the Palestinians justly.

As the Wilson Government to my relief held back from supporting the War in Vietnam, I didn't often mention foreign affairs again but wrote frequently about housing problems—the failure to build Council houses, that Housing Associations could supplement but not replace Council provision, the replacement of slums by houses for sale, high Council Rents and the weakness of the 1965 Rent Act and the 1967 Leasehold Enfranchisement Act, neither of which achieved their declared purpose of protecting tenants from the effects of scarcity or ending the archaic feudal relic of freeholders rights. The Hornsey Housing Campaign Association, based upon experience, warned Richard Crossman about the problems of using Tribunals to fix rents, but we were not heeded. I had an article published in *New Society* on the defects of the 1966 Rent Act, "How Fair are Fair Rents?"

Locally, I wrote supporting comprehensive schools, the iniquities of the Council's proposed banding system with its racist conations about spreading black children between schools, the real needs of schools and the urgency of getting rid of child poverty. Another issue I raised was how the proposed related pension scheme would discriminate against women who comprised two thirds of old age pensioners and were already among the poorest of them. No plan to end poverty among the old can work unless it provides a good pension for all women whether they be single, married or widowed.

An example of my *Hornsey Journal* articles comes from February 1969: 'COUNCIL'S CROCODILE TEARS'.

There's been much talk of Britain's economic crisis. Of the need to cut down expenditure and tighten our belts. Yet it is worth remembering that 1968 was a bumper year for those who own shares. There has been no sacrifice from that sector of the Community.

How many Hornsey families are worth half as much again as they were in 1964 when the Labour Government took power? Very few, except in the richest roads of Highgate. Yet the capital class as a whole has added 50% to the value of the shares, they held in 1964. So, let's have an end to the crocodile tears from both the Government and Haringey Council about how sorry they are about cuts and economies but it can't be helped.

Haringey Council under the Tories are making a great to-do about the £1 million "subsidy" on Council Housing. Why don't they admit that far more than that is paid out in interest on loans? Lower the interest rate and there would be no need of a subsidy. The real solution to the problem of financing our local social services is finding a fairer way of raising the money than the rating system. If Government cut the arms bill by half and used the money for the social services, the problem would be half solved.

If the Government's White Paper on the Trade Unions is allowed to become law, it will help the monopoly capitalist firms to make even bigger profits at the expense of those who do the work.

With a Labour Government putting forward such policies, it is no wonder that our local Tories on Haringey Council think they can get away with rate increases, rent increases, selling off the Council's assets, abandoning the families on the waiting list and cutting down on all services."

As the Election approached the Communist Party's main focus was its opposition to Britain joining the Common Market. I thought at the time that the Common Market was a capitalist cabal and that if we joined it Britain would lose her independence. I wrote in the Hornsey Journal and argued on the doorstep that "we should lose control of trade policy, tariff policy, the ability to control movements of both capital and people, the right to support agriculture in a way which keeps prices down and the possibility of extending public ownership or subsidising underdeveloped area or industries. We should also be forced to adopt a value added tax and to alter our arrangements for financing the social services," I believed this at the time but some of these arguments were not founded on facts. In retrospect left wing politicians in Britain were failing to appreciate the potential benefits of the Common Market and the importance of the joint European commitment to democratic principles and negotiation in place of future wars between European states.

When election day arrived, all my efforts had a disappointingly small return in votes. As expected, Hugh Rossi retained his seat with a comfortable majority over Labour with the Liberals a poor third. I had 624 votes but was not bottom as a Socialist (GB) candidate scored only 176 votes. I was not sorry I had stood, but was ready to focus on other things.

Communist meetings were beginning to be dominated by controversy over our attitude to the Soviet Union. Dubcek had been replaced and his reforms reversed. Some members, who became known as 'Tankies', wanted us 'to show solidarity' with the Soviet Union and stop criticising its take-over of Czechoslovakia. On the other side were the 'Euro Communists', influenced by the writings of Antonio Gramsci, who encouraged communist parties to embrace democracy and abandon sectarianism. It was argued that left wing parties needed to develop social alliances and win hegemonic support for social reforms. In Britain, the leading Marxist historian, Eric Hobsbawn, encouraged the Party to widen its appeal by embracing public sector middle-class workers, and new social movements such as feminism and gay liberation. I agreed with him and the Euro Communists on such proposals and regularly read Marxism Today, but was dismayed at their dismissal of the importance of the Trade Unions. How could a Labour Movement thrive without the inclusion of the largest working-class institutions? It was true some Trade Unions needed to revise their attitudes, especially towards women and even their own role, but brushing them aside was contrary to my understanding of the path to socialism.

As the battles became fiercer, I became alienated: what was the point of a pressure group which didn't know where it stood and whose members spent their time arguing bitterly among themselves? So, my only participation in Communist activities after the early 1970s was attending the Social Services Committee along with Noreen Branson, Editor of Labour Research. The meetings were often interesting but I wondered who would take notice of our ideas. Afterwards, Noreen and I went out for a meal. I found her company so stimulating and enjoyable that I went on going to Social Services meetings long after I stopped going to other CP meetings. I never did resign formally: I just stood aside and watched the CP disintegrate.

Max, however, did formally resign and explained why:

"For a very long time, I had been disenchanted with some of the Party's attitudes and with its methods of work and decision-making. I was particularly critical of what I regarded as excessive willingness to ignore unpleasant events in the Soviet Union and hence take up a genuinely independent attitude to what was happening there. Soviet antisemitism seemed to me to be blatant but one excuse or another was found for playing it down, and on one occasion I stalked out of the Executive in disgust at the obvious dishonest prevarication, for which I blamed in particular two Jewish members. I was only induced to continue after a stormy personal talk with Gollan who badly wanted to avoid an open breach, especially on such an issue.

And in their heart of hearts, my Executive colleagues must surely have been disgusted at the pack of lies the Russians purveyed to us in correspondence explaining the Czech "tragedy"—as it was for me and most of the Party. I found it difficult to credit the utter cynicism with which our Soviet 'comrades', writing 'fraternally', party to party at the highest level, blatantly lied and invented fantasies to replace the harsh, stark facts known to the whole world except those behind what became a veritable iron curtain against the truth.

Paradoxically, although we took the right line on the Czech events of 1968, and indeed on subsequent contacts at international level, my disenchantment was increased. Contacts with the Russians and East Europeans in London were soured and what mattered to me much more, the bitterness over Czechoslovakia extended to the international teachers' sphere. Relations there deteriorated as the Russians became even tougher than before, making contacts sometimes unpleasant."

For Max, the last straw came in 1976. He had been in the Communist Party for just over 40 years when his disillusion finally led to his resigning. As might have been anticipated, this was brought about by changes in the CPs educational policy. For some years, Max had been in an ideological battle with those both outside in Trotskyite groups and within the Communist Party whom he dubbed "pseudo-Marxists and ultra-left sociologists" with "their ignorant and superficial analysis of the school system which they pronounced 'authoritarian' and their claim that 'our state education system is designed to perpetuate the dominance of capitalist ideology.' He was scathing at the Party supporting these 'leftie' views and replacing traditional Marxist views on the dynamic role of education as a political and ideological battleground. Max said they should remind themselves that it was Lenin who translated the Webb's classic work on trade unionism for the education of the Russian workers."

Another development which had had aroused Max's scorn was the decision of the Party's Youth Affairs Committee to sponsor or, as Max said, "not to put too fine a point on it, to create the ridiculous National Union of School Students (NUSS) with close links with the Young Communist League." This was done without consulting the Teachers Advisory Committee. The term 'Union' implied a different, externally active role from that of a debating club or a Society. Though he was no longer attending the Teachers Advisory Committee, Max agreed to take part in its deputation of protest to the Political Committee, led by Gorden McLennan, who was about to replace John Gollan as General Secretary. Max described their unfriendly reception:

"I was not just astonished but horrified at the change in attitude of my one-time colleagues on the Party Executive. What showed through was not only the sheerest bureaucracy—they had agreed in advance not to give way, and to back McLennan—but the silliness of the trendy arguments they used. Instead of taking advice from experienced teachers they were telling us in good old-fashioned party manner what to do."

Max told his comrades that this might well be the last straw for him but he was too absorbed in his NUT work to devote thought immediately on whether to leave or not. Just after this Max opened his TES one morning to find the headline "Unions are 'failing the jobless.'" "The teacher unions have failed to give a lead in the campaign against teacher unemployment," says a Communist Party pamphlet published this week. "The National Union of Teachers in particular was criticised for not supporting the student occupation of colleges and for not extending its sanctions to a refusal to teach classes of more than 30." The pamphlet also spoke about the need "to support the building of a broad left organisation" among teachers at which Max snorted 'as though that had not been the successful politics of Communist teachers for decades.' Max was incandescent with indignation:

"If anyone had given a lead on teacher unemployment it was the union which, as Chairman of the union's National Action Committee, I had good reason to know, as we were conducting a steady and continuous policy of industrial action against local authorities who were attempting to reduce establishments and we had, nationally, bitterly attacked the Government for its policy of cuts, especially those involving the reduction of available jobs. By the time I retired, our estimate was that we had saved some 10,000 jobs."

Max also ridiculed the idea that it was the business of the NUT to support student occupations: "I don't recall us even discussing them—they were a matter for the NUS. We had a regular communication system with the NUS and they had not quarrelled with us—on the contrary, they were appreciative of our efforts to win, by our industrial action jobs for their students on qualification as teachers. As for going on strike for classes of 30, a moment's thought would have shown that this was an absurdly unrealistic policy in 1976, as well an impertinent interference in our democratic procedures."

But it was not just the attack on the NUT which aroused his ire, but the general tenure of the pamphlet and the fact of its publication against the advice of the Education Advisory Committee. It was against all Party procedures and practice for an official publication to attack a union leadership without the fullest agreement of their own comrades in the field. He learnt that the author of the pamphlet had received comments on a draft of the pamphlet from the Secretary of the Teachers Advisory Committee, who had made a number of serious criticisms which were just ignored.

Max then telephoned McLennan, who told him he had not seen the pamphlet and knew nothing about it. Max was told later that Bert Ramelson, the Party's leader responsible for all work in trade unions, also professed complete ignorance of the pamphlet. Max was more than astonished it was inconceivable to him with his long experience of how the Party at King Street operated, that a pamphlet could be issued by the Communist Party without the two top leaders knowing anything at all about it. McLennan said he would look into it and ring him back. Max replied that unless there was a repudiation and withdrawal, he could not with any credibility remain in the Party.

Max was out so I took McLennan's call. He said I should explain to Max that it was only a 'student committee pamphlet', not a 'Party pamphlet' and had been commented on in draft by the Secretary of the Advisory Committee. Max had told me that the Secretary had indeed looked at it earlier and made suggestions for important changes but they had been ignored. So, I told McLellan in no uncertain language that the pamphlet was insulting and Max was expecting it to be immediately repudiated.

When Max came home and I gave him McLennan's message, he thought it was the last straw. He agreed that it was insulting. He said to me "How can McLennan expect me to believe the rubbish about the pamphlet being 'student' and not Party?" He knew then that nothing would be done. Nothing was done. Or, rather, something was done. The pamphlet, a couple of days later, received a major boost in the Morning Star and the text even included impertinent demands by Communist students for changes in NUT policy. Max had no further communication from McLennan, and none from Ramelson—nor did he communicate with them. He had told them he would leave—and so he did.

If that was the way they were now handling trade union affairs, so much the worse for them—it would get them nowhere, nor gain the adherence of more students, and would seriously damage their influence among teachers.

Unsurprisingly, the Press got wind of the quarrel and, when Max was rung up and asked his reaction to the pamphlet, so he told them of his resignation. He did not want to issue a public statement although, when personally cornered by various journalists, he gave his reasons as sharp differences on educational policy and more than a hint of the ultra-left influences to which he objected. He did not accept an offer to write in the Times about how he felt about leaving the CP after so long. He regretted he had not left earlier and wanted to move on.

Margaret: Hornsey Housing Campaign Association

The Borough of Hornsey was created in 1889 and its population and dwellings expanded rapidly. Many of the new buildings were erected by a small number of companies which were responsible for large estates covering several roads of large, three-story houses for renting to middle class families with a head of family working in the city, the professions or local commerce and usually servants living in the attics. Many of the houses built in the Victorian and Edwardian periods were still in use when Max and I came to live in Hornsey. Some of them had been sold and were still occupied by a single family, others had been subdivided into self-contained flats or maisonettes like the one we bought, but the majority had become dilapidated and multi-occupied by working class tenants. At the time that Hornsey became part of Haringey, 70% of the dwellings in the new Borough had been built before 1914; 39% of them were owned by private landlords and housed 51% of Haringey's population.

So, in the 1960s, Hornsey and afterwards Haringey were suffering all of London's housing problems: shortage of housing, dilapidated buildings without modern amenities, insanitary conditions, insecurity of tenure and high rents in decontrolled tenancies, and, multi-occupation. Stroud Green ward was listed in the Milner/Holland Commission Report in 1965 as one of the worst areas for multi-occupation in London.

This explains why 50 people had turned up to the Communist Party Stroud Green Ward meeting in February 1964 described above. At that meeting, it was agreed to set up a non-party association to campaign on housing problems and to help each other. The Hornsey Housing Campaign Association was inaugurated a month later on 19 March 1964 at a meeting in Rokesley School chaired by Harry Sterne, who had been secretary of the 1957 Anti-Rent Bill Association.

Most of those who were at the February meeting came plus a considerable number of other local residents.

Opening the meeting Mr Sterne said that all the fears of tenants about the 1957 Rent Act were being borne out: rents soared when agreements fell in, tenants were frightened of eviction and paid what was demanded or had to leave their homes. An example of how landlords had exploited the 1957 Rent Act had been included on our initial "Who Owns Hornsey?" leaflets. It concluded: "As a result the man who had owned £100 worth of shares in 1960 owned £660 worth at the end of 1962.

WHAT DID THE SHAREHOLDER DO TO GET THIS EXTRA INCOME & CAPITAL?
NOTHING AT ALL!
WHAT DID THE TENANTS DO TO MAKE IT ALL POSSIBLE?
THEY PAID AND PAID AND PAID"

The meeting agreed on the following objectives for the Association:

1. To bring together all people with housing problems or who are concerned about the housing situation.
2. To prepare information on the situation.
3. To give help and advice to individuals; to give publicity to their problems and to mobilise public opinion in their favour.
4. To press for vastly increased Council building in Hornsey and for the full use of the Council's powers of compulsory purchase and other powers.
5. To work for the Repeal of the 1957 Rent Act, restoration of security of tenure and rent control.
6. To campaign at a local and national level for any measures, which in the opinion of the association when they arise, would be likely to speed up solving the housing crisis.

It was agreed that the Association should be non-party: that is open to anyone who agrees with its aims, regardless of his or her political party; and that the Association is not committed to the policy of any party.

There was a general discussion of the range of problems faced by many of those present. The Medical Officer of Health had estimated that there were 600 families statutorily overcrowded in Hornsey and the 1961 Census had shown more than 6,000 people were living at more than one and a half people per room. Fred Moore described the damp walls and crumbling plaster of those who lived as he did in the rat invested Development Area of St Mary's—hardly any of the houses there have a bath and most have only an outside WC. It was decided to send evidence of these conditions to the Milner-Holland Commission as part of the Association's immediate work.

Another problem was the prices leaseholders were being asked to pay at the end of their leases. Mr T.E. Beckley, an Executive member of the Leaseholders Association, said that he would welcome and cooperate with the new Association in any action it takes on this issue.

Two tenants facing eviction then asked what they could do in their situation.

1. Mr Derek Cane, a bus driver living in Hornsey High Street, said his landlord had obtained a court order to evict him and his wife on 24th April. He had been looking for somewhere else to live since October but 'no-one wanted to know' because he had 2 young children. He had applied to the Council but so far without success.

The meeting agreed to organise a petition to the Council supporting his case for Council housing; 600 signatures were obtained in the next fortnight and the petition was sent to the Council.

2. Mrs Kocher had lived in a controlled tenancy in Birchington Road for 20 years when she took in her daughter and son in law who had nowhere else to go. As a result, her landlord gave her notice to quit on the grounds of subletting.

She was so distraught that she was thinking of emigrating. She was advised that she could challenge the landlord's right to evict her and that we would help her.

A Committee of ten members was set up including Mr F. Moore (Holland Road. N8); as Chair and convenor of meetings; Mr H. Sterne (Northwood Hall

N6) as Vice Chair; Mr E.H. Brown (Rathcoole Avenue N.8); as Treasurer and myself as Adviser.

(N.B.: Because of my involvement I sometimes say "we" or "I" rather than "the Association" in this account.)

The Association would need funds so a membership fee of 2/6 was agreed with a reduction to 6p for those who could not afford more.

News of the formation of the Association appeared on the front page of the Hornsey Journal, so we were quickly off the ground. We were able to set up a deputation to the Hornsey Council on 21 April, and Fred Moore, issued a leaflet inviting anyone with housing problems to come to the Town Hall and support our deputation, while Ed Brown circulated leaflets about our aims and becoming a member.

A Public Meeting of the Association was held on 9 June in Crouch End School to discuss its progress and future direction. Almost 90 people attended, some already members and supporters and others attracted by a leaflet given out at the Annual Hornsey Carnival with the message "Today we have a Carnival, but when will we have good homes at a rent we can afford? The landlords are having a Carnival all year round."

The Chairman, Fred Moore, described the achievements of the Association in its first 2½ months: the well-supported deputation to Hornsey Council urging it to catch up urgently on its programme of Council house building and immediately help families facing eviction; the achievement of publicity drawing attention to the misery caused by housing difficulties; and giving help to individual families—2 notices to quit withdrawn, one postponed, a rent reduced, a WC installed and a number of families sent to the Rent Tribunal etc.

The meeting heard with regret that Hornsey Council had decided not to help Derek Cane despite our petition nor any of the other families facing eviction; a resolution was passed protesting at this decision and asking the Council at its next meeting to reverse it. Our Treasurer Ed Brown gave a report about mobile homes and suggested that the Council had access to land on which they could quickly be erected to house families facing eviction.

There was a general discussion of how we could best step up the work of the Association and what our main focus should be. One member said we needed to get into the national press and spread out into other areas. Another asked how could we stop rents rising and how those already excessively high could be brought down? It was agreed that fear of eviction, high rents, dilapidated areas and lack of Council housing were the main problems.

Rent Control had begun in 1915 to prevent profiteering from the shortage of housing and had been maintained with modifications until the Conservative Government's 1957 Rent Act.

Since then, it had ceased to apply not only to higher priced housing but to any house or flat that became vacant. This meant all new tenants had no security of tenure and could be given notice to quit if they couldn't pay whatever rent the landlord demanded. A group of tenants in Oakfield Hall, a large block of flats had asked the Association if we could negotiate with the landlord on their behalf because as individual tenants, they would not be able to resist whatever he asked when their existing leases expired. Another member said it was terrible that British people should be so scared and frightened of their landlord. The meeting was told that there was a Bill before Parliament to prevent evictions without finding alternative accommodation and a resolution was passed to urge MPs to pass it.

Support for the Association's campaigns and its aims continued to grow, and the number of families we were able to help expanded. Fred Moore sent and received letters about the need to change the law from Harold Wilson, Sir Keith Joseph, Michael Stewart (then Shadow Minister of Housing), Ben Parkin MP and several local Councillors.

A meeting was held at St Peter's Hall, Wightman Road on the 15th July 1964 'How to tackle your housing problems' as part of a drive to collect evidence of hardship for inclusion in its submission to the Milner-Holland Commission, which I was compiling. We did not promise to solve the problems of everyone but spread the message that not all cases were hopeless even within the existing law, but tenants must be persistent and refuse to be bullied into accepting unreasonable demands. We also publicised a Labour Party meeting on Leasehold problems on 10th July with Sir Auther Skeffington. Then in September we held a pre-election meeting in the small Town Hall to hear how the Parliamentary candidates would deal with housing problems. The Labour, Liberal and Communist candidates accepted, Lady Gammons declined but Hugh Rossi attended on her behalf. The meeting was chaired by the Editor of the Hornsey Journal.

As soon as the new Labour Government had been formed our Chairman, Fred Moore wrote to Richard Crossman, the new Minister of Housing, on behalf of the Association wishing him success and appealing to him to stop evictions without delay and make it retrospective so that it could apply to cases which had already been through the courts. He urged that future controlled rents should be much lower than current, market rents which had risen fourfold since 1957 because tenants had signed for fear of eviction—a form of blackmail used to push up rents far beyond any 'reasonable' level. Several hundred distressed tenants have attended the Association's meetings and have endorsed the plea that rents be fixed at a lower level.

We ended 1964 with s fund raising pre-Christmas Social and began 1965 by sending a deputation on 6th January to the Housing Committee of the incoming Haringey Council. Our speakers, Mr Bailey, a Committee member living in Hawthorne Road and Mrs Harrison, then our Secretary, living in Huntington Road, spoke on the reasons why a much-increased programme of Council House building was urgently needed and made the following proposals:

1. The adoption of a target of 750 new homes a year in the Hornsey area.
2. Buy all sites coming on the market where there is a possibility of increasing the density and all other sites suitable for Council building. Prevent any further building of luxury flats as half of those recently built were still unoccupied.
3. Try to reclaim sites already acquired by developers but not yet built upon.
4. Make representations to the Government to (a) immediately set up a Land Commission (b) arrange for low interest loans for Council building (c) speed up Compulsory Purchase arrangements.
5. Survey unused railway land in Hornsey such as that in Uplands Road with a view to using it for housing.
6. Speed up work on the existing development areas.
7. Make long-term plans for future redevelopment.
8. Consider the use of mobile homes as a means of using land temporally idle.
9. Buy all properties lying idle for 6 months.
10. Buy all properties where there is a danger of multi-occupation occurring.

In May 1965, we held a meeting attended by 109 members at which a lawyer explained how the new Rent Act would work. All rents would be controlled and tenants would usually have security of tenure. Local Rent Officers would be appointed and both tenants and landlords could apply to them to fix their rent if they considered their existing rent unfair. Rent Officers would set rents on the basis that there were equal numbers of buyers and sellers (i.e., eliminating the effect of scarcity). If either the tenant or the landlord was not willing to accept the Rent Officer's recommended rent, he or she could appeal to a 'Rent Assessment Committee'.

Those present were unanimous in welcoming the security of tenure provided by the Act but worried about the procedures proposed for fixing rents. There was such a big difference between controlled rents and those fixed since 1957 that it would be difficult for Rent Officers to establish what would be a fair rent were there no scarcity. If Rent Officers were to be free to set rents according to their individual judgement, it would be essential for there to be a fixed ceiling based on rateable value as a check. What was the most alarming feature being proposed was setting up Rent Assessment Committees or tribunals. These would be cumbersome, costly and delay decisions and who would be on them? Our experience of the existing tribunals dealing with furnished tenancies had undermined our faith in their impartiality and consistency. Would tenants be given legal aid when appearing before them? So, we sent a long memorandum to Mr Crossman explaining our doubts based on our experience, asking him set a fixed ceiling for rents and above all not to rely on tribunals. We also sent a deputation to the House of Commons to Norman Atkinson. MP for Tottenham. We were in touch with other tenants' associations who were also lobbying Mr Crossman to improve his Rent Act, but it came into effect without any change.

A General Meeting was held on 14th July 1965 to review the work of the Association since its formation and its future aims and activities. Since the election of a Labour Government and the incorporation of Hornsey into a Labour controlled Borough of Haringey the prospects for tackling the housing crisis had seemed brighter but pressure from those in housing need must continue—the landlords would certainly continue to state their case! The Association had already made clear its concerns to the Government about the new Rent Act.

Throughout the period since the Association was formed, we had given advice to individuals in trouble and had dealt with over 50 pleas for help. In many, though by no means all of them, we were able to help mitigate the problems.

This experience had given us a clear picture of the extent of difficulties being suffered and enabled us to draw public attention to them. My report as Advisory Secretary on the range of problems we had come across was submitted to this meeting. It showed that intimidation to force tenants out so properties could be sold (popularly known as 'Rachmanism') was taking place in Hornsey. One tactic was refusing to do urgent repairs and the saddest case we came across was the death of a tenant because of the landlord's long-term refusal to mend a gas Ascot, a death—wrongly in our view-recorded as 'an accident'.

Openly aggressive tactics were also used. One landlord used his key to go into a flat at all hours, even when the female tenant was in bed and shouted at her and vomited over her furniture. We only found out about this case after she had moved out and was living in a single room. There were two cases where landlords used aggressive actions but we were able to help. One nailed the landing window open in mid-winter and when that failed used a solicitor to try to get a court order to evict the tenant on the grounds that she had moved from downstairs to upstairs and was no longer a controlled tenant. With our help and that of local friends, she was able to prove that the move took place just before the 1957 Rent Act became effective so the landlord's case was dismissed. Another case involved an elderly widow in a basement flat. The landlord intimated her by standing and watching her every move and threatening her with violence should she come out, She became ill and the landlord tried to get a court order to evict her, but with our help his case was dismissed and the landlord was ordered to stop harassing her.

There was an even more blatant 'Rachman' type case after my Report was written. A new landlord of a house in Nelson Road began visiting the house, banging on the doors at night and verbally abusing the tenants because they refused to move out. Eventually he took matters into his own hands and early one Saturday morning came with a gang of thugs and threw them and all their furniture out into the road and padlocked the door. I was contacted but didn't know what could be done until Monday morning when the Council Office opened and we could get help to get them reinstated. But in the meantime, what could be done—where could they go? I was at a loss to know what to do.

So, I took legal advice, as I always had done since I took on the role of advisor to the Association, from Sigmund ('Siggy') Seifert, one of Britain's leading experts in Housing Law, who lived in Hornsey. He and his family were close friends and supported the Association. He encouraged me to contact him any time with queries and I had frequently done so, but his advice that day took me aback. He thought for a while then said "Do you have a strong screw driver? You should get the padlocks off the door and reinstall the tenants." So that's what we did. We told the tenants to report what had happened to the Council on Monday morning.

Returning to the Report: the large Company landlords had already doubled and trebled and even quadrupled the rents of the decontrolled properties they owned before the Association was formed and the only course available to us in many cases was publicising the extent of their profiteering. However, there were cases where we were able to intervene to prevent evictions or new rent increases.

One of our first partial successes was in Coleridge Road where a house was rented for £6 a week to a tenant who illegally sublet it for £10 to a family with 7 children, who were living in poverty because of the high rent. The London, City and Westcliffe Company served notice on the tenant for sub-letting but at first refused to recognise the existence of the sub-tenants, who they said were trespassers. So, I wrote to the Assistant Managing Director of the Company, a Mr Landy, at this personal address outlining the whole story and urging him as a humane supporter of charities to offer the family with 7 children the tenancy. This was agreed, but not at the rent being receiving from the absentee tenant (i.e., £6). Instead, £10 a week was demanded. Eventually, I was able to negotiate £8 a week—still unfairly high but the family were able to remain.

There was a sequel to this story 18 months later when the tenant applied to the Rent officer for a fair rent and it was set at £5.15 a week. But London City and Westcliffe appealed to the Rent Assessment Committee; I represented him but could not prevent the rent being raised to £6.15. What was most unfair was that he was ordered to pay £26 to cover the period between the Rent Officer's rent and that of the Rent Assessment Committee. Not surprisingly, the Committee wouldn't allow me to discuss the landlord's profits.

In some cases, we were unable to get landlords to negotiate with the Association. This was the case with the property company which owned the block of flats known as Oakfield Court. They rebuffed us and said that they did not recognise us as representing the tenants whose leases were about to fall in. They then offered 7-year leases to such tenants at higher rents then their already decontrolled rents. Several of the tenants then told us they felt they had no choice but to sign and withdrew their request to us to represent them. All we could do was hope that our representations had led to the landlords moderating their excessive demands.

Attempts to get controlled tenants to move out either because the landlord wanted to raise the rent or sell or sub-divide the property was linked to refusals to do urgent repairs. One landlord tried to evict a tenant who had lived in a house for 23 years but who complained to the Council because the landlord didn't mend a leaking roof for 3 months. The Council mended the roof but the landlord then tried to get the tenants evicted on the grounds that they were 'a nuisance'. She refused to accept their rent for 18 months but eventually agreed to talk to us. She said she didn't want more rent but did want a tenant who would look after the place and not keep demanding that she do repairs. The Council agreed to issue a Purchase Order to break the deadlock.

Furnished tenancies were not controlled but tenants could apply to Rent Tribunals if they thought their rent unfair. The Association urged them to do so but the Tribunals only had power to provide 3 months security and tenants were frightened to apply because landlords might evict them afterwards. One case that received a lot of publicity involved the house next door to where Max and I lived. It had been requisitioned during the War but twenty years later was multi-occupied and in poor condition. I became concerned because a small boy living there was stopping passers-by and begging, saying he was hungry. I considered reporting this to the Council's child protection service but first talked to the tenants.

There were four families all with children occupying one main room each, plus partitioned off 'bathrooms' (with sinks not baths) and kitchens; there were also two bachelors occupying bedsits, and one other room with a bath in a cupboard let unfurnished but really not fit for use, All the tenants were paying incredibly high rents: each had two rent books one for 'unfurnished rooms' and one for hire of furniture. As none of them had controlled tenancies I advised them to apply to the Furnished Tenants Rent Tribunal as a group. An inspection of the property by the Council confirmed it to be in very poor condition and dangerously overcrowded. When the Tribunal met, they were shocked at the condition of the house and the rents being charged and immediately reduced all the rents by half. The Council rehoused the families soon afterwards; the house was sold for redevelopment and became owner occupied.

It was agreed the Association would continue giving advice and helping tenants as best we could while the Rent Act provisions were being set up. our Secretary, Mr Goodwin of Rectory Gardens, reported that 120 people had joined the Association, although many more supporters have signed our petitions and voted for resolutions at meetings. Thanks were given to Fred Moore who had recently resigned as Chairman because of ill health: it was put on record that much of the success of the Association in its early days was due to his enthusiasm and hard work. New members had been co-opted to the Committee during the year, including Michael Seifert, son of Siggy Seifert and a budding lawyer. He was later to become distinguished for his unstinting work supporting trade unions, especially the Miners, so our Association was the first of the many causes he helped. (See The Guardian obituary 6 August 2017).

After our May meeting there was a period of calm and relief at the restoration of security of tenure no more threats of eviction without cause! Meanwhile we waited for the new Rent Officers to be appointed and trained and to see how the new system would work. We recognised that money values had changed since most controlled rents had been set and rents would probably be raised accordingly even though the landlords had made no new investment in their properties and in many cases refused to maintain them in any way despite the availability of grants to help with the costs. So, what would be the extent of the rises recommended by the Rent Officers? Scarcity of housing and fear of eviction had enabled landlords to set all non-controlled rents at what could only be described as profiteering levels—would the Rent Officers bring them down to remaining controlled rents, so similar houses at the same rateable value but currently at vastly different rents would be the same in future? There was nothing more we could do but wait and see.

By early 1966, it was difficult to analyse the pattern Rent Officers were following because it depended on whether it was tenants or landlords who were asking for their help and who was not asking because, like the Oakfield Court tenants, they had just signed new leases and felt bound by them. On the whole, Rent Officers seemed to be supporting tenants in development areas living in dreadful slums but otherwise there was not a clear pattern.

Rent Assessment Committee cases began to be heard. The first reaction we received was from a letter sent to Hugh Rossi and copied to us describing how the couple who was applying for a rent reduction had felt confused and overwhelmed by the formality of the proceedings and by the questioning of the lawyers, surveyors and estate agents serving on the panel or giving support to the landlord, who was asking for a higher rent than that fixed by the Rent Officer. They felt no-one wanted to listen to their case, which they lost.

Soon afterwards, an elderly retired couple who had lived for a long time in South Close, Highgate, asked if I would represent Mrs Norton at a Rent Assessment Committee. I did so at a Hearing that lasted six hours and confirmed all my fears about the use of Tribunals. The case was described in detail in the local press. The key point from our side was that the flat was damp and their bedroom was often unusable and Mrs Norton had to wear a mackintosh in the kitchen when cooking because there was so much condensation and her ceiling was black. In 1939 the rent was fixed at £67, which in 1960s money was £236, but in 1939 the flat was new and in good condition whereas now it was hardly habitable and the landlord had made no attempt to deal with the damp so at least a quarter of the flat was unusable. In the circumstances unless repairs were carried out, we thought £165 was a fair rent.

The Landlord wanted a rent of £348 and the Rent Officer had fixed the rent at £307. Two expert witnesses were called by the landlord, one—presumably an estate agent—said that the landlord could easily find tenants willing to pay a rent of £400. The other said he had inspected the flat and if the tenants had ventilated and heated the rooms properly the walls wouldn't be damp and if Mrs Norton washed her kitchen ceiling regularly it wouldn't be black. I can't remember if I asked him how often he washed his own kitchen ceiling, but I hope I did! The outcome was that the Tribunal confirmed the Rent Officer's rent but I wondered what would have happened if Mrs Norton had had to face the Tribunal alone. The only good aspect of this case was that Mr and Mrs Norton were able to qualify for sheltered housing fairly soon afterwards.

My scepticism about the Rent Assessment Committees was soon confirmed as more cases were reported, including the Coleridge Road case described above which I defended to no avail. Mr Rossi, the Conservative MP for Hornsey, described the Committees as a fraud. My fellow members of the Association were shocked and disappointed at the weight being given to so called 'professional witnesses'—i.e., estate agent and surveyors, gentlemen with the expertise of street traders but not that of professional economists with the competence to analyse the effect of scarcity on rent levels—should that be possible!

Disillusion and concern about how the new Rent Act was failing to bring rent levels down and becoming the tool of landlords spread widely and led to a debate in Parliament in May 1966, led by Frank Allaun MP. A Labour Government, with the stated aim of creating a system fair to tenants and landlords alike, had let loose a landlords' bonanza!

In 1967, the Government passed a Leasehold Enfranchisement Act to deal with the unique English system which gave freeholders the right to take possession when long leases ran out, usually after 100 years, of houses built or owned by others on land the ground landlords owned. This was a critical issue in Hornsey with its large number of Victorian houses.

The Act gave leaseholders the right either to buy the freehold of the house they occupied or to buy an extension of the lease. The price was to be based on half of the change in value of the dwelling before and after the extension as judged by an arbiter. Most ground rents on ancient properties were very low but the whole system was a throwback to feudalism. Land was a natural asset not something resulting from capitalist investment and after 1945 the benefit of a change of land use was very highly taxed in recognition of this. Twenty years later, many thought there was no justification for the proposal to compensate ground landlords for losing the right to take over dwellings that others had paid to build or buy, maintain and occupy. As with the Rent Act instead of a fixed price an assessment panel was tasked with deciding how much ought to be paid.

The removal of the threat to evict people out of their homes without choice was welcomed, but having to pay to buy or extend their lease was seen as unjustified—what had the landlords done to deserve compensation? Even though the amounts were relatively low in the years following the passing of the Act some leaseholders had difficulties. But as the years went by and house prices rose and rose, the compensation given to freeholders seemed more and more unearned and unjustified.

Max and I were a case in point: in 1961 we bought our maisonette on a 99-year lease but were too short of money to buy the freehold of the whole house which was offered to us for £350. The ground rent was a negligible £12 a year and we thought a tenancy for 99 years would more than see us through. About 10 years later we lost contact with our freeholder—the original one had probably died. All attempts to pay our annual ground rent were returned as 'unknown'. It didn't make any practical difference, we and the neighbours above us did our own repairs and maintenance according to our two leases. Almost 40 years later, we and our then neighbours realised that being a leaseholder was a handicap should we want to move, so we began a search to find out who was our current freeholder. Eventually we were given a name and applied to buy the freehold jointly in 1997. The price was fixed by the appropriate body as £89,000—yes, £89,000! For doing absolutely nothing since 1961! This is the unintended legacy of Harold Wilson's Act to enfranchise leaseholders.

The landlords' case for increasing rents had always been heavily reliant on the argument that unless providing properties to rent was made worthwhile, no new building to rent would be done. Despite the dramatic rise in rents and profit in the years after the 1957 Rent Act there were large increases in dividends but hardly any investment by the private sector in building new homes that working class tenants court afford. Ending the housing crisis would depend on Council House building, as it had done since the promise of 'Homes fit for Heroes' in 1918.

The Hornsey Housing Campaign Association had always assumed this, never more so than faced with the disappointing outcome of the Rent Act. Our members looked to the new Haringey Council to provide the impetus for new building that had been lacking by Hornsey Council but were concerned at their proposals to increase Council Rents in July 1967. The Council agreed to meet a deputation from the Haringey Federation of Tenants and Residents Association of which our Hornsey Association was a part. The speakers were Mr P.F. Dennett of the Noel Park Council Tenants Association and myself. Our case was that the Council's own survey had shown that when either household income or the income of the Head of the household were taken into account, Council tenants were among the poorer section of the community.

An increase was an increase even if the tenant was not paying the full rent because of a rebate. For many Council Tenants, higher rents would mean less food.

The Council responded very positively to the deputation and sought our views on what we would regard as a fair structure. They promised to take our views into consideration when considering the future rent structure at their next meeting in September. The Hornsey Journal gave a long and detailed report of our deputation under the heading 'COUNCIL'S **POOR** TENANTS', which gave encouragement to our members. However, the Conservative Party gained control of Haringey Council at the 1968 Council Elections. Nevertheless, the local Labour Party did a serious study of Housing in Haringey in 1970 which tackled the question of rent levels and rebates on Council Housing for the future when they regained control.

The main problem about Council housing was the rising cost of land, house construction and interest rates. New Council building had slowed down when the cost of borrowing from the public Works Loan Board began to rise after the end of 1951 and private loan rates rose and became volatile, making planning difficult. By 1967, programmes of Council building were faltering so the Labour Government passed a Housing Subsidies Act to lower interest costs for local authorities and encourage Council Building. Many Councils, however, still ended with deficits on their housing accounts.

The rising costs of building new homes motivated the Government In 1969 to pass a new Housing Act providing for Government aid to Councils to set up Improvement areas to facilitate slum clearance and encourage the improvement of existing old properties to bring them up to modern standards, which would cost less than building new homes for all those needing housing. This would involve grants to existing landlords and rent increases when work was completed. To ease the cost on Councils, there was also a drive to encourage the setting up of Housing Associations.

The 1969 Act moved forward slum clearance and renovation of some old houses but was no substitute for an enlarged programme of new Council house building and it perpetuated the enrichment of the owners of old houses used for renting at the cost of tenants.

The Labour Party's 1956 Policy document 'Homes for the Future' had recognised that private landlordism had failed, led to exploitation and the growth of slums and must be replaced by Council Housing along with building new houses for owner occupation by those who were able to afford them. It did not include a programme of new private building for rent because landlords were not likely to invest in building new housing for working class tenants because the cost of land and building to a set standard was greater than the limited amounts that such tenants could afford to pay as rent. There was also the view that it is morally wrong for family homes to be a target for long term profit making or their upkeep to be dependent on the decisions of others. Had the Labour Party been in power in 1956, the logic of its conclusion that private landlordism had failed should surely have been to take over unfit properties where the costs of the original investment had long ago been met.

The Conservative 1957 Rent Act had opened the door to big increases in the profits and share value of the owners of existing properties, however old and decrepit.

This trend was modified but not halted by the 1965 Rent Act. The landlords' lobbyists claimed that allowing rents to rise would stimulate new private investment in working class housing but the Wilson Government was misguided to think, as it apparently did, that such investment would happen and that it would move forward progress in overcoming the shortage of decent homes that working class tenants could afford. A new way forward was thought to be not for profit Housing Associations but only a programme of state subsidy could have provided the homes needed. That was true then and remains true today.

Not one of the members of our Association or other working-class residents of the area would have been living in substandard housing had they had any choice, but there was an overwhelming shortage of fit-to-live-in accommodation to rent. For five years, the members of the Hornsey Housing Campaign Association had tirelessly pursued the objectives set out at our inaugural meeting and campaigned along with other tenants' associations against exploitation by landlords and for faster Council building. But their evidence and petitions had not been heeded. The protection offered by old controlled rents against landlord profiteering from scarcity had been lost. The incoming Conservative Government were even less likely to take account of working-class needs. So, by 1970 there was nothing more our Association could do and it withered away. It had been the most united, fact centred and dispute free political organisation I had ever been part of or would ever be again.

Max: Sanctions—The Union's First Steps in Action

The momentum towards action had been accelerating for some time. The NUT Conference in 1967 put forward a hefty salary claim, for some £120 million. The Government offered £24.5 million. The Executive rejected this (as they saw it) paltry offer, and prepared plans for a number of sanctions, which were approved in principle by a Special Conference in June. The Government refused to budge and referred the pay dispute, under the terms of the Remuneration of Teachers Act of 1965, to arbitration whose decisions would become statutorily binding. Max tells the whole story.

"This would normally have been the end of the matter, as indeed the Right on the Executive thought it was. We had made noises; they had failed and that was that. Business as usual. But no! Not this time! A majority of the Executive, impressed by the spirit of the Special Conference and subsequent local expressions of determined militancy, decided to proceed with the preparation of the sanctions while awaiting the arbitration result. Some of us voted for this in the hope of influencing the arbitrators, or at least the Chairman of the Panel who was a government appointee, a line which made sense. Others felt that a safety valve was necessary to let off steam."

"The sanctions selected from the conference package were a refusal to carry out lunchtime supervision of pupils and a warning to LEAs that action would follow if any more unqualified teachers were appointed. Preparations for the actions took place by ballots in selected areas (my area of Brent was one) to secure the necessary majority, now of two-thirds of the membership, not two-thirds of those voting, which would have been a much easier exercise. Some so-called 'leftists' (we were to witness the beginnings of the Trotskyist Rank and File movement, the operation of a wind machine) sneered at these 'half measures'. It was 'all out' or nothing for these parlour revolutionaries. I had never believed in bandying about the word 'strike'—it was too serious a matter for teachers, as indeed for any workers. But the nearest the 'Crank and Guile' mob ever got to a worker was in a bar, as I once told Conference to its great amusement. To my mind we were proposing industrial action 'in teacher terms', something the LEAs and Government clearly understood and feared, especially because of our mainly successful ballots."

"This was remarkable enough during an arbitration process, but what followed was, I believe, unprecedented in the history of British industrial relations. In the middle of the summer holidays, the arbitration tribunal gave its verdict and, as a matter of routine, the Executive's Action Committee met to consider it—the full Executive was on holiday. Lo and behold, the Action Committee, the only Executive Committee vested with such plenary powers, expressed strong dissatisfaction with the award and decided to proceed with the programme of sanctions."

"When the Executive met shortly after it was impossible to overturn the publicly-announced decision which was, therefore, confirmed; the union had succeeded in making history. For here was the respectable NUT not only defying the Government in industrial action but doing so after a statutory settlement had been reached. And the action being taken involved civil disobedience, as we were obliged by law to supervise school meals."

"Within the Executive, it became clear that the decision of the Action Committee was unexpected by and not to the liking of the General Secretary, Sir Ronald Gould, and his closest supporters. He had, in fact, made a gross miscalculation through the besetting sin of those in power, over-confidence and complacency. So convinced was he that the whole operation would never happen because of the inevitable processes of arbitration and its statutory implementation, that he had not bothered to return from Vancouver, though the Conference of the WCOTP which he had been attending was over, for that fateful meeting of the Action Committee. Also, he had not counted on the character and temperament of the President, Denis Gilbert, by no means a 'left' but a very stubborn and dogged man, highly principled and impeccably honest, who was very conscious of his power should he decide to use it and was disgusted with the arbitration result."

"So, the union found itself, in circumstances no-one would have forecast as possible, in a campaign of civil disobedience to overturn an arbitration award on pay sanctified by statute, and to secure the end of compulsory lunch-time duties and the ending of the appointment of unqualified teachers, a pretty tall order for an organisation like ours quite inexperienced in the ways of industrial action. It required a very consciously determined decision, for example of my own members in Brent, to defy both the Government and a friendly local authority in a manner which could lead to retaliation and possibly dismissal."

Though the action proceeded successfully throughout the country in the selected areas and plans were made to extend it, Executive discussions began with both LEAs and the DES to secure a settlement. Max was highly suspicious of these moves, because he wanted a substantial salary settlement and was concerned that the original pay objective of the action was being played down almost into oblivion by official statements and the focus of attention on subsidiary objectives—school meals duties and unqualified appointments—important as these were.

The talks led to the setting up of a Working Party to find an acceptable formula to remove obligatory meals duties and end unqualified appointments. To Max's disgust, a majority of the Executive voted to call the action off subject to satisfactory local negotiations on these issues. Most of his Executive colleagues had no stomach for the fight and were quite resigned to forgetting the salary issue. But even the issue of school meals was not easily settled because neither the Government nor the LEAs, led by Sir William Alexander, wanted to remove the statutory school meals duties from the 1944 Act without some counter-measure which would ensure teachers continuing to perform these duties voluntarily, so avoiding the considerable extra expenditure involved in employing ancillary staff to cover the service.

So, a compromise was evolved whereby the offending sentences of the 1944 Act would be repealed (so ending any statutory obligation on teachers to supervise school meals) and the LEAs would agree to provide ancillary workers on a sliding scale based on the numbers taking meals in primary and secondary schools, but a scale which would not provide full coverage. The gap would be filled by a formula which stated that teachers would regard it as part of their 'professional responsibility' to support the headteacher in carrying out his/her duty to look after the meals service. Not surprisingly, this formula became a major bone of contention not only between teachers and LEAs but between teachers and many Heads and their organisations. Its history is, therefore, of some interest.

Sanctions had been called off on the understanding that meals duties would be ended for ever and no reservations were mentioned. Max and his friends were not surprised, however, when the Report appeared early in 1968 and contained the 'formula' below:

"The Headteacher must retain overall responsibility for the conduct of the school meal, just as he does for all that takes place in and about the school and there is a professional responsibility on the teaching staff as a whole to support the headteacher in fulfilling these responsibilities. It is also important to the teacher, whether head or assistant, that he should be able to enjoy a proper and satisfactory break in which he can relax and rest and, if he wishes, leave the school premises."

This formula aroused the wrath of many of Max's NUT colleagues: it was too blatant a retreat—after a successful operation. And it was more than some of them, right-wing Heads that they were, seemed prepared to stomach. They argued that a law from which a statutory obligation had been removed but which was accompanied by a formula, a masterpiece of civil service prevarication, which said it was the professional responsibility of teachers to assist the Head in an opposite sense to the amended law, would place both Heads and staffs in an ambiguous, invidious and probably impossible position. Besides, the Heads argued, they too wanted to be rid of the duties as it affected their responsibilities, except in the most general way—responsibility for the smooth running of the schools. Meeting on the eve of the Executive, therefore, there was a surge of revolt and the Education Committee threw out the offending passages of the Report to the utter consternation of Sir Ronald and his allies who had committed themselves to its acceptance. Meal's duties were to go—full stop!'

Sir Ronald knew the score and was fully aware of the almost inevitable consequences of no agreement—i.e., the resumption of action—so for him the Committee's decision was a disaster. So 'someone' got to work that Friday night and, lo and behold, when the Executive met next morning, they were presented, by the most vociferous Executive opponents of the formula on the previous evening, with a motion completely changing the Committee's decision! Clearly there had been unprecedented lobbying and arm-twisting. The renegades carried the day and the agreement was finally carried with a minority of only four—Jack Jones, Max and two others. Max commented:

"My other left colleagues had collapsed under pressures whose content I could only conjecture. It was a traumatic decision. It taught me a lot about the realities of people and politics and the difficulties in the way of building the fighting union leadership I had set my heart on. Also, of course, we were saddled with an unworkable formula which could only cause endless trouble in the future. I was convinced and still am that, by standing firm, we would have won, so terrified were the LEAs and DES at that time of a resumption of action."

This was not the end of the story. The formula had to be sold to teachers. The first step was Conference approval when the agreement came up for ratification. There an extraordinary situation occurred as recounted by Max:

"So terrified were the Establishment of any effective opposition to the agreement that they prevented me from speaking by fiddling the speakers' cards. I use this word deliberately.

My card was mysteriously shuffled down the pack which had been handed to the platform by the absolutely honest clerks in order of receipt, as was the conference practice, so that speakers behind me in the queue at the speakers' cards desk were called and my card was never reached because of the closure of the debate.

This was such a blatant fiddle that I managed to force an Executive enquiry into how it had happened. There could be no denial because, behind me in the queue was the Secretary of the powerful Birmingham Association, Gordon Green, later President of the Union, who had been called and who had told John England, his right-wing Executive member, how disgusted he was and that he was prepared to swear to the facts. But the Enquiry came to nothing and the matter was dropped after a nasty suggestion by a senior official that we were casting doubt on the integrity of the clerks, who I knew were absolutely straight. What was, and still is, astonishing to me was the sensitivity of the Establishment that a speech by me would or could scupper the Agreement. How flattering to inspire such terror! Incidentally, there was one good by-product of this unsavoury episode. Shortly after, we introduced a numbered cards system which stopped card shuffling.

So, game and set went to the Establishment even though the Wimbledon Rules had not been observed. But they had not won the match, because the agreement had to be presented to Conference as the ending of lunch-time duties and cold water poured on us doubting Thomases for 'misrepresenting' its obvious contradictions. The 'morning after', therefore, had to be faced—the actual operation of the Agreement on the ground, in the schools, where teachers would insist on what they had been told it meant. A committee was therefore set up by the Executive to prepare an 'explanation' of the text—a Commentary, so to speak, on the Talmud. I could not be kept off it.

We sat for a long time under the tutelage of the craftiest official the union had produced in living memory, the late Bernard Mawby. Bernard was a sound Establishment man who had got on to the Executive in the cold war wave and later preferred a union job and he was, of course, all for the Agreement. There was no need to explain to Bernard how many beans made five. He and I (absolute opposites in outlook in everything you could care to mention) almost at once came to an understanding that there was no alternative to presenting the Agreement as meaning an end to all lunch-time duties. That had to be. Whatever Executive spokesmen had said to the contrary to the management was water under the bridge. There was no possibility of resolving the contradictions. And that suited me fine.

So, having decided (Bernard's suggestion) that we prepare our commentary in the form of a Question-and-Answer document raising and dealing with every possible issue that could arise, we proceeded to do so in a way which, in practice, gave us all we wanted. And no-one dared amend it! For did it not have cachet of the holy St Bernard? And was not St Bernard the patron saint of Executive trouble-shooters? When the LEAs took exception to certain statements in it the Working Party was reconvened in July. But the union could not be moved—the document had to be taken as a whole and the LEAs had to withdraw their objections! It is this document which became the Bible of the union's attitude—on my study wall in school it grew yellow with age but it was never challenged. One just referred to it as the revealed truth. Any attempt to alter it by conceding that any teacher had any professional obligation to do any lunch-time duty was dismissed as heresy. We had the last laugh—it was match to us."

"One final remark. Writing in the Times Educational Supplement in January 1968, I let my hyperbole flow on the consequences of our 1967 action. We had, I said, smashed 'the Shavian image of the teacher as someone who *can't do.*' The profession, I said, 'during the Sanctions campaign gained a new status, a new confidence in itself. Teachers walked 10 feet tall...' That expressed the mood of the time—and the trend!"

The Sanctions Campaign was followed by another step forward for the NUT-affiliation to the TUC. Joining the TUC had for a long time been one of the objectives of the Left within the NUT but its achievement seemed distant. Ideas of political neutrality still had a grip on many members and the TUC appeared inseparable from the Labour Party. Also, let's face it, many looked askance at joining in alliance with the horny handed sons of toil. Were we not a profession?

Joining thus raised fundamental issues. It would mean a more 'industrial' and 'political' approach to many of our concerns and however you looked at it, it brought a union with masses of Tory members closer to the Labour Party. What changed the feeling down below more than anything were the 1967 and 1969–70 actions, climacteric events in our history.

When it became clear that the issue could not be burked, a very reluctant Executive decided to organise a referendum on affiliation in the summer of 1968. What motivated the opponents of the TUC was their confidence that a referendum would bring out the 'silent majority' against affiliation and this would lay the spectre to rest for some time. I was one of the minorities who opposed their strategy. We thought a referendum was premature and felt that we would not secure affiliation till the Executive was itself in favour and made a positive recommendation to conference. The right wing presented themselves as devoted democrats and the referendum was held and lost.

But the expected negative result was far from being the end of the affair. Opinion in the Executive began to change in 1969; some opposed to affiliation on political grounds, had been won over by what seemed to them at first to be Michael Stewart's (one of our sponsored MPs) outrageous refusal as Secretary of State at the DEA to meet us on salaries on the grounds that he negotiated on pay only with the TUC! They had foolishly expected special treatment, while Stewart, always a stickler for the conventions, was keeping to the rules of the political game. Unwittingly, he was moving the union in the direction of the TUC.

We finally secured an Executive majority for a positive recommendation to Conference in 1970. This had been hard-fought reflected the militant transformation which was going on among our members in the strike campaign, and helped on by the very shrewd cooperation of Vic Feather, the TUC General Secretary, who, invited to explain the TUC set-up, behaved with exemplary tact. He gave us all the reassurances we needed against being involved in TUC initiatives with the Labour Party which would have compromised our non-party political position. At Conference the victory was quite substantial and calls for a referendum were just as substantially rejected. So, we were all set to join at the September Congress. It was a historic decision for the whole profession. The union's remarkable strike campaign lent spice to our adherence for it dispelled any illusions that the teachers were a namby-pamby lot.

Our delegation to our first Congress in Brighton was quite excited, especially those members who had opposed affiliation. The sensible ones among them appreciated it would be very difficult to undo.

To be fair to the Executive right wing, I do not recall any efforts in that direction in the years that followed (apart from a few sour remarks), although there was always a hard-line Tory element among the membership who had such yearnings. The left also appreciated that we had to be particularly careful about the TUC's political activities.

At this first Congress, we began laying down the guidelines for participation which have been followed ever since though with a tendency towards greater flexibility of interpretation in recent years. These were that we would vote only on issues that were within the aims and objects of the union and would abstain on all others. Not only the obviously political ones which were debated at Congress. Where there was doubt, we normally had Executive guidance at a meeting held prior to the Congress. This worked well and served to allay the fears of the anti-TUC brigade.

Max: From Strike Leader to President of the NUT

The sanctions campaign was the end of the long era of teachers seeking to gain acceptance as professionals by relying on collaboration with the employers. 'Genteel Poverty' had failed: recognition that teaching required professional skills, parallel with those in the older, generally recognised professions, could not be achieved while their salaries were so much lower not only than other professionals, but also than many other groups of workers. Max and his NUT colleagues were convinced that raising the status of teachers depended on their receiving a proper level of remuneration and that they would need to exert whatever force was necessary until that was achieved.

There were two main problems. First, salary negotiations would be taking place against a difficult economic background because annual inflation rates steadily mounted in the later 1960s and rose to unprecedented heights in the 1970s. Secondly, there was a false perception among many politicians and civil servants that no particular skill was required to teach children and there was widespread ignorance among them of the advances in the study of child psychology and of how the development of children's intelligence from the very youngest age was affected by the quality of the stimulus they received.

Ending the employment of unqualified staff had been one of the objectives of the Sanctions Campaign and a working party had been established to study the issue. A fair number of unqualified personnel, a relic of the bad old days of elementary education, were still teaching in schools as well as the untrained teachers, very common in the Grammar Schools, who had qualified status as graduates. Max regarded untrained graduates as undermining the professional status of teaching just as much as unqualified staff. If I was present when he was speaking on the subject, he would look at me with a smile as he said, "We need to close all loopholes whereby people can be appointed to teach whose only qualification, is that they are warm and breathing."

This was a reference to my one experience of venturing into a classroom. A year or two earlier during a flu epidemic, I had responded to a local appeal for anyone qualified to teach (i.e., including untrained graduates like me) to replace the large number of teachers off sick. I lasted three days and caused havoc. It was a junior school and I was replacing an art teacher. On day 1, innocently, I asked the class what they usually did. "Clay, Miss" they replied, so I told them to get out the materials. Soon there was clay everywhere—on the desks, on the floor, over the children. So, no more clay. The next class said they were learning to do action painting—this wasn't much better, paint everywhere. The School Keeper threatened to resign over the state of the floor (clay footprints had spread from the classroom over the whole school), and some parents complained about the state of their children's clothing. The beleaguered Head suggested I teach them history instead of Art, so on Day 2, I did my best to keep them interested with snippets from the past. On Day 3 I was asked to teach Music—great, I gave each class a choice of gramophone records and each class chose the theme music from the film Exodus. As music was held in the central hall, all the classrooms around the hall heard Exodus all day long and some of the staff were not amused. At the end of the day, the Head told me that the teacher I was replacing was coming back next day—I don't know which of us was most relieved!

So, I totally agreed with Max that without professional training, graduates were inadequate as teachers.

The Working Party Report provided for the immediate cessation of the appointment of 'occasional' teachers who, without regard to proper qualifications or training, had been infiltrated into the profession. It also laid down that 'temporary' teachers, another category whose employment had been abused, should be restricted to qualified personnel awaiting admission to training or to HE and intending to prepare for teaching and they should be supernumerary to establishment, i.e., be 'extras' within the school and for not more than two years. But it allowed the continued appointment as 'instructors', of persons without teacher training for tuition in a number of fields, e.g., musical instruments, sports or games, and certain technical or commercial subjects. Max opposed the inclusion of this latter category owing to its possible wide interpretation and suggested a more limited formula. He thought a stronger line on the issue of instructors could have forced the pace in the training of technical teachers, a category of chronic shortage. He said, "We lost a golden opportunity to begin dealing seriously with problems that still plague the secondary schools. But my main point was that we could not hope for the salary levels we were demanding while admitting that certain teaching jobs could be done without training."

It was not long before salary feeling exploded again. When the majority of the Executive, in February 1969, recommended ratification of an agreement which was to operate from April 1969 to April 1971, Max was part of a very large minority who spoke in opposition at the Special Salaries Conference which followed. The 'increase' awarded actually left teachers worse off, due to inflation, than they had been in 1967. Max pointed out that a Labour Government, operating through its Burnham representatives, was imposing a draconian limitation on teachers' salary increases to 3½% per annum for two years ahead, but allowing other public servants (e.g., airline pilots), very large increases through pure expediency, to avoid embarrassing trouble—'a typical Wilsonian pragmatic approach'. Why pick on us? Became a very potent question among teachers and Max had a clear answer: "They thought we had no teeth and had just shown it by our February acceptance."

Many teachers were suffering genuine hardship because of low pay. Meeting in the neighbouring pub after the February Conference, Max and a few like-minded colleagues pondered their future strategy amidst a noisy and largely discontented crowd of delegates. They came up with what seemed the only viable answer—as it was not possible to break the agreement just passed, they should ask for an 'interim' increase, to try to make good the loss due to the Government's discrimination against teachers. Let Max continue the story:

"At the Easter Conference all went according to plan. We won. The decision was made to go for an interim increase which would almost certainly be backed up by industrial action. The Executive 'majority' was thoroughly trounced both in the debate and the vote. Conference, i.e., vox populi, had turned round since February! In less than two months the minority had become the majority. It was we who had correctly interpreted the mood in the schools and adopted the correct strategy to reflect it."

The Establishment showed up as almost apoplectic blimps, lashing themselves into a fury of hyperbolic vituperation, to the point of incoherent idiocy.

Not least in their fury were our own leaders, including Sir Ronald, in whose opinion the Conference decision was 'a catastrophe.' And Ted Short, the Secretary of State, who was present as a visitor, said "to demand an interim increase during the currency of an agreement was sending the union down a precipice," He was echoed by Bill Alexander, the employers' leader, who pronounced our action as 'disastrous for the future of the education service' and said 'it would end the partnership between Government, LEAs and teachers'. And he added for good measure, that the teachers would not be given one penny, a threat he was bitterly to regret—and not allowed to forget.

There was still much to be done before business started in earnest. First of all, the claim had to be formulated and, in this task, we decided to discuss matters with the NAS to spread support as widely as possible. I was one of the small negotiating groups appointed by the Executive to handle this—they could not afford to keep me out after the ignominy of their Conference defeat. In these talks, it was astonishing that the NAS argued for a sum far smaller than the union was modestly wanting. We finally agreed on £135, a sum which just brought us back to the 1967 real salaries level.

That summer term saw mounting union pressure. London teachers under Sam Fisher's leadership, with Executive approval, organised a magnificent Albert Hall demonstration on a Friday afternoon and, at the beginning of the autumn term, rallies were held all over the country. Feeling ran high as the management stalled and delayed the meeting of Burnham—the fools were playing with a fire laid, they thought, but which would never be set alight! Our publicity, a build-up to the presentation of the claim in October, was magnificent. I was responsible for highlighting the fact that a teacher started on £13 a week, a figure I had worked out as the net take-home pay and which infuriated Sir William. But it was a fact against which his fulminations were useless.

At meetings at which I spoke, I used to quip—looking forward to what I believed was inevitable strike action—"What does Sir William say to himself on entering Burnham? It is not, 'What will the teachers say?' It is 'What will the teachers do?'" This fitted the mood of the time and helped to intensify it.

So, Burnham met at last to consider our claim in the blazing light of boasts that we would get nothing. Like naughty children we should hang our heads in shame and go and stand in the corner till ready to be readmitted to the charmed circle of LEAs and DES. Yet a Marplan public opinion poll showed 64% of the electorate in favour of higher pay for teachers! The management handled themselves with consummate ineptitude. Everything they did played into our hands. After all, if you were going to end up making an offer you might as well produce something that is worth negotiating about.

But no and there was a wave of indignation throughout the union and the profession when £50 was offered. Who did they think we were? These management Bourbons had learned nothing and forgotten everything from the 1967 sanctions. They also were well aware that the union's Action Committee was engaged in a thorough examination of all the possible courses of action in the event of a Burnham breakdown. But Alexander and his colleagues chose to ignore this—presumably with full DES approval. They knew that Sir Ronald was out of sympathy with what we had done and were about to do.

But Sir Ronald, whatever his personal views (and they were quite clear to us on the Executive) had to carry out agreed policy. He was swept along with the tide.

There was a changed mood in the Executive, where even some of the most rabid loathers of industrial action began to reflect the feeling seething in the schools, especially former President, John England, the vociferous Tory from Birmingham who could not be ignored. It was the discrimination that rankled most. It is not merely a pious flight of rhetoric to say that teachers felt keenly the injustice of what had happened; dustmen had been offered 16%, firemen 12% miners 9%, to say nothing of the previous offer to the airline pilots of 15%, while teachers were expected to accept 3½% presented to Parliament by Ted Short with transparently false statistics—another example of the stupid mandarins badly—and dangerously—misinforming their Minister.

There were no clear rules then about action, only about payment of 'sustentation' (strike pay) and when an unofficial action took place in the Midlands, the Executive immediately sanctioned it as well as a series of day and half-day walkouts which spread rapidly. In November, there began another bout of strikes, all officially approved, involving some 150,000 teachers. It must be remembered there had been no experience in the union of strike action since 1924.

We were in the midst of something very big and it needed careful control if it were to achieve our objectives and not just become a spontaneous outburst of indignation. So, while letting the movement rip, we planned extended actions. Two-week withdrawals were the first stage, to begin in December and the movement would escalate as well as continuing to include day and half-day strikes. All in all, it was a remarkable development, the like of which the teaching profession had not seen before. The fact that the first phase of the two weeks' strikes would involve only some 4,000 members (in 81 LEAs) was of no consequence. The management and the public knew that we could call out many thousands more who were clamouring to take part and who were being asked to pay a levy in support of their colleagues. And we were working in close collaboration with the NAS, with the sympathy of very many members in the other teachers' unions, including the Heads.

When we had still failed to achieve a settlement, a second phase of the action began in early January, involving 5,000 members in 24 LEAs, A 'conditional' offer of £100 at the minimum, tapering to £80 at the maximum was immediately rejected. 'Take it or leave it', we were told, 'this is it'. We left it; and a third phase was planned to begin in late January. At the same time, the Assistant Masters Association announced to us its readiness to take part in one-day strikes and the probability of going on to extended strikes in a few areas. And, significantly, we began to consider the possibility of including examinations in our action if the issue remained unresolved in the relevant period, a very sensitive area.

In mid-February, we moved on to extended strikes in much larger areas. Already the 'conditional' offer had been made unconditional, and it was rejected as we were not in sight of our target. It seemed that the management were determined to ensure that the whole school system should be engulfed rather than give way on what, even in 1970, could hardly be regarded as a princely sum. Indeed, already within the union ranks, murmurings began that such drastic action as we were taking should be extended on behalf of a much bigger prize, not merely an interim award.

To all this the management leaders were deaf and the DES acted as though paralysed, in their inability to intervene because of the assurances that they had given Alexander to back him up against these rebellious and turbulent teachers. To the figures of the referendum on strike action that we conducted in January/February throughout the union, which showed overwhelming majorities in support (some over 80%), they were also blind. A fourth inadequate offer failed to stop the extended strikes.

To make the biggest impact the extended strikes were organised in areas which were bound to attract even greater national attention than we already had. We chose the city of Birmingham and two London areas, Southwark in Inner and Waltham Forest in Outer London. I had made the strong point—which was accepted—that we had for this major phase to choose London Associations with reliable leaderships: we could not afford Trotskyist influence which had already become a problem in Inner London. These three areas covered over 7,000 members. I was placed in charge of the Waltham Forest action which was timed to begin on February 23rd.

We were now at a crucial stage of the campaign, with Easter and the operative date of 1 April for payment of the 'interim' approaching. How obtuse our bosses were; how uncomprehending of what was going on; how preoccupied with their own anachronistic conception of how teachers ought to behave, and outraged and embarrassed that this seemed no longer to be so! They had the money to pay; they knew our case was cast iron yet they were utterly at sea in handling the situation, in spite of it being obvious to the whole world that the longer they delayed in making an acceptable offer the worse things would become. We knew that serious alarm was sweeping the Labour Party—both in Parliament and the country—and Ted Short was the butt of sharp criticism for not boldly stepping in.

Two factors speeded up a settlement. First the union increased the levy compulsorily paid by members in areas not striking, thus showing an intensified determination. Secondly, though there were difficulties in securing agreement with the other unions on an examinations ban, the union decided to proceed with one, after much heart-searching, in the summer term. Though I was in favour, I was very troubled about this, both as a sanction per se, but also because of the danger of losing public support. But, having thought the thing through, I became convinced that this was the trump card and that such was its potential that it would never have to be played. A gamble, maybe, but it came off. I felt sure that no government could possibly allow, especially when the margin between the two sides in the dispute had narrowed so substantially, such a sanction to operate. It would have to give way. These were the views I expressed at the joint meeting of all the unions that we held and where opposition to action on exams came from the Heads and the Grammar School Assistant Mistresses.

To emphasise our strength, we called for a National Day of Protest on March 3rd, when Burnham was due to meet yet again. Ten thousand teachers, including a huge contingent from Birmingham, would converge on Parliament for the most massive lobby in our experience, to deal the final blow. I was one of those speaking in a Committee Room in the House to our enthusiastic colleagues; the atmosphere was electric in anticipation of a victory that day in the crucial negotiations. I remember the confusion in Hamilton House where Executive members repaired for a meeting which did not take place because 'negotiations' were still going on. I use the inverted commas because what was happening was an unholy row within the management which prevented normal negotiations.

At long last, Ted Short was prepared to face the facts—the gigantic lobby had shaken the Parliamentary Labour Party. So, he put pressure on the management and finally overrode opposition from Alexander and his mates who were more concerned with saving their faces than winning peace. They never forgave Short for 'ratting' on them. Actually, Short offered them a sop: approval for £120 not the full claim, and this was the settlement finally accepted, a major victory for the teachers.

The value of the award was estimated at £42 millions: the cost of our action was around £3 million. Not bad business, I calculated! It has always puzzled me why Ted did not step in earlier as the money was clearly always available, and so prevent the strikes. I am afraid he was not adroit enough in trade union politics and accepted the advice of his mandarins who were equally maladroit. Decades of cap-doffing by mere school teachers had anaesthetised their chilly minds and hearts against the white heat of a whole profession in action. Ted should have trusted his socialist instincts.

So Max was jubilant. He was fully aware that rising inflation would again undermine teachers' living standards and new battles would need to be fought. He warned also that an apparently innocuous statement attached to the Agreement proposing future discussions in Burnham about restructuring salaries, would be used by the DES and LEA leaders to end the system of 'Basic plus Allowances', whereby the bulk of the money went to that element in the salary bill that embraced all teachers, and to replace it by a system of differentials. Max was right: the management were thirsting for revenge and at the next Burnham meeting put forward an entirely new salary structure of separate scales, which they forced through using arbitration. Max blamed Sir Ronald and other officials who were talking with Ted Short (a union member and sponsored MP) for not briefing the Minister properly about this threat to teacher unity.

But Max's over-riding emotion was elation that the teaching profession had stood up and been counted. He believed the rise of teacher militancy would be permanent and of long-term significance for the profession. There had been no other way of driving home to the public (which backed the strikes) that the professional expertise of teachers needed to be properly valued. Max had played the leading role in the campaign and his supporters urged him to run for President. Max, however, had made up his mind when he was appointed as Head of Willesden High School that he would stay in the school a full five years, so seeing his first, 1967, entry through their fifth-year examinations. So, he resisted throwing his hat in the ring until the 1971 Elections, when he ran as a candidate for office as Vice-President at Easter 1972. Under the NUT system VPs automatically become President in due course so if elected, he would leave school in January 1973, six years after he took up his Headship.

There was little press reference, let alone any campaign, on his CP membership. This he had never concealed and had no intention of concealing. However, he decided not to continue as an Executive member because of lack of time, diminishing interest evidenced by poor attendance and political differences with the CP leadership. John Gollan, the CP General Secretary, immediately telephoned Max at school, asking to see him urgently—that very day if possible. So, he came to see him at home after school. I was present at what proved to be a brief interview. When he came, Max briefly explained his reasons for not continuing, then added: "I have no intention of doing a Dave Bowman on you."

(Dave, a good friend of ours, was a leading railwayman who had resigned from the Party and was accused, wrongly, of doing so in order to run for the Presidency of the NUR where a condition was membership of the Labour Party). Gollan's relief was palpably evident—he had clearly not wanted a resignation of as prominent a trade unionist as Max. He left within a minute or two—satisfied, with no more to say. The whole encounter hadn't lasted more than a few minutes and a small whisky. "What a cold fish," Max said to me, "he should have known me better—that I have a reputation for integrity and would not stoop to electoral expediency on such a question. I would have left long since if I had been an unprincipled careerist." So, he had another whisky to get over the slight.

Max easily topped the poll and was duly announced as Senior Vice-President—the TV News Bulletin flashed his picture on the screen with the brief comment that a communist had been elected NUT President: He enjoyed his victory and celebrated with me, Executive friends and other colleagues. An enormous postbag of congratulations arrived. One that he enjoyed came in a telegram from his old friend Giles, the Daily Express cartoonist, addressed humorously to 'Britain's Top Teacher'—a reference to the way the Express had handled the story. But those he prized most were from old colleagues in

Middlesex who had sponsored and backed him throughout the cold war period. They were delighted that he had come in from the cold.

At Easter, he had to mount two hurdles as the new Senior Vice-President.

"I attended the small private dinner then customarily given by the union Officers to the leading visitors from the Management Panel of Burnham, a curious but traditional courtesy to important guests. There, for the first time, I supped with Bill Alexander with whom I had crossed so many verbal swords. In speaking to Conference next morning, as again was the custom, I quipped about my first engagement as Vice-President: 'Last night I dined with the Borgias…' The week also saw my first personal encounter as an Officer with Mrs Thatcher, when I sat by her at the dinner, again by tradition, given to the visiting Secretary of State. I cannot say I did not enjoy the irony of the experience, including the by no means apolitical conversation—I think she was trying to get to know me, sizing me up. We were to have a stormy couple of years in close encounters."

Max: The President and Mrs Thatcher

When Mrs Thatcher took over the Department in June 1970, none of us had any experience of working with her or even knew her: our only acquaintanceship was through her public reputation as a clever politician with no particular interest in education—that was nothing unusual in the Tory Party. It did not take us long to learn not only that we were dealing with a very tough lady but one who took great pains to master her brief and was a most able and determined fighter for it. Within days of assuming Office, she issued her Circular 10/70 which ended the pressure on LEAS to create Comprehensives. The heat was off and authorities that wanted to maintain selection or return to it would get a receptive hearing. But there was, it seemed, to be no general unscrambling of comprehensive reorganisation by the Government.

In 1969, about a quarter of all secondary children were in Comprehensive Schools. Only 20 LEAS had not yet submitted reorganisation schemes; 30 had adopted completely Comprehensive schemes; 80 had schemes approved and were beginning to be reorganised; 33 had schemes in the pipeline—including some which Labour would not have approved There was therefore, still a long way to go to achieve a fully Comprehensive system. Labour's building cuts had been a big factor in slowing things down. But we were also fully aware that the insistence of a good many heavily Tory Authorities (e.g., Surrey) on maintaining Comprehensive education was an important factor in shaping national Tory policy.

Full of protest and indignation at the new Circular, I went with colleagues to see the great lady and found her reclining on a chaise longue in her room, perfectly coiffured, not a hair out of place, relaxed. Almost languorous, and accompanied only by her private secretary, not the entourage we had been used to under Ted Short. She proceeded to expound her case to which she knew we were opposed, answered all questions with the expertise of a professional, referred those she could not deal with property to the secretary for action and argued with us calmly and politely. We, of course, agreed to differ but left with the feeling that we had the most capable adversary we had seen for years.

I was to see quite a lot of her in the next few years. Especially, after I became Senior Vice President of the Union in Easter, 1972. We met officially on deputations and at conferences and meetings and unofficially at a good many social functions and I developed a healthy respect for her, which I believe was reciprocated. Personal Relations were almost invariably amicable though I was not only a trade union leader (and she did not like unions much) but also a communist (which she liked even less). At parties, I occasionally had to look after her and make sure she had her gin and grub, on which she was always keen, and in whose ambience, she obviously liked to relax. In those days, I used to Sport a purple waistcoat upon which she invariably commented, I objected to one of her affectations which was to call me Maxie, a name both my wife and I detested, but I restrained my feelings even when she once called out 'Maxie' across a huge room in some embassy or other when she spied me in the distance.

Pleasant personal relations ran parallel, however, to sharp and often acrimonious public controversy, especially on the Comprehensive issue and on her famous White Paper, *A Framework for Expansion*. But Mrs T did not dismantle the Comprehensive system and under her regime both Labour and Tory LEAS continued to develop it:

In fact, she closed more Grammar Schools than any other Minister, before or after! In those days though her ideology was doctrinaire, her practice was pragmatic. Ironically, I looked back to the White Paper, which we criticised sharply, almost with nostalgia when Carlisle and Joseph undermined the service under her premiership: those I mused were the good old days.

At the time, I described Framework as "a decision taken in the corridors of power to diminish drastically and permanently the rate of educational advance." Our criticism of Framework was almost entirely due to its too low target, in our view, for future teacher supply with its consequences for pupil-teacher ratios and so size of classes as well as, of course, its failure to provide for higher salary standards.

But one must not forget the commencement of a nursery programme, however small, and the £200 million programme for replacing pre-1903 primary school buildings, if by no means all of them. Neither project had been undertaken by her Labour predecessors. Thus, Mrs Thatcher's practice often belied her preaching, to the advantage of the former, The outstanding example, of course, was her decision to steal Labour's discarded stand and raise the compulsory leaving age to 16. The failure to do so earlier remains a shameful blot on Labour's educational record. The decision in 1971 of the Heath Government (to end free milk except for infants (with means-tested exceptions) was not her personal decision so when it earned her the nasty soubriquet. "Thatcher the milk snatcher." she was bitterly resentful. She supported the Heath squeeze but used to point out sharply that it was Labour that made inroads into the meals service when it had removed free milk from secondary schools.

She was a good 'Heathite' at the Department even though she may have liked to be something else—a latter day Madame Guillotine—which she became later when her theory and practice coincided and serious damage was inflicted on the schools. Educational spending was still going up when she began, but the Heath Government was to slow the rate of increase down in its Public Expenditure approach.

Any hope of an upturn came to a halt with the cuts of December 1973, which she enthusiastically defended to me the day they were announced. They were to mark the commencement of a period of continuous cuts She was all for Tony and Ted then and I am sure very sincerely, but the Barber Cuts ushered in a period of acrimony between Minister and teachers and she was badly served by that dreadful public schoolman, Sir William Pile her Permanent Secretary. Where on earth does the DES pick them up? It must be a special Civil Service jumble sale. The idiot (in the proper Greek sense of the word politically gormless) actually blandly dismissed this fearsome cut package with the words: "Oh, well, the kids will have to sit on broken chairs for an extra year. So what!"

Zombies like Pile help to explain Mrs Thatcher's occasional technical bloomers as when the DES insisted on a Burnham meeting on last day of the Christmas term—a truly absurd day for teachers. When I taxed her with this privately, she was genuinely angry that the public schoolmen whose breeding stables were already on holiday had not bothered to consider that we did not enjoy their privileges. I imagine someone got a thorough dressing down!

This was not by any means the only occasion that I witnessed Mrs Thatcher round on her civil service advisers:

On deputations, it was a not uncommon experience for her to turn to one of them to query whether what she had been told by us was right or to demand why an answer was not forthcoming to a particular question. She was already developing the abrasive manner which was to characterise her Premiership, and who better to practise on than the anaemic bunch of wet willies that populated the reaches of the Department. Hardly any of them had any experience of the education service except as pupils and students, a fact which I uncovered when some years later. I planted a question in the Lords through Norah David, the Labour Education spokesperson there. Of those occupying Assistant Secretaryships and above (i.e., the policy-making grades) only twelve, a small percentage, had any teaching experience, The DES more than any other Department of the Home Civil Service has been resistant to the Fulton proposals for the introduction of greater professionalism into its ranks. They remained overwhelmingly amateur—and wasn't it obvious! In all my years in teacher politics I have never faltered in my total disrespect for the mandarins in the DES who 'advise' their political masters.

In the winter of 1973–4, encounters with Mrs Thatcher and her juniors became increasingly bitter because of confrontations on salaries and the London Allowance. I had already had some brushes with her then faithful acolyte, St John Stevas, when, in a widely-reported statement, I dubbed him an unnecessary Sir Galahad to his mistress, Guinevere, as she could defend herself without his sycophantic incursions into the fray. Stevas had an extraordinary arrogance as a Junior Minister. On one deputation on the London Allowance on which we were in bitter conflict with the Government, I extracted from him what seemed to be a concession—a slight possibility of making progress. Naturally. I issued a press statement to that effect. Stevas, who had obviously gone beyond his brief, immediately sent round by hand a letter denying my report and asking me to retract it publicly. I checked my notes and told him I would do nothing of the kind, whereupon he sent me an official minute of the deputation, without, of course, his damaging remarks, as if to clinch the matter, assuming I would now toe the line. I replied that I was not born yesterday and was not prepared to accept an official minute prepared by one side of a joint meeting. I was fully aware that civil service minutes usually describe what they want to be recorded as history, not necessarily what actually happened. That should have ended the incident, but Stevas, like all arrogant snobs, was a bad loser and tried unsuccessfully to keep the dispute going on a TV programme where we shared a discussion with Eric Briault, the London Chief Education Officer, on the London Allowance. But that encounter did not help him either—he was outraged that his word as a Minister could possibly be doubted.

If I may digress, this was not my only experience of civil service 'minuting' or reporting. Sometime later, during the 'Great Debate', Shirley Williams' Incursion into Bread and Circuses Showbiz, I received a letter from her junior. Margaret Jackson, as she then was (now Margaret Beckett) strongly objecting to something she was told I had said about a statement she was supposed to have made at the London performance of the Circus and would I please withdraw it. I replied that I absolutely agreed she had said nothing of the kind, nor had I said she had and proved to her that t could not possibly have done so. She had been misinformed by her minions for reasons which I could only guess (I had been the most vociferous critic of the whole jamboree and an article of mine on it in the Sunday Times had caused considerable amusement). A long time later I got my reply from Miss Jackson—an unqualified apology.

It is not often that happens in Mandarin-land. There must have been a fearful row, with somebody probably being promoted out of the way as a result.

Mrs Thatcher's tenure of office marked the DES' drive along with LEAs and the NAS to destroy the teachers' Basic Scale. In July, just after she took office, we submitted the largest ever pay claim, one based on the perspectives of the Left. The subsequent conflict did not endear us mutually. But it was the London Allowance that darkened teachers' relationships with her, perhaps more than any other conflict. Of course, she was simply carrying out Heath's wages policy but the fact that she was a London MP should have made her more sensitive and we made full use of it in polemic. We relished this all the more because we knew she had other troubles in Finchley. Some of Finchley's leading Tories (her close friends) were opposed to the Tory Council's pro-Comprehensive policy, which, in spite of her educational pragmatism, she did not like (this was confided to me by one of the local Tory leaders).

She was bitterly opposed to the union's guerrilla strikes at the beginning of 1973 on the issue and this was one of the reasons why in spite of good personal relations, she took the extraordinary step of refusing to attend my induction as President at Easter. I say 'refused' because her excuse (phoney. I believe) was that she had double-booked and had to go to Kuwait (or was it Oman?) to see some sheikh or other rather than maintain the protocol for the Secretary of State to attend, when invited, the major educational conference of the year. Or perhaps she was scared of her possible reception under a communist President. That would have been a gross misjudgement on her part and she was probably, as usual, badly advised by her poodles at the Department. Anyway, she preferred the perfumes of Arabia to the bracing air of Scarborough.

It was true her appearance in 1972 (under a Tory President) had caused a minor sensation because of an unsuccessful attempt at a walk-out which a tiny number of delegates (a curious combination of genuinely angry delegates from Tory Surrey—she had mucked about with their Comprehensive plans—and the usual moblet of Trotskyists. On that occasion, I, along with the other members of the Executive on the platform, had made our displeasure at the 'walkout' clear by giving her a warm welcome. Of course, I was vilified by the trots tor taking part in this—they published a picture of me clapping the Minister—but that was my last worry. I strongly held that if by democratic decision you invite a guest, you must treat her as such, irrespective of her opinions or actions and show the courtesy expected of responsible teachers' leaders. Overwhelmingly the conference agreed.

Anyway, she did not appear in 1973 but took good care to issue a press statement attacking my Presidential address before I even delivered it! (The DES had an advance copy along with the press.) I joked that it was unprecedented for a Secretary of State to do such a thing and got a good laugh on the media about it.

One further incident bears recounting. We were in dispute with the Government over the Industrial Relations Act, in particular their policy that we should submit to the dictates of the Commission for Industrial Relations that it established. This was the background of Mrs Thatcher's request for a private meeting with me at our Christmas party in Hamilton House, where annually the world of education gathered to booze and scoff. I was, as President, receiving and bidding farewell to the guests for most of the evening.

As Maggie was leaving, obviously well-oiled and beaming, she called me aside and suggested we be photographed together. Standing conveniently nearby our excellent photographer Cyril Bernard posted us under a large sprig of mistletoe. I still have the picture, which I forbade the union journal to print. The photo taken, she drew me aside and said, "Come and see me on Monday or Tuesday I want you to explain to me your opposition to the Commission for Industrial Relations. No-one in the office has able to explain the whole business properly to me."

Next morning, I fixed a time with Anthony Chamier, her private secretary, and duly appeared at the House on Monday evening, leaving my patient wife outside in the parked car, "I'll be half an hour at most," I said. Mrs Thatcher had come down to meet me and escorted me to her room. It seemed a mile away, and she casually remarked that she had asked Sir William Pile to come along. My heart sank as I anticipated a half-hour of flannel and fluff-some kind of private relations exercise which would, of course, be a complete waste of time. But how wrong I was! She really did not know the first thing about what the Commission meant for the NUT or the other teachers' unions and Sir William had left her quite ignorant of the main issues. She had not even been told that LACSAB, the technical wing of the LEAS which advised them on such matters, was on our side. No wonder she was puzzled. As I made my points, she remorselessly quizzed the Permanent Secretary, who got more and more uncomfortable and angry when taxed with simply following the line of the Department of Employment without giving any serious thought to what the CIR meant for the education service. He nearly exploded. Yet this was in fact the case.

By this time, in spite of the liberal administration of gin, Mrs T was clearly extremely uneasy and furious with her Grand Panjandrum. It was not that she agreed with me (that was certainly not the case though she was carefully noting all the points and arguing about them). It was that she had been, it seemed deliberately, left ignorant of her Departmental interest in order to maintain Mandarin solidarity behind the Department of Employment's policy, privately agreed by the Permanent Secretaries caucus.

I did not realise it but we had been in conversation for an hour and three quarters and there was my long-suffering wife sitting in a cold car, probably fuming, when we finished. Mrs Thatcher asked Sir William to wait while she escorted me on the long trek to the exit—she was evidently intending him to do penance. She thanked me profusely as she bid me goodnight and, having missed our other engagement. I placated my wife with dinner at the Gay Hussar.

When I saw Sir William at another Christmas function the following evening, he was icy. She must have given him a humdinger of a dressing down. Didn't he think we had a useful meeting? I mischievously asked him. "Not very," he grunted. Sir William was a supercilious, arrogant bureaucrat trying to impress everyone with his superior style, breeding and intelligence. Yet he published a book under his name about the Department some years later that was so unbelievably, unreadably dull and turgid that it was obviously written by an anonymous committee of the most cliche-ridden civil servants in the DES. No-one has ever referred to the book since. It was as stillborn as literature as its presumed author was as an educationist, Sir William was later transferred to head the Department of Inland Revenue, a fate he deserved.

Max: Foreign Trips as NUT President

A President of the NUT has so many foreign visits that it would be tedious to recount them all. I attended national and international conferences and seminars in France, Holland, Belgium and Germany. Exceptional, however, in their interest were trips to Israel, Kenya and Jamaica, the USA and the USSR. Except for Jamaica, Margaret came with me, as was expected of the President's Consort. I had not been to Israel since its 'Palestine' days in 1933 and looked forward eagerly to seeing the changes. These we saw, with the usual hospitality, and liberal doses, inevitably, of propaganda. But, while full of admiration for the enormous achievements of the young state, I cannot say I was re-converted to my early Zionist ideals. I still felt that a more determined will was necessary to come to a settlement with Israel's Arab citizens and there could be no security for its people until this was achieved. Interestingly, our visit preceded by only a few weeks the Yom Kippur War.

We flew from Tel Aviv to Nairobi to the annual WCOTP jamboree in a brand-new Conference Centre in the heart of the city. What a contrast this and the other high-rise buildings (usually belonging to banks and multi-nationals) in Nairobi's main streets made with the desperate poverty evident only a few yards from their doors. It was very unpleasant—and unavoidable—and we retreated with relief for a few days' holiday by the sea at Mombasa. We had said 'hullo' to Jomo Kenyatta, once an anti-imperialist international hero, now the head of a state obviously reeking of corruption. And we were amused when, at our official opening, the President publicly rewarded the school children who put on a show with a day's holiday.

Jamaican teachers had invited me to celebrate the tenth anniversary of their union's foundation and I looked forward eagerly to the visit. After all, I had been (and would be again) responsible for a large school with a majority of children of Jamaican origin. I attended the Conference and toured the island then becoming the scene (in Kingston) of turbulent and violent politics. But what fascinated me were the schools: very large classes under 'traditional' pedagogues, working with limited resources—and a very happy, workmanlike, stable educational atmosphere. Teachers' attitudes amused me in one respect. At a show the union put on, the star piece was a take-off of those elements who were fighting to maintain the Creole patois. They were ridiculed as backward, to the joy of the large teacher audience. I thought ruefully of my own troubles on insisting on good standard English language teaching in Willesden—against the wishes of a tiny number of black politicians.

It all made it easier for me to understand the confusion and unsettledness of our 'immigrant' children transplanted from a Jamaican village, or even a Kingston downtown street, to the delights of West Willesden. This journey was one of the most useful I have ever made, and the pleasure was greater because I knew our sister union was poor and could not afford the lavish hospitality we so often received elsewhere. It was the good will that mattered.

Highlight of the Presidential year is always the 'statutory' visit to the National Education Association Conference in the USA. I had to get a US visa, a matter which concerned union officials, as I was a Communist and Communists were not granted American visas. What would happen if I was refused one—an international incident, I laughed?

Knowing the ways of officialdom at this level, I was not worried, it would all come out in the wash, but I did not wish to embarrass the union.

I applied for my visa in the normal way, filling out the absurd form detailing my political affiliation and all my visits to Eastern Europe since the war, etc. etc., knowing that some behind-the-scenes, high-level approaches had already been made (I think either by George Thomas or Ted Short, or both). With my wife, who was to accompany me—also a Communist—I waited in the milling crowd of visa-seekers for what seemed an interminable period and was about to leave in disgust when an official came over to us, apologised for the delay and took us in to see the head man. He also apologised and made it abundantly clear that he had to go through bureaucratic motions according to the rules. He then told me that the matter would have 'to be referred to Frankfurt' (HQ of the CIA in Europe?) but made it clear it would all be OK. He was the essence of charm and politeness, obviously very embarrassed, and saw us out of the building personally.

A couple of weeks later we got a call from the Consulate. Our visas were there, would I call and collect them? I said I was very busy. Oh dear, don't worry, they would send them round! I was very amused when, a month or so later, we arrived at Kennedy Airport and Passport Control flicked through a book, obviously of dangerous characters, and passed us through ahead of the queue, with expressions of goodwill for a happy visit! When I met my American colleagues, I was told that there had been a minor press effort to draw attention to the proposed visit of the international desperado, Mr Max Morris, which they had scotched by a timely word to the State Department. Needless to say, the visit, which was to Portland, Oregon (following a week's holiday with friends in New York) and tourist trips to San Francisco, Denver and Washington, was a very happy one. American hospitality as is well known is warm and generous. I found American teachers to be very broad-minded politically—a big change from the Cold War days—and extremely interesting educationally. It was a very enlightening experience politically as our visit was at the height of the Watergate scandal that led to Nixon's resignation.

A visit at the end of my Presidential year to the USSR was a contrast, and sadly so. I led a small delegation from the Executive and I had some misgivings because, though I was not a stranger to their country and I knew the Soviet teachers' leaders well personally, they knew that, though I was a Communist, I was critical of Soviet policies and they were aware of my record on Soviet actions in Hungary and Czechoslovakia and did not like it. So, there was a 'certain atmosphere' which led them to push too hard in the propaganda that is inevitable when such delegations go to the USSR. My colleagues also felt this and it somewhat marred the enormous interest of the occasion for us although we fully appreciated the goodwill of the many teachers we met and the efforts they made to look after us in Moscow, Leningrad, Tashkent and Samarkand.

I had long ago come to the conclusion that the Soviet and other East European teachers' leaders were political appointees rather than freely elected union leaders and that their first job was to plug the party line. What was disconcerting was their failure to understand that we knew this. They should have been more intelligent and knowing the kind of people we were been ready to discuss issues frankly as between professional colleagues. This was what we were used to even in a country like Israel where propaganda also looms large in union contacts.

The Soviet education system was full of fascinating problems and these we were entitled to discuss freely.

One incident shows how not to handle foreign educationists, sophisticated in the 'trade'. We went to see a school in Moscow which we were told specialised in the English language. It was an excellent advertisement for Soviet English teaching—children reciting Burns, knowledgeable in British literature—it was a delight to talk to them and be answered in English. On the way back in the car, one of my colleagues who had also asked to see the children's maths exercise books, commented on their very high standard. Was this a selective school, he asked, for very bright children? Oh no, was the reply from a very experienced Soviet teachers' leader whom I knew well, it was just an ordinary neighbourhood school which specialised in English, quite unselective.

My colleague began probing, for there was no way, he believed, that an 'ordinary unselective' school could produce such results in English and maths. Our Russian friend got quite shirty when it appeared that, in fact, the children's 'neighbourhood' was a housing estate for diplomats and high foreign office officials, and we all (I too) suggested that the school was hardly 'unselective'. There seemed to us to be no need for such prevarication—heaven knows Soviet educational achievements are remarkable enough without having to pretend that it is one hundred percent egalitarian. The children we saw were obviously being groomed for the foreign and diplomatic service and for jobs which involved knowledge to a very high standard of English, and were very bright indeed—all of them! Unselective, my foot!

I do not want to convey a wrong impression. We enjoyed the visit immensely and appreciated everyone's kindness, but incidents such as I have described (and there were others) did not create the best impression of our leading Soviet colleagues who, we felt, should have been franker and more open. How these leaders were really regarded by their members we of course never got to know. Officers stayed in office indefinitely till the party decided to change them for some reason—and we would never see them again. Conflicts within the union we never heard about, nor about conflicts with the Government. No wonder glasnost and perestroika created such upheavals within the unions!

Towards the end of my Presidential year an unfortunate incident occurred. Ted Short used to be delighted with my attacks on Government policy and on one occasion it sounded as though he was thanking me officially, on behalf of the Opposition—to my intense (official) embarrassment! But this happy relationship with the union became overcast. We were revising our arrangements for 'sponsored' MPs, of whom he (in common with two other Cabinet Ministers—George Thomas and Michael Stewart) had been one for a long time and there was some feeling against including Ministers as they had publicly to support Government policy in all circumstances. Behind the scenes I argued against this short-sighted view on the grounds that it could only be of advantage to the union to have friends in high places, even if they could not always publicly express their feelings. When the issue was debated in the Executive as I was in the Chair I could not speak, but was quite taken aback when, because of some local vendetta in Newcastle (where Ted was an MP), arguments were used (by the future General Secretary who was a Newcastle man) to remove him from our panel.

I thought this a stupid thing to do to the Deputy Leader (about to become Deputy Prime Minister after the February 1974 Election) and I learned how hurt he was. I decided to get George Thomas to help try to smooth him down by arranging a private meeting, unbeknown to the Executive, for myself and Fred Jarvis to see Ted in the House over a drink. I explained to him exactly what had happened, how much I regretted it and how silly I thought the Executive had been. I felt it to be in the best interests of the union that I should take this step. The meeting was a little fraught though Ted appreciated my effort.

But I am sure the slight rankled and had something to do with the fact that, some years later, he agreed to act as political adviser to the strike-breaking Professional Association of Teachers—an equally foolish action on his part as the Executive's had been on theirs. I'm certain I was right about this incident—a union like the NUT can't afford to throw away any political influence.

Incidentally, I once used Ted's name for my personal, or rather my school's advantage. When I started planning W.H.S. in 1967, I desperately needed a separate phone in my room and met with the usual bland, bureaucratic procrastinations from the Post Office till I threatened to ring up 'my friend, Mr Short', who was then Postmaster General, and get him to intervene. I got my phone the same afternoon!

Margaret: Resuming My Career

The publication of the Robbins Report in 1963 on expanding University education had helped to give me confidence that despite the setback of choosing to study a subject in which there were no vacant appointments, neither when I completed my post graduate studies at Oxford nor at the time when I left the VCH, I would eventually be able to obtain a full-time lecturing post. Five years later I thought it was time to test out my position. I applied for a post as a historian in the new Open University. I thought my extra Mural teaching experience would give me an advantage but instead I was immediately informed that my application could not be considered because I was too old to learn the new techniques required. What—too old at 38 to work in an institution for adult learning? Would a man of the same age have been dubbed too old to learn new tricks? I was indignant but a little alarmed and sought advice from Douglas Johnson, my tutor at Birmingham, by then a professor at University College London.

As already explained, he helped me obtain a commission to write a Historical Association pamphlet on the General Strike and this led to a temporary lecturing post at Queen Mary College. While there I was able to obtain a commission to produce a 'Pelican Original' on the 1926 General Strike in time for its 50th Anniversary, This was a challenge because there were already a number of books about the General Strike and others would be published for the Anniversary, so I needed to find a different approach. I decided that not only would I expand my document-based Historical Association pamphlet by making use of oral evidence but also include a number of special background studies to improve understanding of the economic, social and political condition of England at the time of the strike and also the current views of a selection of trade union leaders about its long-term impact.

So, I bought a tape recorder and set out to collect testimony from some of those still alive who had been involved, including Jim Griffiths, one of the founders of the Welfare State in the Attlee Government and Secretary of State for Wales under Harold Wilson, Betty Harrison of the Textile Workers Union and Vice-President of Bradford Trades Council, Sir Will Lawther, Abe Moffat and many others, including strike breakers and rank and file strikers. This filled my time between leaving Queen Mary until I became the 'President's Consort' at Easter 1973.

I enjoyed these interviews so much that it didn't feel like work at all. I developed an informal method: I behaved as though I'd come for a chat, to see how they were getting along. They knew why I'd arranged to see them and that my tape recorder was on but I had no written list of questions with me nor did I make notes. I just sat back in a relaxed way and left the initiative to them, knowing that most old people are waiting to find someone willing to listen to them. So, I would be invited to stay for tea or supper or asked to visit again. Sir Will Lawther, then very old, insisted I give him a kiss if I wanted to talk to him—so in the interests of history I put aside my women's lib principles and obliged! By dropping in a little question here and there I learnt about what these veterans did during the Strike and how they felt both at the time and later. I used to tell Max not to expect me home early when I was visiting one of them.

My second innovation was to include a number of in-depth background studies, which meant enlisting historians specialising in the fields of British Industry, the Churches and the Poor Law. For general interest, I added a study of writers who had made the Strike the background to their novels. Finally, four regional accounts of the Strike illustrated the differences of its impact in London, Glasgow, Pontypridd in the Welsh mining area and Sheffield in the Manufacturing North of England.

By the time my manuscript was ready to send off, I thought that I had achieved my aim to write a well-rounded account of the General Strike and that my sympathy for AJ Cooke and the miners would be shared by readers. I was very happy when it was well reviewed.

Even before it was published, my commission to write it helped me to obtain a permanent lecturing post in Modern History. This was at the Polytechnic of Central London (originally Regent Street Polytechnic and now Westminster University). Following the setting up of the National Council for Academic Awards (CNAA) in 1964, PCL had begun offering degree courses, including a Social Sciences BA, both full-time and part-time, of which History was a component. One of the Polytechnic's aims was to open the door as widely as possible to those who for social reasons had missed the opportunity to stay on at school. Although less prestigious than a post in the old universities, I was attracted to being part of a new educational development and by PCL's more socially varied intake. I had enjoyed teaching on the Extra Mural Diploma course and saw how it had given a spring board to many of the students to go forward to further study and satisfying careers., I started at PCL in September 1974 and stayed for nearly 12 years. The Head of History, Philip Bagwell, an expert on railway history and the trade union movement went out of his way to make me feel welcome but everyone else from the Dean downwards made me feel invisible because they were not at all interested in me as a new member of staff but only as a source of discussion about Max's activities—the firebrand who had just ended his year as President of the NUT. This was not unexpected and I did not object but I joked that I'd better start going round with a placard saying my name is Margaret. I became friends with a fellow historian, Pat Ryan, whose speciality was the Poor Law and so I asked her to contribute to my book, which she did. We still remain friends.

My invisibility diminished after 'The General Strike' was published but I felt a need to get to know my colleagues better and understand the inner workings of the School of Social Science, so I took on an administrative role as Admissions Tutor. Our students studied more than one subject during their first year before choosing one or two subjects to study in greater depth. Many school leavers were not sure of what they wanted to do after passing their A Levels but most Universities recruited only for single subject degrees whereas our system provided the opportunity for them to discover their aptitudes and interests. The applicants whom I found most interesting were mature students who had not followed the "A" level pathway but now felt ready to study at degree level. Some had taken Access courses and I relied on the judgement of their tutors and admitted all those who they recommended. Others had work experience as their background, so I interviewed them. The Polytechnic's aim was to open the door as widely as possible but I was very aware that it would be no benefit to them to admit those unable to cope.

Although politically in tune with the policy of widening opportunity, I was not an advocate of an open door so I provided information on Access or top-up A level courses to applicants who I judged were not yet ready.

Being Admission Tutor was an enjoyable rather than an arduous task and I had increased the proportion of non-traditional students on the full-time degree to over a third when the Dean became alarmed and ordered me on no account to go as high as 40%. He was worried about the College's reputation if we enrolled a lot of students who would fail or drop out. Time would show that he need not have worried. Only one of the many non-traditional students I admitted was unable to cope and had to drop out. An interesting analysis 3—4 years later of degree results showed that the majority of students were awarded a 2.2 but a higher proportion of the non-traditional students than of the A level intake had obtained a 2.1 or First. At the lower end, only a small number of students overall were awarded 3rds or Pass degrees including a higher proportion of non-traditional students than A level entrants. However, in most cases these students were not disappointed: they said they were pleased to have gained a degree and that learning to study had changed their lives. Education is not just about exam results!

Being Admission tutor enabled me to get to know staff from every subject. I joined the Union—the ATTI—but was a supportive rather than an active member. I chose instead to run for membership of the Academic Council, which I thought badly needed more women members. I was elected a couple of years later and remained a very active member for the rest of my time as a member of staff. We campaigned for all posts to be openly advertised and that appointing committees must have both women and student members. I became a member of what was known as 'the gang of four', constantly pressing the Rector, Terry Burlin, to respect the advice of the Council. Later two of the 'gang' members became Principles/Vice Chancellors of new Universities-Frank Gould of East London and Leslie Wagner of North London and later Leeds Metropolitan. I myself was promoted to Principal Lecturer and Director of the Social Sciences Course and the other female member of the "gang" became Head of Statistics, so our activities did not hold back our careers, which in retrospect is to the credit of Terry Burlin.

Max: Farewell to the Executive

Max's period as President of the NUT coincided with a period of national and international financial turmoil caused by the rise in oil prices and a breakdown of the international monetary system. In December 1973 the Chancellor, Michael Barber, introduced a drastic cost cutting budget, targeting wages and public expenditure, including large cutbacks in education spending. Max immediately led a deputation to Margaret Thatcher, pointing out the inconsistencies with her own 'Framework for Expansion' and the dire consequences of the proposed cuts, but she remained adamant that they were needed.

In February 1974, threatened by a Miners' strike, Ted Heath called a General Election. He failed to win, and in March Harold Wilson returned as Prime Minister of a minority government amonth before Max's period of office ended at Easter. Wilson had reflected during the period of the Heath Government, perhaps on the difficulties of National Planning, and had taken the decision to undo Heath's attack on incomes and cooperate with the Unions. A Liaison Committee was set up to promote cooperation between the TUC and the Parliamentary Party and a 'Social Contract' was drawn up by which the Unions would limit their wage claims in return for the repealing the 1971 Trade Union Act and a substantial social programme including an immediate increase in old age pensions and the establishment of Committees to examine the level of public sector pay.

In May the Houghton Committee was set up to review teachers' salaries. It reported in December giving them a long overdue 29% increase and a salary level more appropriate to their professional responsibilities, although still lower than salaries in other professions. But for a time, teachers were content with their salaries.

Teachers' Salaries continued to be negotiated In the Burnham Committee. The NUT although affiliated to the TUC was not affiliated to the Labour Party and so had no role in the Liaison Committee nor affected by its decisions. Both

Max and I had hoped that the Social Contract would be successful and that the understanding between the TUC and the Labour Party would hold and help to halt inflation. For a time, it did but eventually broke down. Max and I had been friendly for several years with Jack and Evelyn Jones; Max had a close rapport with Jack, General Secretary of the TGWU, who had helped Wilson set up the Social Contact. So, we were disappointed at the Government's failure to see it through. Max was preoccupied with NUT issues but I was immediately upset and frustrated at the failure by the Labour Party to maintain the Social Contract.[4]

Following NUT practice, Max had returned to his school. His Deputy, Sheila Houliston, had followed his approach but she was ready for promotion to a Headship of her own. So, his first task when he went back was appointing a new Deputy. He chose an experienced young woman teacher, Wendy Selly, whom he thought had the right attitudes and would be able to hold the fort whenever he was at meetings or out on NUT business. During his last four years back at school, he resumed his NUT activities, initially as Ex-President and then as Chair of the Salaries Committee, a post he held until his retirement from the NUT in April 1979. After Harold Wilson's unexpected resignation in 1976, James Callaghan became Prime Minister and Shirley Williams Minister of Education.

As pressure mounted on the Government to cut public expenditure as a condition of its loan from the IMF, education expenditure was highlighted as a target for cuts so Max's main focus was opposing them. He did so with added urgency because at stake was the quality and nature of education within the developing comprehensive system.

The Burnham Committee had become over large on both the teachers and Management side by this period and by the time of Max's retirement negotiations over salaries had become very protracted and had broken down, Max blamed Shirley Williams for this by her refusal to accept the terms of reference for the Clegg Committee agreed between teachers and employers. As he was still Chairman of the Salary Committee, he was worried about how to handle the situation at what would be his retirement Conference.

MAX: "When I attended my last NUT Conference at Easter, 1979, in Scarborough, my feelings were very tense. I had devoted the major part of my life to the union and had attended every Conference since 1938, apart from those

---

[4] The best source for understanding its breakdown is Jack Jones's Autobiography, 'Union Man'.

that fell during my army service. 1941–6, So I went off to Scarborough afraid of the inevitable farewells, valedictory speeches and comments.

I could not see how we could avoid recommending action to the Conference as a means of pressurising the Management. If we were to stand back on 'political' grounds we would be in serious danger, for the first time, from the loonies allied to the substantial right wing in Conference through an accusation of playing the Government's game, when the Secretary of State had so patently kicked us in the teeth. It was, after all, a Labour Government which in making the Houghton Award in 1974, had pledged to regularly update it every five years and exactly five years had elapsed since Houghton had begun operating.

Increasing my foreboding was the knowledge that things would have to be done which I had desperately hoped would be unnecessary. Here we were entering into a General Election period which we wanted to result in a Labour win, in spite of all the Callaghan Government's mistakes, and were going to be inevitably plunged into some form or another of industrial action because of the crass stupidity of the Secretary of State who was clearly suffering from a death wish, soon to be politically gratified for both herself and her (temporary) Party.

Determined that we should take the initiative and lead the profession, not be dragged along at the heels of the disruptive and irresponsible tearaways, I drafted an action motion for the Executive on the way up to Scarborough for the pre-Conference Executive. I knew that I would be challenged from a number of quarters, particularly because of the political overtones, so I decided to gather forces carefully. As soon as I arrived, I went to see Jim Murphy who at the Executive meeting would still be Senior Vice-President, but would assume the Presidency the day after, and discussed the situation with him. He agreed to move the motion in the Executive and I then went to see Alf Wilshire, Chairman of the Salaries Committee, a former President and the most respected of the middle of the roaders, a man of impeccable integrity. Alf exactly appreciated the score and agreed to second the motion. With such backing I now felt secure.

When the Executive met, we had a very tough debate, the opposition being led by my Vice Chairman of the Action Committee, my friend Peter Kennedy, who would be President the following year.

Peter was, as I knew, worried about the political repercussions and doubted the support we would get from the membership, and he advocated delay—a course which I thought would give us the worst of all worlds—the Government could afford to ignore us and our members would think we were just prevaricating and lose heart. The line of action we proposed was 'withdrawal of goodwill', i.e., refusal of normal cooperation with the employers, including no voluntary lunch-time duties, no meals accounting, no out-of-school activities including staff and parents' meetings, no use of cars on school business. The action was to start after 72 hours' notice to parents in the new term and could prove very effective. 'All out' strike action we rejected as being unnecessary in the circumstances to achieve our objective. We hoped that at Burnham following Conference we would see a change of heart: the Government would see sense and overrule silly Shirley in time to stop us.

So, at my last Conference, I found myself occupying the centre of the stage following upon the very fine Presidential address by Jim Murphy. I pointed out that, a year ago, the management had persuaded us to call off highly successful sanctions by giving us a commitment to examine the erosion of salaries since Houghton and a pledge to put it right "That commitment," I declaimed, "was clear, precise and unequivocal."

The management had disgracefully reneged and an angry profession was waiting for a lead from Conference to show that the union was not the soft touch they seemed to think it was. Our proposed action would bite deeply into the smooth running of the schools, had pressurised the management last year and could be even more effective now. In a nostalgic phrase, I said we would not tolerate a return to the 'genteel poverty' of the past. Part of my speech was televised and did not please our Labour friends. As for Shirley, she was to lose her seat in an area containing many teacher voters—and she deserved to. She was an unmitigated disaster for Labour.

A couple of days later, on the Monday, I had to return to the attack in moving the Action Memorandum on Educational Standards, our annual set of proposals for effectively improving working conditions for both teachers and children. We were taking, I told Conference, a great leap forward in proposing the step long desired, refusal to teach classes of over 30, for which we were now ready. Instead of being merely an aspiration, it would become a reality by giving the LEAS and Government a year's notice; this showed we meant business, for to have proposed it for operation in the current year would have been hot air as the rates had already been set. There would be no excuse next year for the authorities not knowing what was in store before they made the rates. I emphasised that we meant business and business did not include setting targets we could not achieve.

Our policy was carried overwhelmingly, so that was two up for me at my last Conference, both on fundamental questions.

The Executive had put me down to speak during the week on various other issues but I had privately decided that I had had my lot and withdrew my name after the President, Jim Murphy told me that he was going to interrupt the proceedings, something which was quite unprecedented, quite out of order and could be challenged, to call on me to make a farewell speech on the Tuesday afternoon. (This was a slot which had been reserved for the Secretary of State who had refused to come!)

I had already made a rather emotional (and I hope entertaining) farewell speech at the convivial Executive dinner on the Monday evening.

Here I recalled Old times and Old friends—and opponents—and made the pledge that I would not return to my Old battleground to play a spectator's part like so many of my retired colleagues, even though, as a former President, I was entitled to play a full part in the proceedings.

On the Tuesday afternoon Jim tipped me the wink, interrupted the hitherto traditionally sacred conference arrangements, and asked Conference's permission to allow me to speak. This, to my relief, he got with some acclamation and I uttered my last words to an NUT Conference, the scene of so many defeats and victories over a lifetime.

The Teacher reported the occasion: "Standing Ovation for Past President."

"Tribute was paid to Mr Max Morris, a former President of the NUT who retired from the Union's Executive at the end of the Conference. Delegates expressed their appreciation for his work for the Union with a standing ovation."

The new President, Jim Murphy said Morris had been a central dynamic force in the Union's affairs. He had been described as a major educational figure in Britain. He had always stressed the importance of the relationship between teachers and children rather than the Ideas of theorists.

Mr Morris displayed a high calibre both in the world of education and in the Union, His capabilities such as the ability to make an incisive analysis, had been invaluable to the Union. He had provoked vigorous arguments sometimes but there was no doubt that the effects of his work had been to the good of the Union. Mr Murphy also expressed praise for the work of Mr Morris's wife, Margaret: the Union owed a great deal to Mrs Morris, a historian and author, because of the intellectual support she had given over the years.

In reply, Mr Morris said he was flattered to be allowed to take up a few moments of the time which the Conference would otherwise have spent listening to Mrs Shirley Williams.

He had first attended the Union's Conference in 1938 and the first time he spoke to it was in 1939, 40 years ago this Easter. He had attended every Conference since the end of the war.

The biggest fight that the floor took part in was the one to establish a figure for negotiations. Since that victory in the 1950s Conference had never looked back. The floor had established itself as the voice of the Union. He was brief and emotional as he recalled certain highlights in his union and conference career. The message that he conveyed and which he had also emphasised at the Executive dinner to the union leaders past and present there assembled was that we had achieved in the union what he had always dreamed of as a young militant: the unity of floor and platform which made the union such a powerful force when it moved into action. There were no longer any major issues between the leadership and the mass of our members; there was overwhelming agreement on the main concerns of the profession—salaries and conditions of service. And this was a revolution from the days when the Executive and the mass of the activists were far apart and locked in conflict."

That day, Max withdrew his name from all further debates and began sitting back to enjoy the rest of the week. "In the evening, I had to suffer (and hugely enjoy) the raillery of the annual Press show brilliantly scripted as usual by Tudor David, John Izbicki and Bruce Kemble. I was not absolutely uninvolved afterwards, as I was the guest speaker at the annual Publishers' Dinner, a tribute to the activity I had put in over the years on behalf of much larger book allowances for schools. When it was all over, on Thursday midday, I went off with the Murphy's to Belfast where I was to lecture to the annual Conference rally of the Ulster Teachers' Union and speak at their Conference dinner. I spent much of the time at the Slieve Donard Hotel, where the Mountains of Mourne come down to the sea, in an alcoholic haze induced by their intensive hospitality."

So ended forty years of NUT Conference-going. What on earth would I do next Easter? The Teacher reporter, no doubt over influenced by the conviviality, 'quoted' me as saying: "Next year I shall be in my villa in the South of France, Wild horses won't drag me back." The villa was, of course, a figment of imagination and drawn from a story with banner headlines in the Sunday Express by Lady Olga Maitland, printed during TUC week the previous September, 'Red Max's Riviera Haven'. This referred to the small tumbledown apartment with a large terrace I had purchased with my pension lump sum. Olga had met me at a private dinner party and again, perhaps after over-indulgence, she had committed the not unknown journalistic solecism both of publishing private information and embellishing it to make a news story.

When Easter came around, I did not find as much difficulty as I feared. I went to France to my 'villa', sent a telegram of congratulations to the new President, Peter Kennedy, and happily heard a report of the Conference on the BBC World News. I survived.

Acquiring a New Family

Although disappointed that our hope of having children had not been granted, by 1968 we had become reconciled to the position. We had a full and busy life and neither of us wanted to adopt as Max's brother and his wife had done faced with the same situation. We'd wanted a child of our own not children as such. We never changed this decision but later on fate decided otherwise.

I describe above how becoming an 'Executive Wife' involved attending a lot of local NUT dinners and although I saw it all as a joke, I duly dressed up for the part. This involved going regularly to a local hairdresser. A new shampoo girl appeared one day, called Georgia with a Cypriot surname. She seemed very timid and immature for her age and very vulnerable, so I did my best to chat to her and help her relax. Her English vocabulary was limited and she knew very little about the society we live in and world events. So, my teacher instincts were aroused and my chats with her in the weeks and months that followed were partly geared to helping her learn a little more about the world around her and extend her vocabulary. But mainly, I just tried to jolly her along. After a while, I realised that although immature and ignorant of the ways of the world, Georgia was quick thinking and intelligent. She told me she regretted not having not being allowed to stay at school longer. She fairly soon became a very skilled hairdresser and I made sure she did my hair whenever I went.

I gradually found out her story. She had been born in Cyprus with a life-threatening heart condition, called a 'blue baby'. She was very fragile and not expected to survive for very long. However, because her father had served in the British Navy with distinction, he had British citizenship and the right to send her to England for surgery. She was brought here at the age 6 of by her grandmother and admitted into Hammersmith Hospital. She knew no English and underwent a major, virtually untried operation—she was the 8th patient to have it and the first to survive to adulthood. Still very poorly, she was discharged into the care of her mother's sister, who lived in London with her husband and son. Georgia had to stay in England to have a second operation when she was 13, and was again in hospital for a long time.

Georgia had not seen her own parents since 1960 and felt abandoned by them. It was not until 1971 by which time she was a young woman that she returned to Cyprus escorted by her aunt and uncle to visit her family. She told me about it on her return. Georgia had been eager to have it out with her mother for 'deserting her' but after meeting "this little woman dressed in black living in very simple dwellings and leading a very poor existence," and listening to her three sisters 'who poured kindness and love on her', she learnt that her parents loved her very much and had made the utmost sacrifice by sending her away to save her life. It had made her mother very ill and she had had a heart attack the day she put her child to sail on the ship to England, not knowing whether she would ever see her again. I remember, Georgia telling me on upon her return to England "how could I say anything to that poor woman who did what she thought was best for me."

On her return, her life went on as before—she still went on working at the salon and living with her Aunt and Uncle, who escorted her to work and back home later to make sure she didn't go astray. Her uncle told her that her future was to be married so she needed to be kept safe until then. This meant she had no chance of a social life and was in effect a virtual prisoner. I went on seeing her regularly and enjoyed my hairdressing appointments both for the way she styled my hair and for our chats. It is only in recent years that I learnt from Georgia that she would wait for the door of the salon to open and for me to walk in, then her face would light up as she was looking forward to seeing me and chatting to me. She recalls that she developed a great affection for me to compensate for the loss of her mother. She recalls me telling her about 'canvassing' but didn't have a clue what I was talking about. She said she was just happy to be in my company.

In 1976 at the age of 23, Georgia met Pravine when he came to meet his sister who was a customer at the salon. Pravine was a poor student from Mauritius and had come to England to study building technology and escape poverty. There was an instant attraction between them and Pravine wanted to meet outside of the salon. Georgia tried to explain to him that it would be impossible as her aunty would not approve of such a thing as he was of a different religion, culture and colour, but Pravine thought she was trying to put him off and offered to introduce himself to her aunty. So, it was agreed he would meet her guardians and went with her after work to their house. On meeting him at the front door, her aunt took one look at Pravine and shouted "you have brought shame on my house, you have brought a black bastard to my house, what will the neighbours say" and started punching her in front of him. Pravine was shocked and Georgia begged him to leave, which he did. When Georgia went to work the next day and the staff saw the bruises on her body, they wanted to call the police but Georgia was too scared and stopped them from doing that.

I didn't see her until the next week or I would certainly have urged her to call the police. It was not until many years later that I learnt the extent of the physical and mental abuse that had been done to her as a child and young woman. I asked her why she had not complained and she said she thought being treated that way was normal.

After Pravine had witnessed the beating by the aunt, he wanted to rescue Georgia and they continued to see each other in secret with the help of the staff at the salon. Georgia recalls how when her uncle came to escort her home, he would sit in the front to wait for Georgia to finish work while the staff would let Pravine in through the back of the salon into the staff room where the couple could have some time together, unknown to her uncle. Georgia and Pravine fell in love but they couldn't see each other openly.

She confided in me about what was happening and as Max and I were about to give a garden party to celebrate the publication of my book on the General Strike I took the opportunity to invite Georgia to attend with Pravine. Her Uncle being a supporter of the Cypriot Communist Party knew Max, so could not refuse to let her go, but stipulated that he would come and collect her at the end of the Party. That was the first time she had been able to attend a social function. By agreement, Pravine disappeared before the Uncle arrived.

A few months later Georgia ran away to live with Pravine as her guardians had discovered she was still seeing him and her aunt was going to beat her up again.

By then, Georgia had built up the courage to walk out of the house. As she had never been allowed to go out, all her wages had been put in the bank and Georgia now discovered they had accumulated and she had £7000 in her savings account, which in 1977 was a lot of money. Pravine suggested that she could get a mortgage and buy a house in Middle Lane which was on sale for £15,000. Georgia was very nervous as a woman about going to a bank and asking for a mortgage but to her surprise the bank manager took her seriously and offered her a mortgage only £1000 short of what they needed. I remember Georgia telling me all about this new venture of buying a house while she was brushing my hair. So, I asked her how much was the shortfall and when she said £1,000, I reached into my bag and gave her a cheque for £1,000.

Giving your hairdresser £1,000 out of the blue like that would probably be seen as eccentric or even crazy today but at the time it accorded with my and Max's commitment to living according to our socialist principles. We were not alone in wanting to do this. Many middle-class parents in the Labour Party were on principle sending their children to their local comprehensive schools. When we were first married, we worried about not living 'a bourgeois life style'. Initially I thought we ought not to have a second car. Some socialist friends were more extreme and thought it 'bourgeois' to buy a washing machine, but they then had a baby and we all realised that depriving ourselves was not going to bring socialism nearer.

We had no children to send to the local school but made a stand on how we handled our finances. We were determined to remain members of the working class 'by hand or brain' and not to become capitalists or rentiers. We did not buy stocks or shares either in our early days together nor at any time in our lives. Although we had bought a house it was as a home, not an asset; we both abhorred the idea of becoming a landlord and making money out of poorer peoples' need for a home. This meant that after I was in full time work, we had money to spare even after putting money into insurances, paying subscriptions to various pressure groups (Child Poverty Action Group, Age Concern, Shelter etc,) and building up savings 'against a rainy day'. Max was reluctant to give money to charities to pay for services which ought to be provided by the state because he thought it distracted attention from changes that needed to be achieved through political action. There was nothing particularly socialist about occasionally being a good Samaritan—it wouldn't bring socialism nearer but it didn't undermine our principles. I had been brought up by my mother to help people in difficulties, usually by advice rather than money, but as we had money, why not use it to help someone we knew who deserved help? It gave me pleasure and so Max did not object and left it to me to use my own discretion. Georgia was not the first person I helped, nor would she be the last. So, I played the Good Samaritan role to a small handful of people I judged would benefit during this period of affluence.

Georgia and Pravine settled in their new home but very soon afterwards Georgia got pregnant. She said to Pravine that she could get the pregnancy terminated as they had only just started in life and Pravine was still a student, but Pravine said it was alright they would get married and find a way to manage. So, a wedding was arranged.

By this time, my relationship with Georgia was more than just client and hairdresser. We'd been chatting away regularly for nine years and she'd come to rely on me as an older person whom she could turn to for sympathy and advice. Over the years I had realised she was a very kind; genuine and thoughtful person and I had become fond of her. I enjoyed seeing her and had been happy to help her buy her house.

After the wedding had been arranged, she asked me if I could play the role of her mother at the wedding. To please Pravine's uncle, who had helped them financially, it was going to be a Hindu wedding and the bride had to be supported by her mother at the ceremony. I said of course I'd be happy to do that. I asked Max if would come along. He had already met Georgia and Pravine at our Garden Party so he said he'd come provided he didn't have to play any part in the ceremony. Georgia checked this out and acting on the advice she'd been given, I told Max that he could just sit quietly at the back, which he agreed to do.

So, Georgia was married from our house. A friend of hers came to help her put on a traditional red sari and I put on a nice long dress and off we went. The Hindu priest assembled us ready for the ceremony and then demanded, "Where is the bride's father? We need him here before we can begin." So I asked Max would he please play ball. He muttered a protest but submitted and came along. He smiled and let garlands of flowers be draped around his neck and a red mark made on his forehead. Photographs were taken of us all, including 'Hindu Max'.

So that was the day that Georgia became our daughter. After her son was born, I began helping her with little gifts of food and keeping her company. As I'd never had children, I couldn't give advice on his care. Pravine was conscientious about providing for his family but had male chauvinist attitudes. He came from a culturally different society and had been ill treated as a child which had left its mark. So, he had no idea of English standards of behaviour as either a father or a husband but he looked up to Max and listened to him. All the same, the marriage did not settle down well. Georgia was still timid after being bullied by her Aunt, and had no experience of how to stand up for herself. I was concerned about the effect on Dharam, their son, who sometimes seemed frightened of his father. Other times, if Pravine was in a good mood, Dharam would look at him adoringly. He was a very beautiful baby with great big brown eyes and when he was taken out in his pram people stopped to coo at him.

When Dharam was about two, Georgia became pregnant again. The fact that her heart condition had not prevented her giving birth to Dharam did not mean that she had normal health and during the period she was pregnant she was not well and eventually had to go into hospital. Pravine was in Mauritius and so there was nothing to be done but for Georgia to bring Dharam to stay with us. I felt nervous as I had never looked after a baby (or toddler as he was by then), but necessity is a good teacher. I discovered how to tickle feet and became a proper grandma. I have stayed one ever since. Max too began to get interested in having contact with these young children though the one who totally captivated him was the next arrival, Natasha. When she was not yet three, she did something no child was supposed to do to Max, the Headmaster: she was strutting around the house in my Welly boots and he told her to take them off but she stamped her feet and said "No." He was taken aback—totally flummoxed by this fascinating little creature!

Over time I became a proper surrogate mother to Georgia, although I could never replace her real mother. She says the best thing I ever did was encourage her to go back to school, to learn to read and write. When I first got to know her, I became angry with her uncle for taking her out of school when she ought to have been allowed to stay on and catch up on some of the schooling she had missed. She said she had loved her one year at school between her second operation and leaving. I was very shocked, however, that the School had made no efforts to provide for her special needs nor even make allowances for her fragile state—she was made to walk round the playing field like other children when she was late at a time when she found walking difficult and exhausting.

Because professionally my role involved widening opportunity for young adults who had been disadvantaged in childhood, I was always determined to help her find a way to become educated. But I had to wait a long time. Eventually, when Natasha was ten months old and Georgia 28, we found a way forward. Georgia would drop Natasha to a Creche, her son to school and go to do her 'O' level in English at Kingsway College along with all the teenagers who had failed and were repeating. When Georgia started at the college, she could scarcely put a paragraph together but by the time she had done the year she wrote an essay that the teacher said made her proud. A few years later Georgia met up with the same teacher who informed her that she still was using the story she had written with her 'A' level students. Georgia, couldn't believe that her essay had such an impact. From Kingsway College, she progressed to an Access Course at 'City Lit' for two years. This is where she learned that women could talk, have views and be heard. I remember Georgia telling me how amazed she was that the female students were sitting around the table having a debate on the subject they were studying. By the time Georgia had finished her two years at City Lit, she had written a two thousand words essay on Karl Marx. She was then accepted to take a degree at Middlesex University which—to quote Georgia—"were the best years of my life." She still says the most important thing I ever did for her was encouraging her to study and become her own person. Unfortunately, with education comes freedom and this was the end of their marriage. Pravine blamed me for Georgia having acquired the freedom to think and make up her own mind.

It had taken many years for Georgia and I to build up our relationship and I could never be more than a surrogate mother, but from the moment they were born Max and I were real grandparents to Dharam and Natasha, because they thought we were. They know now that we are not blood relations but it has never made any difference. We did eventually decide to adopt Georgia formally only to discover that in English Law you can't adopt adults. It didn't matter—as far as we and all our friends and acquaintances are concerned Georgia, Dharam and Natasha, and their children are our family. We acquired this family just before Max retired and just after we bought our flat in Menton, which the children later loved visiting. Acquiring grandchildren gave Max a new interest, a new source of amusement and happiness at a critical moment in his life. Nothing was planned it just happened.

Max: The Mandarins Rampant

Control of the education system had long been divided between the Government, Local Authorities and the Teachers, represented by their unions, and struggles between them were endemic. Max thought the biggest problem, even when Labour was in power, was the reliance by Ministers of Education upon the advice of the Civil Servants in the Department of Education, whose senior figures were nearly all educated in the leading Public Schools and whose children would not be affected by decisions about state education. He called them 'the Mandarins' others described them as the 'Establishment'.

It was described above how at the First Labour Conference after the 1945 Election Ellen Wilkinson supported a paper drawn up by the Department on the 1944 Education Act which suggested the working-class children wouldn't need much education for their future employment. She was made to withdraw the document but the officials did not change their attitude nor their assumption that no skills would be needed by the mass of the working class. Even the provision in the 1944 Act for the development of more technical/central schools was ignored. Many years later during the period when the Comprehensive system was being developed the Mandarins set out to influence the curriculum and organisation of the schools and teaching profession.

MAX: "Their objective in this case was subversion of the basic purpose of the Comprehensive and the maintenance of a divided and divisive curriculum as preparation for the age-old class division of jobs which the Establishment regards as natural and immutable."

By the time Max became NUT President, there had been considerable progress towards developing a broader curriculum through both the teacher-led development of Certificates of Secondary Education and the work of the School Council, on which teachers had a major voice. CSE's were available in both academic and vocational subjects, and incorporated course work assessment in addition to examinations. They enabled recognition of a wider range of studies than the University-controlled 'O' and 'A' GCEs.

The School Council had taken over responsibility for curriculum and examinations previously undertaken by the Schools Examination Council and the Curriculum Study Group. It was a non-directive body intended to provide leadership in curriculum, examination and assessment development. Its work was undertaken by committees and working parties on which teachers were the majority. It commissioned research and published reports on its programmes.

The conflicts and issues during the Callaghan years and the main period of Margaret Thatcher's period as Prime Minister were analysed in depth in 'Education—The Wasted Years 1973–86' edited by Max and Dr Clive Griggs (pub. Falmer Press 1988). It contained articles covering all aspects of developments in this period by 13 leading experts in the field of education. Everything in this short account is examined at much greater depth there.

Before he had stood for President, Max had proved to himself and others the advantages of a comprehensive educational structure for children at secondary level with a broad curriculum for all children.

Many other Heads and staff had done their best to do likewise despite the delay in raising the leaving age to 16 and an ongoing lack of resources, including specialist teachers of maths and science and lack of workshops and labs. Max was enthusiastic at the progress being made and convinced that with more financial support the transformation of secondary education could be achieved so that all children would benefit by following a full and broad curriculum.

Max and the teacher unions thought that the priority was getting the curriculum right and that examinations should relate to the curriculum not the curriculum to examinations. The problem was that the Universities and the Mandarins who advised Ministers thought the opposite. An equally fundamental problem was that the weakness of sterling was related to political decisions about the role of Britain in the world after 1945 leading to high spending on our armed forces and armaments. By the 1970s, we had a faltering economy, a sterling crisis, failing industries, unemployment, and a hitherto unknown rate of inflation. The battle for the resources needed to complete the Comprehensive transformation was going to be difficult.[5]

---

[5] See Philip Stevens 'Britain Alone' (2021) for a clear analysis of Britain's economic situation since 1945.

What Max did not expect was that a fresh attack on the principles of Comprehensive education would be taken seriously. He thought that Cyril Burt's theories that children could be classified by measuring their innate intelligence had been debunked years earlier by both leading psychologists and educationalists. Yet when a group of academics influenced by such theories began to publish the 'Black Papers' from 1969 onwards, arguing for a return to 'basics' and selection to counteract what they claimed were falling standards and chaos in schools, they were granted a meeting with Margaret Thatcher and became skilled at getting publicity in the tabloid press. Their claim about general indiscipline in schools was unjustified as demonstrated by an HMI Report covering 1977–78 entitled 'Good Behaviour and Discipline in Schools', but by then the damage had been done by press reports of isolated instances of disorder.

The outstanding case was William Tyndale Junior School in Islington where in 1975 a group of ultra-left teachers were allowing the pupils to do whatever they wanted and neglecting to provide even basic education. Max and the NUT were appalled by this and furious at how it was letting down the children who needed education in order to hold their own in their future adult life and how it was giving teachers a bad name. The ILEA took over the school but the damage had been done. There was a problem also about one of the School Council's reports on teaching children about racism, which was not approved by the Council, but again damage was done by publicity about the issue, even though it had been resolved.

When he became Prime Minister James Callaghan, who had an interest in educational policy although he was traditional in his approach (i.e., he thought working class opportunity could be increased gradually through selection rather than by opportunity for all through comprehensive education), asked Fred Mulley, then Education Secretary for an overview of the position. Mulley was unable to provide one, so the task was given to the DES. Nothing could have made the Mandarins happier as it provided them with the opportunity to claim that what was needed was more intervention by the DES in the schools.

Their 'Yellow Book' was meant to be for the Prime Minister's private use but it became public in 1976. Max thought it was so incorrect and biased that no-one would take it at face value:

"It gave a distorted picture of schools and teachers, and of the Schools Council, whose efforts to reform and democratise as well as broaden the secondary school curriculum and examinations it undermined. It cast doubt in a most biased way on the work of the comprehensives and gave an utterly false impression of the impact of informal methods in the primary schools. Central to its thesis was the assumption of poor performance and declining standards. What might be wrong, they claimed, was overemphasis on students' future role in society rather than their economic roll, with the implication that poor schooling was responsible for Britain's poor economic performance. The 'failure of the schools' became a vogue comment in the media."

There was never an impartial examination of the validity of the statements in the Yellow Book as it was supposed to be a private document. Curiously, in March 1977 Shirley Williams, by then Education Secretary and under pressure from the Tories in Parliament, produced convincing statistics to show how standards had risen. She was backed by the Permanent Secretary, Sir James Hamilton, whose department had just produced the Yellow Book claiming the opposite. Somehow the Press failed to give publicity to this exchange, nor did Shirley Williams. Nor did the press discuss the real reasons why Britain was losing its industrial capacity and suffering increasing unemployment—it was easier to blame the teachers!

After reading the Yellow Book, Callaghan made a speech at Ruskin College, Oxford about the state of education. Understandably given Britain's money problems, he warned teachers not to expect ever increasing budgets. He then attacked permissiveness and the inadequate performance of some teachers as well as 'standards' and lack of accountability. Why were employers complaining? Were the standards of science and maths teaching in comprehensive schools sufficiently demanding? What was available for 16–19-year-olds? How good was the examination system? Most of his questions would have been legitimate had they been asked without the implication that the answers were already known and schools were in a crisis.

I remember at the time Max was less worried than I expected: he knew that the picture being presented was false and had confidence that any objective analysis would vindicate the progress already achieved. He believed the ongoing work of the Schools Council was on the right lines and the educational and social aims of the comprehensive system would be achieved given time and sufficient support. Writing in 'The Wasted Years' he commentated:

"A Labour Prime Minister brought comfort to his Tory enemies in a speech…which took the schools to task for being unrelated to Britain's wealth making processes in industry. As a Labour Prime Minister, he should have castigated the old selective system with its academic neglect of technology in the independent and grammar schools from which British leaders were drawn, leaving the under resourced 'second tier' modern schools for the mass of children. It was this class-biased system, he could truthfully have argued, which had produced an elite which looked down on 'wealth making'—but not wealth enjoying!

And he could have added his deep regret that financial stringency had prohibited successive Labour Governments from fully developing the new comprehensive system by training the specialist teachers needed and equipping the schools with up-to-date workshops and labs. He might have expressed his appreciation of the way the new unselective schools were extending technical education...Concluding he could have pledged more resources for helping to develop a system which could end the class bias in education."

Shirley Williams as Education Secretary did nothing to defend the teaching profession or provide a balanced report of what was going on in schools. Instead, she initiated 'A Great Debate'. Eight public regional Conferences were held to discuss four fundamental educational issues: the aims and content of the curriculum; educational standards and their assessment; the performance of the school system as a whole, including teacher training and the reform of GCSE and CSE; and the school in relation to working life. These questions with their large scope were put to audiences of 200 representatives from the teacher unions, FE, HE, LEAs, parents, industry and the trade unions at conferences in which contributions from the floor lasted 40 minutes flat, meaning those who managed to catch the Chair's eye would have about 4 minutes.

Max derided this as "a publicity exercise in showbiz style, a fanfare for the DES, now publicly entering the 'secret garden'...As a serious contribution to educational debate it was less than null." Yet it opened the door for a flow of papers from the DES and HMI on curricular matters and for battles over the control of the curriculum which would last until long after the 1979 election.

Although Callaghan had not mentioned it in his speech, Max fully realised that the key target of the Mandarins was majority teacher control of the Schools Council. He had heard that the DES at a private meeting in 1975 chaired by John Hudson, the chief DES representative on the Council had voted to kill it off. Max thought the Council could be saved by revising its constitution to provide a greater lay element, which was reluctantly negotiated: "the DES from its esoteric and remote eyrie above Waterloo Station had succeeded in inserting a wedge into the curricular power of the teaching profession and school autonomy." Max was all prepared to fight on.

Although after his retirement he was no longer the spokesman of the NUT or involved in salary negotiations, Max was very much engaged in its battles as a member of the Schools Council and as the elected Chair of the London Regional Examination Board from 1979 until 1990, and as vice-Chair of the Centre for Educational Disadvantage 1975–81. In 1988, he became a Trustee of the NUT: he had vowed not to attend NUT Conferences as an ex-President but becoming a Trustee meant he was required to attend, which he did until his death 20 years later. He supported its campaigns with regular articles in the educational press, l letters in The Guardian and The Times and quite frequent appearances on TV. He enjoyed writing, clarifying facts and carrying out verbal assaults on those he saw as enemies on either the right wing or the ultra-left.

Although educational issues would always be his prime concern, Max felt he was young enough to take on something new as well.

Most of his friends and old colleagues assumed he would be offered some regular employment in the public sector but he had a more realistic appreciation of the public service world, which he said, "was dominated by the bureaucrats whom I had, over the years, beaten with both whips and scorpions. They had had to put up with me, indeed not only play along but even pander to me as long as represented teachers…but I had no illusions about their attitude. It would be anything from unhelpful to vindictive." So, he had no intention of asking for anything.

Then, a while before his retirement, Max received an invitation to visit Roy Hattersley, with whom he had had excellent relations when he was Shadow Education Minister in the Heath period and who was currently Secretary of State at the Department of Prices and Consumer Affairs. Max was mystified and supposed any recent knowledge of him would have come from Hattersley's political adviser, Professor Maurice Peston (later Lord Peston) who lived near us and was a good friend of Max (indeed of us both—I taught his students when working at Queen Mary College). But why would Roy Hattersley want to see Max?

Max: "When I went in to see Roy, we chatted about this and that and he then asked me if I would be interested in becoming Chairman of the Post Office Users' National Council. It was, he said, a body with great potential for playing an active and progressive part in the 'consumer' complex and had latterly been rather quiescent. They were looking for a new Chairman (the previous one had died) to liven things up. He appreciated it was outside my sphere of experience but it was an important body and he would like me to think the offer over.

I asked him a number of questions. We both knew our way around the world of public appointments. Was the post in his gift? Would my Communist background, even though I was now in the Labour Party, not be an impediment? His reply was frank and clear. Before making the offer, he had checked with the PM and Mr Callaghan had cleared it—there was no worry there. The Minister of Industry was also involved—though his relations with Mr Varley were such as to make it 99% sure that the job would be mine if I wanted it. It was, incidentally, a part-time post with a salary/payment of £2000 for which he was very apologetic—it was too little. The amount of time I spent on it would depend on me but it ought not to take up more than two days a week; there was a substantial staff and office."

After thinking it over, Max told Roy he would accept the offer and Roy said that he'd make the arrangements and let Max know. Time went by. Max saw Roy by chance at a social function. Max didn't want to raise the issue, but Roy came over and said that it was taking time but he would be in touch. Max told me he seemed a bit embarrassed. Eventually after the summer holidays Roy contacted Max and said he had failed to get agreement about the appointment. Max was not the least bit surprised but Roy was embarrassed. Over lunch at the Gay Hussar he confided that a retired senior civil servant had been appointed.

Max: "It was perfectly clear what had happened. Even the PM's OK could not overcome the mandarin network when it came to appointments and the mandarins hated me. I was certainly, we laughed, not one of the armies of the Great and the Good—the 'jobs for the boys' brigade. Roy admitted that the Education Department had been consulted. Though, to be fair, Roy added that, if he had been solely concerned, there would have been no problem. Even Roy had not appreciated the weight of the Establishment once the machine got working!"

Someone who did realise this was Tony Benn, who was Secretary of State for Industry 1974–5 but was unable to carry out the programmes he proposed. Later, in his list of why this had been the case, he put as the first reason "Because Civil servants can frustrate the policies and decisions of an elected government."

Max could be very tenacious in his pursuit of a story against the 'Mandarins'. My favourite example is how he built up the case over several years about one glaring example of their failure to recognise the importance of technical education and finally forced them to capitulate:

MAX: "As a member of the University of London Schools Examinations Council and its Examinations Committee I noticed one day in February 1979 in the minutes of the subject panel on Design and Technology (D&T) that the Civil Service Commissioners had upset the panel by stating in quite unequivocal terms its refusal to recognise an A Level in the subject as a qualification for entry to the Executive Grade of the Civil Service, a severe handicap for students in the North East of England taking the relevant courses in schools and FE…even the authoritative Standing Committee on University Entrance had given recognition to design-based subjects as 'intellectually sufficiently demanding to justify consideration by Universities for full recognition'. No matter, the D & T Panel was told:

'The Commissioners have given considerable thought to the position of practical or vocational subjects but in assessing their values for their own purposes they run into difficulty since, in these subjects, success is determined to some extent by a test of practical skill…Bearing in mind the nature of an Executive Officer's work, it was decided that the subjects which could be offered should be of an academic nature or have a very high academic content…The Commissioners agree that a GCE course in Design and Technology requires disciplined study but…they regret that they cannot accept this qualification as having the necessary academic width and depth to satisfy the educational requirements of entry into the Executive Officer Grade…'

I rubbed my eyes in disbelief and raised the matter at the next meeting of our Committee. Their reaction was explosive, which was interesting since the Committee consisted mainly of university professors and lecturers and grammar, or ex-grammar school teachers, who might have been expected not to be too surprised or upset…Sometime in March, with full Council approval, our Secretary wrote to the Secretary of State at the DES and the Secretary of State for Industry. Three weeks later a junior official at the DES replied merely stating "that the DES would make some enquiries before they could make a fuller reply." This was typical Civil Service stalling, as the full facts were available in the correspondence.

When no further letter had been received from Sir James Hamilton (a great public apostle of engineering education), our Secretary wrote again, and again (we are now at the end of February 1980 and the themes of the Great Debate had been taken over by a Tory Minister, Mark Carlisle, in a Government whose public professions were of determination to advance assiduously the cooperation of education and industry). Finally at the end of August, came the earth-shaking reply that the Commissioners had been 'reviewing the subject' and expected to reach a decision shortly.

In November the DES announced that the CSC were now 'favourably disposed...but would like to examine the work undertaken by students and a favourable reply could be expected subject to a satisfactory outcome to this inspection.' The cool effrontery of this latest correspondence was obviously in no way appreciated by these Olympian deities—for they were admitting that they had made their decisions without any knowledge, far less scrutiny, of what was taught in the subject, a decision based on the pure milk of Platonic educational principles, good for all time. And they had done so in the face of all the evidence by the widest spectrum of academic opinion.

Before the issue was concluded, as it soon was by the capitulation of the stupid oafs in Whitehall (why does anyone ever think them clever?), I published in *The Guardian* a feature article telling the whole story up till then, under the heading, 'A Moral Tale'. It was one indeed. Here were two governments, the later one exceeding the former in its public zeal, lecturing the teachers for being old-fashioned in their curricular approaches, demanding that the schools take full account of the importance of manufacturing industry as against the old academic nostrums, promising a thorough overhaul of the content of education to bring those reactionary academic teachers into the 21st century! And they were all the time insisting on the most backward of academic criteria for choosing even a relatively junior grade of civil servant.

People have asked me: how could they expect to get away with insisting that Greek was a suitable A Level subject for the Executive Grade in the Department of Industry or Energy, but not Design & Technology? The answer is that they did get away with it and always had done. The camaraderie of the mandarins was superior to the whims and whimsies or even the policies of Ministers. And as for democracy, that was something Plato wrote about for the elite."

There were three other issues that came up before the change of Government but were passed on to the Conservatives to deal with. First was how to help disadvantaged students: the Centre for Educational Disadvantage was set up in 1975 as an advisory body with a limited budget, and after debating which type of disadvantage should be covered—personal /physical characteristics or social disadvantage including race or sex—was just starting to do useful work when in 1981 it was declared an unnecessary Quango and abolished by Mark Carlisle despite protests by the Chair and Max as Vice-Chair. Max was indignant at it being dubbed a 'Quango', implying unearned perks for Board members, when in actuality the teacher members were unpaid and providing their services free. Having been the headmaster of a school with a high level of Jamaican children Max felt he had experience to offer and that the study of how to deal with all forms of disadvantaged children was important—but not in the eyes of the Mandarins or Thatcher Government.

The role of governing bodies was raised in 1975 in the Taylor Report and much discussed during Shirley Williams reign but left for action by Kenneth Baker as detailed below. Finally, the issue of post 16 exams has been an ongoing issue of trial and error until the present and one on which Max would express his opinion in the following years, but it was still unresolved when he died.

Important as these issues were, Max's main concern throughout the 1970s and 1980s was the development of a suitable curriculum for Comprehensive Schools alongside an appropriate examination structure. In July 1970, after proposals for reforming A Levels had been rejected due to the conservatism of the university, grammar school and other backward-looking vested interests backed by the Mandarins, the Schools Council drew up the proposal, which was accepted, to proceed with studies aimed at replacing O Level and CSE by a single exam so that all pupils could study both technology and traditional academic subjects and be tested in various ways, not just by memory tests.

MAX: "Feasibility and development studies were begun (the paper became mountainous), numberless meetings took place to iron out every possible difficulty, conferences galore were held by the Council, the CSE and GCE Boards jointly and separately until it seemed that, at last, we had worked out a viable new system. This the Council finally agreed in 1976, six years after the original decision, and submitted the proposals to the Department.

That's when our troubles really began! Shirley Williams dithered and delayed, procrastinated and piddled about; she couldn't say yes and she couldn't say no, and finally appointed a committee to examine all the issues already examined in detail over five years with meticulous objectivity. The Waddell Committee sat for a year and recommended (to the consternation of the mandarins and the Minister) a single 16-plus exam. There were more delays and then an acceptance in principle, but a demand from the Minister for further study of how the exam would be controlled at the top, though she had previously agreed that the Schools Council would do the job and was now ratting on that commitment. So, another committee was set up by the Council (on which I sat) which worked out further compromises to satisfy the dithering dame. By this time, it was Easter 1979, and in May the General Election relieved us of Mrs Williams' presence.

Unsurprisingly, the new Minister, Mark Carlisle, placed all developments on 16-plus on the shelf while he examined everything all over again. So, we now entered a further period of Ministerial consultation, though who there was left to consult after ten years of consultation heaven and the mandarins only knew! At last, in February 1980, in a masterpiece of vagueness and ambiguity, the DES appeared to give qualified support for the proposed reform, subject to the production by the Examination Boards of criteria which the Minister found acceptable After seemingly interminable delays in which the monsoon Carlisle was replaced by the sirocco Joseph, the D.E.S. produced a statement of policy in November 1982. As had been feared, the statement was equivocal—Sir Keith would judge the criteria on their ability to maintain O-Level standards.

The GCE and CSE Boards had established a National Joint Council (on which I sat) which was proceeding with the mammoth task through Joint Subject Committees of criteria-building, subject by subject, a job which was only concluded late in 1984. By then, also, the various Examining Groups had prepared, after enormous local effort, a large number of 'interim' joint 16+ syllabuses. These were intended to show the viability of the whole operation. But Sir Keith refused to be hurried and would only promise, under pressure, to give his decision by the summer of 1984. In the meantime, he began commenting in detail on the criteria.

Yet already the Schools Council, which had done all the basic work, had been sentenced to death. In 1981 a specially chosen don, Mrs Trenaman, was appointed to examine the work of the Council but contrary to DES hopes, she produced a favourable Report. Nevertheless, Sir Keith ignored her Report in favour of accepting the 'malevolent' advice of the DES. The announcement of the abolition of the Council was made in April 1982, just when it was making its greatest impact under the leadership of John Tomlinson. It was finally closed in 1984 and replaced by two bodies, the Secondary Examinations Council, which was entirely government appointed, and the School Curriculum Development Committee on which the LEAs managed to secure representation along with the

Mandarins. Teacher representation was ended on both bodies. The experience and professional knowledge of teachers was dispensed with in favour of central control alongside an emphasis on privatisation and individual enterprise.

Max was disappointed that Keith Joseph had given in to the mandarins. "Sir Keith is the only Minister I have met who actually spoke for himself on educational matters. His comments though sometimes very reactionary were also often well-informed and sensible, though it was impossible to expect total agreement over hundreds of pages of closely-written and argued criteria for a varied range of school subjects. To our delight, the Secondary Examinations Council, the body he had personally set up and appointed to take over the examination functions of the Schools Council, so which he had to consult, came to the 'firm and unanimous' conclusion that the single, 16-plus should be approved and go ahead. History had once again repeated itself and yet another committee had confirmed the Schools Council's conclusions. The Minister acquiesced and the new exams finally began in 1988."

Keith Joseph, although right-wing in his views and his advocacy of parental choice and vouchers, was always correct and polite in discussion with teachers. A most amazing example of this was when he was due as Education Secretary to be the main guest at an NUT dinner hosted by Max in the House of Commons the day after the Brighton bombing on 12 October 1984. The room he was in was damaged and his wife injured. Naturally the NUT expected he wouldn't be coming, but they got a phone call apologising that he would have to come in a dusty suit as his dress suit had been lost in the bombing. And he came. I sat next to him and when he found I worked in HE, he initiated a serious discussion about its problems, as well as being gracious to Max about the combined exam now going ahead. None of Callaghan's secretaries of State had shown any such respect to the NUT.

Kenneth Baker who succeeded him was said by Max to be "more direct, less subtle with an air of absolute certainty, not beset by any intellectual doubts." He was appointed in 1986 and in his four years in office dismantled the long-standing shared control of education policy between the Government (guided by the Mandarins), the Local Authorities and the Teachers. Baker believed in private initiative, competition between schools, selection and parental choice and had no use whatsoever for the input of teachers in decision making of any kind. He also set out to limit the role of Local Authorities, which had already started by cutting back their access to funding. The percentage of the Rate Support Grant paid by the Government, which was 60% in 1979, went down to 52% in 1884–85 and to less than 47% under Baker.

His first target was the Burnham Committee. By 1986, it had become a very cumbersome body for a number of reasons. First, ever since the NUT lost its role as the sole representative of teachers, the NAS and some of the other unions represented clashed with the NUT over the breakdown of salaries between the Basic Scale and differential payments; secondly, all the unions vigorously opposed proposals from the Management side to include conditions of service in the negotiations and finally, delays were caused because of a secret agreement made in 1965 that the Government would impose in advance an overall limit on how much the Management (L.E.As) could offer.

Salary settlements in 1974 and 1981 did not emerge from Burnham negotiations but from judgements by Committees set up to rectify low pay in public services. Teachers had welcomed the Houghton Agreement but it had been destroyed by inflation which left them far below the salary level of any other profession seeking to recruit graduates. Although they gained from the findings of the Clegg Committee., they were disappointed to be reliant on them. Since then, the Burnham Committee had failed to reach agreement during negations and there had been strikes by both the NUT and NAS over salaries. Parents in general supported teachers' demands for pay appropriate to their responsibilities but became frustrated by the number of strikes in 1984 and 85. Kenneth Baker took advantage of this to impose central control. His Teachers' Pay and Conditions Act came into effect in 1987. It abolished the pay negotiation rights of the teaching profession, imposed a new salary structure and laid down conditions of service.

As was said at the time, "Government power can be used to impose a settlement but what parents are interested in is a good education for their children…High quality education depends ultimately on inspired leadership and inspired teaching in the schools. A profession which has had to submit to superior power, its contract of employment imposed instead of freely negotiated, may go through the motions of teaching…but the spark of enthusiasm, the high morale which fosters good work is likely to be missing."

Few Committees of Enquiry in education have created such controversy as Tom Taylor's Report which reviewed the role of governing and managing bodies in schools and their relationship to LEAs, Heads and staffs, parents and pupils. The idea of an Enquiry originated under the Thatcher regime at the DES and was put into operation by her Labour successor, Reg Prentice, but despite many hours of discussion nothing was formally decided until 1980, when an Act was passed requiring all schools to have parent governors elected by secret ballot.

Max was in no way opposed to involving parents in Governing Bodies and had invited as many parents as the hall could hold to his school's Prize Day and annual Report to his Governing Body on the school's progress, but Governing Bodies were not regularly involved with schools in the 1960s. However, parents were involved through Parent Teacher Associations and the development of pastoral care systems brought teachers into contact with individual parents so problems could be jointly tackled. Max conceded that School Boards, although not necessary, might become a useful link between individual schools and the local community, although he did not envisage them having a major role.

Six more years went by until Kenneth Baker enacted legislation about the future role of Governing Bodies and another two until this was finalised as part of his 1988 Education Act. Since then, every aspect of running a school has been the responsibility of Boards of Governors. Instead of being a useful support for the schools, they were transformed into a link in a chain of command. It was laid down that "they were to be in the direct line of formal responsibility between the LEA and the head of the school…there is no area of the school's activities in respect of which the governing body should have no responsibility nor one on which the head and staff should be accountable only to themselves or to the LEA. This approach would facilitate the definition of a clear and straightforward line of responsibility and authority running from the LEA through the governing body and the head to every person engaged in running the school."

Max thought the system being set up was absurd and unworkable, time wasting and confusing. He believed in delegation and team work but under the leadership of a Head with ultimate control and responsibility. How else could any large and complex organisation be effective? Head teachers had always been responsible to Local Education Authorities but LEAs didn't run the schools or control the curriculum, that was the responsibility of the Schools themselves under the leadership of the Head teacher.

After 1988, Head teachers lost their authority to School Boards composed of less than one-quarter staff, some parents, pupils, ancillary workers (i.e., caretakers, cleaners and clerical workers), representatives of the various political parties and representatives of 'the community', e.g., an ethnic minority activist, member of a chamber of commerce or trades council, the local branch of CASE or member of ACE.

"Just imagine" Max mocked, "such a motley cast performing the Taylor comic opera, constantly reading reams of reports, attending committees and sub-committees, being available for the Head to consult them at all times of the day on disciplinary matters, keeping a watch over the teaching methods, ensuring that the agreed curricula were in no way departed from, and attending Governing Bodies." Both he and I much later became members of Governing Bodies but he always said "Thank Goodness I'm not a Head under such a system" and I thought his original reactions had been absolutely correct and Governing Bodies were totally unsuited to carry out all the tasks laid upon them and could make an absurd amount of extra work for Head teachers unless they had the sense to avoid it. The Head of the first School for which I was a Governor pointed out that it would take 40 hours a week of her time if she attended all the committees of its Governing Body.

The 1988 Education Act was the worst of the Baker changes not only because of replacing the authority of Heads by School Boards but above all because it established total central control of the curriculum. Teachers were not opposed in principle to a national curriculum, it was what the Schools Council had been working towards, but the Baker curriculum was totally prescriptive and rigidly detailed, leaving no room for teacher initiative and adaptation to the needs of the children in front of them. Worse still was the accompanying examination system and accountability through Ofsted and League Tables.

The curriculum covered ten subjects and was split into 4 stages ending at ages 7, 11, 14 and 16, with formal, centrally organised assessment at the end of each stage, not as an aid to teaching, but for the purposes of bureaucratic control and accountability through Ofsted and League tables. When put into effect, English children became the most frequently tested in the world so much so that in 1993 all the teacher unions boycotted the key stage exams and even the Head HMI thought they were distorting the curriculum, so they were modified and tests at 14 abolished. Nevertheless, testing, Ofsted and League tables became the norm, along with parental choice, selection, encouragement of private schools and Assisted Places. Kenneth Baker even created a new type of School, City Technology Colleges, totally outside the control of the Local Authorities.

All ideas of equal provision or cooperation between schools was thrown out and dismissed as a teachers' vested interest. Comprehensive Schools still existed but their purpose and aspiration to provide a full range of opportunities for all children regardless of class background was sabotaged. The Mandarins had won and Max's hopes were unfulfilled. He refused to be discouraged and based his hopes on a future Labour Government coming to power.

Margaret Enters Management

Once Max finished his year as President and my role as his 'Lady Consort' was over apart from occasional social events, I carried out my long-term plan to concentrate on my own career. As described above, I became a lecturer in history at the Polytechnic of Central London and stayed there twelve years. I was very happy there and had no desire to move. I enjoyed the mixed range of students of different ages and backgrounds; on the evening course we had quite a few active trade unionists including the 'bell ringer of Dagenham' a renowned strike leader. Halfway through my time there, I was appointed Director of the Social Sciences Degree, which by then was the largest Course in PCL. This meant I had an office and a secretary but I continued to teach and still considered myself an academic.

I continued being an active member of the Academic Council and was pleased that we achieved our main objective to end crony appointments and ensure that all new vacancies were publicly advertised and that appointment committees contained at least one woman, one student, one ethnic minority member and an outside adviser in the relevant subject. This worked well. Deans in each School were at that time democratically elected by academic staff and there was going to be a vacancy in 1986 in the School of Social Sciences. I had received 70% of first votes for Academic Council membership in 1985 and was expected to be elected as Dean the following year.

However, in line with the beginning of the move in HE towards central control by management, the Rector decided to end the system of election and replace it by appointment. I opposed the change on political grounds but didn't think it was directed against me personally. I thought Terry Burlin might appoint me anyway; he was very correct and impersonal, but I had always got on with him reasonably well despite being part of the 'troublemakers' on the Academic Council.

By chance, I saw an advertisement for the Director of Modular Studies at City of London Polytechnic, which had pioneered modular studies degrees and had a large multi-subject Modular course. It had always been run by a male scientist so I didn't think a woman historian would be appointed, but I decided to apply as a gesture of independence: if I were shortlisted it might stop Terry Burlin taking my services for granted. I thought this plan had failed until I received a letter inviting me to come to an interview in two days' time bringing with me a statement of objectives for the future of the Degree on an A4 sheet of paper. I thought this late invitation was very odd and later found out that that NATFHE (previously the ATTI) at City Poly had raised objections because no women had been shortlisted, so two of us had been added at the last minute.

Anyway, I got out my Amstrad and did as required and went along that Friday assuming I must be a token addition and wasn't going to get the post. So, in a very relaxed way I told them my views on modular degrees and how they should be managed (a subject on which I was used to holding forth). They said I would be phoned that evening if offered the post, but I went home had a meal with Max and popped out to see a friend and thought no more about it. To my surprise when I returned Max said "they are offering you the post and seemed put out you were not here waiting for news. You are to let them know on Monday if you accept."

On Monday morning, I went along to see Terry Burlin and told him that I had been offered the City Poly post but wasn't sure about leaving PCL, hoping he'd say he would like me to stay. To my utter astonishment, he leapt to his feet, gave me a warm hug and said "Many Congratulation." So that left me no choice but to accept the offer.

The Modular Degree at City covered a much wider range of subjects than that at PCL but was run on the same principles, yet there was a major difference between the role of Modular Director at the two Polytechnics which I only fully realised on my first day. The Provost, Michael Edwards, who had a business background, welcomed me and told me that I was in charge and could choose whatever staff I wanted as my Assistant Directors and other supporting staff. There were two acting Assistant Directors who had applied for the top job, but I shouldn't worry about that I could choose whether to keep them or not. (Oh dear! that was awkward—what was I letting myself in for?) He then said that I would be chairing the Modular Studies Board, consisting of about 30 members including all the Heads of Department, some of whom disagreed with the existence of modular studies, but I shouldn't let them disrupt the meetings. I would also be chairing all the Modular Examination Boards and would be responsible for making final decisions after discussion with borderline students. I didn't exactly quail, I was very experienced at chairing committees, but it seemed to me that I was facing a difficult time ahead compared with life at PCL.

Finally, he told me I would be part of the Senior Management Team which set policies and the Budget along with himself, the Deputy Provost, two Assistant Provosts, 3 Deans (I had the same status as the Deans), the Finance Director and Legal Secretary. The Senior Management team was responsible to ILEA, soon about to be abolished by the Thatcher Government. The Polytechnics were converted into independent Universities in 1992 with a Board of Governors and City Poly became London Guildhall University with Governors mainly drawn from the City.

Although City Poly also had an Academic Council there was clearly less consultation with staff than at PCL. I found out later that the main challenge to the Management at City Poly came from the Union, whose intervention about women candidates had led to my appointment. As a member of the Union, I wondered whether I would face conflicts of interest being part of Management. I asked the Provost if I would be doing some lecturing in History as part of the job but from his reply, I realised that my lecturing days were over. Like it or not, I was moving into full-time management. My salary was enhanced by moving to City Poly but I had been perfectly satisfied with my existing PCL salary and hadn't needed to move. I had never had any training in management skills apart from a word of caution from one of my 'Gang of Four' colleagues, Leslie Wagner, who when I became Director of the PCL course warned me to watch my back and abide by existing regulations even if I wanted to change them.

Despite my qualms, I had taken the post and intended to do my best in it for the sake of the students on the course. An HMI Report a year earlier had said the Scheme was well organised and well taught and the standards achieved by students were generally high. There were staff in most departments committed to supporting it. So, my role would be to maintain and defend it rather than fundamentally change it. I soon settled in and got to know the colleagues who believed in it—and those who didn't!

I learnt to keep the Modular Studies Board strictly to its agenda—at my first meeting I did this so successfully that the meeting lasted less than two hours, compared with previously 4 or 5 hours, and the members sat on at first not believing it was over. Academics like discussion and I was never able to contain it quite as well once they got to know me.

This was the period when instead of providing money for all HE institutions, the practice began of making them compete for money to carry out specific developments or gain prizes for having already achieved a particular objective. I had been Director of the Modular Degree for nearly 4 years when in 1990 a prize for widening access was offered, financed by British Gas. I thought City Poly's Modular Scheme met all the criteria and prepared an application. Twenty-seven other institutions also applied but City Poly won. One factor in our favour may have been that when the British Gas representative came to visit us, I had with me Gordon Kirkwood, who was in charge of our community and Access work and visibly impressed him with accounts of recruiting members of the local Bangladeshi community.

Outside recognition is a great help in gaining internal respect: Roderick Floud, by then Provost, was delighted at our gaining this prize: £3,000 was not going to solve City's financial problems but it gave it added status. I was delighted at this recognition of the validity of modular studies—I knew well that the main credit belonged to my predecessor and the staff who helped him design the Scheme but I had worked hard at putting together the application. I thought that our winning this prize would encourage the other Directors of Modular Schemes in our Modular Users Group.

Our application outlined three key features:

THE OPEN DOOR: encouragement of applicants without traditional educational qualifications; outreach work among local communities in Tower Hamlets, Hackney and Docklands; links with Access courses at Further Education Colleges; the provision of places for students with modest A level results from socially or educationally deprived backgrounds; direct entry into the 2nd or 3rd year with credit from previous study or work experience; a vigorous and well monitored Equal Opportunities policy.

STUDENT-CENTRED FLEXIBILITY: students choose their own programme from a wide range of subjects and modules within them, and can change subjects in the light of their developing interests or aspirations; unusual combinations of modules are encouraged if they are academically sound; there is opportunity to experiment with new subjects; Diagnostic testing in the first semester and resit exams at the end of the first year give time for students to reach fixed academic standards; Students can study full or part-time to suit their circumstances in each semester, and may if necessary interrupt their studies for an agreed period.

CONTINUOUS SUPPORT AND COUNSELLING: all students have a coordinator of Studies who advises them on the academic coherence and viability of their programme; students can also seek personal advice from professional counsellors in the Student Advice Centre; and in each subject there are Senior Tutors who provide advice on modules in that subject, professional exemptions and careers.

Although we'd won the prize, I had realised soon after I was at the helm that there were weaknesses in having a student advice service without a central, purpose-built Advice Centre. All students were allocated a Coordinator to advise them on the viability of their programme throughout their course but the coordinators were located in subject departments and given the role because they had spare time, rather than keen to do it or well informed about the Scheme outside their own departments. Students would come into the set of offices in Jury Street where I and my administrative assistants had offices asking for extra coordinating help. A budget of £250,000 was distributed between the departments to cover the cost but without any check on whether it was being spent effectively. Now seemed a good time to put a case forward to the Senior Management team to use this budget in a more effective why by setting up an Advice Centre with administrative staff manning a counter and interview rooms where a small team of trained Academic Coordinators could be available. The Coordinators would remain attached to their Department but released for a set amount of time to work in the Advice Centre.

This was so obviously a more efficient way to provide advice to students on their programmes and enable me to supervise how it was being carried out that the Senior Management team accepted my arguments but queried whether free space was available. So, I went on a tour of Calcutta House and came across a large unused area where the Biology department used to have its teaching rooms and labs before it was closed down. I got a ladder so I could see over the internal partitions. It was derelict and in a poor state but in a good central location. I consulted an architect and drew up plans with him for the new CAS (Credit Accumulation Scheme) Centre. Space was tight and my future office would not be spacious nor that of my secretary and the interview rooms were even smaller, but the Centre would be fit for purpose. Students would know where to go and there would always be staff ready to listen and give informed advice. Building work took time but eventually we took possession. It improved our relations with students and enabled the Scheme to operate more efficiently. After we became

London Guildhall University most courses conformed to a set format within the modular, semester system. Being in the same building as the Registry staff was an asset during the change to the modular format and the computerisation of module details. This enabled us to check more quickly that a student wanting to change modules had the correct prerequisites.

Although some of the Business School Heads were sceptical of Modular degrees, we developed relations of mutual tolerance. Making sure when approving student programmes that they respected departmental prerequisites was essential to cooperation. The stress points came after Modular Examination Boards if I proposed allowing students to repeat who they thought would never pass and claimed teaching them would be a waste of their time. I did not lightly hold to my decisions because repeated failure is demoralising for students, but in most cases my optimism was justified. Unfortunately, not always, and I learnt to recognise when students with mental health problems needed specialist help before continuing.

The most distressing experience I had there occurred after I had interviewed an overseas student called Joy Gardner and given her permission to repeat a year. She had experienced various personal problems but was capable of passing.

So, I gave her a hug, wished her success in her repeat year and promised to confirm to the Home Office that her right to remain should be extended (the usual procedure was for the Home Office to check whether overseas students were still enrolled and attending or not). Two or three days later I heard on the news that Joy had been killed while resisting the police who had come to deport her saying her right to remain had run out. How could that have happened? I was very shocked and angry but could do nothing.

London Guildhall University was required to organise Validation of its own courses after 1992. Two years earlier the London College of Furniture had been merged with City Poly but had no degree level courses; the lecturers there were proud of their expertise in making furniture and musical instruments and their graduates were sought after so they were not convinced that expanding their courses to include background modules was necessary, but were eventually persuaded being on a degree course would have advantages for their students and widen their career options. Even when their first-degree course was ready for validation the staff who designed it had doubts about whether it would be approved. There would be two outside specialists on the Validation Board, four members from other departments and a Chair—me in this case. The Validation routine began with a meal together the evening before the event to discuss informally our views of the programme. It became clear that the outside members had doubts, so I would be chairing an event where there was a lack of confidence among both the applicants and the assessors. I would need if I could to create a relaxed atmosphere. Fortunately, the staff did overcome their diffidence and win over the two outside assessors. So, the course was validated and would prove to be successful and in demand.

This outcome led to my being asked to chair other Validation Boards during my remaining time at London Guildhall. I was also invited to be an outside member of Validation Boards at other Modular Users Group Universities. In the early 1990s, serving on other Universities' Validation Boards was not paid except for expenses, nor was giving guest lectures at other universities. it was seen as a reciprocal service between members of an international Academic Community; However, this would shortly come to an end with University Managements wanting compensation when their staff worked elsewhere during normal working hours. Financial considerations were beginning to dominate the way Universities were run and adding to the pressures on teaching staff. External Relations Departments were extended in the competition to recruit overseas students. I myself was not directly concerned apart from acting as liaison with a University in Paris with which we ran a joint degree—I looked forward to my annual visits there.

Guildhall was even more financially vulnerable than most other Universities because it rented instead of owning most of the buildings it used. As a member of Senior Management, I was party to financial discussions but could do nothing except worry about how staff could teach ever increasing numbers of students with diminishing budgets. The size of tutorial groups and seminars grew, which increased the amount of marking to be done without increasing the hours credited. Temporary contracts began to be offered for nine months, ending in June instead of a full year, despite union protests.

This was the period when Universities began employing Accountants as business consultants but I was surprised when our Provost commissioned advice from one of the big firms to help him decide organisational issues. The Accountant came, listened to the views of the three Deans and myself and put them together in a Report, and charged £250,000. Why didn't the Provost just ask us directly and save the money? He would have had to decide between our differing views – wasn't that what he was paid for?

Management demands for greater accountability in the use of staff time was applied to all departments and the Government's requirement for a system of yearly appraisal was put in place. Even if carried out sympathetically, the threat of dismal was inherent in the process. I had a very good team: a deputy Director who dealt with student problems; another who handled Admissions, and two Assistant Directors one to oversee our outreach and Access work and a statistician who liaised with the Registry and Heads of Department to ensure our information was always up to date and correctly entered on both computer records and handout material for students. We meet briefly every Monday morning to plan the week and usually had a Friday afternoon meeting and a glass of wine, sometimes with my secretary and a couple of administrative staff, before going home. I duly went through the appraisal process with them but felt it was unnecessary. Everyone was on a tight schedule and the Modular Degree was so essential a part of the University's work that I could not be asked to reduce staff but only to ensure that they put in their full number of working hours.

I myself was appraised by the Deputy Provost, Max Weaver, to whom I formally reported. He was a lawyer, who spent his free time playing the trumpet with the Salvation army and in the University orchestra. He was absolutely straight and rule abiding but also caring and humane. Although he would never speak out of line, I realised he was worried about the pressures financial problems were placing on staff. Despite our very different backgrounds and interests, we worked amicably together. As might be expected, he took appraisal seriously but it caused no problem between us and I was very glad that he was my immediate superior. Even though he was a teetotaller, if we had worked late, he would come into the bar for a glass of lemonade so I could have a glass of wine.

Another new edict from the Provost was that all staff except those receiving outside research funding must be available on the premises throughout their working day. I was disconcerted to be told by him that this rule would apply to members of the Senior Management team. I thought this was unnecessary and inappropriate. It would impede my ability to get things done because despite the best efforts of my secretary, when I was in my office, I was constantly interrupted. It was more efficient to do reports or other work requiring concentration at home. Indeed, for several years I had written the next year's Student Handbook while formally on our summer holiday in France, fitting it in for an hour or so on occasional days after our early morning swim and breakfast.

I was interested in doing it and it hardly counted as work. Now I would need to go back home earlier and compile it in my office, which would take much longer.

For the first time, I began to think about retirement but I didn't want to go early because I needed to build up my pension as I had not worked full-time when young.

Also, the Teachers Widows Pension Scheme was only set up not long before Max retired, so my widow's pension should he die first would be very small. This worried him more than it did me: I would have an adequate pension without working on until I was 65. I still enjoyed running the Modular Degree but was concerned about where the University's financial problems were leading.

Staff morale sank and a staff survey organised by NATFHE in May 1994 showed that 67% of the staff felt that stress was affecting their work; and 86% felt senior management showed little interest or total disregard for staff opinion. There was a meeting of NATFHE to discuss possible strike action or withholding students' examination results. I sympathised with the teaching staff but was very concerned about the last suggestion because of the damage this would inflict on those graduating. So as a member of NATFHE I went to its meeting and appealed for them not to do that: I received 4 votes of support and over a hundred against, but was shown no antagonism as I was speaking as Director of the Modular Scheme and not on behalf of Management—indeed I'm not sure everyone realised I was part of the Senior Management Team. The target of staff anger was the Provost and the Deans, especially the Dean of Business.

At a Senior Management Team meeting, the Finance Director began saying that the Modular Degree was excessively complicated and streamlining it would reduce costs. In reply, I pointed out that its flexibility and range were its strength and attracted students—only London Guildhall and Oxford Brookes University offered such a wide choice. My remarks were noted rather than answered.

I was not at all surprised when a fortnight later the Personnel Officer made an appointment to see me. He said it was absolutely necessary to streamline the Modular Degree and it would be easier for someone new to take on the task. I was due to retire in less than 15 months' time but they would like me to accept retirement sooner. He offered me what was financially a fair deal; I would be served a redundancy notice and receive an appropriate sum in compensation. I would immediately cease attending Senior Management Team meetings but they would like me to continue running the Modular Scheme until a new Director could be appointed. This would take some time, so I would still be responsible for that summer's Exam Boards and preparations for the Year beginning in September 1994 and possibly the whole autumn term and would be paid the equivalent of my current salary until no longer needed. I accepted this offer. I regretted the need to streamline the Scheme and didn't want to be involved in doing it. I blamed the Government's failure to provide adequate funds for the Universities.

In the event, the search for my replacement ended up with an internal candidate, Eric Collier, who had been one of my first Assistant Directors until moving on to become Head of the Accountancy Department. I was very pleased because I knew he believed in the principles underlying the Scheme. In the end, I didn't leave until the end of the Spring term 1995. I left on good terms with all my colleagues, though sad at the reasons. I was given a splendid leaving party to which my daughter and grandchildren were invited. Some years later my granddaughter obtained a degree in Business studies there.

I am still in touch with some of my ex-colleagues still living but, as I had feared, London Guildhall University was unable to overcome its financial problems and had to merge with North London University as London Metropolitan University in 2002. The modified Modular Degree Scheme continued within the new University, It seemed a pity to waste my experience of Validation Boards so Max Weaver suggested I apply to join the team of auditors of the Higher Education Quality Council. He himself had served a term as an Auditor and on his recommendation, I was accepted in the early summer of 1964. Auditors usually served for 3 years, which would take me two years after retiring. It was not a paid post but there were generous expenses. I likened it to joining a very elite club, whose members were well looked after but expected to meet exacting standards when taking part in its mission. New auditors attended an induction course and observed part of an Audit in progress and all auditors were required to attend general meetings to review how the system was working and possible modifications. HEQC was based at Edgbaston and used Birmingham University's hospitality suite for its Conferences. We were moved between different discussion groups and It was very interesting meeting the other Auditors all of whom had different backgrounds and specialities and were expert in their fields. There were more male auditors than women but not by a large majority. Each Audit was carried out by a team of three Auditors with backgrounds appropriate to the Institution being audited. They were assisted by a secretary who made all the practical arrangements and acted as the scribe.

HEQC Audits were not concerned with the academic content of individual courses but with the mechanisms and structures used by institutions "to monitor, assure, promote and enhance their academic quality and standards in light of their stated aims and objectives." All Audits were organised under the following headings: Systems for Quality Assurance; Design, Approval and Review of Programmes; Teaching, Learning and the Student Experience; Assessment and Classification of Awards; Feedback and Enhancement Processes; Staff Appointment and Development; Promotional Material; Collaborative Provision and ended with Conclusions and Points for Commendation and Consideration.

Student feedback was a very important part of the process and meetings with different groups or informal lunches with students were often our most revealing indication of what went on behind the paperwork. Large numbers of staff and students were interviewed between the three auditors e.g., on my first audit at Paisley we met 150 staff and students, at Bath we held 24 meetings covering 180 staff and students and at the College of Ripon and York St John we held 21 meetings involving 95 staff and 50 students. Later audits at Wrexham, Norfolk and Loughborough were similar. At tea-time each day, we met alone with our Secretary to discuss and record our findings before dinner. Although for three days, our presence dominated the Institutions being audited, they did not need to prepare fresh paperwork and we were accepted as being there to help rather than judge. My six visits were mainly to new developing institutions who were pleased to be offered extra guidance. This made audit visits a pleasant experience, which was enhanced by getting to know the other two auditors over dinner in our hotel or nearby restaurants.

I had another opportunity to make use of my Validation experience. In the autumn of 1995. I received a request for help in a letter from Kevin Porter, then Registrar of the Royal College of Music. Kevin had previously worked in the Registry at London Guildhall and we had shared visits to Paris organising the joint degree there. He said the Royal College needed to create a Degree ready for Validation but, like the College of Furniture in the past, many of the staff were not interested or convinced it was unnecessary because Royal College students wanted to spend their time in one-to-one tuition and practice so they could become singers or instrumentalists.

However, not all would succeed and for those who might become teachers or follow a different occupation having a degree would be an asset. Some background written modules had been devised but the College lacked experience of blending together a degree course and organising the procedures required. The Deputy Director responsible was feeling overwhelmed so would I help her for a small fee? So, I visited the College and spent an afternoon discussing her problems with her and took away her paperwork. I spent two days clarifying the necessary processes and who should be responsible. I then returned and spent an afternoon going over my recommendations. It had been fascinating being there with music in the background—a different world. Although I had done what I was asked, I was aware that for some students the requirement to give time to anything other than practising would seem irrelevant and I was not sure that wanting all of them to do so was right. The College would hopefully realise who were best excused.

As my period as an auditor was nearing its end, I began to look for something else useful I could do. A friend suggested I could become a lay chair of National Health Complaints Panels. There was a system at the time to give an opportunity to patients with a grievance about their own or their relatives treatment to take their complaint to a Panel which could examine whether it was justified or not. If it was found justified, the aim was to find a way to prevent such a problem happening to anyone else and hope that the complainant would feel comforted by the acknowledgement that they had been right and that steps would be taken to prevent it happening in future. A complainant whose case was found justified was not offered compensation and could still sue for damages. Apparently very few did. The Panels consisted of a lay chair, a second lay member, and two or more medical advisers. The NHS provided training for lay members and only accepted those deemed capable of carrying out the role. Partly because I had myself been subjected to an unnecessary operation when I was 21 and had been left with life-long problems, I decided to apply and after training began serving as a Lay Chair. This was a voluntary post with travelling costs only. Some of the cases were heartrending, some unjustified and some the result of accidental mistakes. I served from 1997 to 2002, handling an average of 2 or 3 cases a year. It seemed to me a very worthwhile use of my time and I only gave it up when the NHS changed the system to a paid role with fixed time commitments, greater than I wanted to fill. I also thought it would destroy the ethos of the service.

After leaving the Communist Party, Max had joined the Labour Party hoping that at the next change of Government it would support the policies, he and the Teacher Unions had been advocating. I very much hoped this would happen.

However, I decided when starting to work at City Poly that I wanted to concentrate on my job there and did not want to re-join the Labour Party. I had become pessimistic—to put it crudely, I was losing confidence that the Labour Party was fit for the job. It had been set up enable the working class to achieve recognition of the value of their contribution to the British economy and enable them to participate in deciding the future direction of Britain. In 1918, the Party became committed to socialism and public ownership of key sections of the economy. Yet class structure and differences in wealth, living standards and power had not fundamentally changed.

My book on the General Strike had ended by quoting the historian A.J.P. Taylor's letter to the Times after the success of the Miners' strike in 1972:

"Fifty years ago, the miners were driven back to the pits by the lash of hunger. Successive Governments combined indifference and brutality…Now the miners have avenged the defeats if 1921 and 1926."

When I was writing my book and used that quotation, I too felt jubilant but by the time it was published in 1976 realism had set in. The Miners' victory was already being undermined by inflation and their future was bleak. Although nationalised, the industry had not received the technological investment needed to compete internationally and was declining. Miners' wages and conditions were again below those in other industries and their future was bleak should the Conservative Party under Mrs Thatcher win the 1979 Election. The Labour Party was trying to prevent that by offering a 'Social Contract' and I strongly supported that but feared that the lack of unity over policy which had discouraged me in the 1950s had become deeply embedded. I would go on voting for Labour but I saw no need to expose myself to frustration by going to argumentative ward meetings between left and right. Perhaps Max with his prestige and connections might be able to help effect changes.

Mitterrand, the Social Democratic Leader in France, was about to become President with a very left-wing, socialist programme. Maybe, just maybe, the British Labour Party would follow the same course but I was pessimistic. I did not want to share my views with Max—time would tell and I wanted Max's hopes to be fulfilled, so the last thing I wanted was to discourage him. I decided early in our marriage that there was no point in arguing when we saw things differently because we were both sure of our arguments and not easily convinced otherwise. We agreed on objectives and time alone would show who was right. My decision about not again becoming a member of the Labour Party meant we would not be going to meetings together but we continued to spend all our leisure time together, including giving and attending dinner parties to discuss politics. I might not want to go to LP meetings but continued my deep concern about political developments.

Max Joins the Labour Party

Despite his CP past, Max had no difficulty being accepted as a member of the Labour Party. He was still a leading figure on the NUT Executive and was supported by Nikki Harrison, Chairman of the Haringey Education Committee. So, the members of the Crouch End branch saw him as an asset and went out of their way to welcome him. One day there was a knock on the door and a lady stood there and said that we didn't know her but she was Jean Brown and had come to invite us to a Labour Party Social at her house nearby. Max was out but I said I was sure we'd be pleased to come. Later I found out the event had been organised for the purpose of meeting him. He began regularly attending ward meetings and was fairly soon elected as branch Chair and as a representative on the Constituency GC.

Max also joined the Socialist Educational Organisation, the only educational body formally affiliated to the Labour Party. Its President was Caroline Benn and, in the past, he had often collaborated with its members on campaigns over comprehensive education. A Haringey branch of the SEA was set up which soon became very active at both local and national level. He was elected to the SEA's National Executive Committee and fairly soon became Vice Chair and in the mid-1990s, Chair.

After the 1979 Election, Michael Foot became Leader of the Party and did his best to keep it united. He appointed Neil Kinnock as Shadow Secretary of State for Education. Max knew Neil well through his wife, Gladys, who was a keen Brent NUT member. He regretted that Labour were now in opposition and that Neil had not been in post earlier instead of Shirley Williams, the procrastinator, or some of the previous Labour Education Secretaries. He knew Neil would give such support as he could against the Tories and the Mandarins in their determination to exclude teachers from policy making.

When Kinnock became Labour Leader after the 1983 Election, he appointed Giles Radice as his successor as Shadow Secretary of State for Education. Giles valued the advice of the SEA and frequently had meetings with Max and other members of its NEC. During his period of office, he often spoke on joint platforms with Max. On one occasion, he came to supper at our house to meet a group of educational experts. When Giles was followed by Jack Straw, he too held meetings with the SEA, but had no personal rapport with Max. At the annual Labour Party Conferences, it was customary for the SEA to move the main motion on education, which Max did several times after he became Chair.

In 1984, Max was elected as a Haringey Councillor in a by-election in White Hart Lane ward and soon became very involved in case work. He was on the Council during the Rate Rebellion of 1984-5. Unfortunately, at the 1986 Election the ward was won by the Conservatives. Despite losing his seat, Max continued to be widely consulted about Council affairs and frequently met with some of the Councillors and officers. All in all, he became an active Labour Party member.

Not all the local LP members were pleased he had become a member as Max was aware:-

"The hard and Trotskyite Left in Hornsey saw to it that, once I was admitted, I was marked as an enemy, smeared as a reactionary (which amused all my friends and did not even irritate me, so stupid was the characterisation) somewhere to the right of Genghis Khan! The smear was reinforced as the now Hornsey & Wood Green Constituency came increasingly into the grip of young mindless militants, usually without the slightest base in the Labour Movement, and many with only the shortest span of membership straight from either the Militant Tendency Young Socialists or other factions such as the International Marxist Group, Socialist Workers' Party, Workers' Revolutionary Party and the fifty-seven varieties of trot splinter groups."

Within the NUT, Max had always opposed and ridiculed those he called 'the trots' for their lack of understanding of the necessity for a trade union to organise carefully planned action and avoid indulging in wild cat strikes. Once he became a member of the Labour Party, he adopted a similar attitude to supporters of the Militant Movement.

MAX: "A few of us 'moderates' (including Nikki Harrison and Maurice Peston) used occasionally to meet together before the Constituency General Committee or after our Crouch End Branch meeting or at other times to try to devise a practical strategy to defeat the trot mob who ruled the roost in Hornsey. The fact of Trotskyite penetration of the London Labour Parties was palpable and could not be gainsaid. We did our best to limit the damage, an example of which was my successful organisation of the move which prevented Tariq Ali, the notorious Trotskyite, being accepted into the party. He lived in my area and had to seek admission through our branch. His application was personally handed in by Jeremy Corbyn, the Hornsey Party Leader at the time.

Tariq Ali was never one to hide his light under a bushel and the issue soon achieved wide national publicity. At the crucial meeting we had the largest attendance ever known in a branch meeting anywhere—the fruit of painstaking organisation on our part. We refused Mr Ali's application by an overwhelming majority. The affair was not completely over but I claim this as the first successful blow against the trots in London, such was the significance of this cause celebre. Our victory had widespread repercussions—we had been helped nationally by Neil Kinnock as well as Ron Hayward of the NEC. Happily, the growth of hard left cum Trotskyite influence in the Labour Party nationally, but especially in London, has been stopped—something necessary if Labour was ever to return to Government."

On one occasion, David Owen had spoken to a Crouch End ward meeting and a number of members stayed afterwards to have a drink and a chat with the former Foreign Secretary over the parlous state of the Hornsey and other London parties in thrall to the trots. Owen confessed himself astonished at how far things seemed to have gone and promised to alert the high ups. Sometime later, after the formation of the SDP, Max read an account by Owen in which he described a meeting he had had in Hornsey which finally convinced him that it was impossible to reform Labour—so far had things gone in favour of the ultra-left. He had expressed no such view at the time and Max and his friends found it disconcerting to hear that they had caused or in any way contributed to the formation of the SDP, to which they were all opposed.

The Tariq Ali meeting had taken place in our large Victorian sitting room but not being a member, I was not qualified to attend. This was as well as I wasn't convinced that keeping out Tariq Ali was all that essential. I did sympathise with those who were losing patience with endless theoretical battles centred on events in Soviet Russia: I thought British politics needed to be based on British experience. It may have been difficult working with the group around Jeremy Corbyn, though he himself was not a member of a Trotskyite group. Apparently, meetings were becoming unruly, with speakers being shouted down and personally abused, which certainly needed controlling.

The Leaders of the Militant Movement made clear they were disciples of Trotsky but I thought Max was too sweeping in characterising all its supporters as beyond the pale. During my late 1960s campaigns about housing we cooperated without the slightest problem with a couple of members of the Fourth International. I thought it would be undemocratic to bar from membership of the Labour Party men or women having their particular views. Also, I had recently come across various supporters of Militant through work and found them reasonable enough. Maybe I was wrong to generalise from limited contacts. The Labour Party was supposed to be a broad church and I thought that having as wide a membership as possible would help, not hinder, the Labour Party to win future elections.

Max said he wanted to support the 'Tribune' wing of the Labour Party. He had been a keen reader of *Tribune* from its foundation in 1937. It had published his articles on education and had been a reliable ally during his twenty years of campaigning to abolish selection and class differentiation in secondary education. I myself began reading *Tribune* as a student and it played a key role in forming my political views. Labour Politicians including Bevan and distinguished journalists and writers including Michael Foot and George Orwell edited and wrote for it. Their 'Keep Left' foreign policy called for Britain to take an independent stance and not be tied to supporting either American or Soviet policies but to work for peace and the ending of wars and colonial oppression. There was a Tribune Group in Parliament and it was the forum for Labour Party discussion throughout the Attlee Government and the following years in Opposition. Michael Foot, who became an MP, was one of the founders of CND and *Tribune* was seen as its journal. However, unlike the more right-wing socialist think-tank, the Fabian Society, the owners of *Tribune* did not build up a membership base but relied for influence on the sales of their newspaper, which stood at 40,000 during the first Attlee Government but had dropped to less than 10,000 by the time Max joined the Labour Party.

The Labour Left in Parliament had always strongly supported trade unionism and welcomed Max joining the Labour Party as did Jack Jones, General Secretary of the TGWU, whom we knew well. For the first approximately two years after the War ended reconstruction, funded by repayable loans from America and high taxation had enabled the Attlee Government to achieve its aim of full employment. These years were good years for trade unions in other countries as well as Britain, because wages and salaries increased their share of the national cake compared with pre-war. Some text books call this 'The Golden years' because wages increased year by year.

This had ended before Max joined the Labour Party. Keynes' pre-war warnings about the consequences of policies favouring banks and financiers instead of industry were again being borne out. Unemployment was rising and technical innovations such as containerisation in the docks were reducing demand for workers. In addition, the breakdown of the Bretton Woods system in 1971 had removed the ability of states to control the exchange rate of their currencies or the movement of capital, leading to monetary crises, rising prices, particularly of oil, and rampant inflation. City Financial leaders and the Conservatives used rising wages as the scapegoat for these problems even though by then wages were no longer keeping pace with rising prices.

Harold Wilson and the leaders of the largest trade unions realised the danger of the situation and made an effort to find a new way to work together in face of the rapid rise of inflation and unemployment. A Trade Union and Labour Party Liaison Committee was set up in 1972. This brought together representatives of the Government and Trade Unions, led by Jack Jones of the TGWU. The Unions insisted that effective price control must be in place if Wilson wanted wage claims to be moderated, and Michael Foot pressed for legislation to be prepared for improving Employment Law. Dennis Healey said a wealth tax could be considered—although he never proposed one.

After the March 1974 Election was won, many of the measures planned were quickly put in place: The Industrial Relations Act was repealed, a Health and Safety Act was passed, the Advisory, Conciliation and Arbitration Service (ACAS) was set up. The October 74 Election was won with a better, though still small, majority, but inflation continued soaring—prices rose by 17% and wage increases averaged 25%. If what was called 'the Social Contract' was to be saved, wage inflation would need to be curtailed as well as prices.

Jack Jones put forward the suggestion that for the coming 12 months all wage increases should be for a flat sum. This was a totally novel idea and he wasn't sure that Harold Wilson and the rest of the Cabinet would go along with it or that he could win the support of the TGWU and the TUC, but after negotiation it was agreed that all workers and salary earners should have a £6 increase during the coming year. A high level of compliance resulted in inflation falling by over half—from 25% to 12%. The overwhelming majority of workers in industry were not opposed to another year of flat rate restraint as it favoured the lower paid, but professional and managerial staff and the-white collar unions wanted the return of differentials.

Max and the Teachers were not directly involved as they had a separate negotiating system through the Burnham Committee. They were already starting to lose the benefits of the Houghton Report but were not being offered any increase. Their case was vigorously taken up in Tribune. The major Trade Unions and public sector workers such as the teachers fully supported each other's demands but had not discussed what was the first priority. Jack Jones had no doubt it was expanding economic growth, as he made clear at a crucial by-election in Coventry: "Some public expenditure has to be restrained to help convert our candy-floss economy into a thriving industrial society. The key battle is not about public expenditure—it is the battle for the very industrial heart and life of Britain. Are we to have jobs—to make things on which we can survive—or will we continue to drift into a super-salesman's Britain where there are no jobs for working men and women but plenty of secret bank accounts in Switzerland or the Cayman islands?"

The NUT were not affiliated to the Labour Party and could not vote on Labour Party affairs even in the TUC. Max knew Jack was right but as Chair of the NUT Salaries Committee he went on pressing the case of the Teachers for an increase to keep pace with inflation—as they were being offered nothing, he didn't see this as trying to make teachers a special case. The priority was keeping Labour in power and Mrs Thatcher out of Downing Street. Max keenly followed the progress of events. With inflation responding to the constraint on wage increases, the trade unions felt they had made a contribution to slowing inflation and wanted the next effort to be directed at carrying through the Government's side of the Social Contract by doing more to keep down prices and boost the economy, including state support for cooperative as well as nationalised enterprises and public services. However, Dennis Healey as Chancellor would not allocate extra financial support. Eventually the Cabinet agreed to have one more year of controlled wage increases, after which collective bargaining was restored. Oil prices were still soaring and Inflation and unemployment soared correspondingly. The Trade Unions had wanted to continue the Social Contact as a means to keep Labour in power but it broke down in the 'Winter of Discontent' and Mrs Thatcher became Prime Minister.

I was as disappointed as Max at the end of the Social Contract and the outcome of the election. Max consoled himself by battling on fighting back against Tory education policies and hoping that the next election would see Labour return to power. Despite Mrs Thatcher's lack of popularity and continued unemployment, loss of industries and a weakening economy, I realised that his hopes would not be fulfilled after the 'Gang of Four' broke away and set up the SDP in March 1981, followed shortly afterwards by an electoral Alliance with the Liberals. Under the first-past-the post British voting system this would ensure that the Conservatives would win the next election. To make matters worse, in 1982 the Falklands War led to a wave of patriotic support for Margaret Thatcher, who decided to take advantage of her new popularity to call an election in June the following year. As expected, the 1983 Election was won by the Conservatives, with Labour second and the SDP Liberal Alliance third, having won 25% of the votes but only 23 MPs. Nothing could better illustrate why the Liberal Party had long campaigned against First Past the Post. It was leading to the election of governments only a minority of the electors supported, and prevented anything like fair representation of third parties. In 1983, Margaret Thatcher was supported by less the half of those who voted (42.7% on a turnout of 72.7% i.e. only 31% of the electorate). Reading the popular press at the time you would never realise this but imagine she had the support of the whole nation!

The Labour Cabinet was divided in 1983 and Michael Foot, presumably knowing that the Tories would win anyway, decided that instead of patching together a compromise manifesto, the electorate should be given the opportunity to vote for a programme matching the aims and purpose for which the Labour Party had been created. The 1983 Election Manifesto is usually dismissed as a "suicide note" but what it contained is rarely examined. Max and I voted for it with enthusiasm because it put forward policies to enable Britain to avoid a future of British economic decline, increasing unemployment and working-class poverty.

Max and the SEA cooperated with Neil Kinnock in formulating the Education section of the 1983 Manifesto, which was extremely detailed and worth reading today.

It covered all stages of education: free nursery education for all under-fives whose parents wanted it; improved funding of primary schools to reduce class sizes and improve learning materials; "secondary schools aiming at a high standard of achievement among all pupils in the variety of academic and other activities which are essential parts of fully comprehensive education"; prohibition of all forms of selection such as the eleven plus; "all schools should be required to maintain a broad, balanced and comprehensive curriculum with genuinely equal opportunities for boys and girls appropriately and ethnic minorities"; there should be closer contact between home and school; School meals and milk should be restored to offset the inequalities in nutrition and health highlighted in the Black Report; Private schools are an obstacle to a free and fair education system so assisted places would be abolished, along with charitable status and other tax privileges, such as being excused Vat; where appropriate and private schools would in time be integrated into the Local Authority sector; the rigid A Level system with its over-specialisation would be replaced with a broader programme of study promoting flexibility and breadth in learning; student grants not loans and an end to corporal punishment.

The education section of the 1983 Manifesto has recently been compared with the 2017 Manifesto, 34 years later. Both were lengthy and detailed. What Max would find immeasurably sad is that so many of the 1983 proposals to benefit children of all classes and aptitudes were still listed as future proposals in 2017 and 2019, and some had been lost on the way.

The 1983 Manifesto was forward looking and detailed on other issues: emergency programmes to rebuild industry and end mass unemployment; renationalisation of the industries privatised by the Government; higher taxes for the rich including a wealth tax and lower ones for the poor; a Development Plan, power to invest in, purchase or take temporary control of individual companies; a National Investment Bank; exchange controls to counter currency speculation and stop capital flowing overseas; build more Council houses but end Council House sales, help owner occupiers; withdraw from the EEC; abolish the House of Lords; Work for peace and eliminate British nuclear weapons.

Michael Foot is remembered for losing a General Election by the worst margin of any Labour Leader, but with FPTP would Labour have done better with a different manifesto? Eight million voters cast their votes for this programme. It voiced the aspirations of the trade unions and the economic interests of the population of the British industrial regions. It was forward looking. The vested interests of the ruling elite and beneficiaries of capitalism were bound to do all they could to prevent it being given serious consideration. The Labour Party had been created to advance the interests of the working class and the Manifesto showed how this could still be achieved.

After the Election defeat, Michael Foot resigned and Neil Kinnock was elected as Leader. Less than a year later, the Miners' Strike began and occupied political attention from March 1984 until a year later. The wisdom or otherwise of the strategy followed by the miners is still a matter of debate. Max went along with Kinnock's criticisms of Arthur Scargill but the details of the miners' procedures were complex. As the author of 'The General Strike' my sympathy was strongly with the miners and I thought the miners should be fully supported whatever the technical niceties and I was shocked at the violence used by the police.

At PCL, where I was working, the Union organised meetings for the Miners' Wives and collections for the miners who were increasingly suffering as the months dragged on. The miner's cause was just, but their tactics failed and Margaret Thatcher began dismantling the British mining industry.

Once in power in 1980, the Conservatives Immediately went ahead with their plans to reduce state activity, centralise control and weaken the role of Local Government by cutting back funding. Max had been protesting for years about reductions in Education grants but the Government now set out to limit all Local Government expenditure. Any Council deemed to be overspending would have its rate support grant cut. When this began to be carried out those Councils with schemes for developing and regenerating their areas protested and raised their rates so they could carry on with their plans.

The Government then introduced a Bill to limit the amounts that Councils could raise in rates. This was a major change—since the 19th-century towns and cities had taken pride in their public gardens, buildings and facilities and since the end of the First World War Local Authorities had been responsible for building Council Housing and regenerating slum areas. Labour Councils would be most affected but Conservative Councils also valued their independence. Ted Heath led a large group of Conservative MPs to oppose the Bill and there was opposition in the House of Lords on the grounds that limiting the right of Councils to raise money was undemocratic and unconstitutional. Mrs Thatcher refused to listen and in June 1984 the Act was pushed through.

Many Labour Councils were dismayed and Liverpool decided immediately to take a stand. Labour had won control of Liverpool in 1983 and the new Councillors had ambitions to rescue their City from decline due to falling population, unemployment and decaying slums. It was determined to carry through its programme and decided to copy the slogan of George Lansbury and the Poplar Councillors in 1921: "Better to break the law than the poor." The Poplar rebels spent six weeks in jail for refusing to pay Poplar's London precepts, but won their struggle when Lloyd George passed the 1922 Local Authority Powers Act, which spread the cost of Poor Law support over all the London boroughs and gave Poplar the help it needed. Lansbury later became Leader of the Labour Party and his stand in 1921 is part of Labour Party legend. Inspired by their example, Liverpool initiated a deficit budget In 1984 but the balance of power was very different from 60 years earlier and Margaret Thatcher a very different opponent from Lloyd George.

The key members of the Liverpool Labour Party were members of Militant, although a number of the Councillors including John Hamilton, an SEA member and Leader of the Council, were not. Throughout the next two years the Council won increasing support in elections. Council meetings from March until the summer of 1984 were spent discussing whether to put forward a deficit budget (which would not be legal) or buy time by not submitting any budget at all. Two meetings with Patrick Jenkin, Secretary of State for the Environment, took place: the first in June ended in deadlock with Liverpool Council still without a budget but in July Jenkin said he could offer Liverpool an extra £20m for housing. Liverpool approved a legal budget a few days later. This was widely seen as a victory for its confrontational strategy.

The next stage of the battle would begin in the New Year when Councils would be due to submit their budgets for the 1985–6 Council year. A list of 18 Councils to be capped was issued including Haringey.

All but two of the Councils selected were held by Labour and began to meet to discuss how to react, along with a few other Labour Councils who feared they would be next. It was agreed to delay or refuse to submit a budget. Liverpool would have preferred to submit a deficit budget but agreed to follow the majority line.

At the Labour Party Conference in October, Neil Kinnock tried to discourage any action outside the law. One argument put forward in reply to him was that the capped budgets would not be enough to enable Councils to carry out their statutory obligations; "So the question is not shall we break the law but which law shall we obey?" The NEC statement called for unity in opposing the rate caps without mentioning illegal actions specifically but two composites were passed which did: one proposed support for Councils framing budgets "which could be defined as technically illegal," and the other support for any Council "forced to break the law as a result of Government action."

Most of the capped Councils had failed to submit a budget for the 1985–6 financial year by February, already past the usual deadline. Jenkins agreed to meet them as a group, but made threats not concessions except in one or two small adjustments. Including one for Haringey, but the main cap remained. At a meeting in March Haringey Council voted unanimously not to submit a budget. A few days later, however, the Leader of its Council George Meehan, put forward a legal budget for the Councillors to consider later. Meehan saw meeting the legal obligation to set a budget as urgent to protect the Council from penalties so at the next meeting he formally proposed taking an immediate decision on his proposed budget. Only 12 Councillors supported him, including Max, while the majority voted to postpone a decision until the end of April. George Meehan resigned and Bernie Grant became Leader. Eventually the Council, like the majority of the Councils planning defiance, capitulated and tabled a budget. Haringey's Budget continued to be capped for the following years, which limited progress on council house building and other desperately needed projects.

Only Liverpool and Lambeth held out and were surcharged. Liverpool put forward a deficit budget. They were given legal advice to provide redundancy notices to cover the rights of their workers. They panicked and delivered them by taxi, which they later saw as a tactical mistake, especially as they had no intention of making anyone redundant, but it caused dissension at the 1985 Labour Party Conference a week later. Neil Kinnock had been opposed to Councils breaking the law but had not been supported at the previous Conference, and now he reacted with anger and mockery to the idea of a Labour Council delivering redundancy notices by taxi. Neil Kinnock was a brilliant orator and his speech is seen as an outstanding example of his mastery as he laid bare the failures of the Thatcher Government but it was his scathing criticism of Liverpool Council which hit the headlines.

A month later Labour's NEC suspended the Liverpool District LP and began an inquiry which eventually led to the expulsion of all the Liverpool Militant members. The Council, however, found a way out of its problems and was able to complete a large part of its Regeneration Programme which had included 5,000 Council houses, 7 Sports Centres, 6 new nurseries, new parks and the creation of 1000 new jobs. The surcharges owed by 47 Councillors were paid off by trade union and public donations.

The Council transferred £23m from its capital to its revenue account and £30m was borrowed from Swiss banks to replenish the capital account. So, in

November 1985 a legal budget was approved. Derek Hatton, the leader of the Militant members in Liverpool, admitted that sending out redundancy notices had been a serious tactical error, but said the campaign had been justified and achieved its objectives.

Opinion within the Labour Party was divided and some left-wingers criticised Kinnock for what they called a "witch-hunt" against Militant which had distracted attention from the battle against the Tories and would not help Labour win the 1987 Election. However other members thought he had been justified in disassociating the Labour Party from the actions of the Militant Movement. Max certainly thought this. I certainly didn't, but as I was not a member at the time felt I should not be outspoken. It would be difficult to judge the effect on the electorate by the result of the 1987 Election because the split of the anti-Tory vote between the Labour Party and the SDP Liberal Alliance would in any case ensure the Conservative Party would remain in power.

The issue of Labour's attitude to the Militant Movement came up again a few years later over opposition to Thatcher's poll tax, which replaced Rates by an equal 'Community Charge' on all residents, rich and poor alike, which was obviously unfair and beyond the means of many working-class families. It was introduced in Scotland in 1989 and immediately ran into difficulties. Local Authorities had no lists of who should pay and many people didn't pay either because they were too poor and couldn't pay or because they felt the system was totally unfair, so evaded being registered or deliberately didn't pay. Anti-poll tax groups sprang up, some joined the All-Britain Anti Poll Tax Federation organised by the Militant Movement in November 1989 or another group called '3D' (**D**on't Register, **D**on't Pay, **D**on't Collect) and there were hundreds of non-politically aligned local 'Anti Poll Tax Unions' after the poll tax began to be levied in England and Wales from March 1990. Major Demonstrations took place in London, Glasgow and other large towns. The London March attended by around 200,000 turned into a riot going on into the night and causing physical damage and leaving 113 people injured and 339 arrested. Militant who had called the march disassociated themselves from the violence and blamed heavy-handed policing and anarchist groups for turning a peaceful march into a riot.

The exact number of those who failed to pay is not clear but at least 30% in some areas. Several hundred served jail sentences for continued noncompliance, including Terry Fields, a Liverpool Labour MP and member of Militant. Punk bands featured the song 'Don't pay the poll tax' and one opinion poll showed

78% of those questioned thought it should be scrapped. The Labour Party Conference in 1988 had agreed that the Poll tax was totally unfair and promised that it would immediately be repealed if the Party won the next Election. Neal Kinnock was opposed to encouraging what he saw as illegal actions so the Conference voted against endorsing proposals for a campaign of non-payment when the poll tax began to be levied. Even when the campaign began gathering widespread popular support, Kinnock held the Labour Party back from taking part and was unsympathetic towards those jailed for refusing to pay the tax. He told Terry Fields.

"Law makers shouldn't be law breakers" and warned that encouraging non-payment was allowing the Militant tendency to take over the Labour Party.

Meanwhile the Conservative Party set about protecting itself from the biggest movement of civil disobedience in modern British history. First Margaret Thatcher was induced to resign and all three candidates to replace her declared they would get rid of the poll tax. John Major who became Prime Minister put forward proposals in 1991 to replace it with a Council tax on properties according to their rentable value which would come into effect in 1993. In the meantime, so many were refusing to pay that the task of prosecuting them became unmanageable, while those evading registering reduced the number of electors on the electoral roll. Polls had shown a strong surge for Labour in the first year of the poll tax but it lessened after Major became PM and Labour's call, "Time for a Change," lost its potency. Britain's participation in the 35-nation Gulf War, which forced Iraq out of Kuwait and its oil fields in March 1991, made Major popular with some voters. By the time of the 1992 General Election the polls were predicting either a hung Parliament or a small Labour majority.

This did not happen. The Conservative Party had been given time to regroup and yet again became the Government despite receiving a minority of the votes cast. The main difference from 1987 was that the Conservative popular vote went down from 42.2% to 41.9 %, Labour's went up from 30.8% to 34.4% and the Liberal Democrats (replacing the SDP Liberal Alliance) down from 22.6% to 17.8%. The number of MPs elected for each party was Conservative 336 (41,943 votes per MP), Labour 271 (42,608 per MP) and Liberal Democrat 20 (299,980 per MP). Before the election the new Liberal Democrat Party could not agree which Party, they would support in case of a hung Parliament These figures clearly show how even with a clear majority of all voters not wanting to support the existing Government, unless the two largest minority parties had agreed an electoral pact in advance, the Conservatives would continue to govern the country.

Neil Kinnock resigned and John Smith became the Leader of the Labour Party. Max was depressed at the result, although pleased that our own constituency, Hornsey and Wood Green, had elected a Labour MP for the first time. I too was disappointed that another Tory Government had been elected but had a different view from Max about why this had come about. I had not agreed with Neil Kinnock's handling of events since his attack on Liverpool Council in his speech to the 1985 Labour Party Conference. His powerful critical focus would have been better directed not on Militant but on the undemocratic new laws the Conservative Government had just passed which had taken away the ability of Local Authorities to provide for the needs of their constituents.

I saw nothing wrong with nonviolent civil disobedience and thought it a necessary adjunct of democracy. Not endorsing the popular revolt against the Poll tax had been a wasted opportunity to show that the Labour Party was on the side of the working class and the poor. Just saying "if you vote for us and we win the Election, we'll abolish the Poll Tax" doesn't give much comfort to families facing bills they can't pay and imminent destitution. Attacking Militant, which had played a prominent part in organising the boycott, would have seemed uncalled for by those taking part in it. So, I was not altogether surprised at the result of the election.

Labour's defeat in 1992 made me reflect about how the trade unions and the Parliamentary Party have never been fully on the same wavelength since 1918 when the Trade Union members of the already existing Labour Party and a small number of socialist societies, most prominently the Fabian Society, had agreed on Sidney Webb's new Labour Party Constitution and Socialist Programme which added individual membership to that of affiliated trade unions and socialist societies. I keep turning over in my mind why the class structure is so little changed and why the Conservatives Party has been in power for so much of the period since 1918. I have added my final thoughts on these issues to these Memoirs in a section entitled 'In Retrospect'.

For the immediate future I kept my thoughts to myself. Max was entrenched in his attachment to Kinnock and his attitudes and there was no point in my telling him that I saw things differently. I could have reminded him that he had led his staff out of school on an 'illegal' strike, or that I had supported picketing tenants illegally occupying flats during a rent strike or that I had not only marched for CND but also lain in the road for the Committee of 100. It wouldn't change anything; we were both set in our ideas. I was due to retire in two years and I thought our priority was to concentrate on making the rest of our time together enjoyable. Political activity had dominated our lives but not to the exclusion of everything else. There were still issues and campaigns which we both supported strongly, including the Anti-Aparthide movement. We rejoiced when Nelson Mandela walked out of prison and after I retired visited South Africa. We also were both early supporters of Compass and I remember speaking at one of their meetings on education.

We followed with enthusiasm the development of the Soviet Union after Gorbachov became General Secretary in 1985 and attempted to develop detente with America to end the Cold War and limit nuclear weapons. He wanted to maintain the Soviet Union but introduce democratic systems and end the one party state. We were saddened when he lost power to Yelsin followed by Putin, who abandoned Communist ownership and seized all the Soviet Union's public assets. This was seen in the West as a great victory for capitalism but led to the emergence of those we now call the oligarchs. Max and I thought the fall of Gorbachov was a tragedy for the prospect of world cooperation and peace.

It was time to ease up. In a year's time, Max would have his 80th birthday so we could celebrate that and spend more time in our holiday home in Menton, including with our family. Go more often to the theatre and concerts. Max was too much the Party Loyalist to give up politics so he would want to continue attending Labour Party events and I was still as addicted as ever to following economic and political developments. Despite my criticisms, I had always voted Labour so I would re-join the Party and the Socialist Educational Association after I retired and keep him company at meetings and hope that we could avoid voting differently too often.

The Blair Years and After

Max and I expected the years between 1992 and the 1997 election to be politically fairly uneventful. The Tories had run out of steam and were having problems over Black Friday and EU policy. We regarded John Smith as traditional middle of the road Labour and felt he could be trusted to bring back Labour values and policies after the next election. He had appointed Ann Taylor as Shadow Education Minister and set up an Education Commission which was ready to report when sadly he died. We were prepared to have an open mind about hitherto unknown Tony Blair, although concerned when he immediately proposed updating Clause Four of the Labour Party Constitution. This had last been attempted by Hugh Gaitskell in the 1950s in an attempt to end a commitment to socialist policies. Was this just media directed tactics or an indication of his future direction?

When Ann Taylor reported the findings of her Commission, including abolishing League Tables and replacing A levels with a broader curriculum, Tony Blair was non-committal but talked warmly about A Levels. In the autumn, he replaced Ann by David Blunkett and publicly confirmed that Chris Woodhead would be continuing as Chief Inspector of Schools. This alarmed the teacher unions.

Max as Chair of the SEA was eager to have meetings with David Blunkett, the new Shadow Education Secretary and sound him out about the plans of 'New Labour'. He wanted to make sure that 'New Labour' would be implementing the Commission's Report and that it would abide by the existing Labour commitment to end class inequality by merging the surviving grammar schools with their local comprehensive schools and ending selection at 11+. The SEA was all set to challenge any backsliding on previous commitments. However, at the 1995 Labour Party Conference David Blunkett forestalled conflict by saying "Watch my lips: no selection, either by examination or interview, under a Labour Government."

Life was not all politics for Max or work for me and we spent our summers in Menton. First, we had to make a totally derelict flat habitable and then install a pull-down bed in the sitting room so we could entertain friends and family as planned. One strange coincidence happened: Jack Jones and his wife Evelyn were spending two or three days with us on the same weekend as *Le Monde* published a photo of Jack and an article about 'the most powerful man in Britain'. We had new French neighbours above but had assumed they were probably typical members of the French 'bourgeoisie'. The day Jack and Evelyn left, our French neighbour waving a newspaper appeared on the balcony above and asked in exited French "was that really Jack Jones on your terrace yesterday?" It emerged that although a high-ranking civil servant he was the son of a Communist miner and his wife the daughter of a leading Communist dock worker from Marseilles. We became good friends from then on, visiting each other's homes and going on holidays together in Scotland and Ireland.

I had plans to celebrate Max's 80th birthday in Menton in 1993 but they were doomed. He went there early. Hotel rooms were booked and friends were making travel arrangements. On the last day of term, after chairing exam boards for 3 days, I caught an evening flight to Nice where our relative Myron was waiting to drive me to Menton. He told me Max was ill but wouldn't go to the doctor till I arrived. I was horrified to find him doubled up with prostate pain.

So, he spent his birthday in hospital in Nice having surgery. The French health service was excellent in every way except the food, so I spent his birthday week driving to Nice everyday with titbits for him. Fortunately, he quickly recovered.

As we already had a Labour MP in Hornsey & Wood Green, the local branches began canvassing and money raising activities very early. We got to know our MP well as Max and I were quite often invited to a friends' Friday 'Sabbat' along with Barbara Roche and her husband. Max had long ago ceased to be religious but enjoyed these reminders of his young days and remained proud of his Jewish heritage. I liked taking part in the political discussions although by agreement with Max refrained from dwelling upon our opposition to the policies of the Israeli Government.

Election day came, Tony Blair became Prime Minister, Barbara Roche was re-elected with an enormous majority and became a junior member in the Government, initially in the Board of Trade. So now we would find out exactly what 'New Labour' was planning to do.

'Education, Education, Education' was to be the priority and plans to increase school budgets and finance new school buildings were exiting and welcomed, but the honeymoon quickly went sour. Within days of becoming Prime Minister, Tony Blair made clear he was going to take direct personal control of education policy. 'Standards and Effectiveness' were to be the priority and centrally set targets for literacy and numeracy were immediately laid down. Not only did the Government set targets but it produced daily teaching programmes which teachers would be required to follow. Ofsted in future would judge schools not only on meeting targets but also on conformity with the Governments recommended teaching methods. There was no consultation with the Teachers' unions nor with the SEA before a White Paper entitled 'Excellence in Schools' was released outlining the new system of central control of England's state funded schools.

Teachers who had spent 3-or 4-years becoming graduates, including the study of children's development and different teaching methods, were no longer to apply their expertise and experience but rely instead on following set programmes, regardless of the background or stage of development of the children in front of them. Tony Blair himself, and those he most closely relied upon (Chris Woodhead, Andrew Adonis and Michael Barber) had themselves been to Public Schools and Oxbridge and had no experience of state schools. The DFE set up a Standards and Effectiveness unit to monitor the exam results of schools. It soon had 100 staff recruited though Civil Service procedures, which normally resulted in a high proportion of Public-School alumni in senior positions So the future managers of state education were from a different social class from the majority of its pupils and, unlike teachers, lacked professional training and experience of teaching children.

League tables listing each school's results were to be made public and parental choice of schools encouraged. School budgets were tied to the number of pupils whose parents applied to send their children to that school so schools high in the League tables would thrive and others would be forced to get better results or cease to exist. A number of Education Action Zones were set up bringing together parents, governors, and business people in areas where schools were getting poor results with the task of attracting sponsorship and investment from the private sector. This had limited success and was later abandoned.

Tony Blair not only retained Ofsted and League Tables from Kenneth Baker's legacies but also privately sponsored schools. The original City

Technical Colleges, independent of their local education authorities, hadn't been very successful but in the year before the election the Conservatives had created a few sponsored 'specialist schools'. Soon after taking power Blair declared, he was in favour of such schools and announced that any Local Authority secondary school doing reasonably well could apply to become a specialist school responsible to a private sponsor instead of their LEA. This was state sponsored privatisation because not only did local authorities lose ownership and control of their schools to various businessmen who could afford £50,000, but specialist schools were allocated higher state funding than other secondary schools. To make it worse from Max's perspective, Specialist Schools were allowed to offer 10% of their places to applicants deemed to have an 'aptitude' for their specialist subjects. This was just as class biased as selection by the 11+. There was no scientific way aptitude could be measured so schools could pick 'easy to teach' middle class children. The teachers' unions were appalled at this reintroduction of class division in the provision of state education and sceptical about the idea that businessmen of all sorts were automatically qualified to run schools. There were 196 specialist schools under the Tories before the election and 2500 by ten years later.

In addition to specialist schools, other different types of school were created. City Academies were schools deemed by Ofsted to be failing and were taken away from their Local Council and allocated to a sponsor and in some cases provided with a new school. There were also Foundation Schools, other types of Academies, and later Free Schools. Local Government Authorities still controlled those of their schools not privatised but LEAs were in future to be organised by a system of paid Cabinets instead of elected Committees. Government grants to LEAs were drastically reduced forcing them to outsource some of their functions.

On the good side, money was poured into schools and school buildings and the Government stated that its aim was to end the exclusion of poor children from the benefits of education. 'Sure Start' the 'Every Child Matters' programme and Maintenance grants for students staying on after 16 were great innovations and it is a tragedy they were not permanently embedded in the Educational system. Teachers warmly welcomed the publication of the Tomlinson Report but it was never implemented. Unfortunately, the surviving legacies from the early years of New Labour's Educational programme were the ones that Max and the Educational Unions saw as against the interests of children, teachers and the development of a skilled labour force—i.e., excessive testing linked to selection and streaming at an early age, Ofsted and League tables, an over-prescribed and narrowly academic curriculum, privatisation and reduction of the role of local authorities.

Max was distressed at the effect he believed continual testing and League tables were already having both on children and on the teaching profession. He found it hard to believe that the Labour Party was throwing overboard the accumulated understanding of children's educational needs as outlined in the Plowden Report. 'Half our Future' of 1967 and the work afterwards of the Schools Council.

How could 'New Labour' be following in the steps of Kenneth Baker and Margaret Thatcher and promoting the ideology of competition instead of cooperation? Children and Schools were to be judged by their results at Key Stage One (the 7+ test) and at Key Stage Two (at 11) as well as O and A levels. Just as many of the 75% of children who failed the old 11+ carried into adult life a sense of failure and inadequacy, children as young as 7 who failed to score the target grades for Key Stage One became prone to discouragement and seeing themselves as future failures. Headteachers whose pupils failed to reach set targets became at risk of being sacked, which pushed teachers into teaching to the test. Max's predicted that the result of this system would be large scale Truancy and a rise in Exclusions and that children from poor backgrounds would be the main victims.

After overcoming his incredulity and anger, Max wrote an article for the Socialist Educational Association Journal, urging a change of policy. He was Chair of the SEA and was taken aback when the Editor informed him that the Secretary of the SEA for the last 17 years, Graham Lane, had vetoed its publication. Maybe after being in post so long, he had come to regard himself as in charge of the organisation and had shown signs of this at a meeting in Birmingham the previous year when he started pulling Max's arm while he was speaking trying to interrupt him. I was in the audience and amused at this little tussle but for a Secretary to embargo the publication of an article by the Chair was totally unheard of.

At the next SEA NEC meeting in London, Max was ousted from the Chair, a position to which he had been democratically elected by the SEA membership. The next Chair of the SEA, Peter Holland, has provided me with an account of what happened:

"At the meeting, I was seated between Caroline Benn, President of the SEA and Tony Pearce (a fellow member from Staffordshire). There had been tension between Max and Graham Lane in the morning session. Very soon after the break for lunch, Lane invited David Benn the Editor of the SEA Journal, 'Education Politics' to speak. He immediately moved a vote of no confidence in Max as chair, which he must have been put up to at lunch. Caroline muttered to me sotto voce 'It's a coup' but did not feel she should side with either group. The vote of no confidence was carried At that time, Staffordshire had a very strong branch of over 70 members, built up by Brian Lovatt and Joanna Tait (the Chair before Max). At the next branch meeting our members were appalled by our reports on the action of the NEC and resolved to continue to support Max. After a while Max and Margaret came to an informal discussion at Joan and my home in Stone. There were one or two others present, probably Joanna and Brian. We decided to put up 18 names, the number on the NEC, to stand against Lane's team in the election which would have to follow. Max thought I should be put forward as chair. At our next branch meeting Tony Pearce agreed to stand as General Secretary, Malcolm Green as Treasurer, Joan Holland and Irmgard Green as members. Max enlisted others from his branch and members from southern branches came forward (including some whom Max didn't even know personally). In the end, we had 18 names to put forward.

The NEC continued its meetings under the Vice-chair, a Lane supporter, but they were fruitless as the Committee was so divided. This was a great disappointment as Blair had only recently been elected as PM and the SEA was losing its opportunity to, influence education policy. We were 'advised' by Stephen Byers, a junior education Minister, to support the policies that were being put forward. I think it was at the AGM that Lane urged us, at the Party's bidding, to change our name from Socialist Educational Association to New Labour E.A. Fortunately, this was defeated. Max's supporters thought the SEA would have no purpose if we rubber-stamped whatever the Party put forward. The election was organised by the NEC of the Labour Party (trust having broken down completely within the SEA). Our group's mantra was 'critical friends.' This clearly identified us and we took 17 of the 18 places, including all the officer positions."

Max had decided not to stand for re-election as Chair as he did not want the issues to be about his personal position but about the educational policies which should be supported by the SEA as the Party's only affiliated educational body.

Our membership had made clear their support for the proposals of the 1994 Education Commission and advised against the adoption of 'Excellence in Schools'. For 80 years, the SEA's reason for existence had been to provide the Labour Party with informed advice about educational policy. It had been listened to and its role recognised at National Conferences, even if our recommendations were not always fully accepted. It would be a denial of our purpose to become a rubber stamp. We did not want to oppose the leadership of the Labour Party but hoped they would accept that we could contribute to its success in the role of 'critical friend'.

To Max's surprise, I volunteered to become Editor of *Education Politics* and become involved in SEA's debates and programmes. This was a considerable commitment but I thought it would be a good use of my time as my period as an Auditor for the Higher Education Quality Council had recently ended and being a Lay Chair of the NHS Complaints Committee was only intermittently demanding. There were not many HE members on the NEC so I would be able to help in that policy area. For five years, I produced 5 or 6 issues a year of *Educational Politics* containing 12 foolscap pages of reports and analysis of educational matters. With Max's help, I was able to draw upon articles from many leading educationists of the period. We saw this as a serious contribution to current thinking about educational policy, which could benefit the Labour Party, should they be prepared to make use of our expertise.

This they were not prepared to do but not because the SEA did not agree with New Labour's educational policy but because Tony Blair didn't want the advice of experts in any policy area and wanted to change the process of decision making. Ever since I began lecturing on British history in the late 1950s I'd contrasted the democratic procedures for deciding future Labour Party policy with the Conservative Party's reliance on the decisions of their Leader. In the Labour Party, the process began in the branches which could pass resolutions for Conference, which then went to their Constituency GC. If endorsed, they were placed on the Conference agenda along with resolutions from trade unions and affiliated societies. Obviously, a composting system had to take place to establish a workable Conference timetable but the principle was that the votes of Conference were binding on the Party for the year ahead.

Another democratic feature was the election by Conference of Shadow Cabinet members, which could be constraining on the Leader, but continued until 2011. The Cabinet or Shadow Cabinet might decide that it would not be practical to take action on an agreed policy but they could not change it until the next Conference.

The system was cumbersome and had weaknesses which could be addressed. John Smith before his death had been proposing changes to a 'one man on vote' system rather than the block system of the trade unions. The principle of grassroots involvement in the preparation of the agenda for Conference was never openly challenged. The leaders of New Labour, however, wanted to be able to initiate the Conference agenda themselves instead of leaving it to the outcome of the traditional system. They prepared the ground for this by creating a large 'Policy Forum' to widen policy debate over key areas. Membership of the Forum and its subject groups was based on representation from each area of the country rather than subject expertise. The specialist affiliated Societies were allocated 3 places which meant most of them did not have members on the Forum examining their area. This idea of "widening" the debate resulted in practice the Government or Shadow Cabinet organising the Forum meetings and in effect pre-empting the agenda of Conference. The outward form was retained but branch resolutions were limited to issues not already discussed in the Forums. A later examination of the effectiveness of the National Forum way of working suggested it needed changing but so far it remains in place.

Although critical of the changes being introduced in education many of our members were reluctant to be publicly critical because of the scope of the building programmes for schools but even in relation to this, its most popular programme, there were serious misgivings about the use of Public Private Initiatives for covering the costs. Max became involved in this issue as one of three Labour Party Governors at Fortismere School, a successful large Comprehensive school serving a racial and socially mixed population, which our grandson had attended. The School was offered a new science Lab and Sixth Form Centre to be financed by PFI. The Chair of the Governing Body, Elizabeth Osman, one of the Labour Governors, allowed Max to move a motion expressing concern about burdening the school for the next 30 years with paying for the costs of the work because it would be much cheaper to use money from the Public Works Loan Fund with low interest rates. The Haringey Council, however, was adamant that they must follow the Government's guidelines, so to remove opposition from Max and his fellow Labour Governors, their appointments as Governors were terminated. So that was that!

The school continued under Andrew Nixon as a non-selective Comprehensive School, deemed one of the hundred best such schools in England, until his retirement in 2005. His successor wanted to turn it into a selective school aimed at high flying children from well to do backgrounds. To Max's horror, the School became a Foundation School in 2007, despite opposition from 70% of the parents.

Max and my focus was so centred on education developments and the SEA that we were slow to react to the beginning stage of 'Blair's Wars' but were appalled at his support for NATO's illegal intervention in Kosovo, including dropping bombs on civilians and generally exacerbating instead of solving the problems of the area.

I had never ceased to support CND and was appalled that a British Prime Minister could think that peace keeping could be achieved by war and thousands of deaths. He was too young to remember the Second World War but plenty of those who lived through it were still alive and would feel as I did.

After Bush declared "A War on Terror" in response to 9/11 and threatened to invade Afghanistan, although the bombers did not come from there. Max and I were not able to attend the key meeting in Friend's House to stop the war before it began to but both Max and I were there in spirit. Tony Blair did not listen and became a keen supporter of the idea that democratic forms of Government could be imposed on 'backward nations' by invasion and occupation. He saw bringing about regime change in such countries as a moral mission. We saw it as evil warmongering and a reversion to the imperialist illusions of the past.

The invasion of Afghanistan took place in 2001 but the American desire for revenge for 9/11 was not appeased and Iraq was chosen as the next target. In 2002 and early 2003, nearly three million British citizens took to the streets to demonstrate their opposition to the planned invasion. Trade Unions and other organisations held meetings. Max and I as delegates to our Labour Party Constituency GC meeting urged our MP to oppose the war as did the majority of the delegates. She replied that if only we had read 'the Dossier' on Iraq's accumulation of weapons of mass destruction, we would understand. After the meeting, we told her privately that she was being naïve but to our regret she was not one of the Labour PMs who voted against the war.

Max remained in the Labour Party but I left it when the Government voted to participate in the Iraqi War and could not bring myself to vote in the 2005 election for our sitting MP, who lost her seat to a Liberal. This gave me no pleasure but strengthened my longstanding conviction that the British electoral system was unfit for a democracy. Since 1945, because of the use of First Past the Post, we have had only two Parties able to form a Government—Labour or Conservative—both of which supported the war on Iraq. There was no way of expressing a view on key Issues of peace or war through the ballot box in any meaningful way. British political involvement was limited to taking part in factional struggles within one of the two main parties or voting for a party which would have no chance of obtaining a fair representative number of MPs in Parliament, let alone winning power.

Max was 90 in August 2003 and to cheer him up I organised with the help of the NUT a Celebration of his life to take place before teacher and political friends and colleagues left on summer holidays. It was held in Hamilton House and Jack Jones, himself also 90, acted as Master of Ceremonies. The NUT had assembled a photographic display on the screen which was played alongside reminiscences by of some of those pictured, Wine flowed and I had organised snacks. There were lots of people there and Max sat on a Chair so everyone could take turns chatting to him. Jack was as ebullient as ever and Max back on his old form. It was just a wonderful evening.

Afterwards we went to Menton for the summer, swam, drank and ate with friends, played with our grandchildren and tried to ignore all that was happening in the world. Back in London we concentrated on SEA meetings and I finished my 5-year stint as Editor of Education politics. After the split, we changed the SEA Constitution to limit the length of service of Officers to 5 years to ensure a turnover in the leadership. Max had been getting deaf and this limited his participation in to-and-fro debate, even though I did my best to tell him what was being said. He could still make a good speech on whatever was the main theme of the meeting, right to the end of his life.

After Gordon Brown replaced Blair, I re-joined the labour Party so I could help Max at branch meetings, though they were very small gatherings. Relations between the Government and the SEA were reopened to some extent but the Party listened more to Think Tanks financed by wealthy donors, such as Progress, then to the member-financed SEA. Max was getting frail as well as deaf but could still enjoy going to meetings. As described above he attended the 2008 Annual Conference and made a speech about his first attendance in 1938, 70 years earlier.

He still enjoyed our winter sun-seeking holidays and although he ceased to go swimming, he still loved going to Menton and sitting by the sea. We celebrated his 95 birthday with breakfast and a glass of champagne as we had done for years. He was not well the next week and the doctor was concerned about his heart but her pills seemed to be having an effect. On the morning of the 26th of August he said he would like to have dinner that evening by the sea to celebrate feeling better, so I booked our restaurant.

Later that morning, Max did something unusual: I was just sorting the flat out in a routine way getting ready to go out that evening when he. beckoned me over and said "come and sit down and talk to me." So, I sat down and he continued "I've been thinking about what would have happened to you if I'd not decided to look after you?" We'd been married for nearly 50 years and had never had this type of discussion. I was taken aback and amused at the old-fashioned idea that he'd married me to look after me as that was not exactly how I remembered it. For several years, I had been looking after him not vice versa, but I didn't want to say that, so I just smiled and got up and went on getting ready while he went back to reading his book.

Max liked to look smart when we went out. So, in the early evening he put on his latest jacket and I drove us down to the restaurant. As we settled down someone on the beach kicked a football which landed on our table and gave Max a shock but he appeared to get over it. Later we were busy, happily having a very erudite discussion about the merits of the steak with gorgonzola sauce, which he was eating, against the steak with green sauce I was eating, when he suddenly choked and fell forward on to the table. The waiter very quickly called a police ambulance and the medics screened off our table, ushered me aside and attended to him. I was in shock and a waiter gave me a brandy while I waited. Sometime later the doctor in charge came and told me Max was being transferred into their ambulance so they could continue treating him while taking him to hospital in Nice, He said I'd be in the way in the ambulance but a police car would take me behind the ambulance to the hospital. I was surprised at this and wondered if such service would be offered in England.

At the hospital I was taken to a waiting room, offered a coffee and told I could rest there and they would let me know how Max was later. Eventually a Doctor came and told me they were still trying to resuscitate Max but were doubtful about whether they would succeed. If I wished I could stay where I was until the morning, when they would let me know the situation.

So, I stretched out on a bench and tried to rest. In the morning, the Senior Professor came to see me. He said that although Max was still alive, sadly he was fading and would die in the next few hours but I could spend them by his bedside. He explained that although he was not able to reply, Max was not completely unconscious and would be able to hear me if I talked to him. I found out this was true. For the next four or five hours, I sat by his bed and whenever I spoke to him, he smiled. I could see on a gauge that his blood pressure was falling and that the doctor would soon tell me he had died. I was very tired and very grateful when my grandson arrived at the hospital. He had managed to get a flight from London to Nice at 7am, then rescued my car from outside the restaurant in Menton and came to find me in the hospital. He went out and got some food and sat with me during the last couple of hours. We were both pleased when he smiled at the sound of Dharam's voice—Max would have been pleased that someone was there to look after me when he died, which happened about 4 in the afternoon. Dharam stayed in Menton for over a week to help arrange for his cremation and the placing of his ashes in the Garden of Remembrance in Menton.

Thirteen years have now gone by. For the rest of that year, I was in a daze partly through sheer tiredness and partly because too many deaths had occurred one after another. In June, Pierrette, our neighbour, had died after a long period of a form of dementia. She and Marcel had teamed up when she was 14 and he a year older, 60 years ago. Her death was expected and a release, but left Marcel bereft. The death of our relative, Myron, a month later was a total shock, neither expected nor clearly explained. Ever since he bought a flat in Menton a couple of years after us, he had served as the brother I never had, and I had been relying on him for practical and moral support when Max died. So, his death was a double blow to me. I had realised Max would not keep going for ever and was relieved that he passed away without suffering. I was glad that I had out lived him because he had become very over dependent on my being there in his last 2 or 3 years and could not have coped. My own health had held up well for someone with reduced lungs since the age of 21, but I had no energy left. I stayed on for some weeks in Menton before returning to London. There was a memorial meeting for Max in late November.

After Christmas with the family, I began to give thought to adapting to widowhood. I decided I would go on spending long summers in Menton in memory of the past, but also that when there I would do something I'd enjoyed when young, but not done for 50 years, and start playing duplicate bridge. So, I joined the Menton Bridge Club, and started going to tournaments in various holiday resorts.

My main life in London would continue around the SEA and attending all the NEC meetings. After a while, I was elected an Honorary vice President and served in that position until recently. I also took over from Max as Chair of the Haringey SEA and fronted our campaign to try to prevent Haringey's Schools becoming Academies, with limited success. The Hornsey and Wood Green Labour Party recaptured the seat from the Liberals in 2010 with a candidate I could warmly support and Ed Miliband was elected Leader of the Party, so I recovered some hope for the future.

Meetings between the leaders of the SEA and the Shadow Ministers resumed although our old position as the main adviser on education policy was not recovered. The SEA and a number of other education pressure groups including CASE teamed up to organise conferences on future education policies. These continued after Jeremy Corbyn became Labour Leader. I was not a personal fan of his but mainly supported his policies and welcomed the upsurge of younger members he attracted. It grieved me that the Party was so divided and became ever more focussed on its sectarian divides than in uniting to challenge the domination of financial interests in the running of Britain.

Ever since I was 21, I expected not to have a long life and I was astonished that I was still alive after 80, less alone that I'd live to be over 90. After Max died I did not at first think of trying to rescue his manuscript from the drawer in order to take the advice of those publishers who suggested adding human interest to it. I thought it would be too big a task and I'd not live long enough to complete it. However, I eventually stopped being negative and now I've finished it. I hope it will help deepen understanding of past left-wing struggles.

In Retrospect

When choosing which incidents in our lives to include in these memoirs, I selected those which seemed historically of interest but now, looking back, I keep returning to the question posed in our introduction: "Why after a more than a hundred years since 1918 is Britain in its present condition?" The simplest answer is because the Conservative Party has been in power for the majority of the years since Labour replaced the Liberals as their main opponent. But why did that happen? Why did the aspirations of the early Labour Party remain unfulfilled? How far back do we need to go to pin point the circumstances which have enabled the Conservative Party to hand over the British economy to international financiers and create such an unequal society that millions of our citizens are dependent on food banks and live in a state of constant anxiety and stress?

Poverty, hunger, exploitation and wretched living conditions were the lot of much of the working class in the early 19th century and were the background to demonstrations for the right to vote in Parliamentary elections from Peterloo in 1919 onwards. The growth of trade unions and their increasing militancy over the next eighty years helped raise wages for sections of the working class but did not change Britain's deeply divided class structure nor lesson working class conviction that obtaining representation in Parliament was essential. By 1884/5 when over half the male working class had obtained the vote for both Parliamentary and local elections, it became clear that having a vote was not enough without a political party to campaign for trade union and working-class concerns.

The Independent Labour Party was set up in 1893, led by Keir Hardie, a miner who became a trade union organiser and independent MP. He believed in pacifism and a generalised socialism based on a secularised Christianity and was instrumental in setting up the Labour Representation Committee in 1900. He was its first leader when it became an organised Parliamentary Party in 1906. His pacifist views were shared by many of the members of Methodist and other Christian congregations existing among the working class at the time.

The conviction of the Trade Unions of the importance of having a voice in Parliament was quickly confirmed by the passing of the 1906 Trade Disputes Act which established the legal rights of workers to withhold their labour and trade unions to organise strikes without being held responsible for any losses they might cause employers. That the right to strike is a basic human right, marking the difference between being a worker and a slave, was recognised in the United Nations declaration of human rights after the Second World War. It was achieved in Britain in 1906 by cooperation between Asquith's Liberal Party and the new Labour Party. Despite the efforts of the Conservative Party ever since 1906 to undermine or limit its effects it remains in force today.

Not all trade unionists were socialists but there was a growing number who were and maybe a larger number still who supported the Cooperative Movement. A number of socialist societies advocating various forms of socialism came into being. The Social Democratic Federation was based on Marxist theories and was set up in 1881 by H.M. Hyndman and supported among others by William Morris, George Lansbury and Eleanor Marx. Its offshoot, the British Socialist Party, was affiliated to the Labour Party from 1911–1920. The Fabian Society, set up in 1884 by a group of mainly middle-class intellectuals, was another of the founders of the Labour Party. It espoused the improvement of society by socialist ideals but rejected the ideas of Marx and believed change could only be achieved slowly, little by little, by winning Parliamentary elections. It became a 'think tank' for the Labour Party and Sidney Webb prepared the Labour Party's 1918 Constitution, which provided for the admission of individual members. Until then the Labour Party consisted of affiliated trade unions and socialist societies with the right to nominate candidates for election as MPs or representatives on local bodies such as School Boards, Poor Law Guardians and Councillors.

Labour Manifestos were produced for all General Elections from 1900 onwards. The first one had a long list of policies including not only immediate social reforms—old age pensions, housing, work for the unemployed, adequate maintenance for children, etc.—but also, Income Tax, Government contribution to the Rates, Nationalisation of Land and the Railways, Abolition of the Standing Army, the People to decide on Peace or War, and the legislative Independence of all parts of the Empire. It ended, "The object of these measures is to enable the people ultimately to obtain the Socialisation of the Means of Production, Distribution, and Exchange, to be controlled by a Democratic State in the interests of the entire Community, and the Complete Emancipation of labour from the Domination of Capitalism and Landlordism, and the Establishment of Social and Economic Equality between the Sexes."

The Manifestos of 1906 and 1910 added to the list of specific policies including reducing the burden of rates and taxation for shopkeepers and ensuring that the benefit of increases in land values should be used to relieve ratepayers instead of going to people who had not earned them. The commitment to socialism was repeated without being specific about different theoretical approaches. Many of the concrete proposals would be helpful to the working class in a country with a mixed economy as well as a fully socialist state and had enabled cooperation with the Liberal Party. Elected representatives from affiliated organisations were still able to promote their own views but the 1906 Manifesto ended with a call for unity: "The Labour Representation-Executive appeals to you in the name of a million Trade Unionists to forget all the political differences which have kept you apart in the past."

The outbreak of the First World War destroyed the unity which was being developed. Despite the hopes of the Second International and previous Labour Party statements that "war is made by the rich to make them richer," when recruiting began the majority of the working class both in Britain and abroad rallied to support their own governments. Some of Labour's Leaders kept to their pacifist beliefs: Keir Hardie was trying to organise a general strike against the war when he died in 1915; and Ramsay MacDonald resigned as Leader of the Party so he could continue opposing it. When conscription began quite a large number of Labour Party supporters became conscientious objectors for religious, moral, ethical or political reasons. However, when a Coalition Government was set up, Henderson and some other Labour leaders became ministers.

By 1918, the mood was sombre. So many soldiers and sailors had died and others had been left disabled. The British economy had been weakened, so would there be work for demobilised soldiers? Labour's Manifesto for the coming election called for 'a peace of reconciliation'. Sidney Webb prepared an extended statement of the socialist aims of the Labour Party in "Labour and the New Social Order" and a new Constitution which included what became known as 'Clause Four': "to secure for the producers, by hand or by brain, the full fruits of their industry and the most equitable distribution thereof that may be possible upon the basis of the common ownership of the means of production, and the best obtainable system of popular administration and control of each industry or service." Resentment of profiteering during the war led to a proposal for the entire abolition of profit-making armaments firms. What was totally new were proposals to create a Labour Party with individual members in every constituency, and representation on the Executive and Annual Conferences from constituency members and women members. as well as affiliated trade unions and socialist societies.

In both documents principles and aims were very explicit: "The Labour Party stands essentially for revolt against the inequality of circumstances that degrades and brutalises and disgraces our civilisation"…"conscious and deliberate cooperation is productive of life and progress"…"the Party is unreservedly democratic in its life with the widest possible participation in power and consent…it supports internationalism and the role of the League of Nations…it repudiates Imperialism and domination over other races…it believes in the right of each people to live its own life in its own way."

In the 1918 Election, the Labour Party stood in 351 seats and increased their MPs to 57 but while this was disappointing it had not been a normal election. Lloyd George's decision to continue the Coalition Government and hold a General Election only a month after the war ended resulted in an overwhelming vote of confidence in his leadership. The composition of the new Parliament was determined by his giving "Coupons" to those supporting the continuation of the Coalition but not to other MPs or candidates including members of his own Party. Asquith had remained Leader of the Liberal Party but was not a member of the Coalition Government. He had wanted to return to single Party government for the Election, but the Liberals were divided: 147 accepted a Coupon and stood as Coalition Liberals and were elected, but only 36 of the 277 Asquith Liberals who stood were elected. Labour representation would grow in future elections but the Liberal Party would never again form a Government, which was a warning about the electoral danger of internal Party splits and conflict.

The immediate outcome was that three quarters (379) of the new Coalition MPs were Conservatives, including more businessmen and bankers than in the past. Before the war, Lloyd George had been one of the Liberal Party architects of the early welfare state and of taxing the rich, but being dependant on Conservative support would limit his power despite his personal standing. This proved to be the case and the Coupon Election was to be a key factor in the domination of Conservative views between the Wars.

After the Soviet Revolution led to civil war, fears that the British Government would intervene on behalf on the White Army led to a vigorous 'Hands Off Russia' Campaign including the London Dockers' refusal to load the Jolly George with arms for Poland to use against the Red Army in May 1920. Originally the Campaign was a spontaneous rank and file movement but when Lloyd George raised in Parliament the possibility of sending British troops to help Poland against the Red army a National Council of Action was set up by the official leadership of the Labour Party and TUC, hitherto opponents of 'direct action'. The threat of British intervention was withdrawn which encouraged them to have confidence in their ability to influence events.

The TUC and the Labour Party strongly supported the legal right of individual trade unions to strike in defence of their own living standards or in support of strikes by related unions but there were many differing opinions within the Labour Movement about the use of Direct Action for political ends (See my *The General Strike. Pub by Penquin 1976*). Before the war there had been some support, especially in the Welsh coalfields, for the use of a General Strike to take over the mines, but there has never been more than very limited support in Britain for syndicalism as a route to political power. This did not deter Conservatives from attributing every manifestation of trade union militancy to revolutionary intent in order to discredit the Labour Party.

While the threat of being taken into an anti-Soviet War had been averted, Labour's hope of progress towards its economic programme was stalled. Before the War, coal mining was Britain's biggest industry and provided a tenth of the value of all British exports. The Miners Federation of Great Britain was set up in 1889 and had had won negotiations over pay and conditions, helped by the 1908 Eight Hours Act and 1911 Coal Mines Act. The miners work was arduous and dangerous but better paid than other industrial workers by the outbreak of war. By then, the British coal industry was being challenged by the growth of mining in other countries, especially America and Germany, using better equipment and organisation. The British Industry was handicapped by having over 1,500 companies or individual owners of collieries and about 4,000 landowners with the right to royalties for the use of the land occupied by collieries. The threat to Britain's economy was so obvious that a motion to nationalise the mines was tabled in Parliament but had not been debated before war broke out.

During the war, the Government gradually assumed control of all aspects of the economy, including coal mining. The leaders of both sides of the industry accepted, albeit grudgingly, that national interests must transcend class interests. As Lloyd George recognised, this attitude would not last after the war ended but he also understood that Britain would lose out in world markets unless the coal industry was modernised. Miners wages had failed during the war to keep up with rises in the cost of living but mine owners profits had been protected, so in February 1919 the Miners put in a claim not only for immediate rises and full pay for demobilised miners until they found work, but also for keeping the mines in public control by nationalisation. When their demands were rejected, they voted to go on strike but Lloyd George persuaded them to hold back while a Royal Commission considered the future of the British mining industry. He offered them the opportunity to nominate members to represent the Miners' case, a hitherto unknown procedure, so they nominated Sidney Webb. R.H. Tawney and Herbert Smith (leader of the NUM), No Royal Commission has ever been more thorough than that held under Mr Justice Sankey, nor has any case won such widespread public support as that made by the miners' representatives. Nationalisation, they argued would not just benefit the miners, "it would benefit the whole community and be a profitable investment for the nation." Revelations about the wartime profits and royalties of the owners being £25m more than the total pre-war capital of the industry led consumers, both industrial and domestic, to feel cheated when they remembered the prices they had had to pay. The Wartime Chief Inspector of Mines testified to the inefficiency of the Owners. Justice Sankey as Chairman was won over by the evidence and his massive Report supported the Miners proposals.

Three supplementary Reports were produced one by the miners along the lines of the main Report and reinforcing the reasons why the miners should be involved in the management of the nationalised mines, one from the Owners who opposed any change except small pay increases, and one from the independent businessmen on the Commission who agreed that fundamental change was necessary but proposed the unification of the industry around a limited number of owners.

It was all in vain because Lloyd George could not get the Conservative majority in the Coalition Government to agree.

The bankers and businessmen on the Coalition bench had a different aim—they wanted to bring prices down so Britain could restore the Gold Standard in the interests of maintaining London as a financial centre. For Britain, it was a missed opportunity to revitalise its industrial economy. For the miners and the Labour Party, a bitter disappointment. The day Lloyd George announced that the Government would not be going ahead with nationalisation the miners felt cheated—had setting up the Commission been a hoax? They felt even more betrayed when the Government handed the mines back to the Owners in March 1921. Events moved on after that towards the General Strike.

(On a personal note, I still have a copy of the three volumes of the Sankey Commission which I acquired when writing *The General Strike.* The third volume with the Reports is so heavy I can't any more lift it down, but I look at it sometimes with sadness and think how the General Strike and the mass unemployment of the inter war years might have been averted if its main recommendations had been adopted—but that wasn't to be. If the financiers, owners and manipulators of wealth want to select a date on which to celebrate the beginning of their control of the British Economy, they could choose the day that Parliament binned the Sankey Report, sixty years ahead of the advent of Margaret Thatcher.)

Despite this major setback, Sidney Webb's hopes that the Labour Party would reunite around the new Programme seemed to be going well and the rift between those who had supported the war and those opposing it gradually healed and in 1922 Ramsay MacDonald was again elected Leader of the Party. However, he and some of the other senior leaders of the Party began to make winning elections their sole priority. He quickly became opposed to the Labour Party formally supporting trade union militancy on the ground that strikes would deter voters from supporting the Labour Party. This was contrary to the spirit and purpose behind its formation as defined in the 1918 Statement, "The New Social Order." In particular, he opposed Strikes and in 1926 gave no support to the miners, even though their strike was purely in defence of their living standards.

The Minority Labour Governments of 1924 and 1929–31 were able to carry out important social reforms, especially the growth of Council Housing, but wages fell, unemployment soared and the class structure remained rigidly divided. MacDonald's lack of commitment to the aims of the Labour Party culminated in his returning as Prime Minister of the National Government in 1931 after the majority of Labour MPs had refused to support further wage cuts and reductions in unemployment benefit.

While still its leader, MacDonald began to disassociate the Labour Party from all left-wing movements of any kind and talked of moving "ever upwards" rather than of Socialism, which he feared would be equated with Communism. Although the Hands-Off Russia Campaign had won formal support from the Labour Party, attitudes towards the Soviet Union after it became established were to be a source of sharply divided opinions and splits in the years that followed. Individual members of the British Socialist Party had played a prominent part in the Hands-Off Russia Campaign along with other members of the Labour Party and Trade Unions, but when in 1920 they joined up with other smaller left-wing groups to form the British Communist Party and it affiliated to the Communist Third International, the Labour Leaders decided to disassociate the Party from any connection with it. When it applied to affiliate to the Labour Party it was rejected both immediately and later.

After the forged Zinoviev Letter was used to discredit the 1924 short-lived Labour Government, the Labour Party declared in its 1929 Manifesto that Tory scaremongering had won the last election and asserted that Labour was 'neither Bolshevik nor Communist'; thereby implying that having Communist views would be discreditable. Some Socialists had already become critical of the Russian Government under Stalin and opposed to equating communism or socialism with Soviet Russia, but others including members of the British Communist Party insisted that the Soviet Union was a beacon for Marxists worldwide. Beatrice and Sidney Webb were favourably impressed by a visit there in the early 1930s but were deemed over credulous by others. Lack of unity and conflict among different sections of the Labour Party in their assessment and response to the Soviet Union were to be a major problem from then until many years later—always to the benefit of the Conservative Party.

During the period of the Great Depression and the National Front Government, campaigning about the effects of mass unemployment dominated trade union activity and lessoned concern about ideological divisions. Communist members took a leading role in organising Hunger Marches and trade union and Labour Party members of every viewpoint rallied to organise facilities for their reception on route. When the rise of Hitler became a threat antagonism to Communism was partially replaced by calls for a united front against Fascism although its leading advocates such as Stafford Cripps, founder of Tribune, were then expelled from the Labour Party. When finally, both Russia and America became Britain's Allies in the war against Hitler, ideological differences within the Labour movement were put aside for a while. They regurgitated later and were a major issue between the followers of Tribune and those of Gaitskell in the 1950s and afterwards.

Despite the bitter disappointment of the formation of the National Government, Labour made progress in Local Elections and in 1934 captured control of the London County Council. Herbert Morrison, who had been a conscientious objector in the First World War, had become an LCC Councillor in 1922 and was Minister of Transport in the 1929–31 Labour Government. After 1931, he became the leading member of the Labour Group on the LCC, which was already running some aspects of London transport. In 1933, he wrote a book, 'Socialisation and Transport' outlining the advantages of a public transport service and how he thought a public Corporation should be run by a Board of Directors. When he became LCC Leader, he put his theories into effect by setting up the London Passenger Transport Board covering all aspects of transport—buses, trams, trolley cars and the Underground.

The first Chairman of the Board was Lord Albert Stanley, Baron Ashfield, a leading businessman who had been recruited by Lloyd George in 1916 as a Coalition MP and President of the Board of Trade. When he left the Commons in 1920, he was appointed to the Lords as a Conservative Peer and returned to business as Chairman of the London Electric Railway. He served as Chair of the London Passenger Transport Board from 1933 to 1947. He was without question a very capable businessman but his appointment was against the existing policy of the Labour Party that publicly owned enterprises should be democratically run by the workers with experience in the industry. It would have been difficult in such a complex and segmented a business as London Transport but it's successful launch didn't justify abandoning the general principle of democratic involvement in management.

In 1935, when Morrison ran against Attlee for the Leadership of the Labour Party, he was defeated but he had established his claim to be among the senior leaders of the Party. During the War he was Home Secretary. He developed the use of advertising skills and had a major role in writing 'Let us Face the Future'. After the 1945 victory, Attlee appointed him as Deputy Leader and Leader of the House of Commons although he had no great regard for him. He was given responsibility for preparing plans for the Nationalisation of key industries. Because his views on organisation and management of nationalised enterprises by appointed businessmen or Civil Servants were known, his appointment to this role was not welcomed by the trade unions, who believed their knowledge and experience had a great deal to offer and would be useful in ensuring the success of the new enterprises.

During and after the war, Shop Stewards had cooperated in helping achieve efficient running, but their role was not included in plans for the future, not even for minority representation on the new Boards, as was the case in some other countries.

The Sankey Report on Coal Nationalisation had recommended democratic involvement of the miners in running the industry not just as a democratic principle but to help achieve success, but this was brushed aside when nationalisation finally happened. A businessman, Lord Hyneg, was appointed Chair of the Coal Board when it was set up. Most of the other members were not coal face workers but had other roles in the industry and as such were members of the NUM, but they were appointed in their individual capacity not to represent the workforce. This was not satisfactory to either the NUM or the men appointed. They mainly left to join a Staff Association and before long were campaigning to be regarded as Civil Servants and paid accordingly.

The main concern of Attlee and Morrison seems to have been maintaining control of economic planning rather than thinking what would best facilitate the future efficiency or development of the nationalised industries. There was very little thought given to transforming their organisational structures or to investing for the future. Their financial results were seen as part of the general budget in the short term. After the 1951 Election and the restoration of Conservative Governments, the attitude towards the nationalised industries became grudging tolerance of their existence and opposition to an extension of their number. The opportunity to strengthen their role in the economy with the help of the Trade Unions had been lost.

Returning to critical turning points, a Speakers Conference of both Houses of Parliament held way back in 1916 had a lasting effect on Britain's political future, if only by leaving things unchanged. The various Reform Acts since 1832 had altered the number of constituencies and electors but without sorting out how future Governments would be decided. Historically, after an election the Party Leader obtaining majority support among newly elected MPs was invited to become Prime Minister and his Party became the Government. At local level, there was no uniformity in either the size of constituencies or the number of seats allocated to each one. From 1884, there was a move towards using single member constituencies and 'First Past the Post', but it was not complete and there was an awareness that the use of single seat constituencies and FPTP might result in no Party winning the support of a majority of MPs or one Party winning a disproportionate share of seats compared with votes.

In the 1910 elections, the Conservatives under Balfour had a higher vote than the Liberals under Asquith but the Irish National Party and the Labour Party MPs, even though not formally running jointly with the Liberals, were ready to support a minority Liberal Government. But what, it was asked, would have happened if this had not been the case?

The changes taking place became a major source of controversy. Both Liberals and Conservatives were motivated by wanting to prevent the enlargement of the number of Labour MPs. In 1916, a Speakers Conference was set up with members from both Houses of Parliament to try to come to an agreement. Neither of the main parties wanted FPTP to be generally implemented and the use of either the Alternative Vote (AV) system, with the reallocation of losing votes in a single constituency until one candidate was left, or the Single Transferable Vote (STV) using larger constituencies with several seats, which was thought to be fairer in towns, were proposed. In the end, a Bill prepared by the House of Lords ending FPTP and the introduction of AV was put to a free vote of the Commons, but was rejected. This led to the continued use of FPTP although some multiple constituencies and multiple voting remained.

Although all the elections between the wars used FPTP, which led to discrepancies between the number of votes cast for different parties and the number of MPs elected, it wasn't the main reason why the Conservatives were in power for most of the period. Lloyd George's Coupon election in 1918 with its large Conservative majority was followed by the Conservatives winning majorities in 1922 and 1924. No Party obtained a majority either of votes cast or MPs elected in 1923 or 1929 and there was only a small difference between the Labour and Conservative results but as the Liberals obtained a fifth of the seats and were opposed to Conservative policy on tariffs, they agreed in both years to support the formation of a Minority Labour Government. From 1931 the National Government, mainly comprised of Conservatives, first under MacDonald then Baldwin, had a clear majority. It was not until after the Second World War that the potential problem of using First Past the Post, discussed in 1916, became evident.

Before the 1945 Election, Attlee appealed to electors to vote Labour and not waste their votes on other parties if they didn't want to return to the unemployment and hardship of Conservative rule between the Wars. This appeal struck a chord, especially with soldiers, and Labour won the election with 47.7% of the national votes and 393 MPs. The Conservatives took 36.2% with 197 MPs. while 50 MPs were elected from other parties. In 1948, the Government decided to pass an Act to remove anomalies such as plural voting and complete the division of the country into single member constituencies of roughly equal size. Extra constituencies were created and boundaries redrawn.

Although not cited as an objective of these changes, the effect of combining single member constituencies with "First Past the Post" was as predicted in 1916—i.e., it drastically weakened representation of parties other than the two biggest parties, the Labour and Conservative Parties. After 1948, the ability of minority parties to play a balancing role in Hung Parliaments, as it had in 1906 and 1910 and the 1920s, virtually ceased as the number of their MPs fell far below their share of the national vote. The 1948 Act made it virtually impossible for other or new parties to achieve significant representation in Parliament.

Another long-term effect of the Act was to break the relationship between the overall national vote and the outcome of elections. Not only were adherents of minority parties virtually disenfranchised, but the outcome even between the two big parties was no longer determined by which of them had a bigger share of the national vote. This was because of the effect variations in the spread of votes within constituencies could have on the number of MPs elected.

It is one of ironies of history that the Labour Party has been the loser from Attlee's 1948 Act. Although the Attlee Government was losing momentum and experiencing difficulties, there didn't need to be an election in 1951. Thanks to the efforts first of Hugh Dalton and then Stafford Cripps as Chancellors of the Exchequer, economic recovery was beginning to take place and Attlee could have continued in power. In the 1951 Election, there was a very high turnout (82.65%) because faced with the return of Churchill, electors still remembered his pre-war policies, and voters rallied behind the Government.

Labour won 48.8% of the national vote compared with 48% for the Conservative candidates but it was the Conservative Party who gained more seats—321 against 295. Only 9 MPs were elected from other parties. The history of Britain might have been different if the overall votes gained by each party had been matched by the number of their MPs. More of the electorate had wanted

Labour to stay in power than had wanted the return of Churchill but instead the Conservatives took over and it was 13 years before there was another Labour Government.

The seriousness of the outcome of this election has been down played by both historians and contemporary commentators, who have dwelt upon the following years as a period of post war consensus or 'Butskellism'. Max's accounts of struggling to overcome class bias in education and my experiences of working with the Hornsey Housing Campaign Association provide a different perspective of the practical effects of the change of Government. Economic policies began to be centred on the interests of finance rather than providing full employment.

An even more outstandingly undemocratic outcome because of the use of First Past the Post came later after the 'Gang of Four' set up the Social Democratic Party, which joined with the Liberal Party to form an alliance to fight the 1983 Election. The Gang of Four were all respected intellectuals but lacked an understanding of basic arithmetic if they didn't anticipate that splitting away from the Labour Party while the FPTP system was in use would ensure victory for the Conservative Party without providing any chance of substantial representation for themselves. This proved to be the case: the Conservative popular vote went slightly down, the Labour Party vote also went down but it still obtained 27% and the Alliance obtained 25% of the national vote, but when this was transformed into seats the Conservatives went up to 397 MPs, Labour down to 269 MPs. and the Democratic Alliance only obtained 23 MPs. This was hailed by the press as a great Conservative victory and a big defeat for Labour, but it was hardly a victory for democratic choice of Government! The same voting pattern enabled Mrs Thatcher to remain Prime Minister in!987 and the Conservatives to cling on in 1992. It wasn't until 5 years later that the Conservative hold on power came to an end after 18 years. Even back in 1979, when the Thatcher transformation of Britain began, and she defeated James Callaghan, she still was supported by less than half of those who voted and a smaller proportion still of the electorate.

As well as enabling Conservatives to form the Government for the majority of the period since 1945, there has been a second cost to our use of 1948 Act electoral system—a gradual loss of public confidence in Parliamentary Democracy. Many electors have ceased to believe that using their votes will affect the result except in marginal constituencies, make a difference to their own lives or enable new policies to be considered. Politics has become a media game. We judge other countries' electoral systems by high participation rates without bribery or coercion, but our own turnout rates have dropped steadily since 1951 when it was 82.65%. It fell to 76.8% in 1955 and went on falling down to 71% in 1997, when New Labour was elected. It then fell down to 59% in the next election in 2001—meaning 40% of the electorate saw no point in casting their vote, and the Blair Government was re-elected by the votes of less than 25% of the total electorate.

In 2019, only 43.6% of those who voted supported Boris Johnson. As the turnout was 67.2%, he was the choice of approximately 30% of those entitled to vote, yet—as in 1997—the result was described as a landslide. We must not be hypnotised by pollsters and the media into thinking our current system of governments chosen by the votes of a minority of the electorate equates to Lincoln's definition of Democracy—"Government of the people, by the people, for the people."

Our voting system could have been changed when it was evident it was leading to government by parties representing only a minority of the electorate, so it cannot by itself explain why the Labour Party has not achieved the aims of its founders. Trade unionists, who were numerically the largest part of the membership in 1918, were suffering under the existing status quo and wanted to bring an end to class divisions, poverty and exploitation as soon as possible. After the Labour Party was set up, they hoped for faster progress but until it could win an election and form a Government, they continued to use trade union action to try to defend their members: i.e., strikes when negotiation failed, demonstrations, withholding rents and boycotts. When Ramsay MacDonald abandoned the Labour Party in 1931, the Trade Unions hoped that antagonist attitudes to trade union action would no longer have a place in it.

Most of the Labour MPs in Parliament during the first two Labour Governments were working class in origin and a majority had been trade union officials: only 20 out of the 191 MPs elected in 1923 were members of the Fabien Society of whom 5 were members of the First Labour Government. Changes in the composition of the Labour Party initiated in 1918 by the creation of individual membership and constituency branches had reversed the balance of Labour MPs' backgrounds by 1945. Trade union members continued to belong to the Party through their trade unions but only a minority took out individual membership in local constituency branches so the rest of constituency branch members belonged to socialist societies or were Cooperative Society members or members of local or parish councils or just concerned individuals.

There were still a considerable number of Trade Unionists both in Parliament and the Government but in 1945 well over half of the Labour MPs were Fabian Society members (229 out of 393 including Attlee himself).

This did not mean they were all of middle-class backgrounds nor that they were right-wing because a considerable number of Fabians were writing articles for Tribune at this period, but it was a cultural change. The early Fabian Society membership included some working-class members but mainly consisted of middle-class intellectuals. Their commitment to socialist ideas was what united them and the Trade Unions but the Fabians had less sense of urgency—on the contrary, they made a virtue of step-by-step progress. They recognised that there would be fierce opposition to the transformation of Britain into a socialist state and thought that obtaining a Parliamentary majority and winning power would require skill and patience.

However, respecting all existing laws until they were changed by Parliament could mean leaving in place laws that were class biased or clearly unjust, and not taking action of any kind at the implementation of new laws which took away existing rights. There can be no criticism of the commitment of the early Fabians but most of their membership did not face personal hardship living within the existing status quo. While this was no longer necessarily true by 1945, there was a measurable difference between the class composition of the trade union movement and that of constituency members in parts of the country.

There were also changes in social and cultural attitudes between 1918 and 1945 within the working class. Sidney Webb and his contemporaries saw themselves as representing 'workers by hand or brain' but after 1945 many "workers by brain" preferred to see themselves as 'middle class'. To what extent this affected political attitudes is not clear cut but had some relevance to the divisions between the right and left wing of the Labour Party.

During the early years of the Attlee Government, the priority given to full employment and the drive to restore peacetime industries together with the nationalisation of key industries brought the Trade Unions and the Parliamentary Party closer together but there remained a gulf between the different wings of the Party. It did not correspond to a simple division between members with a trade union background and those from a Fabian or other background but that had some relevance. The right wing of the Parliamentary Party together with older Trade Union leaders, such as Arthur Deacon, were timid about challenging the status quo, compared with a new generation of leaders in the large trade unions such as Jack Jones and Hugh Scanlon who were more proactive in their approach and believed that giving priority to the growth of industry was essential in national as well as working class interests.

Victory in 1945 was the first opportunity for the Labour Party to put into effect the socialist principles of 1918 which remained written into its Constitution. The Labour Manifesto in 1945 concentrated on domestic policy and despite struggling with war debts the Government began to put in place the Beveridge Plan for a Welfare State, a National Health Service, the 1944 Education Act and other reforms. There were many difficulties to be overcome in setting up a National Health Service but with the perseverance of Aneurin Bevan it was achieved, whereas in Education the class prejudice of the existing Education Department, which maintained working class children only needed the basics, held up progress for twenty years as Max has described. Admission to the Civil Service was by examination but the form of the tests were based on the syllabi of the Public Schools and no change had taken place in the social structure of the top Civil Servants since before the First World War. Attlee himself went to Haileybury College followed by University College, Oxford and may have thought it didn't matter.

Austerity, rationing and high taxation were necessary and generally accepted in the years immediately after the war. The continuation of conscription after 1948, however, was not seen as necessary by all party members or the general public and was part of the issues concerning Britain's role in the world that were to lead to conflict within the Labour Government. Attlee had joined the Wartime Coalition under Churchill in 1940 and had served as his Deputy Prime Minister since 1942 and had been either acquiescent or positively supportive of the way Churchill had been running the British war effort. British and American troops had cooperated in action where necessary. Although the Coalition was dissolved and an election had taken place there was no expectation of an immediate change of policy while Britain and America was still at war with Japan.

The Yalta and Potsdam Conferences had agreed a division of responsibility for ending the war and establishing government in three main zones, plus allocating to France a part of Germany and the areas of its previous Colonies. In most cases before the war had ended the armies of the four powers were already in occupation, if not in complete control, of the areas agreed as their responsibility. Attlee had replaced Churchill and Truman Roosevelt at the July/August Potsdam Summit with Stalin, but the agreements made at Yalta were mainly confirmed at Potsdam. Churchill was not only very determined to limit Stalin's areas of control but equally determined to eliminate Communist influence in the British controlled areas. After British troops occupied Greece, he wanted to enable the restoration of the pre-war monarchy. This had led in December 1944 to the massacre by British troops of a peaceful cross party gathering of Partisans, including the Communists who had been allies against the German occupiers. This was an unprovoked atrocity but later whitewashed as repression of a Communist uprising. Attlee claimed not to have been aware of it happening.

As Prime Minister Attlee took close control of the direction of foreign policy and worked very closely with Ernest Bevin, sometimes without consulting other members of his Government. Bevin had been an outstanding Minister of Labour and National Service during the War but his appointment as Secretary for Foreign Affairs was problematic as he was blunt and unsubtle and fiercely anti-communist. He lacked diplomatic skills and was out of his depth faced with implementing the Britain's self-serving but unrealistic Balfour Agreement of 1917.

His view of British interests was based on a willing subservience to America. Supporters of the Tribune Group within the Government totally disagreed: they wanted Britain to follow an independent path and not become an ally of either America or Russia. The Bretton Woods Conference in 1944 where Keynes' proposals for a world currency were defeated in favour of the dollar had made clear America's determination to dominate world finance and replace the British Empire. There would be no equality only subservience in having a 'special relationship' with America. The Tribune followers preferred Britain to follow its own path. Their slogan was "Keep Left" and implement the socialist policies in the Labour Party's long-standing programme.

The War was not over when the Election took place and Japan still had powerful forces. Truman advised Attlee of his intention to drop Atomic bombs on Hiroshima and Nagasaki but the extent of death and devastation they caused were a shock even after six years of unrelenting warfare. The Japanese accepted defeat a few days later and the end of WW2 was celebrated.

Britain was deep in debt, but Attlee seemed as determined as Churchill to maintain the role of a Great Power. Even though American economic interests were not the same as those of Britain, as was made clear by the immediate ending of Lend Lease and the long-lasting debt repayments imposed, he continued to act in alliance with America after the end of the war without any pause or public discussion of the terms of their post WW2 relationship. It was as though all that was involved was just tidying things up now the war was over. The aim of America under Truman was to assert its own leading position in the World and prevent the spread of Communist regimes. To this end, he wanted the territories occupied by the Western Allies at the end of the war to be restored to their pre-war status: Monarchy to be restored in Greece, the Dutch Empire restored in Indonesian and the French Empire in Indochina, even if it meant suppressing independence movements which had been cooperating with the Allied Forces during the war and instead enlisting Japanese ex-servicemen.

Attlee was not yet Prime Minister at the time of the December '44 atrocity in Greece but in the following years British troops were used to help the right wing in the Greek Civil War ensure the restoration of the Monarchy. By 1947 the cost was proving too great and Britain prepared to hand over its role in Greece to America. British troops also took part alongside the Americans in the suppression of the Independence movements in Indonesia and Indochina. There was not a great deal of knowledge or understanding of events taking place far away from Britain. If questions were asked, Communist insurgencies were blamed or the threat of Russian expansion.

It was only later that the use of many thousands of British soldiers and the extent of the death toll in Indonesia, Vietnam and Cambodia was realised. There was no public discussion of whether it was in British interests to support American policies in this way, nor of whether Britain should continue maintaining a large Army and prolonging conscription in order to support American aims. It seems that Attlee just assumed that being in partnership with America was in Britain's interest, even though key members of his Cabinet including his first two chancellors of the Exchequer, wanted Britain to be independent of alliances.

Since 1918, the Labour Party had been committed to dismantling the British Empire ("the Labour Party repudiates Imperialism and domination over other races…it believes in the right of each people to live its own life in its own way"). It was not be possible in any case to hold on to India and negotiations were already under way for India and Burma to be granted independence, but Attlee seemed reluctant to let go of most of our other colonies. He did not openly renounce Labour's past commitment to end colonialism and allow our colonies to pursue independence and self-government, but Malaysian hopes of independence in return for their help in fighting the Japanese had been disappointed and outbreaks of conflict between the independence movement, which included Communist groups, and the British occupying forces began.

The involvement of Communists in Malaysian battles for independence was used to justify all out repression, including extra judicial killings of unarmed civilians, killing of livestock, bombing villages, and destroying crops by herbicide. It was presented by the press in Britain as defence against Communist aggression and would continue for several years after the Conservatives took over in 1951. However, profits by British owners from the tin mining industry and rubber plantations in Malaya were greater than from all British industrial exports, and the use of British troops to suppress the Malaysian Uprising in 1948 looked very like a return to retaining the British Empire by force to protect British investments.

In the first three years of the Attlee Government, although there were fundamental differences of opinion within the Cabinet about the foreign policies being pursued, they were not brought out into the open because of the urgency of dealing with immediate post war problems. There were almost equal numbers in the Government of right-wing members and supporters of Tribune. Stafford Cripps, the founder of Tribune as Chancellor of the Exchequer and before him Hugh Dalton, had the task of keeping Britain afloat financially and there were others in important positions, including Bevan as Minister of Health and George Straus, the co-founder of Tribune and the future Barbara Castle as a Tribune Trustee. Attlee respected their work but didn't consult them on foreign affairs, although he knew they would not agree with his decision to tie Britain into dependence on America and its anti-Communist campaigns. He carried out the negotiations over acquiring a British Atomic Bomb in secret and took the decision without obtaining full Cabinet approval.

The year Britain began its campaign of repression in Malaysia, Stalin took over control of Czechoslovakia. Stafford Cripps had no hesitation in condemning his actions but did not alter his opposition to turning the Cold War into a hot war nor his belief that it was in Britain's interests to be independent and not a committed ally of either America or the Soviet Union. Cripps more than anyone understood Stalin and the Soviet Union because he had served as British Ambassador in Russia in the first two years of the war and had been responsible for negotiating the alliance with Stalin after Hitler invaded Russia. He had always had reservations about Stalin's regime and had never joined the British Communist Party but he had advocated cooperating with it against the appeasement of Hitler and had supported retaining normal diplomatic relations with Russia after the war in 1948, although strongly criticising Stalin's treatment of the countries within the Eastern bloc, he thought the devastation and economic weakness of the Soviet Union after the war would prevent it being a danger to the West. As Chancellor he wanted to reduce the cost of expenditure on the armed forces in order to increase it on housing and welfare.

Open conflict within the Cabinet became inevitable when in 1950 America demanded Britain increase its defence spending as the price for its financial help. The outbreak of the Korean War in 1950 brought things to a head within the Cabinet. Opposition to the use of British troops was spreading among many on the left and pacifists both within and outside the Labour Party. Just at this moment. Stafford Cripps became critically ill with cancer and had to retire. Attlee replaced him as Chancellor by Hugh Gaitskell, whose first Budget included high expenditure on the armed forces so that Britain could support the war in Korea.

This could only be paid for by cuts in expenditure on welfare and the National Health Service. Bevan, now the leading 'Tribunate' supporter of Tribune views in the Cabinet, immediately resigned along with Harold Wilson and John Freeman.

The Korean War went ahead. When the Japanese forces occupying Korea were defeated in 1945, the country had been 'temporarily' split at the 38th Parallel— with US troops liberating the south and the Russians moving into the north. The Koreans wanted to be united as a single state but the division between North and South was prolonged under the auspices of the United Nations Security Council. In the north the Russians set up a communist state—the Democratic People's Republic of Korea (DPRK) under Kim Il Sung. In the south, the Americans established the Republic of Korea under Syngman Rhee. On 25 June 1950, the Democratic Peoples Republic launched an attack on their southern compatriots. The United Nations Security Council led by the USA. and in the absence of Russia, passed a resolution to begin "a police action" to help the South. Attlee was not enthusiastic but felt obliged to supply troops as requested. For the United Nations to set in motion 'a police action' could be seen as a legitimate activity, and altogether 25 nations agreed to take part, but supporting an all-out war was contrary to its founding principles. Yet that was what followed. America provided the main impetus, control and 90% of the forces for what became a global containment of Communism.

The Korean War was the most destructive conflict of the modern era, with approximately 3 million war fatalities and a larger proportion of civilian deaths than in World War Two. It led to the destruction of virtually all of Korea's major cities, thousands of massacres by both sides, including the mass killing of tens of thousands of suspected communists by the South Korean government, and the torture and starvation of prisoners of war by the North Koreans. By the end of the war in 1953 Korea had become among the most heavily bombed countries in history. Chinese casualties were also very high after the Chinese were drawn in. British troops began arriving in August 1950; the exact number of soldiers sent to fight is not verified but estimates range from 60,000 to 100,000. All the records agree that quite a large proportion were conscripts serving their stint of national service rather than regular soldiers. British loss of life was over 1,100 and many others were injured. Commonwealth forces were also among the British contingent, which was the largest after that of America itself. Britain also sent battleships and aircraft to Korea.

Participation in the Korean War was the key turning point in British politics because it led to an openly divided Labour Party which has since spent its energy fighting among itself. The cost of participation in the war and developing a 'British' Atomic bomb led to financial constraints and cuts to welfare provision to the extent that the original aim of the Beveridge Report to provide 'a floor' against poverty has never been achieved. There would be no need for Universal Credit if paying national insurance gave the right to receive benefits sufficient to avoid poverty or if a child allowance ensured that no child could go hungry—the original aims of the Welfare state.

There was a brief period of unity between Gaitskell and Bevan in opposition to the Suez crisis and Anthony Eden, but it was ended by controversy over nuclear disarmament. 'Butskellism' was not a consensus of the Labour Party and the Conservatives, but only of the right wing of the Labour Party and the Conservatives. The policies promoted by the Tribune Group had more in common with those in the Labour Party Constitution than those followed by Attlee and Bevin in relation to foreign policy, attitudes to peace and war or the dissolution of the Empire, but the opportunity to create a united party was lost.

It did not recur despite the efforts of Harold Wilson, who refused to provide British support for the Vietnam War despite continual pressure from America.

In retrospect, it would have been far better if the Labour Party had got rid of FPTP in 1951 instead of calling an election and had then split into two separate parties and allowed the electorate to be involved in deciding what policies they wanted to support. Of course, it wasn't ever going to happen that way.

Roll forward fifty years to the period of Blair's Wars based on the arrogant, post imperialist belief that dropping bombs and taking over control of countries in less developed parts of the world would benefit them and lead to their becoming democracies. Max and I were united from the beginning in opposing the concept of the 'War on terror'. During the prelude to the invasion of Iraq an estimated three million people in Britain took part in demonstrations and marches opposing British participation in America's impending invasion. Max and I were too old to march but took a stand as delegates to the Hornsey and Wood Green Constituency Labour Party when our Local MP, Barbara Roach, defended the impending invasion. She failed to convince the majority of the members present. She told us if only we had read the 'Dossier' we would understand. So, we told her she was naïve to trust in it. In the end 140 Labour MPs voted against the war but it went ahead, just as the Korean War had gone ahead.

The problem for all those opposed to the Iraq war was the lack of a Party to represent their views in Parliament because our voting system only gave voters a viable choice of two parties, both of which formally supported the war. In the 2001 Election 40% of the electorate abstained which indicated the amount of doubt about Government policy. After the war began, I resigned from the Labour Party but had no way of using my vote to express my opposition to the war, so I joined the Stop the War Movement and abstained from voting for Labour in 2005. Max remained a party loyalist but strongly opposed the policy being followed both over Iraq and education, so during the last years of his life we were in closer accord than sometimes in the past.

Again and again over the years, since 1951, a divided Labour Party has left the field open to a right-wing Conservative Party. A democratic state enables all citizens to have the opportunity to vote for a party that can uphold their beliefs and opinions within Parliament. This was not the case at the onset of the Korean War nor when the invasion of Iraq began over 50 years later. Nor is it the case today. Pacifist views within the Labour Movement have not been supported by the Labour Party but it is impossible within the current electoral system for any new Party to gain significant representation—at the last election it needed over 800,000 supporters of the Green Party to obtain one voice in Parliament. The 2022 local elections demonstrated that support for that Party is growing rapidly but this cannot be reflected in the next General Election nor the fair representation of any other new Party.

The recent criminal attack by Putin on Ukraine has highlighted the long standing differences within the Labour Movement on foreign and defence policy, no-one is justifying the Russian action nor immediate need to support the Ukrainians, but there is a profound difference of view about its historical background. Opposition to the Iraq war and Tony Blair's use of military intervention to bring about regime change in other countries led to the formation of the Stop the War Organisation which I joined not long after it was created. Modern warfare is inhuman is its killing and maiming of soldiers and civilians alike and destruction of buildings and services. Its effect on the planet undermines the attempt to prevent global warming and the stockpiling of nuclear weapons is a danger to the survival of life on earth. In these circumstances, it is the duty of governments to pursue diplomacy to settle disputes between nations and avoid provoking or declaring war.

Finding a way to bring an end to existing wars, including the war in Ukraine, is difficult and requires international cooperation and care for humanity alongside, and as a contribution to, the survival of our planet. However the Labour Party under the leadership of Keir Starmer has forbidden Labour MPs to support meetings organised by 'Stop the War' or propagating its views. I am still a member and voted for Keir Starmer as Leader because he promised to unite the Party. I did not anticipate when I did so that he would forbid discussion of views, and an historical analysis, which, rightly or wrongly, I support.[6]

The extent to which the Leader of the Labour decides the Party's policies and imposes them on the Party has changed dramatically since the resignation of Harold Wilson in 1976. Wilson said that as Prime Minister he was 'the first among equals' within the Cabinet and accepted that policy was decided by the members of the Party at Annual Conference and that when in opposition Conference was responsible for electing members to serve in the Shadow Cabinet alongside the existing Leader. There was no constraint on free discussion nor rules on publication of different views. The only constraint was the expectation of loyalty to the elected Leader and the decisions of the last

---

[6] Stop the War has just published a pamphlet under the title 'Nato. A War Alliance'.

Conference on policy. This was in complete contrast to the Conservative Party where the Leader once elected decides policy. This was always the case but Margaret Thatcher tightened the grip of the Leader.

The breakaway of the 'Gang of Four', an act of disloyalty to the then Leader Michael Foot, was defended as impatience with the way policy was being decided and the left wing gaining control. The next Leader, Neil Kinnock, thought its lesson was that Labour Leaders must enforce discipline and if members want to win elections they must avoid unauthorised actions because not maintaining unity behind the Leader reduced his prestige and the Party's chance of winning the next election. Tony Blair as Prime Minister carried this approach further and centralised decision making in his own hands, disassociated the Party from socialist aims by changing Clause Four, and weakened the role of the Trade Unions except as money providers thus undermining traditional conventions about the division of authority within the Party.

Boris Johnson has gone further in this direction and developed government by cronies but that just makes it more important that the Labour Party clarifies the role of its Leader. Should he or she be a boss, an umpire, or a champion of those who voted for him or her?

I did not bother to vote in the 1955 election because the Labour Party spent all its time attacking each other. I wonder if that is why in recent years turnout among young electors has been low? What is certain is that if the Labour Party is to remain 'a broad church' and play a positive role in the future its leaders and officials must find a way to unite the Party, which Keir Starmer promised to do but has not yet done. In fact he has heightened it by the treatment of two of his predecessors: he has chosen to make Tony Blair, the war monger, his mentor but has taken away the membership of the left wing but politically unsophisticated Jeremy Corbin.

The extent and effect of factionalism within the Labour Party has just been analysed in the Forde Report, a very serious and detailed examination of the workings of the Party from 2015 – 2019. Its key findings are that "factionalism is so deep-rooted that the Party found itself dysfunctional" and that "factionalism within the Party has seen it fail the electorate and has undermined the democratic process." Max and my memoirs demonstrate that much of the Report could have been written at almost any date after 1951. Its key recommendation, with which I completely agree as would Max were he still alive, is that equal respect must be shown to all its members whatever their class background, be they right-wing or left wing, Christian, Jewish, or Muslim, black or white, male or female and whatever their sexual orientation. To which I would add the importance of respecting the democratic right of all citizens, whatever their political affiliation, to freedom of thought and expression. The advent of social media has created problems about distinguishing private discussion exploring ideas or making jokes from public advocacy. As a lecturer I sometimes when running seminars used the technique of being devil's advocate which would surely get me into trouble today! Holding anyone to blame for their ideas recorded on Facebook when young but later renounced or just forgotten is a form of persecution. So is making lists of forbidden organisations that members must not join – left wingers might well object to some of the think tanks that right wing members have joined.

One very recent current and encouraging development has been the revival of independent Trade Union activism rather than relying on the Labour Party and political solutions alone. The Trade Unions were the majority component in the formation of the Labour Party but once the Party came in sight of power it ceased to respect the role of the trade unions, The fear by its Leaders that supporting strikes would lose votes goes back to Ramsey MacDonald and would appear to be influencing Keir Starmer.

No Trade Union wants to have to strike in order to obtain fair wages – least of all to organise a General Strike which has just been mentioned as a possible last resort. With an increasing proportion of families living in poverty and well over a third of our children hungry, the situation of both wage and many salary workers is no longer tolerable. It is too late to wait for political action and the current trade union leaders are responding in the only way they can and deserve unstinting support, especially from the Labour Party. Unfortunately, Keir Starmer has cast doubt on his support by sacking Sam Tarry, the Shadow Minister for Local Transport who was originally given promotion by Corbyn, for attending a picket line and voicing his support. Politics allows no room for errors of judgement and however much now Starmer declares his support of the strikes it is unlikely that the trade unions will trust his leadership in future. However most trade union leaders don't want to end their affiliation to the Labour Party and want it to put forward positive plans for the future.

Whether trade union militancy will bring about significant change is yet to be seen. Some success has been achieved in negotiating improved offers from employers but there is a long way to go. The most difficult political and electoral challenge is winning confidence for a different economic policy The two Tory candidates to replace Boris Johnson are promising to develop an economy that will attract investment and cut taxes, but in practice are even more extremely right wing than the austerity policies which have brought about the sorry state of Britain today, Yes, investment is needed but not by keeping wages low to woo asset-striping hedge fund managers and companies who hide their profits in overseas tax havens. Their competition will show which of them will cut most taxes and most reduce the ability of the Government to fund public investment. Poor Britain whichever of them becomes Prime Minister in September! Max fifty years ago when he was NUT President, even in his worst nightmares would not have envisaged that, less than 200,000 Tory Members would be able to impose upon Britain a complete economic ignoramus as Prime Minister!

Keir Starmer is saying Labour policy will be based on "growth, growth, growth" but at the same time is insisting that a future Labour Government would respect the classical neoliberal rule that borrowing must be limited to planned future income. That would tie our hands behind our backs! The alternative is new initiatives to raise and use the money needed for growth, Waiting for the Leader of the Party to produce a brand new Manifesto rather than adapting, modifying and building upon the last two manifestos doesn't seem necessary and isn't making good use of the expertise within the Party. Interesting ideas are being developed in some regions, especially in the wider Manchester area and Wales, involving reginal government and the formation of Cooperatives. A proposal being floated is to replace the House of Lords with a body comprising representatives of the different nations and regions which would help to decentralise government and hold Britain together.

In 2018, a group of leading economists and academics set up the Progressive Economic Forum "to highlight the dangers and failings of austerity, provide alternative progressive policies to rebuild the economy, deconstruct economic myths and coordinate the response to the failure of Government Policy." Many of their proposals were used in the 2019 Manifesto including for shorter working hours and a pilot of Universal basic income. A simple version of their proposals has been published.[7] It includes floating Building Britain Bonds for the general public to buy (like the War Bonds that helped finance Britain in the Second World War). The Party is in touch with the PEF and hopefully, John MacDonnell's experience as Shadow Chancellor will also be put to use. In case,

---

[7] 'The Return of the State; Restructuring Britain for the Common Good' Agenda publishers 2021.

there is a sudden General Election Starmer and his front bench urgently needs to get help to produce an innovative programme quickly.

It is clear that the role of the state in regulating monopoly capitalism and developing state and Cooperative enterprise must be renewed. Absolute poverty and child hunger must be eliminated **urgently (not just reduced!**) and general inequality reduced both in Britain and worldwide. Undeveloped countries must be given aid whatever their regimes.

Max and I did our best as campaigners but our visions for the future have not been fulfilled. It will be up to the younger generation to find a way forward but it won't be easy. Lord Acton warned that "all power corrupts but absolute power corrupts absolutely," as Stalin proved even when power was used in the name of the working class. An American political commentator, Ostrogorsky, warned as early as 1909 that those elected as leaders of political parties soon start pursuing their personal interests instead of those of the voters who elected them (a particularly apposite warning in Britain today!). Changing society by democratic methods is difficult as Marx explained theoretically and Ralph Miliband explored in relation to more recent experience. It is essential to protect democratic principles and procedures where they exist—never more so than now when they are threatened by media manipulation. Saving the Planet should be the priority and 'Liberty, Equality and Fraternity' should be reborn as our slogan.

Margaret Morris
August 2022

Ingram Content Group UK Ltd.
Milton Keynes UK
UKHW020023070423
419773UK00006B/622